UF
100 Documented Incidents.

The Unexplained Archives.

Dear Reader,

Welcome to *UFOs: 100 Documented Sightings*. I'm Claudio Bocchia, a writer with a deep fascination for the mysteries that surround our world. In this book, you'll embark on an in-depth exploration of various UFO-related events, from the famous "Battle of Los Angeles" in 1942 to the most recent sightings.

Each chapter delves into a specific incident, offering a comprehensive analysis of witness testimonies and official responses. You'll uncover the investigations carried out, the conclusions drawn, and the ongoing debates within the UFO community and among skeptics.

This book is for anyone intrigued by unidentified aerial phenomena and eager to understand the wide range of theories, personal accounts, and the evolution of public perception regarding UFOs.

Your feedback is invaluable, and I would love to hear your thoughts. Reader reviews play a crucial role in helping other enthusiasts discover this book. If you enjoyed your reading, please consider sharing your experience.

Thank you, and happy reading!

Claudio Bocchia

Table of Contents

Foreword.

Dear reader,

The world is filled with uncertainties, but isn't the fundamental question: Are we alone? This question, as old as humanity itself, continues to fascinate us and push us to look beyond our planet. In our quest to understand the universe and our place within it, this question remains at the heart of many scientific, philosophical, and even popular discussions.

Over the centuries, our perspective on the universe has evolved dramatically. Once, we considered ourselves the center of a finite and ordered cosmos. Today, thanks to advances in astronomy and space sciences, we know that we are just a small part of a vast and mysterious universe that extends far beyond our solar system, into distant and unexplored galaxies. Each discovery of a habitable extrasolar planet, each unusual signal picked up by our telescopes, renews speculation about the possibility of life elsewhere.

This possibility confronts us with a fascinating duality: on one hand, the excitement and hope of discovering that we are not alone, and on the other, the profound philosophical and existential implications that this would entail. How would our society react to the confirmation of the existence of other intelligent life forms? What would be the impacts on our beliefs, our cultures, our sciences, and our international relations?

UFOs, often relegated to the margins of serious discussion, play a central role in this ongoing investigation. Whether they are interpreted as misunderstood natural phenomena, artifacts of advanced technologies, or even extraterrestrial vehicles, they stimulate our imagination and our desire to understand the unknown. Through this book, we explore not only the incidents and testimonies but also the vast implications of these observations.

We invite you to dive into this exploration with an open and critical mind. Perhaps by examining the enigmas we have gathered here, we can together approach an answer to this universal question: are we really alone in the universe? The answer to this question could not only redefine our future, but also our understanding of our own existence.

Introduction.

Scientists' stance on UFOs.

Scientists approach the question of UFOs with methodological rigor based on the fundamental principles of physics and astronomy. An argument often put forward by the scientific community concerns the astronomical distances that separate stars and galaxies. For example, crossing our own galaxy, the Milky Way, would require traveling about 100,000 light-years, a distance that makes interstellar travel practically impossible with current or foreseeable technologies. This reality poses a major problem for the hypothesis of visits from extraterrestrials from other star systems or galaxies.

Furthermore, many UFO testimonies describe behaviors that defy the known laws of physics, such as sudden movements at very high speeds without any visible form of propulsion, or the ability to change direction instantly. These descriptions often conflict with principles such as gravity and the conservation of momentum. For most scientists, such phenomena remain highly suspect and are generally attributed to perception errors, optical illusions, or misinterpretations of more conventional natural or artificial phenomena.

The scientific community maintains that any extraordinary claim requires equally extraordinary evidence. So far, concrete, measurable, and reproducible evidence of extraterrestrial technologies or vehicles has not been provided. This leads most scientists to remain skeptical about the idea that the observed UFOs are vehicles of extraterrestrial origin.

Position of ufologists on UFOs.

On the contrary, ufologists are often more open to the possibility that UFOs could be manifestations of advanced technologies from extraterrestrial civilizations. They argue that, although we do not understand the technologies involved, this does not mean they cannot exist. According to them, it is arrogant to assume that humans possess all possible technological knowledge, and that extraterrestrial civilizations could have solved challenges such as superluminal travel or advanced propulsion methods that are currently unknown to us.

Ufologists also highlight the numerous cases where objects have been observed performing maneuvers that seem impossible with our current technology. For them, this could indicate that these entities or their crafts are capable of manipulating physical forces in a way that we do not yet understand. This perspective is often reinforced by reports of close encounters and testimonies from credible individuals who claim to have seen or interacted with these phenomena in a way that seems to exclude more down-to-earth explanations.

In conclusion, while scientists demand empirical evidence in accordance with known physical laws, ufologists are ready to consider that the limits of our current understanding of the universe do not yet cover all the possibilities of existence. These fundamental differences in approaches and beliefs underpin the great divide between the two groups in the UFO debate.

THE BATTLE OF LOS ANGELES: THE UNIDENTIFIED OBJECTS INCIDENT.

DATE: February 24-25, 1942.
COUNTRY: United States.
STATE: California.
CITY: Los Angeles .

On the night of February 24 to 25, 1942, just a few months after the United States entered World War II following the attack on Pearl Harbor, the city of Los Angeles was the scene of an extraordinary event that caused panic and confusion among its inhabitants and military authorities. This incident, known as "The Battle of Los Angeles," began with the observation of unidentified flying objects in the night sky of the Californian metropolis. At a time when fear of an enemy attack was at its peak, the presence of these objects triggered a series of intense defensive reactions.

The anti-aircraft spotlights were quickly activated, sweeping the sky in search of the enemy. Shortly after, the AAA (Anti-Aircraft Artillery) opened fire, launching a salvo of shells towards the detected objects. The sky lit up from the explosion of the shells and the spotlights, creating a surreal scene that was observed by thousands of residents awakened by the noise of the explosions and sirens. The military authorities were on high alert, and the confusion was exacerbated by the lack of clear information about the exact nature of the threat.

The incident lasted several hours, during which the objects seemed to move slowly in the sky, sometimes remaining stationary, defying conventional explanations. Despite the intensity of the bombardment, no enemy aircraft debris was found, and there was no confirmation of an attack. After the incident, authorities issued various statements, some suggesting that it was a false alarm due to war nerves, while others maintained that the objects had not been identified.

The "Battle of Los Angeles" remains one of the most mysterious and controversial incidents involving unidentified flying objects. It raises questions about wartime preparedness, information management, and the possibility of other unconventional explanations. This event has also had a lasting impact on popular culture, inspiring various films, documentaries, and conspiracy theories about alien visits.

The Observation.

The observation began shortly after midnight, when the radars of the American military detected an unidentified object approaching the coast of Los Angeles. The radar operators, already on high alert due to the fear of a Japanese attack, tracked the object as it slowly moved towards the city. The exact nature of this object has never been clearly identified, which contributed to the atmosphere of tension and mystery surrounding the event.

The description of the object varies according to the testimonies. Some observers reported seeing a large zeppelin-shaped object, while others described a formation of several smaller objects. The confusion was exacerbated by the darkness of the night and the searchlights sweeping the sky for the enemy. These powerful light beams, combined with the smoke from anti-aircraft explosions, made visual identification of the object even more difficult.

The weather conditions that night were relatively clear, although visibility was partially reduced by the presence of smoke from the numerous anti-aircraft fire. The moon was almost full, which provided some brightness, but was not enough to clearly illuminate the sky. The wind was weak and did not significantly affect the trajectory of the shells or the dispersion of the smoke.

The exact time of the observation was recorded from 02:25, when the alert was given and the anti-aircraft batteries were authorized to open fire. The bombardment lasted until about 04:14, during which thousands of shots were fired at the object or objects in question. Despite the intensity of the fire, no confirmed debris from the object was found, which added to the mystery of the incident.

The nature of the object observed during the Battle of Los Angeles remains a subject of debate and speculation. Descriptions vary and testimonies are often contradictory, making it difficult to form a coherent picture of the event. What is certain, however, is that the incident caused a great stir among the population of Los Angeles and left an indelible mark in the annals of UFO sightings.

Testimonials.

One of the first witnesses, Katie, a resident of Santa Monica, reported seeing several luminous objects in the sky shortly after midnight. According to her, these objects did not resemble any airplane she had seen before: they were oval-shaped and emitted a brilliant light. Katie described how these objects moved slowly in the sky, sometimes stationary, before suddenly disappearing on the horizon.

James, an anti-aircraft projector operator, provided a detailed testimony of his observations. He was one of the first to spot an unidentified object using his projector. James described the object as being extremely bright and much larger than any known aircraft at the time. He also noted that the object seemed to have superior maneuverability, moving against the wind with apparent ease.

Sergeant Mitchel, a member of the coastal defense, testified to having received the order to fire at the objects after they had been spotted by several spotlights. According to him, despite multiple anti-aircraft artillery salvos, the projectiles seemed to have no effect on the object, which continued its slow and steady progress across the sky.

Another important witness, Lieutenant Smith, an air force pilot, reported being on alert that night but did not receive the order to take off. From his position on the ground, he observed the events and confirmed the descriptions of the objects as being unusual and not in line with the planes of the time. He highlighted the confusion and agitation among the military personnel about the exact nature of the threat.

Finally, Eleanor, a local journalist, documented the reactions of civilians during and after the incident. She collected testimonies from local residents who described a range of emotions from curiosity to terror. Many reported feeling a sense of unreality, as if what they were seeing could not be true. Eleanor also noted the psychological impact of the incident on the community, with people fearing an imminent invasion, whether of human origin or otherwise.

These testimonies, although varied, paint a picture of a night of intense confusion, aggressive military reactions, and observations of objects that witnesses struggled to explain with the knowledge of the time.

The Investigation.

What began as an air raid alert quickly turned into one of the greatest hoaxes in UFO history. The subsequent investigation attempted to unravel the facts of a chaotic night marked by fear and confusion.

In the hours that followed, military and governmental authorities began to investigate the incident. The Secretary of War at the time, Henry L. Stimson, was informed and ordered an immediate investigation. The military questioned witnesses and examined reports from radar stations and observation posts. The testimonies were varied and often contradictory, some claiming to have seen a large zeppelin-shaped object, while others reported several small flying objects.

The initial reports from the military authorities suggested the possibility of an enemy attack. However, no concrete evidence was found to support this theory. The army's final report concluded that the incident was probably due to a "false alarm" caused by tense nerves and a misinterpretation of objects such as weather balloons. This conclusion did not satisfy everyone, and numerous alternative theories continued to circulate, including that of an extraterrestrial visit.

The investigation also examined the damage caused by anti-aircraft fire. Several buildings and vehicles were damaged, and there were several civilian casualties due to falling shell debris. These tragic aspects of the incident were documented in the report, but were often overshadowed by the mystery surrounding the object itself.

Over the years, the incident of the Battle of Los Angeles has remained a subject of fascination and speculation. Despite investigations and official reports, many questions remain unanswered. The lack of tangible evidence and contradictory testimonies have left the door open to numerous interpretations and theories. The official investigation, although thorough, failed to provide a definitive explanation, leaving this event as one of the most intriguing in the history of UFO sightings.

Theories and Speculations.

The first theory, and the most immediate at the time, was that the incident was an enemy attack, specifically a Japanese aerial incursion. This hypothesis was supported by the high tensions following the attack on Pearl Harbor and the fear of a Japanese invasion on the west coast of the United States. However, no concrete evidence has ever been presented to support this theory, and the Japanese government subsequently denied any involvement in the incident.

Another popular explanation is that of a misunderstanding caused by the nervousness of the American troops, exacerbated by the context of war. According to this theory, what the military took for enemy planes could have simply been weather balloons or even clouds misinterpreted by the spotlights and the effects of the anti-aircraft defense. This hypothesis is reinforced by the fact that no enemy plane debris was found.

Some ufologists argue that the observed objects were of extraterrestrial origin. This theory is fueled by witness testimonies who described the objects as having unusual shapes and movements, not corresponding to the planes of the time. Moreover, the fact that the numerous artillery shots failed to shoot down the objects adds to the mystique of this theory. However, this explanation is often dismissed by experts and historians who consider it implausible and without tangible evidence.

Another less common speculation suggests that the incident could have been a psychological operation orchestrated by the American government to test the responsiveness and preparedness of the west coast defenses. This theory proposes that the objects sighted could have been American planes used in this exercise. However, this idea remains controversial and largely speculative, with little evidence to support it.

Finally, some researchers have suggested that the incident could be related to rare atmospheric phenomena or optical illusions caused by particular weather conditions. This explanation attempts to find a middle ground between observations of strange objects and the lack of material evidence of an attack or extraterrestrial visit.

DATE: December 5, 1945.
COUNTRY: United States.
STATE: Florida.
CITY: Fort Lauderdale.

On December 5, 1945, a mysterious and unexplained event occurred over the Atlantic, in the region known as the Bermuda Triangle. That day, five torpedo bombers from the US Navy, designated as Flight 19, disappeared without a trace after taking off from the Naval Air Station in Fort Lauderdale, Florida. The flight was a routine training mission, led by Lieutenant Charles Taylor, an experienced veteran of World War II. The planes, TBM Avengers, were equipped to withstand difficult flying conditions and were considered very reliable.

The planned mission was to follow a triangular route, starting with a flight east from Florida to the Bahamas, then north before returning to base. However, shortly after the start of their mission, communications between Flight 19 and the base began to reveal a series of worrying problems. Lieutenant Taylor reported that his compass was not working properly and that the visual landmarks did not match what they should be. Despite attempts to guide them back to base, confusion increased and communications became increasingly fragmented.

Finally, the last messages received from Flight 19 indicated that the pilots were completely disoriented and did not know in which direction Florida was. After several hours of erratic flight, contact was lost. A search and rescue operation was immediately launched, including the dispatch of another plane, which also disappeared, deepening the mystery. Despite intensive search, no debris from the planes or any sign of the crews were ever found.

The incident of Flight 19 has become one of the most famous and enigmatic cases associated with the Bermuda Triangle, an area of the Atlantic Ocean notorious for the unexplained disappearances of ships and aircraft. This mystery continues to spark speculation and theories, ranging from unusual natural phenomena to paranormal activities, although no definitive explanation has been universally accepted.

The Observation.

The flight was led by Lieutenant Charles Taylor, an experienced pilot. The mission consisted of a simple navigation exercise that was to follow a triangular route. The first segment of the flight was to take the planes east from Florida to the Bahamas. Then, the flight plan called for a turn north for the second segment, before returning to the starting point to complete the triangle.

However, shortly after the start of the mission, problems began to arise. Lieutenant Taylor reported by radio that he was disoriented and could not determine his exact position. He mentioned that the compasses on his plane were not working properly, adding to the confusion. Radio communications picked up by the base and other ships indicated that Taylor thought the flight had ended up over the Gulf of Mexico, northwest of Florida, when they were actually northeast of their starting position.

As the afternoon progressed, the weather deteriorated. Weather reports began to indicate an increase in cloud cover and an increasingly rough sea in the area where the flight was supposed to be. Communications between the flight group and the base became increasingly sporadic, with messages often fragmented and difficult to understand.

The latest communications received from Taylor were increasingly urgent, indicating that he was trying to find a way back to Florida but visibility was low and flying conditions difficult. He encouraged the other pilots to stay in tight formation and to conserve their fuel as much as possible. Night was beginning to fall, and with it, the chances of accurately locating the planes were rapidly decreasing.

The last transmission received from Flight 19 was a confused message, mentioning that the water was white and they didn't know where they were. Shortly after, contact was definitively lost. Despite a vast search and rescue operation launched immediately after the flight's disappearance, none of the planes or any of the crew members were ever found. The weather conditions during the search were extremely poor, with rough seas and reduced visibility, which complicated rescue efforts.

Testimonials.

The flight leader, Lieutenant Charles Taylor, was the main witness to this incident, albeit indirectly since his communications were recorded by the base. At the start of the exercise, everything seemed normal, but shortly after, Taylor reported that his compass was no longer working correctly. He expressed his confusion about his exact position and that of his squadron. The other pilots in the group also reported similar anomalies with their navigation instruments.

Another key witness was Lieutenant Robert F. Cox, another pilot who was flying near the area at that time. He heard Taylor's communications and tried to help him determine his position. Cox reported that Taylor seemed disoriented and unsure of which direction to follow to return to base. He also noted that the weather conditions had become increasingly difficult, further complicating navigation.

The radio operators at the Fort Lauderdale naval base, where the flight had taken off, also witnessed the radio exchanges. They tried to guide Taylor and his squadron back to the base, but the communications were intermittent and marked by great confusion. At one point, Taylor even mentioned that he and his squadron were heading towards the Florida Keys, which was geographically incorrect and added to the perplexity of the situation.

Finally, another indirect but crucial testimony comes from subsequent research reports. After the disappearance of the flight, a vast search operation was launched. The testimonies of the crews of the ships and planes involved in this search revealed that no trace of the planes or pilots was ever found, despite improved weather conditions and a relatively calm sea.

These testimonies together paint a disturbing picture of a group of experienced pilots faced with an inexplicable situation that led to one of the greatest enigmas of aviation. The precise details of their observations and communications continue to fuel speculation and theories about what could be behind the strange phenomena in the Bermuda Triangle.

The Investigation.

The initial investigation was conducted by the United States Navy immediately after the disappearance of the planes. The initial reports indicated that the flight, led by the experienced instructor Lieutenant Charles Taylor, had encountered navigation problems shortly after taking off from the Fort Lauderdale Naval Air Station in Florida. Intercepted radio communications suggested that Taylor was disoriented and that the planes' compasses were not functioning properly.

The search began shortly after the last radio transmission from Flight 19. Despite the scale of the operations, which included hundreds of ships and aircraft, no debris from the Avengers was found. The Navy's investigation had to rely primarily on the testimonies of other pilots and on the recordings of communications between the aircraft and the base.

The testimonies collected during the investigation revealed that the weather conditions were relatively mild at the time of the flight, and that other pilots flying in the area had not reported similar technical problems. This led to speculations about Taylor's mental state and competence, although those who knew him described him as an experienced and competent pilot.

The Navy released an official report in 1946, concluding that the incident was due to "unknown causes or reasons". This vague conclusion fueled public speculation and gave rise to various theories, including those suggesting paranormal phenomena or extraterrestrial interference, although nothing of the sort was mentioned in the official reports.

In the following years, other investigations were conducted, including by civil organizations and independent researchers. These investigations often sought to verify the weather conditions, navigation errors, and even the possibility of a collective mechanical failure, but none have managed to provide·a satisfactory definitive explanation.

Declassified archives from years later showed that the Navy had considered several scenarios, including the hypothesis that the planes could have flown in circles until they ran out of fuel. However, the lack of concrete evidence and debris made it impossible to confirm this theory or any other.

The investigation into Flight 19 remains one of the most mysterious and debated in the annals of military aviation. Despite decades of research and speculation, the exact fate of the planes and their crews has never been elucidated, leaving an indelible mark on the Bermuda Triangle region and on popular culture.

Theories and Speculations.

The first theory suggests that magnetic anomalies in the Bermuda Triangle region could have disoriented the pilots of Flight 19. The Triangle is known for its magnetic variations that can affect compasses. The aircraft's navigation instruments could have been disrupted by these anomalies, leading the pilots off their planned course and possibly running out of fuel at sea. This hypothesis is supported by reports from the time indicating that the flight leader, Lieutenant Charles Taylor, had expressed confusion about his geographical position.

Another popular theory is that of extreme weather conditions. The Bermuda Triangle is known for its sudden and violent storms that can arise quickly and without prior warning. Some researchers believe that Flight 19 could have been caught in such a storm, thus losing control or suffering critical damage that would have led to their loss. This theory is reinforced by the fact that the weather was reported as being particularly turbulent on the day of the disappearance.

In addition to natural explanations, there are more controversial and fantastic theories. One of them is alien intervention. Some ufologists and conspiracy theory enthusiasts suggest that the planes were "absorbed" or destroyed by UFOs. Although this idea is widely rejected by the scientific community, it continues to captivate the public's imagination and stimulates a multitude of speculations and fictional stories around the Bermuda Triangle.

Another speculation involves advanced technology or unknown phenomena, such as portals to other dimensions or small black holes. These ideas, although extremely speculative and without concrete evidence, are sometimes discussed in the context of mysterious disappearances in the Bermuda Triangle. They suggest that the region could be a hotspot for physical phenomena not yet understood by current science.

Finally, there are those who believe that the disappearances are simply the result of cumulative human errors combined with natural hazards. The Bermuda Triangle is a frequently traveled area for navigation and flight, which statistically increases the chances of accidents. Advocates of this theory argue that the legend of the Bermuda Triangle is a mix of myths amplified by coincidences and misinterpretations of events.

Conclusion.

The disappearance of Flight 19 in the Bermuda Triangle remains one of the most intriguing and discussed aeronautical mysteries. Despite decades of research and investigations, no definitive explanation has been found to clarify what happened to these planes and their crews. Theories vary widely, including magnetic anomalies, human errors, unfavorable weather conditions, or even supernatural phenomena. This incident greatly contributed to the legend of the Bermuda Triangle as an area of unexplained dangers and unsolved mysteries. The families of the missing and the scientific community continue to search for answers, hoping one day to understand the events that led to this tragic disappearance.

THE GHOST ROCKETS INCIDENT, SWEDEN.

DATE: Summer 1946.
COUNTRY: Sweden.
STATE: Not applicable.
CITY: Various localities across Sweden.

The "Ghost Rockets" incident in Sweden during the summer of 1946 represents one of the first major waves of UFO sightings in Europe after World War II. At that time, Europe was still in full reconstruction and the political climate was marked by increasing tension between the Eastern and Western blocs, foreshadowing the Cold War. In this context, reports of unidentified flying objects caused great concern among populations and governments. The "Ghost Rockets" were mainly described as missile-like objects, but with no clear identification as to their origin. These observations were reported mainly in Sweden, but also in other Nordic countries. Witnesses described objects crossing the sky at high speed, sometimes accompanied by whistling noises or explosions. The Swedish government, taking these incidents very seriously, launched an official investigation. Despite numerous theories, ranging from technological explanations such as experimental missiles to natural phenomena or collective hallucinations, no definitive explanation has been provided to date. The "Ghost Rockets" incident thus remains an intriguing and unresolved chapter in the history of unidentified aerial phenomena.

The Observation.

On August 9, 1946, near Lake Kölmjärv, located in the north of Sweden, around 6:30 pm, several witnesses observed a strange object crossing the sky at an impressive speed. The object, described as cylindrical, was about 15 meters long and had a shiny metallic appearance. It showed no visible wings or signs of conventional propulsion such as propellers or reactors.

The weather conditions were clear with an unobstructed sky, which allowed for very sharp visual observation. The object was seen moving from north to south before abruptly plunging into the lake with a muffled noise, suggesting an explosion. However, no trace of debris was found in subsequent searches, adding a layer of mystery to the incident.

Witnesses also reported that the object made no engine noise before the impact, which is unusual for a craft of this size. The flight path was stable, with no signs of turbulence or deviation, suggesting precise control or navigation. After the impact, a column of smoke was observed rising from the point of impact on the lake, but it quickly dissipated.

This specific incident is part of a larger wave of similar observations across Sweden, where over 2000 reports were recorded in 1946. These observations were often accompanied by descriptions of objects plunging into lakes or crashing to the ground, but without leaving recoverable debris or concrete evidence after site inspections.

The absence of tangible debris and the ephemeral nature of the observations have led to great speculation and thorough investigations, both nationally and internationally. Despite this, the exact origin and nature of these "Ghost Rockets" have never been clarified, leaving this incident as one of the great unsolved mysteries of the modern era of ufology.

Testimonials.

One of the earliest significant testimonies comes from a pilot of the Swedish Air Force, Captain Gösta Carlsson. On July 10, 1946, while he was flying near the city of Malmö, Carlsson observed what he described as a bright, streamlined object crossing the sky at an incredible speed. According to his report, the object made no sound and left no visible trail, unlike the jet planes of the time.

Shortly after, on July 19, a collective observation was made by a group of swimmers on a beach near Stockholm. They described seeing a silver, cigar-shaped object diving into the nearby lake before disappearing without a trace. This observation was particularly disturbing as several witnesses reported seeing the object briefly emerge from the water before flying off at high speed.

Another notable testimony is that of Erik Reuterswärd, an amateur astronomer. On August 12, 1946, Reuterswärd was observing the night sky from his private observatory when he noted the presence of an unidentified flying object. He described the object as being oval-shaped with an intense light emanating from its center. The object moved erratically, changing direction several times before disappearing on the horizon.

On August 28, 1946, a group of geologists working in northern Sweden also reported an observation. They described an object similar to a rocket, with a trail of fire at the back, crossing the sky at a dizzying speed. The object was seen for several seconds before vanishing, leaving the witnesses perplexed about its nature and origin.

Finally, one of the most detailed testimonies was provided by a Swedish army officer, Lieutenant Lars-Erik Blom. On September 5, 1946, while he was on patrol near the Norwegian border, Blom and his unit observed a bright object crossing the sky. The object, described as metallic and cylindrical in shape, was followed for several minutes. Blom noted in his report that the object seemed to be under intelligent control, performing maneuvers that defied the capabilities of aircraft of the time.

The Investigation.

The "Ghost Rockets" incident in Sweden, which primarily took place in 1946, sparked a vast investigation conducted by Swedish authorities with the collaboration of military and international organizations. The first sightings of these mysterious flying objects, resembling rockets or missiles, were reported shortly after the end of World War II, and testimonies multiplied across the country.

The initial reaction of the Swedish military authorities was to treat these observations with great caution, given the context of the time, marked by the emerging Cold War and international tensions. The Swedish Air Force quickly set up a special unit to investigate these phenomena. This unit was composed of aeronautics specialists, meteorologists, and physicists.

The initial stages of the investigation involved gathering testimonies from people who had observed the "Ghost Rockets". These testimonies came from various sources, including pilots, air traffic controllers, and ordinary citizens. Common descriptions included elongated objects with a luminous trail, crossing the sky at high speed and sometimes accompanied by a whistling or explosion sound.

In parallel, the military authorities analyzed the available radar data and aerial photographs, but these efforts often did not corroborate the visual observations. This added a layer of complexity to the investigation, as it was difficult to determine the exact nature and origin of these objects without concrete material evidence.

In response to the increase in the number of reports and the lack of clear answers, the Swedish government has sought international assistance, particularly from the United States and the United Kingdom. Experts from these countries have participated in the investigation, bringing their expertise in aeronautical technology and intelligence.

As the investigation progressed, several theories were explored to explain the observations. Among these, the hypothesis of missile tests or experimental devices by the Soviets was often mentioned, although no concrete evidence was found to support this idea. Other theories included rare weather phenomena or space debris.

Despite months of intensive investigations, the inquiry into the "Ghost Rockets" never reached a definitive conclusion. The final reports highlighted the lack of tangible evidence and left open the question of the origin of these objects. This lack of a clear answer has helped fuel speculation and conspiracy theories around this incident, which remains one of the great unsolved mysteries of ufology.

Theories and Speculations.

One of the most common theories is that the Ghost Rockets were missiles or experimental devices, probably of Soviet origin. At the time, the Cold War was beginning to take shape, and the Soviet Union was actively engaged in the development of new military technologies. Some experts suggest that these objects could be tests of ballistic missiles or other types of weapons that the USSR was not yet ready to publicly unveil. This hypothesis is supported by the fact that several of the observations were made near the Baltic Sea, a strategic area for the Soviets.

Another explanation suggests that the Ghost Rockets could be misinterpreted meteorological or astronomical phenomena. Meteors entering the Earth's atmosphere could be mistaken for flying objects, especially by witnesses not trained to recognize these phenomena. This theory is often dismissed by ufologists who argue that the trajectories and behaviors of the reported objects do not match those of meteors.

Some researchers propose a psychosocial explanation, suggesting that the observations of the Ghost Rockets could be the result of some kind of "mass hysteria" or collective psychosis, fueled by post-war tensions and the fear of a new confrontation. According to this theory, witnesses may have projected their anxieties onto natural phenomena or ordinary planes, perceiving them as exotic or supernatural threats.

Finally, there is inevitably the theory that attributes the Ghost Rockets to extraterrestrial visitors. This idea is popular in the UFO community, where it is speculated that these objects could be probes or exploration vessels from other civilizations.

THE INCIDENT OF MAURY ISLAND.

DATE: June 21, 1947.
COUNTRY: United States.
STATE: Washington.
CITY: Maury Island.

The Maury Island incident, which occurred on June 21, 1947, is one of the first reported UFO sightings in modern history, preceding the famous Roswell incident by a few days. Located in the state of Washington, Maury Island is part of the Vashon Islands archipelago, a peaceful and sparsely populated place, which makes the event all the more intriguing. On that day, a local businessman named Harold Dahl was sailing near the island's coast to collect driftwood, a common practice in the region. What started as an ordinary workday took an extraordinary turn when Dahl and his crew observed six unidentified flying objects in the sky. According to witnesses, these objects were circular in shape with a hollow center, resembling flying "donuts". Dahl reported that one of the objects malfunctioned and began to lose altitude, even ejecting what appeared to be metallic debris, which damaged his boat and injured his son. After the incident, Dahl was approached by a man in black, who allegedly warned him not to discuss what he had seen. This account has become a key element in the "Men in Black" mythology associated with UFO sightings. The Maury Island incident remains a fascinating and mysterious case in the study of unidentified aerial phenomena, fueling debates and theories about extraterrestrial presence and government responses to such events.

The Observation.

Around 3 o'clock in the afternoon, the sky was partially cloudy but visibility remained excellent, an ideal weather condition for a day of work at sea. Suddenly, Dahl spotted six flying objects of circular shape, hovering about 600 meters above his boat. These objects, with an estimated diameter of nearly 30 meters each, were metallic and seemed to emit a glow that was not due to the reflection of the sun. Their surface was smooth, without any visible marks or external structures like wings or windows.

Dahl reported that these objects moved with astonishing precision, in tight formation, before one of them began to lose altitude, as if it was in trouble. This object briefly stabilized before resuming its descent, dangerously approaching Dahl's boat. In his testimony, he described how this object began to eject some sort of material resembling lava or molten metal, which fell into the water and onto the deck of his boat, causing property damage and, tragically, injuring his son and killing his dog.

The other objects, seemingly reacting to their companion's distress, positioned themselves above it, forming a sort of lid or shield. Shortly after, the object in difficulty righted itself and they all resumed their initial formation before speeding off to the west, disappearing from Dahl and his son's view within seconds.

The incident, which only lasted a few minutes, left Dahl deeply shocked and perplexed. He noted that the water around his boat was bubbling and hot to the touch after the debris fell, suggesting that the ejected material was extremely hot. The debris later recovered by Dahl was metallic in nature, very light and blackened by heat.

This detailed observation report by Harold Dahl constitutes one of the first documented cases of UFOs where debris was recovered after a close encounter. Despite the absence of photographic evidence, the precision of the details provided by Dahl and the physical damage observed on his boat have fueled discussions and speculations for decades.

Testimonials.

One of the first witnesses, Harold Dahl, was working on a rescue boat near Maury Island when he observed six saucer-shaped objects in the sky. According to his testimony, these objects were in formation and seemed to be made of a shiny metal. Dahl described one of the objects as being in trouble, losing altitude before stabilizing. Shortly after, this object began to eject what appeared to be lava or a similar material, which fell into the sea and onto the deck of his boat, causing damage.

Fred Crisman, another witness who accompanied Dahl, corroborated this observation. He added that the debris falling from the objects had not only damaged the boat, but had also killed their dog, who was on board, and injured Dahl's son. Crisman described the objects as being silent but having a disruptive effect on their environment, noting that the sea water was boiling under the objects as if it was heated by an intense force.

A third witness, an unidentified woman who was on the beach of Maury Island, reported seeing the objects from a different perspective. She described seeing five objects in perfect formation, with a sixth seeming to have technical difficulties. This observer also mentioned the presence of a strange substance falling from the sky, which she compared to "molten metal".

The testimonies of these main observers were supplemented by those of several other local residents and visitors to the island, who reported seeing similar objects in the sky around the same time. Some described the objects as emitting a brilliant light, while others noted an unusual silence during the incident, interrupted only by the sound of debris falling into the water.

These collective testimonies provide a coherent overview of the incident, although the exact details vary slightly between witnesses. What remains constant in the accounts is the presence of unidentified flying objects exhibiting behaviors and technological characteristics that do not correspond to aircraft or natural phenomena known at the time.

The Investigation.

The initial reactions were marked by a certain urgency, given the period of tension post-World War II and the beginning of the Cold War. The military authorities, particularly the US Air Force, were the first to respond. Investigative teams were dispatched to the island to question witnesses and examine the sites where the objects had been spotted.

The testimonies collected during the investigation were varied but often consistent on certain details. Witnesses generally described flying objects of discoidal or oval shape, sometimes accompanied by bright lights and high-speed movements. These descriptions fueled speculations about the possibility of advanced technology, perhaps non-terrestrial.

The initial reports from military investigators attempted to rationalize the observations by attributing them to natural phenomena or confusion with conventional aircraft. However, the lack of concrete evidence and the persistence of testimonies led to a deadlock in the investigation.

Faced with the inability to provide a definitive explanation, the authorities have classified a large part of the investigation results. This lack of transparency has fueled conspiracy theories and public distrust towards official explanations.

In conclusion, despite the efforts made, the investigation into the Maury Island incident has not been able to completely demystify the reported events. The declassified documents from the following years have only reinforced the aura of mystery surrounding this incident, leaving many questions unanswered.

Theories and Speculations.

One of the most widespread theories is that of extraterrestrial intervention. This hypothesis suggests that the observed object was a spacecraft of non-earthly origin. Supporters of this theory base it on several elements, such as the description of the object, which did not correspond to any known device at the time, and the behavior of the pilot, who seemed to perform maneuvers impossible for a human aircraft. Moreover, some witnesses reported seeing strange life forms near the object, which reinforces the idea of an extraterrestrial origin.

Another theory put forward is that of a secret military project. According to this hypothesis, the observed object could be a prototype of an airplane or drone secretly developed by the government or the military. This theory is supported by the fact that the incident occurred shortly after the end of World War II, a period marked by intense research and development in the field of aviation. Supporters of this hypothesis also point out that the government may have been motivated to conceal the true nature of the object for reasons of national security.

A third theory suggests that the incident could be the result of an optical illusion or a mistake. Some experts in optics and meteorology have suggested that particular atmospheric conditions could have created deceptive visual effects, making an ordinary object appear as an inexplicable phenomenon. This hypothesis is often invoked to explain other UFO sightings, but it remains controversial in the case of Maury Island due to the specific details reported by the witnesses.

Finally, there is a less conventional theory that suggests the incident could be related to paranormal phenomena or parallel dimensions. This hypothesis is generally less accepted by the scientific community, but it attracts the attention of some paranormal researchers. According to this theory, the object could be a manifestation of forces or entities from another dimension, which would explain its unusual appearance and abilities.

KENNETH ARNOLD'S OBSERVATION: THE INCIDENT THAT POPULARIZED THE TERM "FLYING SAUCER".

DATE: June 24, 1947.
COUNTRY: United States.
STATE: Washington.
CITY: Near Mount Rainier.

On June 24, 1947, an unusual event occurred that would not only captivate the public imagination but also give birth to a new term in the lexicon of unidentified aerial phenomena: "flying saucers". That day, Kenneth Arnold, a private airplane pilot and American businessman, was flying from Chehalis, Washington, to Yakima, Washington, in his CallAir A-2 plane. As he approached Mount Rainier, Arnold decided to slightly alter his route to assist in the search for a military transport C-46 that had crashed in the area. It was during this deviation from his initial route that Arnold spotted a series of bright objects in the sky. According to his testimony, these objects were flying at an incredible speed, far exceeding that of any plane of the time, and seemed to be moving in a linear formation. Intrigued and somewhat disconcerted, Arnold observed the objects for several minutes, trying to understand their nature and origin. What he saw that day and how he described the incident to the media not only sparked a wave of interest in UFOs but also introduced the term "flying saucer" into popular vocabulary, a term that would become synonymous with mystery and speculation in the decades to come.

The Observation.

The objects, numbering nine, were moving at an incredibly high speed, which Arnold later estimated to be about 1,200 miles per hour, much faster than any plane of the time. They were flying in staggered formation, and Arnold described them as being flat and rather circular, with some sort of tail or wing. What particularly caught his attention was the way these objects bounced in the air, like saucers skipping on water, which led Arnold to describe them as "flying saucers", a phrase that would become famous worldwide.

The flight path of the objects seemed to be from northwest to southeast, and they crossed Arnold's field of vision in just a few seconds, quickly disappearing behind a mountain range.

The weather conditions that day were ideal for flying, with little or no wind and no clouds on the horizon. This not only allowed Arnold to clearly see the objects, but also eliminated some conventional explanations such as reflections on clouds or optical illusions due to particular atmospheric conditions.

Arnold's observation quickly made headlines and sparked considerable public and media interest in unidentified aerial phenomena. This incident is often considered the starting point of the modern era of UFOs, and the term "flying saucer" has become synonymous with UFO in the collective imagination.

Testimonials.

Arnold described the objects as being flat and rather circular in shape, with a wavy motion that allowed them to reflect the sun's light like mirrors. He compared their movement to that of a disc skipping on water, which later originated the expression "flying saucer", although Arnold specified that the objects were not exactly disc-shaped. This observation lasted several minutes, giving him enough time to thoroughly detail what he was seeing.

In addition to Arnold, there were other indirect testimonies that corroborated the observation of unidentified flying objects in the same region and at the same time. A forest ranger named Fred Johnson, located on Mount Adams, reported seeing six flying objects around the same time as Arnold's observation. Johnson noted that his compass began to behave erratically when the objects were visible, which could indicate magnetic interference caused by the objects.

Another testimony comes from a couple who were on a boat on the Columbia River, who reported seeing similar objects a few days before Arnold's sighting. Although their report was not as detailed, their description matched Arnold's regarding the speed and formation of the objects.

These testimonies, although less detailed than Arnold's, add a layer of credibility to the incident, suggesting that what Arnold saw was not an isolated phenomenon or an illusion. The accumulation of these observations contributed to the interest and subsequent investigation of UFOs by authorities and researchers.

The Investigation.

As soon as Arnold's report reached the authorities, the United States Air Force took the initiative to investigate these claims, as part of what would later become known as Project Sign. This project was the first official operation of the US Air Force aimed at collecting, analyzing and interpreting data on UFOs. The investigators first thoroughly questioned Arnold, seeking to understand precisely what he had observed. Arnold described the objects as being disc-shaped, shiny and reflective, moving at an incredibly high speed in a way that seemed to defy the laws of physics as known at the time.

The military authorities also collected testimonies from other witnesses who reportedly saw similar objects in the same area and at the same time. These additional testimonies added some credibility to Arnold's report, suggesting that what he had seen was not the product of his imagination or a simple misidentification.

In parallel, aeronautics experts from the military tried to determine if what Arnold had seen could be explained by natural phenomena or known technologies. They examined various hypotheses, including reflections on the cockpit or weather balloons. However, none of these explanations fully matched the descriptions given by Arnold and other witnesses.

The investigation took a more complex turn with the analysis of the weather and atmospheric conditions of that day, as well as possible optical illusions due to light and reflection. Scientists specializing in optics and meteorology were consulted to assess these aspects. Despite these efforts, the explanation of Arnold's observations remained elusive.

The final report of the Project Sign on this incident has never been fully disclosed to the public, and the conclusions reached by the military authorities have remained ambiguous. Some declassified documents suggest that the air force could not provide a definitive explanation and maintained the possibility that the observed objects could be of non-terrestrial origin. However, this position has not been officially adopted by the US government.

The Kenneth Arnold incident thus served as a catalyst for a series of government investigations into UFOs that would continue for decades. Each new sighting was often compared to Arnold's, and his case remained a reference in the study of unidentified aerial phenomena. Despite the accumulation of reports and data, the mystery of the objects that Arnold saw that day remains unsolved, fueling curiosity and debate about UFOs to this day.

Theories and Speculations.

The first and most popular of the theories is that of the extraterrestrial visit. This hypothesis suggests that the objects observed by Arnold were spacecraft of non-earthly origins. Supporters of this theory often cite the speed and seemingly impossible movements of the objects, as described by Arnold, which seemed to defy the laws of physics known at the time. Moreover, the absence of any known technology capable of reproducing such phenomena at that time strengthens this perspective for many.

Another theory put forward is that of natural or atmospheric phenomena. Some researchers have suggested that what Arnold saw could be the result of mirages or particular light refractions, caused by unusual atmospheric conditions. This explanation is often supported by scientists who point out the possibility that rare but natural optical conditions could create illusions of flying objects.

A third hypothesis concerns secret or experimental technologies. At the time of Arnold's observation, the Cold War was underway, and both the United States and the USSR were actively developing new aeronautical technologies. Some theorists suggest that the objects could be experimental aircraft or drones unknown to the general public and even to most military personnel. This theory is sometimes supported by declassified documents showing interest and investment in advanced aerial technologies during this period.

Furthermore, there are those who believe that Arnold's observation could be a mix of several of these explanations. For example, it could be a misunderstanding where Arnold saw experimental aircraft, but due to particular atmospheric conditions, these aircraft took on a strange and unidentifiable appearance. This hybrid theory attempts to combine scientific and skeptical elements to provide a more down-to-earth explanation while acknowledging the limits of our understanding of secret technologies.

The debates around these theories are often lively and polarized. Ufologists and skeptics meticulously analyze the details of Arnold's observation, each firmly defending their interpretation of the facts. Discussions frequently focus on the credibility of the witnesses, the plausibility of human technologies of the time compared to the maneuvers described, and the reliability of natural or atmospheric explanations.

These controversies and speculations continue to generate significant interest, both in the scientific community and among the general public, illustrating the complexity and enduring appeal of unidentified phenomena in our sky. The Kenneth Arnold incident remains an emblematic case, often revisited for its implications in our understanding of UFOs and their place in popular and scientific culture.

Conclusion.

The incident involving Kenneth Arnold in 1947 is a pivotal moment in the history of ufology, marking the beginning of the modern era of UFOs. Arnold's observation of several unidentified flying objects near Mount Rainier not only introduced the term "flying saucer" into popular lexicon, but also stimulated global interest in unexplained aerial phenomena. Despite numerous theories and speculations, the accuracy of Arnold's observation details and the nature of the objects he saw remain a subject of debate. This incident continues to fuel curiosity and research on UFOs, highlighting the enduring fascination for the unknown and unexplained in our sky.

THE ROSWELL INCIDENT: THE MYSTERY OF THE DEBRIS FROM AN UNIDENTIFIED OBJECT.

DATE: July 1947.
COUNTRY: United States.
STATE: New Mexico.
CITY: Roswell .

The Roswell incident remains one of the most mysterious and discussed events in the history of UFO sightings. In July 1947, something crashed near Roswell, New Mexico, sparking speculations and conspiracy theories that still persist today. Initially, military authorities announced they had recovered debris from a "flying disc". However, this claim was quickly retracted, giving way to an official explanation that the debris came from a weather balloon. Despite this statement, many eyewitnesses reported seeing materials with strange properties, as well as bodies of non-human beings at the crash site. These testimonies have fueled a rich UFO lore, placing Roswell as a pillar of pop culture associated with aliens. The incident also engendered lasting mistrust towards the American government, many believing in a cover-up of the real facts concerning UFOs and extraterrestrial life.

The Observation.

This event took place near Roswell, New Mexico, a region that, at the time, was sparsely populated and primarily used for agriculture and livestock. The initial observation of the debris was made by a local farmer, William "Mack" Brazel, who discovered strange materials scattered on his ranch located about 75 miles north of the city of Roswell.

The discovery was made early in the morning, just after a series of violent storms that had swept the region. The weather conditions around the time of the incident were marked by frequent lightning and heavy rains, which initially led to the belief that the debris could be the remains of a weather balloon or other equipment affected by the bad weather. However, the nature and appearance of the materials found by Brazel did not correspond to those usually associated with such equipment.

The debris discovered covered a large area of about 200 meters in diameter. They included numerous fragments of shiny and metallic materials, as well as pieces of what seemed to be thick paper or plastic. Some witnesses who saw the debris described very thin metal sheets that were incredibly light and resistant. These sheets could be crumpled or deformed, but returned to their original shape without any sign of folding or damage. In addition, there were metal rods with strange symbols that did not resemble any known writing.

The exact time of the debris discovery is not clearly documented, but it is generally accepted that Brazel found the scattered materials early in the morning, after the storms of the previous night. Visibility was good at the time of discovery, despite recent rains, and the day was beginning to dawn, providing sufficient natural light for detailed observation.

The debris emitted no sound, movement, or detectable radiation, which added to the confusion about their origin and nature. The impact area showed no crater or ground mark typical of a high-speed collision, suggesting that the materials had landed or had been scattered with relatively little force. This observation led to speculations about the possibility that the debris had been deployed or dropped from a relatively low altitude.

In summary, the observation of the debris from the Roswell incident describes an event where unidentified and unusual materials were found scattered over a large area after a night of intense weather conditions. The description of the materials, combined with the absence of significant ground damage and the unexplained nature of the symbols observed on some fragments, continues to spark interest and debate among researchers and the general public.

Testimonials.

The key first witness to this incident is Mac Brazel, a local farmer who discovered strange debris on his land near Roswell, New Mexico. Brazel described the materials as being very light and unbreakable, unlike anything he had ever seen. He mentioned that the debris included thin metal sheets, rigid rods, and pieces of plastic that resembled paper, but were impenetrable.

Another important witness is Sheriff George Wilcox, who was one of the first to be informed by Brazel. Wilcox contacted the military authorities at Roswell Air Base, which triggered an official investigation. The sheriff reported that Brazel was visibly upset and confused by the discovery, insisting that the materials were not conventional.

Major Jesse Marcel, intelligence officer at the Roswell base, was sent to recover the debris. Marcel reported that the materials had unusual properties, such as the ability to return to their original shape after being crumpled, and that they were extremely light and durable. He also mentioned the presence of symbols resembling hieroglyphs on some metal fragments.

Lieutenant Walter Haut, the public relations officer of the base, was tasked with drafting and releasing an initial press release stating that a "flying disc" had been recovered. However, this statement was quickly retracted, and a new explanation was given, asserting that the debris was in fact from a weather balloon.

Finally, General Roger Ramey, commander of the 8th Air Force, played a key role in managing the incident. Ramey organized a press conference where he presented debris that he claimed to be from the weather balloon, contradicting the initial descriptions of the materials by Marcel and other witnesses. This action sowed doubt and confusion among the public and the media.

These testimonies, although varied, highlight the unusual nature of the debris and the speed with which the military sought to control the narrative of the incident. The contradictions between the initial reports and the subsequent official explanations have fueled speculations and conspiracy theories that persist to this day.

The Investigation.

The official investigation was conducted by the United States Air Force. The debris was sent to Fort Worth, then to Wright Field in Ohio for further analysis. According to military reports, the materials examined were those of a weather balloon from the Mogul project, a top-secret program intended to detect Soviet nuclear tests. This conclusion was officially adopted and the case was closed, at least temporarily.

However, interest in the Roswell incident has not diminished, and many alternative theories have emerged. Faced with public pressure and persistent theories of a cover-up, the Air Force launched a new investigation in the 1990s. The 1994 report, titled "Case Closed: Final Report on the Roswell Incident", reaffirmed the conclusion that the debris came from a balloon from the Mogul project. The report also included testimonies from people involved in the recovery of the debris, who described materials that matched those used in weather balloons.

In addition to the analysis of materials, the investigation also collected eyewitness testimonies. Many of these testimonies were contradictory, some claiming to have seen extraterrestrial bodies and others not. The air force attributed these accounts of bodies to a misinterpretation of crash test dummies, which were used in military experiments around the same period.

The investigation into the Roswell incident remains a subject of intense debate. Despite the official conclusions, many researchers and UFO enthusiasts continue to question the version of events presented by the government. Declassified documents and testimonies collected over the years have only added to the complexity of the case, making the Roswell incident one of the most emblematic and mysterious cases in UFO history.

Theories and Speculations.

The first theory, and undoubtedly the most popular, is that of the extraterrestrial craft. According to this hypothesis, the debris found near Roswell, New Mexico, would be the remains of a non-earthly spacecraft. This theory is supported by several testimonies from people who had access to the site of the incident, who described the recovered materials as being of a nature and technology unknown on Earth. Moreover, some reports mention the recovery of extraterrestrial bodies, which would reinforce the idea of a non-human origin of the object.

Another theory put forward is that of a secret military experiment. According to this perspective, the debris at Roswell could be the remnants of a classified military project, such as a spy balloon or a new experimental aircraft. This hypothesis is supported by the fact that the area of the incident is close to several military bases, including that of Roswell, which was at the time a very active Air Force base. Skeptics of the extraterrestrial theory suggest that the US government could have orchestrated a cover-up to hide the details of a sensitive defense project.

A third theory suggests that the incident could be the result of confusion or misinterpretation of the events and objects involved. Some researchers believe that the debris could have come from a regular weather balloon or another conventional aerial object, which may have been misidentified as something more mysterious or exotic due to the collective hysteria about UFOs at the time.

Finally, there is a conspiracy theory that the Roswell incident was an elaborate hoax staged by the US government in order to divert public attention from other more important or sensitive issues at the time. This hypothesis suggests that the authorities could have used the UFO story as a smokescreen to cover up internal or international operations or political issues.

The controversy escalated when witnesses began to report that they had been pressured to keep quiet about the incident, and some even claimed to have seen extraterrestrial bodies recovered from the site. These testimonies fueled speculation about a possible government cover-up.

Over the years, the Roswell incident has become a cultural phenomenon, inspiring films, books, and television shows. Despite investigations and reports, including those from the United States Air Force in the 1990s that concluded the incident involved a top-secret surveillance balloon and not a UFO, many questions remain unanswered for UFO enthusiasts and skeptics.

THE AZTEC INCIDENT.

DATE: March 25, 1948.
COUNTRY: United States.
STATE: New Mexico.
CITY: Aztec.

The Aztec incident is an event that has captivated the imagination of UFO enthusiasts and paranormal phenomena researchers for decades. Located in the small town of Aztec, New Mexico, this incident is often compared to that of Roswell, although it is less publicized. According to the accounts, an unidentified flying object would have crashed on the desert plateaus near Aztec in early spring 1948. What distinguishes this incident is the alleged recovery of an almost intact device and several alien bodies inside the apparatus.

The first reports on the Aztec incident emerged in the 1950s, but it was Frank Scully's book "Behind the Flying Saucers", published in 1950, that really brought this case to light. Scully detailed how scientists and military personnel allegedly recovered a 30-meter diameter flying disc, as well as the bodies of 16 small humanoids. These claims have been widely discussed and controversial, with some asserting that the story was an elaborate hoax, while others believed in the cover-up of a real extraterrestrial encounter.

Over the years, the Aztec incident has been the subject of numerous investigations and research. Declassified documents, witness testimonies, and field research have attempted to unravel the truth from the false in this complex story. Despite the skeptics, many researchers continue to believe that something extraordinary indeed happened on that day in March 1948, adding an intriguing piece to the puzzle of UFOs and extraterrestrial presence on Earth.

The Observation.

The observation took place early in the morning, around 5 o'clock, when visibility was still limited by pre-dawn darkness. However, the sky was exceptionally clear that day, with no clouds on the horizon, allowing for a clear view of the object. The weather conditions were calm, with little or no wind, and a cool temperature typical of early spring mornings in the region.

Witnesses reported that the UFO moved with remarkable precision, without any engine noise or other mechanical sound. It seemed to float in the air rather than fly, moving slowly over the desert landscape before coming to a halt. At this point, the object was described as stationary, suspended a few meters above the ground. This phase of the observation lasted several minutes, giving the witnesses enough time to observe in detail the external structure of the UFO.

The surface of the object was apparently seamless and without visible assembly, which added to the strangeness of the apparition. Moreover, some witnesses reported seeing some sort of portholes or small circular openings along the circumference of the object, although no movement or sign of life was observed through these openings.

After hovering in the air for a while, the UFO began to emit a series of flashing lights, varying from red to blue, then to white. This light show lasted a few moments before the object began to move again. It accelerated impressively, without any apparent increase in noise or turbulence, and disappeared over the horizon within seconds.

The entire observation lasted about an hour, leaving the witnesses both amazed and perplexed by what they had seen. The precision of the details observed and the duration of the event allowed for an unusually high amount of data to be collected on the appearance and behavior of the object, making the Aztec incident an important case study for ufologists and researchers in unidentified aerospace phenomena.

Testimonials.

One of the first witnesses, a petroleum engineer who was working in the region, reported seeing a silver disc about 30 meters in diameter hovering and then slowly descending to the ground. He described the object as being perfectly circular with a sort of dome on top, and without any visible markings or windows. The engineer also noted the absence of engine noise, which left him puzzled about the propulsion method of the craft.

Another witness, a local police officer who was called to the scene shortly after the alleged crash, corroborated this description. He added that when he arrived, he saw several bodies around the craft, which seemed to be small in size and dressed in tight suits, made of a material he had never seen before. According to him, these bodies did not resemble any known earthly creature.

A rancher from the region also testified, claiming that he had seen the object descend from the sky early in the morning. Intrigued, he had approached the site before the arrival of the authorities. The rancher described a chaotic scene with debris scattered around the main craft, and confirmed the presence of the strange bodies mentioned by the policeman.

A radio technician, who was an aviation enthusiast and had heard about the incident from friends, went to the scene to see for himself. He reported that the craft had a smooth and reflective surface, and it seemed to be made of an unknown metal. He also mentioned that the object had apparent damage on one side, as if something had hit it or if it had hit something during the landing.

Finally, a member of the military, who preferred to remain anonymous, shared that his unit had been dispatched to secure the site and recover the debris. According to him, the operation was of the utmost confidentiality and they had received strict orders not to disclose anything about what they had seen. However, he confirmed that the object recovered did not resemble any device or technology known at the time.

These testimonies, although varied, paint a consistent picture of an extraordinary event that continues to raise questions and theories to this day. The details of the observations, although sometimes diverging on minor aspects, converge on the description of an abnormal craft and its non-human occupants, thus posing a persistent challenge to conventional explanation.

The Investigation.

The investigation began immediately after local authorities were alerted by witnesses who reportedly saw a flying disc crash on the Hart Canyon plateau, near Aztec. The first responders on the scene were local police officers, quickly joined by members of the United States Air Force. According to some unofficial reports, the military quickly secured the area, establishing a strict perimeter and prohibiting access to civilians and the press.

The testimonies collected during the initial investigation indicate that the recovered object measured about 30 meters in diameter and had a disk shape. Several witnesses also reported the presence of non-human bodies inside the craft, which added an additional dimension to the case. These witnesses included local residents, hunters, and even some of the first police officers to arrive at the scene.

The military authorities conducted a more thorough investigation, the details of which remained largely classified. However, subsequently declassified documents revealed that the Air Force had carried out a series of technical analyses on the recovered object. These analyses aimed to determine the nature of the material used for the construction of the UFO, as well as its possible flight capabilities.

The final report of the army, which was partially declassified decades later, concluded that the incident was the result of a misunderstanding. According to this report, the object in question was actually a very advanced weather balloon, part of a top-secret American government project. This conclusion was widely disputed by the UFO community, who accused the government of cover-up.

In addition to military and government investigations, several civilian ufology groups have also conducted their own investigations. These groups have gathered additional testimonies, often contradicting the official conclusions. They also pointed out several inconsistencies in the army's report, particularly regarding the speed at which the army cleaned up the site and the nature of the materials recovered, which did not match those typically used in weather balloons.

The investigation into the Aztec incident remains a subject of intense debate among researchers and UFO enthusiasts. Despite the decades that have passed, many questions remain unanswered, fueling conspiracy theories and speculation about the possibility of a government cover-up. Declassified documents and testimonies continue to be analyzed by those seeking to understand what really happened that day in Aztec.

Theories and Speculations.

The first theory, and perhaps the most popular, is that of the extraterrestrial craft. According to this hypothesis, the object that crashed in Aztec was a spacecraft of non-Earth origin. Supporters of this theory rely on testimonies from people who allegedly saw the wreckage or the bodies, as well as on documents that allegedly leaked from the government. They argue that the American government recovered the wreckage and the bodies to study them in secret, as part of a broader effort to understand and exploit extraterrestrial technology.

Another theory put forward is that of the secret military experiment. Some researchers believe that the object that crashed could have been an experimental American device, such as a spy balloon or a prototype of an advanced technology aircraft. This hypothesis is often reinforced by the context of the Cold War, a period during which the United States and the Soviet Union were actively developing new aeronautical technologies and testing secret weapons. Supporters of this theory argue that the government could have concealed the true nature of the incident to prevent sensitive information from falling into enemy hands.

A third theory concerns a possible hoax or exaggeration of the facts. Some skeptics suggest that the Aztec incident could have been a fabrication or an exaggeration on the part of those who initially reported it. They suggest that the story could have been embellished for various reasons, such as the desire to create a media sensation or to financially benefit from the growing interest in UFOs at the time. This theory is often supported by the lack of concrete physical evidence and inconsistencies in the witness accounts.

Finally, a last speculation revolves around the idea of a confusion with another incident. It is possible that the witnesses misinterpreted a more mundane event, such as the crash of a conventional plane or the fall of a meteor, and that this was subsequently transformed into a UFO story. This theory is sometimes used to explain why there is little consensus or clear evidence regarding what actually happened in Aztec.

Despite the lack of tangible evidence and lingering doubts, the Aztec incident remains a subject of fascination for ufologists and conspiracy theory enthusiasts. It is often cited in discussions about the alleged concealment of UFO information by the U.S. government and continues to be studied and debated in circles interested in the UFO phenomenon.

THE CHILES-WHITTED INCIDENT, ALABAMA: AERIAL ENCOUNTER WITH AN ELONGATED OBJECT EMITTING FLAMES.

DATE: July 24, 1948.
COUNTRY: United States.
STATE: Alabama.
CITY: Montgomery.

The Chiles-Whitted incident is an emblematic case in the history of UFO sightings, deeply impacting the UFO community and studies on unidentified aerial phenomena. In the early hours of July 24, 1948, two experienced pilots from Eastern Air Lines, Captain Clarence Chiles and co-pilot John Whitted, witnessed an extraordinary event that defied their understanding of aviation and physics. As they were piloting a DC-3 near Montgomery, Alabama, they suddenly spotted a strange and luminous flying object. According to the pilots' descriptions, the object had an elongated shape, similar to an airplane fuselage, but with no visible wings. What particularly struck them was the presence of flames or some kind of propulsion at the rear of the object, emitting intense light that illuminated the night sky. The object passed by their plane at a dizzying speed, before abruptly ascending into the sky and disappearing. This encounter lasted a few seconds, but it left a lasting impression on the witnesses and raised many questions about the nature of the observed object. Official reports, including those from the American Air Force, attempted to analyze and rationalize the incident, but no definitive explanation was provided, thus leaving this event shrouded in mystery.

The Observation.

On July 24, 1948, an unusual event occurred in the night sky over Montgomery, Alabama, involving pilots Clarence Chiles and John Whitted, both employees of Eastern Air Lines. While they were piloting a DC-3 at about 5,000 feet altitude, at 2:45 in the morning, they witnessed a strange and disconcerting apparition that would mark the history of UFO sightings.

The object observed by Chiles and Whitted was elongated in shape, similar to an airplane fuselage, but without the wings usually visible on conventional airplanes. The size of the object was impressive, estimated to be about 100 feet long. What particularly caught the attention of the two pilots was the intense brightness emanating from the object, as well as flames and a glowing red light at the rear, giving the impression that the object was propelled by some kind of jet.

The weather conditions that night were clear, with almost perfect visibility under a starry sky, which allowed for a detailed observation of the incident. The moon was low on the horizon, which minimized natural light interference and accentuated the brightness of the observed object.

According to witness descriptions, the object was moving at a staggering speed. It was first seen approaching the plane head-on before changing trajectory and passing at a blistering speed on the side of the DC-3. The object's passage was accompanied by a high-pitched whistling, perceived by the pilots, and a wave of heat felt throughout the cabin, a phenomenon that added to the strangeness of the experience.

The observation lasted a few seconds, but it left an indelible impression on Chiles and Whitted, who both insisted that the object did not have the characteristics of a conventional airplane, neither in terms of structure nor flight behavior. The accuracy of their report, combined with their experience as pilots, added considerable weight to their testimony.

Testimonials.

On July 24, 1948, two experienced pilots from Eastern Air Lines, Captain Clarence Chiles and co-pilot John Whitted, witnessed an extraordinary event while they were piloting a DC-3 near Montgomery, Alabama.

Around 2:45 in the morning, while they were flying at about 5,000 feet altitude, Chiles suddenly spotted an intense light approaching their plane at a dizzying speed. At first, he thought it was a jet, but he quickly realized that the object did not match any known aircraft. According to his testimony, the object was about 100 feet long and had a streamlined shape, resembling a rocket or a missile, but much wider.

Whitted, who also observed the object, confirmed Chiles' description. He added that the object had two rows of windows emitting a bright light, giving the impression of interior lighting. Both pilots reported that the object emitted red and orange flames from the rear, which seemed to be a propulsion system. The object passed at an estimated distance of only a few hundred feet from their plane, before abruptly ascending into the sky and disappearing.

Another witness, a passenger named Clarence McKelvie, confirmed seeing an intense light pass by the plane, although he could not describe the object as precisely as the pilots. His testimony, however, corroborates the fact that something unusual happened that night.

The impact of this encounter was not limited to these visual observations. Chiles and Whitted reported that the plane had been violently shaken when the object had accelerated to rise into the sky. This physical disturbance was further evidence that the object had interacted in some way with their immediate environment.

The detailed descriptions of the object, combined with the physical effects felt, make this incident particularly notable in the annals of close encounters with unidentified objects. The testimonies of the pilots, both considered reliable and experienced, add a layer of credibility to the incident, distinguishing it from the many other less well-documented UFO reports or those from less reliable sources.

The Investigation.

The initial reaction of the authorities was to take this testimony very seriously, given the credibility of the two pilots. The American Air Force, under the auspices of Project Sign, which was then in charge of investigating unidentified aerial phenomena, immediately launched a thorough investigation. The investigators collected the testimonies of the pilots, who described the object as being streamlined in shape, measuring about 30 meters long, with rectangular windows and a tail emitting an intense red light.

The initial reports from the pilots were supplemented by checks of the weather conditions and other commercial or military flights in the region at that time. No particular weather phenomena or other aircraft were identified that could explain the observation.

The investigation also included the analysis of psychological and physical impacts on the witnesses. The pilots were subjected to medical and psychological examinations to assess their health status and reliability. The results confirmed that both men were in excellent physical and mental condition, thereby strengthening the credibility of their testimony.

The military authorities examined several hypotheses, including that of a secret experimental aircraft or a rare natural phenomenon, but none of these explanations could be definitively proven. The final report of Project Sign concluded that the descriptions of the object and the conditions of the observation did not correspond to any known aircraft or natural phenomenon at the time.

However, this conclusion did not put an end to speculations and alternative theories. Other investigations and analyses were conducted by civilian ufology organizations and independent researchers, who often criticized the approach of the military authorities, suggesting a possible withholding of information or a misinterpretation of the data.

Despite numerous investigations and the passage of time, the Chiles-Whitted incident remains an unsolved case and continues to fascinate and divide experts and UFO enthusiasts. The testimonies of the pilots, as well as the lack of a convincing explanation, continue to fuel the debate about the possible presence of unidentified flying objects in our airspace.

Theories and Speculations.

One of the first theories put forward was that of a meteor. Skeptics and some scientists suggested that what the pilots had seen was nothing more than a bright meteor quickly crossing the night sky. This hypothesis is supported by the fact that meteors can sometimes create illusions, especially when observed from particular angles, and can appear larger or closer than they actually are. However, this theory has been widely contested, notably because the pilots' descriptions of the object included specific details such as windows and an apparent structure, which is atypical for a meteor.

Another proposed explanation is that of an experimental balloon or a secret device tested by the military. During the Cold War, many tests of new aircraft were conducted in secret, and it is possible that Chiles and Whitted may have observed one of these devices. This theory is reinforced by the fact that the US military and government have often been reluctant to disclose information about their secret projects. However, no document or concrete evidence has ever been presented to support this hypothesis.

A third theory, more marginal but still present in the UFO debate, is that of the extraterrestrial visit. According to this perspective, the object observed by the pilots would be a spaceship from an advanced civilization elsewhere in the universe. This idea is often supported by ufologists who cite the apparently advanced technology and unusual flight capabilities of the object, as arguments indicating a non-earthly origin. However, this theory is generally rejected by the scientific community, which demands more tangible and reproachable evidence before seriously considering the extraterrestrial hypothesis.

Finally, there are those who believe that the incident could be the result of a hallucination or a misunderstanding by the pilots, perhaps due to fatigue or other psychological factors. This explanation is often seen as an attempt to rationalize the incident in the absence of solid material evidence. Nevertheless, both pilots were experienced and respected, which makes this theory unconvincing to many.

THE GORMAN DOGFIGHT INCIDENT: A NATIONAL AIR GUARD FIGHTER PILOT ENGAGES A UFO OVER FARGO, NORTH DAKOTA.

DATE: October 1st, 1948.
COUNTRY: United States.
STATE: North Dakota.
CITY: Fargo.

On October 1, 1948, an unusual event occurred in the night sky over Fargo, North Dakota, capturing the attention of UFO enthusiasts and aviation experts. That night, Lieutenant George F. Gorman, an experienced pilot of the Air National Guard, had a close encounter that became famous as the "Gorman Dogfight". Gorman, who had served as a fighter pilot during World War II, was conducting routine flights near Hector Airport in Fargo. Around 9 p.m., after escorting a Piper Cub to landing, he decided to stay in the air to practice night maneuvers. That's when Gorman spotted an unidentified flying object. According to his report, the UFO was a bright light moving at a speed and with agility that exceeded the capabilities of his fighter plane, an F-51 Mustang. Intrigued and determined to examine the object more closely, Gorman engaged in a pursuit that lasted nearly 27 minutes. The object and Gorman executed a series of complex aerial maneuvers, the UFO seemingly skillfully evading Gorman each time. The incident ended when the UFO suddenly accelerated at a phenomenal speed, disappearing into the night, leaving Gorman alone and perplexed. The Gorman Dogfight incident remains one of the most documented and discussed confrontations between a military aircraft and a UFO, raising questions and theories that still persist today.

The Observation.

That evening, Gorman was participating in a routine mission with other planes from the National Guard. After the other pilots had landed, Gorman decided to stay in the air to practice night flying maneuvers. At around 9 p.m., as he was preparing to land, he spotted an unidentified flying object and decided to approach it for a closer look.

The object that Gorman reported seeing was oval-shaped and emitted a bright light. It measured approximately six to eight feet in diameter, according to his estimates. What particularly intrigued Gorman was the object's ability to perform aerial maneuvers with agility and speed far surpassing that of his own plane, a P-51 Mustang, which was one of the most high-performing fighters of the time.

The chase, which lasted about 27 minutes, saw the UFO perform a series of evasive maneuvers. Gorman tried several times to approach the object, but it always seemed able to escape with disconcerting ease. At one point, the object passed so close to Gorman's plane that he had to make a sudden maneuver to avoid a collision. The object then gained altitude very quickly, leaving Gorman far behind.

The weather conditions that night were clear with excellent visibility, which allowed Gorman to maintain constant visual contact with the object throughout the duration of the incident. The clear sky also helped ground controllers to track part of the engagement via radar, although the object did not consistently appear on their screens.

The incident finally ended when the object made a vertical ascent at a phenomenal speed and disappeared from Gorman's view. Exhausted and perplexed, Gorman eventually landed at Fargo airport, immediately reporting the incident to his superiors as well as local authorities.

This observation remains one of the most detailed involving a military pilot and a UFO, primarily due to the accuracy of Gorman's testimony and the duration of the engagement. The technical details of the object, such as its ability to perform high-speed maneuvers and its apparent ability to avoid collision with ease, continue to arouse interest and speculation.

Testimonials.

Gorman describes the object as being a bright light, with no visible solid structure, measuring about six to eight inches in diameter. According to his testimony, the UFO is capable of high-speed maneuvers and sudden accelerations, well beyond the capabilities of his own aircraft, a P-51 Mustang. He reports that the object has the ability to make tight turns and seems to be guided by an intelligence due to its ability to dodge his attempts to approach.

During the pursuit, which lasts about 27 minutes, Gorman reaches speeds of up to 400 miles per hour and climbs up to 14,000 feet. The object and Gorman's plane approach within a few feet of each other several times, creating a high-risk situation for the pilot. Gorman also notes that the object makes no audible noise and has no external features such as wings or windows.

The ground controllers at Hector Airport in Fargo, as well as the control tower staff, confirm having seen the object both visually and on radar. Controller Lloyd D. Jensen reports that the object appears on the radar as a small echo, moving at variable speeds and abruptly changing direction.

After several unsuccessful attempts to intercept the object, Gorman loses sight of the UFO when it makes an abrupt vertical movement. Exhausted and running out of fuel, Gorman finally decides to return to the airport. He lands without incident and immediately reports the event to his superiors.

The Gorman incident is quickly handled by the Air Force, which launches an investigation. Gorman is thoroughly questioned by Air Force officers and representatives of Project Sign, a US Air Force initiative aimed at investigating unidentified aerial phenomena. During his interrogation, Gorman remains firm in his position, insisting that the object was neither an atmospheric phenomenon nor a conventional aircraft.

This testimony from Gorman, corroborated by the radar and visual observations of ground controllers, remains one of the most documented and discussed incidents in the study of unidentified aerial phenomena. The subsequent official explanation, suggesting that Gorman might have confused a weather balloon with the planet Jupiter, is widely disputed by ufologists and remains a subject of intense debate.

The Investigation.

The investigation began immediately after the incident, when Gorman landed and reported his experience to the military authorities. He described the UFO as a bright light capable of high-speed maneuvers and exceptional agility, defying the capabilities of the aircraft of the time. The initial stages of the investigation involved collecting testimonies from Gorman himself, as well as other witnesses on the ground and in the control tower of Hector Airport in Fargo.

The military authorities also examined the radar data to see if the object had been recorded. However, the reports were contradictory; some radar operators claimed to have detected an unidentified signal, while others observed nothing unusual. This disparity added a layer of mystery to the incident and complicated the investigation efforts.

In the following weeks, aeronautical experts from the Air Force analyzed the descriptions of the object and the movements reported by Gorman. They tried to determine if the UFO could be an experimental aircraft, an atmospheric phenomenon, or something else. The technical analysis included comparing the flight capabilities of the UFO with those of known aircraft at the time.

One of the most crucial parts of the investigation was the thorough questioning of Gorman by Air Force officers. They examined every detail of his account to ensure the consistency and reliability of his testimony. Gorman maintained his version of events throughout, insisting that the object was neither a conventional aircraft nor a weather balloon, as some had suggested.

The Blue Book project, which took over the investigation at a later stage, classified the Gorman incident as "unresolved". The investigators could not provide a definitive explanation, despite examining all available evidence. The final report noted that the flight characteristics of the UFO, as described by Gorman, did not match any known natural or technological phenomenon at the time.

Theories and Speculations.

One of the first theories put forward is that of a mistake with a weather balloon. At the time, it was common to use balloons for atmospheric observations, and some have suggested that Gorman might have confused one of these balloons with a UFO. However, this theory is often contested due to the detailed description given by Gorman of the object's fast and seemingly controlled movements, which seem incompatible with the movements of a balloon subjected to air currents.

Another popular hypothesis is that of an optical illusion or hallucination. Skeptics argue that Gorman, flying alone at night, could have fallen victim to visual fatigue or temporary disorientation, leading to a misinterpretation of what he was seeing. This theory is reinforced by the fact that night flying conditions can create various deceptive optical phenomena, such as reflections or mirages.

Some researchers have suggested that Gorman may have encountered a prototype of a secret airplane or an experimental drone. During this period, the United States was testing several new types of aircraft, and it is not inconceivable that one of these devices could have been mistaken for a UFO. This theory is supported by the fact that the incident took place near a military base, where such tests could have been conducted.

On the side of extraterrestrial theories, some ufologists argue that the Gorman incident is proof of the visit of extraterrestrial vehicles. They cite the apparently intelligent behavior and superior maneuvering capabilities of the object as indications that the object could not be of human manufacture. This perspective is often reinforced by comparisons with other UFO incidents where similar features have been reported.

Finally, there are those who consider the incident as a case of "war nerves" or paranoia related to the Cold War. At that time, the fear of an aerial attack or an invasion was palpable, and it is possible that this tension influenced Gorman's perception, leading him to interpret an ordinary phenomenon as a potential threat.

THE MCMINNVILLE INCIDENT: TWO ICONIC UFO PHOTOS CAPTURED BY A COUPLE IN MCMINNVILLE, OREGON.

DATE: May 11, 1950.
COUNTRY: United States.
STATE: Oregon.
CITY: McMinnville.

On May 11, 1950, in the small town of McMinnville, Oregon, a couple, Paul and Evelyn Trent, captured two photographs that would become iconic in the field of UFO sightings. That day, Evelyn Trent was outside their farm, feeding the rabbits, when she spotted a strange metallic object in the sky. Intrigued, she called her husband, who, equipped with his camera, managed to quickly take two shots of the object before it disappeared at high speed.

These photos were first published in a local newspaper, the "Telephone-Register", and then gained national notoriety after being picked up by "Life" magazine. The images show an object with a discoid shape, with an apparent structure under its base, floating in the sky. The authenticity of the photos has been the subject of many debates. Photography experts and scientists have examined the shots on various occasions, some claiming that it was a hoax, while others supported their authenticity.

The McMinnville incident remains an important case study for ufologists and continues to spark interest and curiosity, not only among experts but also among the general public, due to the clarity and quality of the photographs taken by the Trents. These images are often cited as some of the most convincing evidence of the potential existence of unidentified flying objects and have contributed to fueling the debate on extraterrestrial presence.

The Observation.

That day, around 7:30 pm, Evelyn Trent was in her garden, busy feeding her rabbits. The sky was clear, with a few scattered clouds, and visibility was excellent, which is typical for a spring evening in the Pacific Northwest region.

Suddenly, Evelyn spotted a strange object in the sky. She described it as metallic, with a very distinct shape resembling a disk or a saucer. The object seemed to reflect the light of the setting sun, giving it an almost silvery glow. Intrigued, she called her husband, Paul Trent, who was inside the house.

Paul, after hearing his wife's call, rushed with his camera, a Kodak Roamer, which used 620 format films. He managed to take two photographs of the object before it disappeared at high speed towards the west. The photos show a disk-shaped object with an apparent dome on top, suspended in the sky without any apparent sign of propulsion or emission.

The two images captured by Paul Trent have become among the most analyzed and discussed in the history of ufology. The object photographed did not resemble any known aircraft of the time, and its ability to remain stationary, then accelerate rapidly without noise, was contrary to the capabilities of aerial vehicles of the time.

The light of the setting sun, combined with the clarity of the sky, provided ideal conditions for photography, which allowed for capturing precise details of the object. Photography experts who examined the negatives afterwards concluded that the photos were not tampered with and that the object was indeed present in the sky at the time of the shots.

This McMinnville incident and the photographs taken by Paul Trent continue to be a source of fascination and study, offering a rare and valuable insight into a phenomenon that, to this day, still raises many questions and theories.

Testimonials.

Evelyn Trent described the object as being circular in shape with a raised center, resembling a "flying saucer", a popular term at the time to describe unidentified flying objects. According to her testimony, the object was silent and seemed to reflect the sunlight on its metallic surface, giving it an almost silvery glow. She estimated that the object was at a relatively close distance, which allowed her to distinctly see its shape and contours.

Paul Trent, for his part, confirmed his wife's observations. He added that the object moved without any perceptible noise and without any disturbance of the air around it, which was unusual for a flying object. The photos he took that day clearly show a disc-shaped object with a smooth and metallic appearance, suspended in the sky. Paul Trent insisted that he had never seen such a craft before and had no explanation as to its nature or origin.

The photos taken by Paul Trent were subsequently published in a local newspaper, then caught the attention of national media and UFO researchers. The images have been analyzed by numerous experts and institutions, including the United States Air Force as part of Project Blue Book, an official UFO study program. While some analyses have suggested that the photos could be authentic, others have hypothesized that they could be the result of a hoax. However, the Trents have always maintained that their encounter was real and that they had no reason to fabricate such a story.

The McMinnville incident remains an emblematic case in the study of UFOs, mainly due to the clarity and quality of the photos taken by the Trents. These images continue to be studied and debated by researchers and skeptics, each seeking to understand the true nature of what the Trents saw that day in May 1950.

The Investigation.

As soon as the photos were published in the local newspaper, the "Telephone-Register", interest in the case exploded, prompting the United States Air Force to intervene under the auspices of Project Blue Book, an official program tasked with studying unidentified aerial phenomena. The investigators from Project Blue Book quickly made contact with the Trents to obtain direct testimonies and examine the original negatives of the photographs.

The initial stages of the investigation involved verifying the authenticity of the images. The Army's photography experts analyzed the negatives to detect any possible alterations or overlays. The results of these analyses were controversial: some experts concluded the photos were authentic, while others suggested the possibility of a hoax, particularly due to the absence of motion blur in the images, which would have been expected given the supposed speed of the object.

In parallel, investigators questioned other witnesses in the McMinnville area to corroborate the Trents' account. Although a few people reported seeing unusual phenomena in the sky at that time, no other tangible evidence was collected to support the existence of a UFO.

The analysis of weather and aerological conditions was also a key component of the investigation. Investigators examined weather data to see if natural phenomena could explain the appearance of the object. However, no abnormal conditions were recorded that day, leaving experts perplexed about the nature of the photographed object.

Over the years, the McMinnville incident has been the subject of numerous reassessments by independent researchers and UFO organizations. More modern analyses, using advanced image processing technologies, have attempted to determine the size, speed, and distance of the object from the camera. These studies have often led to divergent conclusions, some reinforcing the theory of an unidentified flying object, while others lean towards a more prosaic explanation, such as a small plane or a weather balloon.

Despite the efforts made, the official investigation was never able to provide a definitive explanation. The Blue Book Project ultimately classified the McMinnville incident as "unresolved", leaving open the question of whether the photos represent a genuine UFO or a more conventional object misidentified. This lack of clear conclusion has fueled numerous theories and speculations, making the McMinnville incident a persistent case study in the field of ufology.

Theories and Speculations.

One of the most common theories is that of the authenticity of the UFO. Many ufologists and researchers believe that the photos show a real extraterrestrial craft. This hypothesis is often supported by the fact that the photos have been analyzed by several photography experts who found no evidence of falsification or superimposition. Moreover, the testimonies of the Trents, who maintained until their death that the object was real and that they had no particular photography skills to fake such images, reinforce this theory.

However, there is also strong opposition to this interpretation. Some skeptics argue that the object could be an elaborate hoax or a mistake. A popular theory among skeptics is that the object was actually a mirror or a porthole detached from agricultural equipment, which would have been suspended by nearly invisible wires to create the illusion of a UFO. This hypothesis is often reinforced by the analysis of shadows and light in the photos, which some experts deem inconsistent with a flying object.

Another speculation concerns the possibility that the object might be a weather balloon or another type of balloon. At the time, the use of balloons for various scientific and military research was common, and it is possible that the Trents mistakenly photographed one of these balloons. This theory is often disputed because the descriptions of the object by the witnesses do not typically match the appearance or movements of a balloon.

Furthermore, some researchers have suggested that the incident could be linked to secret military experiments. In the context of the Cold War, the United States conducted numerous tests of new aircraft and aeronautical technologies. It is therefore plausible that the observed object was a prototype of an airplane or drone being tested, which was not yet known to the public. This hypothesis is difficult to verify due to the defense secrecy surrounding such projects at the time.

Conclusion.

The two photographs taken by Paul and Evelyn Trent in 1950 in McMinnville, showing a discoidal object in the sky, have been widely circulated and analyzed, sparking both fascination and skepticism. Despite numerous investigations, including that of the US Air Force's Blue Book project, the authenticity of the photos has never been definitively proven or refuted. This incident illustrates the complexity and challenges associated with interpreting UFO evidence and continues to captivate researchers and the general public. The McMinnville photos remain a valuable case study for understanding how visual evidence of UFOs is scrutinized and debated in the scientific community and among ufology enthusiasts.

THE UFO SIGHTING OF MARIANA IN GREAT FALLS, MONTANA.

DATE: August 1950.
COUNTRY: United States.
STATE: Montana.
CITY: Great Falls.

In August 1950, Nick Mariana, the general manager of the semi-professional baseball teams of Great Falls, captured images that are among the first UFO videos ever recorded. That day, Mariana was at the Great Falls baseball stadium with his secretary, when they both spotted two bright objects in the sky. Mariana, who had his camera with him to film a game, quickly began recording the objects. The images he captured clearly show disc-shaped objects, moving at an incredible speed and without any noticeable noise.

The incident quickly attracted media attention and was one of the first to be seriously studied by the US Air Force, as part of what would later become the Blue Book project, a series of studies on UFOs conducted by the American military. The investigators of the Blue Book project examined the films and interviewed Mariana and his secretary. Although the Air Force eventually concluded that the objects were probably reflections of the sun on two fighter planes, this explanation did not convince many researchers and ufologists, who pointed out the abnormal movements of the objects and their appearance that did not match that of planes.

Mariana's observation remains an emblematic case for UFO enthusiasts and continues to spark debates and theories. It highlights the complexity and challenges associated with interpreting UFO sightings and distinguishing between conventional explanations and unexplained phenomena.

The Observation.

That day, around 11:30, Mariana was at the Legion Park baseball stadium, accompanied by her secretary, when something unusual in the clear and sunny sky caught her attention.

The weather conditions were ideal for clear observation: the sky was devoid of clouds, visibility was excellent and there was only a slight breeze. These conditions allowed a clear view of the mysterious object.

Mariana spotted two bright objects, reflecting the sunlight, moving at an incredible speed in the sky. The objects were round in shape and had a metallic appearance. They seemed to be spinning on themselves while flying. Intrigued and aware of the rarity of what he was observing, Mariana quickly ran to his car to retrieve a 16 mm camera with which he began to film the moving objects.

The filmed sequence, which lasted about 16 seconds, clearly shows the disc-shaped objects flying at high speed. They were moving from west to east, and at one point, they seemed to perform some kind of aerial maneuver, as if they were piloted or controlled. The objects emitted no perceptible sound, which added to the strangeness of the observation.

The analysis of the objects' speed, based on the film, suggests that they were moving at a speed greater than that of jet planes of the time. This characteristic, along with the absence of noise and the ability for advanced aerial maneuvers, clearly differentiated these objects from any known conventional aircraft.

The precision of the details captured in Mariana's film was a key point in the study of this incident. The images not only show the shape and apparent structure of the objects, but also their brightness and reflection of light, which has led to numerous speculations about the nature and construction material of the observed objects.

This Great Falls incident has become a classic case studied by ufologists and has been included in several government research projects on unidentified aerial phenomena. The clarity of the observation, the quality of the film, and the perfect weather conditions have made this encounter an often-cited example in discussions about credible UFO sightings.

Testimonials.

This event took place in August 1950, and the testimonies collected mainly come from Nick Mariana, the general manager of the Great Falls Electrics baseball teams, and his secretary, Virginia Raunig.

Nick Mariana was the first to observe the unidentified flying objects that morning. According to his account, it was around 11:30 when he spotted two bright objects in the sky. These objects, round in shape and silver in color, seemed to be spinning on themselves while flying at high speed. Mariana described the objects as being "like two inverted flying saucers, one above the other". He estimated that the objects were moving at a speed greater than any plane he had ever seen. Intrigued and aware of the importance of his observation, Mariana ran to get his 16mm camera and managed to film the objects for a few seconds before they disappeared over the horizon.

Virginia Raunig, who accompanied Mariana that day, also confirmed having seen the objects. She specified that the objects were extremely bright and that they were moving at an incredible speed. She added that the objects made no audible noise, which was unusual compared to airplanes. Raunig also mentioned that the objects had left a bright trail behind them, which made their observation even more spectacular.

The testimonies of Mariana and Raunig were taken very seriously by the UFO community and by the authorities of the time, notably because Mariana had managed to capture the objects on film. This film was subsequently analyzed by several experts and institutions, including the US Air Force, which at the time was leading the Blue Book project, a series of studies on UFOs.

In addition to Mariana and Raunig, other indirect witnesses reported seeing similar objects in the sky of Great Falls that day, although their observations were not documented with the same precision. These additional testimonies helped to strengthen the credibility of the incident and to generate considerable public and media interest around this case.

The Investigation.

The investigators interviewed Mariana and Raunig, reviewed the film, and analyzed the meteorological and aeronautical conditions of the day of the incident.

The initial reactions of the military authorities were to rationalize the observation as being reflections or conventional aircraft. However, the analysis of the film by Air Force experts revealed that the objects were moving at a speed and with a maneuverability that did not correspond to those of the aircraft of the time. Moreover, no military or civilian aircraft were reported in the area at that time.

The investigation took a controversial turn when Mariana accused the Air Force of tampering with his film before returning it to him. According to him, some of the clearest images of the objects had been removed. The Air Force denied these allegations, stating that the film had been returned in its entirety.

The testimonies collected during the investigation varied. Other witnesses in the area reported seeing similar objects, while some experts suggested that the objects could be misinterpreted natural phenomena, such as meteors. However, the analysis of the movement of the objects in the film and their appearance did not match that of meteors or other known natural phenomena.

The official investigation concluded that the observations were "unexplained" but did not explicitly state that they were of extraterrestrial origin. The Blue Book Project classified the incident as unresolved.

The Mariana incident has had a lasting impact on the UFO community and has contributed to fueling the public and scientific debate on the possible presence of unidentified flying objects and their origin. Despite the decades that have passed since the incident, the details of the investigation and the images captured by Mariana continue to spark interest and speculation.

Theories and Speculations.

One of the first explanations put forward is that of the American Air Force, which suggested that what Mariana had filmed was nothing more than reflections of two F-94 Starfire fighter jets. This theory is supported by the fact that Malmstrom Air Base, located not far from Great Falls, was active at that time and frequently used this type of aircraft. However, this explanation has been widely contested by Mariana and other witnesses who claim that the observed objects looked nothing like conventional aircraft, particularly because of their apparent speed and erratic movements in the sky.

Another popular theory among ufologists is that of the extraterrestrial craft. This hypothesis is fueled by the speed and maneuvers of the objects, which seem to defy the capabilities of the aerial technologies of the time. Moreover, the Mariana film was analyzed by several photography and cinematography experts who concluded that the images were not faked. However, this theory is criticized by skeptics who argue that visual evidence is not sufficient to confirm the presence of extraterrestrial crafts and that interpretations can be biased by pre-existing beliefs.

A third explanation considers the possibility of an optical illusion or a rare atmospheric phenomenon. Some researchers have proposed that the particular weather conditions that day could have created unusual mirages or reflections in the sky. This theory is often dismissed by those who have studied the film and noted the clarity and consistency of the objects' movements, which appear to be solid objects with a defined trajectory.

Finally, there are those who believe that the incident could be linked to a secret military project or tests of new aerial technologies. This hypothesis is supported by the proximity of Malmstrom Air Base, which could have been the site of advanced prototype testing. However, no official document has ever confirmed this theory, and it remains speculative.

THE FORT MONMOUTH INCIDENT: UFO OBSERVATIONS AT FORT MONMOUTH, NEW JERSEY.

DATE: September 1951.
COUNTRY: United States.
STATE: New Jersey.
CITY: Fort Monmouth.

The Fort Monmouth incident is a case of UFO observation that took place in September 1951 at Fort Monmouth, New Jersey. At that time, the Cold War was at its peak and international tensions strongly influenced public perception of unidentified aerial phenomena. Fort Monmouth, an active U.S. Army installation in the development and testing of electronic communications and surveillance equipment, was a strategic location for such observations. The context of the incident involves several credible witnesses, mainly military personnel and technicians, who reported seeing unidentified flying objects moving at speeds and with maneuvers that exceeded the capabilities of aircraft of the time. These observations were made over several consecutive days, and each testimony was meticulously recorded and analyzed by military authorities. The incident sparked a thorough investigation by Project Blue Book, a series of UFO studies conducted by the US Air Force. The detailed reports and subsequent investigations not only contributed to a better understanding of the surveillance capabilities of the time, but also fueled public and scientific debate about the possible presence of unidentified flying objects in American airspace.

The Observation.

That day, specifically on September 10, the weather conditions were clear with excellent visibility, which is a crucial detail, as it allowed for detailed observation without obstruction by atmospheric phenomena such as fog or rain.

The event began early in the morning, around 11:00, when several army radar technician students, who were training at Fort Monmouth, detected an unidentified object on their radar. The object was moving at an unusually high speed, much higher than that of conventional aircraft of the time. The estimated speed was about 700 miles per hour, a feature that immediately caught the attention of the radar operators.

Shortly after the radar detection, a T-33 training plane pilot, who was flying in the area at that time, reported seeing a flying object that did not match any known type of aircraft. The description given by the pilot was that of an oval-shaped object, with a smooth and metallic surface, which reflected the sunlight. The object had no visible wings or apparent means of propulsion, which clearly distinguished it from planes and helicopters.

The visual observation lasted about twenty minutes, an exceptionally long duration for this type of encounters. The object was seen maneuvering with agility, performing quick movements and changes of direction that defied the capabilities of the planes of the time. On several occasions, the object approached at high speed, stopped abruptly, then accelerated again, all without producing any audible noise.

The intensity of the observation increased when the object was seen heading east, towards the Atlantic Ocean, before suddenly disappearing from the witnesses' view and radar screens. This sudden disappearance, as well as the speed and maneuvers of the object, left the observers perplexed and without a conventional explanation.

The Fort Monmouth incident was taken very seriously by the military authorities, who immediately launched an investigation to try to determine the nature and origin of the observed object. The testimonies of the radar technicians and the pilot, combined with the recorded radar data, constituted a solid basis for the analysis of this event. However, despite the efforts made, no definitive explanation was found at the time.

Testimonials.

These observations took place over several days and involve different witnesses, mainly radar operators and pilots.

The first testimony comes from two radar operators, Sergeant James Barton and Corporal Edward Nugent, who were working at the Fort Monmouth air traffic control center on the morning of September 10, 1951. They detected an unidentified object on their radar, moving at an unusually high speed, estimated between 700 and 800 miles per hour. The object was tracked for about 30 seconds before disappearing from the radar screen. Both men described the object as being clearly different from conventional aircraft, both in its speed and its flight behavior.

The same day, a little later, an army test pilot, Lieutenant Wilbert Rogers, reported seeing a flying object at high altitude while he was conducting a test flight near Fort Monmouth. According to his testimony, the object was oval-shaped and shone in the sunlight. He observed the object for about two minutes before it disappeared at a speed greater than that of his plane.

On September 12, another incident involving several witnesses took place. This time, it was a group of cadets from the air force school who observed a similar object. The cadets, under the supervision of Lieutenant George T. Gregory, were in formation outside when they spotted a shiny metallic object in the sky. The object was moving erratically, changing direction several times before rising rapidly and disappearing from sight. Lieutenant Gregory estimated that the object was moving at a speed far greater than that of any known aircraft at the time.

In response to these observations, an investigation was conducted by the Blue Book project, the US Air Force unit responsible for studying unidentified aerial phenomena. Although the investigation concluded that there was no threat to national security, the testimonies of radar operators and pilots continued to raise questions and debates among researchers and UFO enthusiasts.

The Investigation.

This case involved several observations of unidentified flying objects by qualified military personnel, which triggered a series of official investigations conducted with particular rigor.

From the first observation reports, the command of the air base took the initiative to meticulously document the testimonies of radars and visual observers. The descriptions reported objects moving at speeds and with maneuvers that did not correspond to conventional aircraft of the time. Witnesses described objects of various shapes, some evoking discs, others more elliptical shapes, moving at high speed without notable noise.

In response to the seriousness of the testimonies, the Air Technical Intelligence Center (ATIC), which was part of the Air Force Intelligence, was tasked with conducting the main investigation. The ATIC sent investigators on site to question witnesses, examine radar recordings, and assess all available evidence. The goal was to determine the nature and origin of the observed objects, as well as to assess any potential threat to national security.

The investigators collected detailed testimonies and tried to correlate these accounts with radar data. The radar reports confirmed that the objects had been detected moving at varying speeds and altitudes, sometimes remaining stationary, then suddenly accelerating. These characteristics were not typical of the aircraft of the time, which added a layer of mystery to the investigation.

During the investigation, ATIC consulted various experts in aeronautics, meteorology, and physics to analyze the available data. Despite these efforts, many aspects of the observations remained without a convincing explanation. The experts were unable to attribute the observations to meteorological phenomena, weather balloons, or known aircraft.

The final report from ATIC concluded that the observations were credible, but could not provide a definitive explanation. The report emphasized the need to continue monitoring and analyzing UFO observations, recognizing that such incidents could have significant implications for national security.

This incident also influenced government policy on UFOs, leading to the creation of more structured projects like Project Blue Book, which aimed to systematically investigate UFO sightings and determine their potential threat. The Fort Monmouth incident remains an important case study in the annals of ufology and continues to be cited as an example of how UFO sightings are handled at the government level.

Theories and Speculations.

The theories put forward to explain the observations at Fort Monmouth vary widely, ranging from conventional explanations to more exotic hypotheses. One of the earliest theories suggests that the observed objects were in fact weather balloons. At the time, it was common to use balloons for atmospheric measurements, and it is possible that the radars misinterpreted these floating objects as unidentified flying objects. However, this theory has been widely contested, particularly because the testimonies of pilots and radar operators described movements and speeds that did not correspond to the flight characteristics of a balloon.

Another explanation put forward is that of a mistake with conventional aircraft. At that time, the Fort Monmouth region was an active air corridor, and it is plausible that the observations were the result of a misidentification of military or civilian aircraft. However, this theory also struggles to explain the detailed descriptions of erratic movements and exceptional maneuvering capabilities reported by witnesses.

Among the unconventional theories, some speculations suggest the presence of experimental devices, either of American origin or foreign. During the Cold War, the United States and the Soviet Union regularly tested new aeronautical technologies, and it is possible that what was observed was a secret prototype. However, no declassified document has so far confirmed this hypothesis.

The extraterrestrial theory remains one of the most popular and controversial. It posits that the observed objects were vessels of non-earthly origin. This hypothesis is often supported by descriptions of sudden accelerations and antigravitational movements that seem to defy the laws of physics as we know them. Despite its appeal to the general public and some researchers, this theory lacks concrete evidence and is often rejected by the scientific community.

Finally, there are those who suggest that the incident could be attributed to rare natural phenomena, such as atmospheric mirages or electromagnetic anomalies. These phenomena can sometimes create illusions of flying objects, especially when observed through devices like radars or telescopes, which can amplify perception errors.

The variety of testimonies and technical data collected during this incident makes the analysis particularly complex and open to interpretation. Despite numerous investigations and analyses, the incident remains one of the many unsolved cases in the history of ufology, illustrating the inherent challenges in understanding and explaining such phenomena.

Conclusion.

Despite the thorough investigations conducted by the Blue Book project, no satisfactory explanation has been found for the objects observed at Fort Monmouth. The testimonies of radar technicians and pilots, as well as radar recordings, suggest that the observed objects possessed flight capabilities superior to any known aircraft at the time. This incident underscores the complexity and mystery that still surround unidentified aerial phenomena today, and continues to arouse interest among both researchers and the general public.

THE WASHINGTON D.C. INCIDENT: WAVE OF PANIC FOLLOWING THE DETECTION OF UNIDENTIFIED OBJECTS.

DATE: July 1952.
COUNTRY: United States.
STATE: District of Columbia.
CITY: Washington D.C. .

The Washington D.C. incident in July 1952 remains one of the most publicized and controversial events in the history of observing unidentified flying objects (UFOs). This series of events took place over several consecutive nights, attracting the attention of the public, media, and government authorities. At that time, the Cold War was at its peak, and the fear of a technologically advanced attack from the Soviet Union was omnipresent in the minds of Americans. It was in this context of tension and suspicion that the radars of Washington National Airport and Andrews Air Force Base began to detect unidentified flying objects moving at speeds and with maneuvers that exceeded the capabilities of aircraft of the time. The radar observations, corroborated by visual testimonies from pilots and citizens, triggered a series of reactions ranging from questioning to panic. The objects were described as being luminous and capable of sudden movements at high speed, defying the laws of physics as known at the time. The American government, under pressure to clarify the situation, had to publicly intervene to try to calm the population and demystify the observations. This incident not only marked the annals of encounters with UFOs but also influenced aviation policy and the management of classified information concerning unidentified aerial phenomena.

The Observation.

Over several nights, unidentified flying objects were observed in the sky of the American capital, causing an unprecedented wave of panic and media interest.

The most notable observation took place on the night of July 19 to 20, 1952. Around midnight, the radars of the Washington National Airport (today the Ronald Reagan Washington National Airport) began to detect objects moving at speeds and with maneuvers that far exceeded the capabilities of the aircraft of the time. These objects appeared sporadically on the screens, sometimes disappearing only to reappear elsewhere.

The air traffic controllers, intrigued and worried, observed these radar anomalies for several hours. The objects seemed capable of remaining stationary, then suddenly accelerating to supersonic speeds, behaviors that were not associated with conventional aircraft of the time.

Visually, witnesses on the ground and in surrounding planes described the objects as being oval or circular in shape, with bright lights, often white in color, but sometimes with shades of blue or red. These lights did not blink like those of planes, but rather seemed to pulse or vary in intensity.

The observation reached a peak of intensity when several of these objects were seen simultaneously at different locations in the Washington sky. Pilots flying nearby were contacted by air traffic controllers and some visually confirmed the presence of the mysterious objects. One pilot even reported that one of these objects approached his plane before moving away at an incredible speed.

The weather conditions during these observations were clear with few clouds, which eliminates the possibility that the observed objects are weather phenomena such as lenticular clouds or atmospheric mirages. The visibility was good, which allowed many witnesses on the ground to clearly see the objects in the night sky.

This incident lasted several nights, with similar observations made on subsequent nights. Each time, the objects mainly appeared between midnight and dawn, thus maximizing the number of witnesses due to the darkness and clarity of the sky.

In summary, the Washington D.C. incident of 1952 is characterized by multiple observations of unidentified flying objects, detected both by radar and visually, behaving in a manner that does not correspond to known aircraft or natural phenomena of the time. These observations were accompanied by clear weather conditions, which strengthens the credibility of the visual testimonies.

Testimonials.

The testimonies of this event come from several credible sources, including air traffic controllers, pilots, and even members of the police.

One of the first witnesses to this incident was Edward Nugent, an air traffic controller at Washington National Airport. Nugent observed seven strange objects on his radar, moving in a restricted airspace. These objects did not conform to the movements or speeds of conventional aircraft. Nugent described the objects as being "hovering, then moving at incredible speeds, like nothing I had ever seen before."

Harry Barnes, another air traffic controller, corroborated Nugent's observations. Barnes reported that the objects disappeared and reappeared on the radar screen, changing direction with astounding agility. He also noted that the objects sometimes seemed to follow commercial planes, causing concern among the pilots.

One of the pilots, Captain S.C. "Casey" Pierman, flying for Capital Airlines, was a key witness to this incident. While he was in flight, Pierman observed six bright objects moving at high speed. He described the lights as being "white and bright", moving at a speed he estimated to be much faster than any plane he had ever seen. Pierman followed the objects for about fourteen minutes before losing sight of them.

The observations were not limited to aviation professionals. A Washington D.C. police officer, named John Baxter, reported seeing objects similar to those described by air traffic controllers and pilots. Baxter observed several lights moving at high speed in the night sky, changing direction abruptly and without any apparent noise.

These testimonies, among others, contributed to the magnitude of the Washington D.C. incident. The descriptions of the objects' movements, their ability to change direction quickly and disappear from radar, as well as the consistency of reports from different professional witnesses, fueled debates and speculations about the nature of these objects for decades. The incident not only captivated the public, but also drew the attention of military and government authorities, leading to more in-depth investigations into unidentified aerial phenomena.

The Investigation.

This phenomenon has triggered a series of official investigations conducted by various American government agencies, including the Air Force.

Everything began when a radar at Washington National Airport detected several unidentified objects in the night sky. These observations were quickly confirmed by other radars in the region. Faced with the increasing number of reports and media pressure, the Air Force launched an official investigation to determine the nature and origin of these objects.

The initial reactions of the military authorities were to rationalize the observations as natural phenomena or radar errors. However, the testimonies of civilian and military pilots, who reported seeing flying objects with extraordinary characteristics, complicated this explanation.

The investigation was primarily conducted by the Blue Book project, an Air Force initiative dedicated to the study of UFOs. The investigators examined radar data, collected testimonies, and analyzed weather conditions during the incidents. They also questioned air traffic controllers and eyewitnesses.

One of the key aspects of the investigation was the analysis of radar recordings. The Air Force's radar experts attempted to determine if the signals could be attributed to atmospheric anomalies, such as temperature inversions, which could reflect radar signals to the ground and create echoes of false objects. However, this theory did not fully match the rapid movements and flight formations reported by the witnesses.

The testimonies of the pilots were particularly disturbing for the investigators. Several experienced pilots described objects moving at incredible speeds, performing maneuvers that defied the laws of physics known at the time. These descriptions added a level of credibility to the reports, putting investigators under pressure to provide a plausible explanation.

Faced with the inability to provide a definitive explanation and the fear of public panic, the Air Force organized a press conference. Major General John Samford, then director of Air Force intelligence, stated that the majority of UFO sightings could be explained by conventional phenomena, but he also admitted that some cases remained unresolved.

In conclusion of the investigation, the final report of the Blue Book project on the incident attributed most of the observations to radar errors and misinterpreted weather phenomena. However, this conclusion did not satisfy all observers, and the Washington D.C. incident remains a subject of debate and speculation among ufologists and skeptics.

The incident had a lasting impact on the management of UFO observations by the American government, leading to more structured policies and ongoing monitoring of UFO reports by specialized agencies.

Theories and Speculations.

One of the first theories put forward was that of temperature inversions. According to this hypothesis, particular weather conditions could have caused radar anomalies, creating echoes of false objects. Skeptics and some meteorologists argue that temperature inversions, which involve a layer of warm air over a colder one, can refract radar waves in unusual ways, creating illusions of objects moving in the sky. However, this explanation does not take into account the consistent visual testimonies of pilots and air traffic controllers who reported seeing lights moving intelligently and coordinated in the sky.

Another popular theory is that of extraterrestrial intervention. This hypothesis is supported by many ufologists who argue that the movements and maneuvering capabilities of the observed objects do not correspond to any known technology of the time. Moreover, the fact that these objects could disappear and reappear quickly, change direction at high speeds, and execute tight turns without slowing down, suggests for some a technology far beyond the human capabilities of the time.

Some conspiracy theorists suggest that the incident could be linked to secret experiments by the American government. They speculate that the United States might have been testing prototypes of advanced aircraft or drones, and that the Washington incident could have been a staged event to assess public and defense system reactions to an unknown aerial intrusion. This theory is often reinforced by the fact that the military initially downplayed the events before officially acknowledging them, which could indicate an attempt at concealment.

Finally, there are those who believe that the incident could be attributed to psychosocial phenomena. According to this view, the collective fear of alien invasion, fueled by the media and popular culture of the time, could have led to a kind of mass hysteria where witnesses were predisposed to interpret ordinary phenomena as extraordinary. This theory is often used to explain why so many people reported similar observations despite the absence of concrete physical evidence.

The variety of explanations offered reflects the complexity of the incident and the mystery that continues to surround it, making it a fascinating case study for those interested in unidentified aerial phenomena.

THE ADAMSKI INCIDENT.

DATE: November 13, 1952.
COUNTRY: United States.
STATE: California.
CITY: Desert Center.

George Adamski, a restaurateur and amateur philosopher passionate about astronomy, claims to have encountered an extraterrestrial spaceship and its occupant in the California desert, near Desert Center. Before this event, Adamski had already made a name for himself in UFO circles for his photographs of what he claimed to be spaceships. On November 13, 1952, accompanied by several witnesses, Adamski ventured into the desert, where he said he observed a large cigar-shaped ship. According to his account, a small saucer-shaped ship detached from the latter and landed not far from him. Adamski left his friends at a distance and approached the craft alone, where he allegedly met a being he described as being of human appearance, coming from Venus. The entity, named Orthon, allegedly communicated with Adamski telepathically, sharing messages of peace and warning against the dangers of the nuclear age. This incident catapulted Adamski to the status of an iconic figure in UFO communities and sparked a lively debate about the veracity of his claims.

The Observation.

That day, Adamski, accompanied by several witnesses, was in the California desert, near Mount Palomar, where he ran a small restaurant and an amateur observatory.

The observation took place in the early afternoon, under a clear and sunny sky, which offered perfect visibility. According to Adamski and his companions, the UFO initially appeared at a considerable distance, resembling a bright point in the sky. Gradually, the object approached, allowing for more detailed observation. Adamski described the UFO as having the shape of a classic saucer, with a transparent dome on top. The object measured about 10 meters in diameter and was composed of what seemed to be a shiny metal, emitting a soft glow.

The object stabilized at a short distance from the ground, floating without any perceptible noise, which intrigued Adamski and his companions. They noted that the UFO produced no visible disturbance of the air or sand beneath it, suggesting advanced levitation or anti-gravity technology. Adamski used his telescope to take several photographs of the UFO, which show a disc-shaped object with precise details, such as portholes or marks on the hull, which were not visible to the naked eye.

During the observation, which lasted about 30 minutes, the object performed several maneuvers in the sky. It executed movements that seemed to defy conventional laws of physics, such as sudden accelerations and abrupt stops, high-speed vertical ascents and descents, and lateral movements without changing orientation. These movements left the witnesses perplexed about the nature of the technology used.

The Adamski incident was particularly striking due to the clarity and duration of the observation, as well as the number of witnesses present. The ideal weather conditions that day allowed for an unambiguous observation, which is rare in cases of UFO sightings. The detailed description of the object and the photographs taken by Adamski contributed to making this incident an important case study for ufologists and skeptics.

Testimonials.

George Adamski, the main witness of this event, provided a detailed account of his experience with a purported extraterrestrial spacecraft and its occupant. According to Adamski, on November 20, 1952, while he was in the California desert with several friends, he observed a large flying saucer-shaped object that landed not far from him.

Adamski described the object as having a metallic brightness, with a transparent upper dome through which he could see silhouettes. After a few moments, a door opened and a being emerged from the ship. Adamski described this being as resembling a human, of perfect beauty, with long hair and fitted clothes made of an unknown material. The extraterrestrial, whom Adamski named "Orthon", allegedly communicated with him telepathically, sharing messages of peace and warning of dangers associated with the use of nuclear energy.

The other witnesses present, including Alice Wells and Lucy McGinnis, confirmed having seen a strange object but were not close enough to observe the direct encounter between Adamski and the entity. However, they attested to Adamski's excitement and seriousness when he returned to them after the incident. Wells mentioned having seen Adamski talking to a figure near the ship, although too far away to distinguish the details.

Another witness, George Hunt Williamson, who was also present that day, claimed to have observed strange footprints in the ground near where the ship would have landed. These footprints, according to Williamson, had unknown symbols that could be related to an extraterrestrial language. Williamson also took casts of these footprints, which he later used to support Adamski's account.

In addition to these direct testimonies, photographs taken by Adamski of the flying object have been widely circulated. Although these images have been subject to controversy and accusations of falsification, they remain an integral part of the Adamski incident file. Critics argue that the photos could be hoaxes, while Adamski's supporters consider them as tangible proof of his experience.

The Investigation.

The investigation into the Adamski incident began shortly after he made his experience public. The military authorities, notably the US Air Force, quickly showed their interest in Adamski's account, mainly because of the national security implications that the presence of unknown craft in American airspace could entail. The Air Force, through Project Blue Book, its program tasked with studying unidentified aerial phenomena, took the initiative to collect and analyze information related to this incident.

The initial stages of the investigation involved detailed interviews with George Adamski himself. The investigators examined his claims about encountering a spaceship and a being he described as coming from Venus. Adamski provided photographs of the ship he claimed to have taken during the incident. These images were meticulously analyzed by Air Force photography experts, who sought to identify signs of falsification or features that could corroborate Adamski's version of events.

In parallel, eyewitnesses who were present during the incident or who had observed unusual phenomena in the region at that time were also questioned. These testimonies were crucial to corroborate or refute Adamski's statements. However, the accounts were often contradictory or lacked precise details, making it difficult for investigators to draw definitive conclusions.

The authorities also consulted scientists and aerospace experts to assess the plausibility of the technologies described by Adamski. The descriptions of the spacecraft and its flight capabilities were compared to the technological knowledge of the time to determine if they could be technically feasible without resorting to non-earthly technologies.

As the investigation progressed, attention also turned to Adamski's personality and motivations. Investigators explored his past, previous activities, and potential affiliations to understand if he could have reasons to fabricate such a story. This part of the investigation revealed that Adamski had a long-standing interest in occultism and ufology, which raised questions about the credibility of his claims.

Despite the efforts made, the official investigation was unable to provide a definitive explanation or conclusively validate Adamski's claims. The conclusions of military and government reports tend to be cautious, indicating that while some photographic evidence and testimonies were deemed intriguing, there was not enough evidence to confirm the existence of extraterrestrial visitors or advanced technologies. Investigators also noted that the evidence could be interpreted in several ways and that Adamski's claims, although fascinating, lacked sufficient independent corroboration to be accepted as facts.

Theories and Speculations.

One of the most debated theories is that of deliberate hoax. Some skeptics argue that Adamski may have fabricated the entire story for fame or financial gain. They point out inconsistencies in his accounts and the lack of tangible evidence such as clear photographs or independent corroborating testimonies. Moreover, critics highlight the fact that Adamski was a skilled storyteller and had a clear interest in occultism and paranormal phenomena before his alleged encounters, which could indicate a predisposition to fabricating extraordinary stories.

Another theory suggests that Adamski may have been a victim of hallucinations or delusions, possibly due to undiagnosed psychological disorders. This hypothesis is supported by the fact that Adamski described extremely precise and complex details of extraterrestrial technologies and civilizations, which could be the result of a hyperactive imagination combined with altered mental states. However, this theory does not take into account the many followers and witnesses who claimed to have seen unidentified flying objects and even extraterrestrials in the company of Adamski.

A third perspective suggests that Adamski's narratives could be a form of metaphor or allegory, reflecting his own utopian ideals about society and humanity. According to this view, the "peaceful and advanced" aliens he described would symbolize a longing for a better world. This interpretation is often adopted by those who see Adamski not as a liar, but rather as an idealist using the narrative of aliens as a means to promote values of universal peace and harmony.

Finally, there is a minority who consider Adamski's claims as potentially credible, or at least worthy of examination. These individuals, often ufologists or researchers in paranormal phenomena, argue that certain elements of Adamski's stories, such as the descriptions of the spacecraft or certain astronomical knowledge he possessed, were too advanced for the time to be simply invented. They suggest that, even if some aspects of Adamski's stories could be embellished, there might be a kernel of truth in his encounters, perhaps linked to phenomena still unexplained.

Each of these theories has its supporters and detractors, and the debate around the Adamski incident continues to be a subject of fascination and controversy in the field of ufology and beyond. Discussions continue on forums, in books, and at conferences, each trying to unravel the mystery of what George Adamski really experienced, or claimed to have experienced, more than half a century ago.

Conclusion.

Although many skeptics dismiss his claims as fabrications or hallucinations, he has undeniably had a profound impact on popular culture and the perception of UFOs. Adamski's accounts paved the way for other contactee stories and helped popularize the idea that extraterrestrial beings could not only visit Earth, but also communicate with its inhabitants. Despite the lack of concrete evidence supporting his encounters, Adamski's story continues to fascinate and divide opinions, illustrating the complexity and enduring appeal of unresolved mysteries related to UFOs.

THE KINROSS AIR FORCE BASE INCIDENT, MICHIGAN: MYSTERIOUS DISAPPEARANCE DURING A UFO INTERCEPTION.

DATE: November 23, 1953.
COUNTRY: United States.
STATE: Michigan.
CITY: Kinross.

Located in the state of Michigan, Kinross Air Force Base was a strategic point for the air defense of the United States during the Cold War. On November 23, 1953, an unusual event occurred, involving the mysterious disappearance of a US Air Force fighter plane and its pilot, First Lieutenant Felix Moncla. That day, an unidentified flying object (UFO) was detected by the radar at Kinross Air Force Base. Faced with this unexplained detection, an F-89C Scorpion fighter plane piloted by Moncla, accompanied by radar operator Robert Wilson, was dispatched to intercept and identify the object. Communications between the plane and the base were normal until the radar showed that Moncla's plane had merged with the unidentified object on the screen, after which contact was lost. Despite intense searches and investigations, neither the plane nor the bodies of the crew members were ever found, leaving behind a mystery that endures to this day.

The Observation.

On November 23, 1953, an unusual event occurred in the sky above Lake Superior, near the Kinross Air Force Base, located in the state of Michigan, United States. That day, the weather conditions were relatively clear with moderate visibility, although low clouds had formed over the lake, making visibility variable at times. Around 6:22 p.m. local time, an unidentified object was detected by the radar of the air defense system. The object was moving at a speed and with flight characteristics that did not match any known aircraft at the time.

The detected object was circular or oval in shape according to the radar operators' reports. It seemed to move at a constant speed, then suddenly accelerate inexplicably, before slowing down again. Its size was not clearly established, but estimates based on radar readings suggested it was larger than a conventional aircraft. The color and texture of the object could not be determined due to the lack of direct visibility and reliance on radar instruments for tracking.

In response to this mysterious appearance, an F-89C Scorpion fighter jet, piloted by Lieutenant Felix Moncla, with Second Lieutenant Robert Wilson as radar operator, was dispatched to intercept and identify the object. The Scorpion took off from the air base and headed towards the position indicated by the radar. As the plane approached the object, ground operators closely watched the radar screens, noting that the two signals, that of the plane and the unidentified object, began to converge.

At a certain point, the radar signals from the plane and the object overlapped. It seemed that the plane was about to reach the UFO, or at least pass very close. However, instead of two distinct signals separating after such a maneuver, there was only one signal left on the radar. This phenomenon lasted a few moments before the single signal completely disappeared from the radar screens.

The incident took place in an area of Lake Superior that was notoriously difficult for search and rescue operations, due to its deep and often turbulent waters. The disappearance of the radar signal caused great concern among the base staff and immediately triggered a search operation. Despite intensive efforts, neither the plane nor its occupants were found, and the unidentified object was no longer detected on any subsequent radar.

This incident remains one of the most enigmatic and discussed cases in the annals of UFO sightings, mainly due to the unexplained disappearance of the plane and its pilots, as well as the absence of debris or other physical evidence confirming a crash or a close encounter. The precise details of the observed object and the exact circumstances of the disappearance remain a mystery, fueling various theories and speculations among researchers and the public.

Testimonials.

According to the testimonies of ground radar operators, the unidentified object was moving at a speed and with maneuvers that did not correspond to those of a conventional aircraft. The operators observed on their screens that the blip representing the F-89 approached the object, then the two signals merged into a single point. After this merger, the single blip continued its path before completely disappearing from the radar.

Lieutenant Wilson, from the plane, radioed that they were approaching the object and trying to visualize it. However, shortly after, the communication was abruptly cut off. No other message was received from the plane. Efforts to reestablish contact with the F-89 were in vain, and the plane and its occupants were never found.

Intensive searches have been conducted, involving planes and ships from the Coast Guard, but no debris from the missing plane has been located. The weather conditions were good at the time of the incident, and nothing in the usual flight profile of the plane explained such a disappearance.

The testimonies of the radar operators, who were interviewed separately, all corroborated the same sequence of events. They described the object as initially stationary, then moving at high speed, performing abrupt maneuvers that defied the capabilities of an aircraft of the time.

This case was officially attributed to an "unknown cause" by the Air Force, and despite various theories, no satisfactory explanation has been provided as to the nature of the object or the fate of Lieutenant Moncla and Lieutenant Wilson. The testimonies of the radar operators remain the only concrete clues as to what might have happened that day, fueling speculations and theories about encounters with unidentified aerial phenomena.

The Investigation.

The initial investigation was conducted by the Air Defense Command, which immediately launched a search and rescue operation to find the missing plane and its pilot, First Lieutenant Felix Moncla, as well as the radar operator, Lieutenant Robert Wilson. Despite intensive searches involving planes and ships, no debris from the plane was found, and the unidentified object that had been detected on the radars also disappeared from the screens without explanation.

The initial reports from military authorities suggested that the plane may have been the victim of a collision or malfunction, but no concrete evidence was found to support these theories. Testimonies collected from the radar operators at the air base indicated that the unidentified object and the fighter plane seemed to merge on the radar before completely disappearing, which added a layer of mystery to the incident.

In the face of a lack of clear answers and increasing pressure from the public and media, the Air Force tasked Project Blue Book, its official UFO study program, with conducting a more thorough investigation. The investigators from Project Blue Book examined radar data, interviewed additional witnesses, and analyzed the weather and aeronautical conditions of the day in question. However, the final report from Project Blue Book concluded that the incident was unresolved, citing a lack of physical evidence and the simultaneous disappearance of the plane and the unidentified object as the main obstacles to a definitive conclusion.

Over the years, the Kinross incident has remained a subject of speculation and theory among ufologists and paranormal researchers, many suggesting that the plane may have been "absorbed" or destroyed by the UFO. However, despite the numerous theories, no concrete evidence has emerged to support these claims, and the incident remains one of the many unsolved cases in the archives of the Blue Book project.

The investigation into the Kinross incident highlighted the challenges associated with understanding and interpreting encounters with UFOs, as well as the limitations of the technologies of the time to track and analyze such phenomena. Despite the efforts made by the Air Force and other agencies, the disappearance of the F-89 Scorpion and its occupants remains an unsolved mystery, leaving ongoing questions about what really happened that day over Lake Superior.

Theories and Speculations.

One of the most widespread theories is that of instrumentation or radar error. Some aviation and radar technology experts suggest that the equipment of the time was not as reliable as today, which could lead to erroneous readings. According to this hypothesis, what the radar detected as a UFO could have been a ghost echo or a technical problem, and Moncla's plane could have crashed due to pilot disorientation or a mechanical failure unrelated to the UFO.

Another popular theory is that of extraterrestrial intervention. This speculation is fueled by testimonies and reports describing flying objects with seemingly impossible aeronautical capabilities for the time. According to proponents of this theory, Moncla's plane could have been captured or destroyed by the UFO during the interception attempt. This idea is often reinforced by accounts of UFO wreckage recovery and unknown technologies, although these accounts are generally unverified and controversial.

A third hypothesis concerns a possible confusion or military misunderstanding. It is suggested that the object Moncla was supposed to intercept could have been a spy plane or an experimental drone, not recognized by radars as being an American craft. In the climate of the Cold War, tests of new equipment were common and often secret, which could explain the lack of recognition and the subsequent confusion that could have led to a tragic accident.

Some researchers also put forward the idea of a government cover-up. This theory suggests that the details of the incident were deliberately obscured by the authorities to hide sensitive information, perhaps related to secret military tests or encounters with unexplained phenomena. Supporters of this theory point to inconsistencies in official reports and the absence of found debris, which, according to them, indicates a desire for concealment.

Finally, a less common explanation but sometimes discussed is that of an atmospheric or geophysical anomaly. Lake Superior is known for its sometimes extreme weather conditions and unusual natural phenomena. Some scientists and meteorologists suggest that phenomena such as mirages, St. Elmo's lights, or magnetic anomalies could have been misinterpreted as UFO activities, leading to fatal confusion for the pilot.

THE KELLY-HOPKINSVILLE INCIDENT: ENCOUNTER WITH MYSTERIOUS CREATURES.

DATE: August 21, 1955.
COUNTRY: United States.
STATE: Kentucky.

On August 21, 1955, in the small rural town of Kelly, near Hopkinsville, Kentucky, a family had a terrifying experience that forever marked the community and paranormal phenomena researchers. That evening, after a quiet day, the Sutton family, composed of several adults and children, returned to their isolated farm. Shortly after their return, at dusk, their tranquility was abruptly interrupted by the appearance of strange little creatures. These beings, described as having large pointed ears, bulging and shining eyes, and skin similar to that of metallic silver, seemed to come straight out of a science fiction movie. The terrified family barricaded themselves in their house, claiming that the creatures were trying to get in. What followed was a long and distressing night, where the Suttons had to defend their home against these unknown visitors. The incident quickly attracted the attention of the media and researchers, but despite the investigations, there are still many unanswered questions. Was it a mistake with wild animals, a hoax, or something much more mysterious? The Kelly-Hopkinsville incident continues to fascinate and mystify, and remains a prominent case in UFO studies.

The Observation.

Around 7:00 PM, Billy Ray Taylor, one of the residents of the Sutton farm, went out to draw water from a well located outside the house. It was at this moment that he saw a bright object in the sky. According to his testimony, the object had a round shape and emitted a multicolored glow, crossing the sky at an incredible speed before suddenly disappearing behind a grove not far from the house. Intrigued but also frightened, Taylor hurriedly returned inside to inform the other occupants of the house of what he had just seen.

Shortly after Taylor's return inside, the occupants of the house began to hear strange noises outside. Curious and somewhat anxious, Taylor and another man, Elmer "Lucky" Sutton, decided to investigate. To their great surprise, they were confronted with a small creature about a meter tall, with oversized arms in relation to its body, clawed hands, and an oversized head in relation to its slim body. The creature's skin seemed to have a metallic texture under the dim light.

The weather conditions that night were clear with few clouds, making visual observations relatively easy, despite the darkness of the countryside without public lighting. The moon was almost full, providing natural light that helped to distinguish shapes and movements in the darkness.

Faced with this unexpected apparition, Sutton and Taylor, panicked, ran to the house to look for weapons. Armed, they returned outside where they saw the creature approaching the house, floating rather than walking, which added to the strangeness of the scene. They opened fire several times, but the bullets seemed to bounce off or be ineffective against the creature, which temporarily retreated into the darkness.

Over the following hours, several other similar creatures appeared around the house, seeming to float through the fields and sometimes perch on the roof or peer through the windows. The occupants of the house continued to resist, using firearms and barricading themselves inside. This confrontation lasted until the early morning, the creatures finally disappearing with the arrival of the first light of dawn.

The detailed description of the creatures and the object observed by Taylor at Kelly has fueled many theories and speculations, but no definitive explanation has ever been established.

Testimonials.

That evening, in a small farm near Kelly and Hopkinsville, in Kentucky, several members of the Sutton family as well as friends present reported having seen and interacted with mysterious creatures.

Billy Ray Taylor was the first to report an anomaly. According to his testimony, as he was drawing water from a well located outside the house, he saw what he described as a flying saucer with multicolored lights, crossing the sky to finally disappear behind a line of trees near the farm. Excited and somewhat scared, he returned inside to inform the others of his discovery, but was initially met with skepticism.

Shortly after Taylor's return indoors, the family and their friends began to hear strange noises and see shadows moving around the house. It was then that Lucky Sutton, the main tenant of the house, spotted a strange figure at the window. He described the entity as being about a meter tall, with long, thin arms, clawed hands, pointed ears, large, bright eyes, and skin that seemed to have a metallic hue under the moonlight.

Panicked, Lucky and Billy Ray grabbed firearms and began shooting at what they believed to be assailants. According to their accounts, the creatures seemed to float instead of walk and, when hit by bullets, emitted a metallic sound, as if the projectiles were bouncing off metal.

Glennie Lankford, the matriarch of the Sutton family, also testified to the presence of the creatures. She described a scene where several entities seemed to gather around the house, appearing curious but not aggressive. She recounted that the creatures had large ears, which were the most distinctive feature, and that their movements were jerky, like mechanical.

During the night, the confrontation continued, with several attempts by the creatures to enter the house, all repelled by the men's gunfire. This series of events lasted several hours, until the family decided to leave the house as a group to seek help at the local police station.

The testimonies from that night were corroborated by the police officers who visited the farm after the incident. They noted signs of damage caused by the shots and a palpable atmosphere of fear among the witnesses. Although skeptical at first, the officers could not ignore the sincerity and obvious distress of the Suttons and their friends.

The Investigation.

The investigation into the Kelly-Hopkinsville incident began immediately after local authorities were alerted by the residents of the Sutton farm, located near the small town of Kelly in Kentucky. On August 21, 1955, several members of the Sutton family reported seeing an unidentified object land near their property, followed by encounters with small strange creatures. The testimonies of the family members and neighbors quickly attracted the attention of local and national authorities.

The first responders on the scene were police officers from Christian County, who were joined by representatives from the Kentucky State Police. The latter conducted detailed interviews with witnesses, who described the creatures as being about three feet tall, with large ears, bright eyes, and thin bodies. The witnesses also reported that the creatures seemed to float instead of walk and that they were extremely fast.

In response to the extraordinary nature of the claims, the American military, notably members from Fort Campbell Air Base, were consulted. Military investigators visited the Sutton farm to examine the site and search for physical evidence of a UFO landing or the presence of creatures. Although the military found traces and impacts that seemed to indicate unusual activity, no conclusive evidence was publicly reported.

The investigation also involved scientists and ufologists, who examined the testimonies and physical evidence. The investigators tried to determine if the experience could be explained by natural phenomena or misunderstandings. However, despite the efforts made, no definitive explanation was found.

The conclusions of the military and governmental authorities were cautious, indicating that there was not enough evidence to support the existence of extraterrestrials or an unidentified spacecraft. Nevertheless, the incident continued to be a subject of fascination and speculation, fueling the debate about the possible presence of extraterrestrials and how governments handle information related to UFOs.

The testimonies collected during the investigation were widely disseminated and analyzed in the following years. The members of the Sutton family, in particular, were in the spotlight, some suggesting that their story might have been influenced by cultural phenomena or media pressures. However, they maintained their claims, adding a layer of mystery and complexity to the whole affair.

In summary, the investigation into the Kelly-Hopkinsville incident failed to provide a clear explanation and left many questions unanswered. The interactions between the witnesses, local authorities, military investigators, and researchers have created a complex narrative that continues to be studied by researchers in paranormal and UFO phenomena.

Theories and Speculations.

The first theory is that of extraterrestrial visitation. According to this hypothesis, the observed creatures were beings from another planet or another dimension. This idea is supported by the description of the creatures - small in size, with large ears, bulging eyes, and skin that seemed to reflect light. Proponents of this theory argue that the movements and behaviors of the creatures, as well as their unusual appearance, do not correspond to any known animal on Earth.

Another popular explanation is that of a hoax or misunderstanding. Some skeptics suggest that witnesses may have misinterpreted wild animals, such as owls, under the influence of fear and confusion. The large eyes and nocturnal behavior of owls could have been misinterpreted as those of extraterrestrial entities. Moreover, psychological tension, amplified by rural isolation and local legends about supernatural creatures, could have played a role in the witnesses' perception of the events.

A third theory concerns psychological and sociological phenomena. Some researchers believe that the incident could be a case of sleep paralysis or hypnagogic hallucinations, where individuals between the state of wakefulness and sleep see "intruders" in their immediate environment. This condition could be exacerbated by stress or fear. Furthermore, the impact of the media and science fiction films of the time could have influenced the witnesses, predisposing them to interpret ambiguous stimuli as being of extraterrestrial origin.

A fourth perspective is that of secret military experimentation. Some ufologists and conspiracy theorists suggest that the incident could have been the result of an undisclosed government test, involving advanced technologies or chemical substances that could have caused hallucinations or altered perceptions in the witnesses. This theory is often reinforced by the context of the Cold War, a period during which many secret tests were conducted by the American government.

Finally, there are those who consider the Kelly-Hopkinsville incident as an event still unexplained, possibly due to a combination of several of the above factors. This multidimensional approach suggests that the complex interaction between the environment, the psychology of the witnesses, and possible external influences could have created a unique experience that is difficult to strictly categorize into a single explanatory box.

Conclusion.

Despite numerous investigations and analysis of testimonies, no definitive conclusion has been reached regarding the nature of the events of that August night in 1955. The descriptions of the creatures and behaviors reported by the Sutton family add a layer of mystery, often compared to science fiction scenarios. Skeptics lean towards a psychological explanation or a mistake with wild animals, while UFO believers see it as proof of extraterrestrial visitation. What is undeniable is that the incident deeply affected the witnesses and continues to inspire debates and research on unidentified aerial phenomena and their possible implications.

THE LAKENHEATH-BENTWATERS INCIDENT.

DATE: August 1956.
COUNTRY: United Kingdom.
STATE: Not applicable.
CITY: Lakenheath and Bentwaters.

The Lakenheath-Bentwaters incident, which occurred in August 1956, involves several testimonies from radar operators and pilots from the British and American air forces, who reported sightings of unidentified flying objects in the sky of Eastern England. Prior to this incident, the period was marked by intense Cold War activity, where aerial surveillance was at its peak, particularly due to the fear of a Soviet attack. The Lakenheath and Bentwaters air bases, used by the US Air Force and the Royal Air Force, were strategic points for defense and surveillance in this region. The night of the incident, the weather conditions were clear, allowing for detailed visual and radar observation of the reported phenomena. The events of that night were meticulously recorded and analyzed, but remain shrouded in mystery to this day, fueling various theories and speculations about the nature and origin of the observed objects.

The Observation.

This case involves several testimonies from radar operators and pilots, providing a series of technical and visual details that enrich the narrative of this event.

The observation began around 9:30 pm, when the radar operator of the Royal Air Force (RAF) stationed at Lakenheath, in Suffolk, England, detected an unidentified signal on his radar screen. This signal was moving irregularly and at a speed far exceeding that of conventional aircraft of the time. The radar operator described the object as having extremely agile behavior, capable of changing direction at acute angles and accelerating at a staggering speed without any visible preparation.

Shortly after the first detection, a second radar post, located at Bentwaters, also picked up the object on its system. The operators at Bentwaters confirmed the observations from Lakenheath, noting that the object seemed to play with the radar beams, avoiding them or diving into them with a precision that seemed to defy the capabilities of the aircraft of the time.

Around 10:00 PM, a RAF Venom fighter jet was dispatched to intercept the object. The Venom pilot reported seeing a bright, circular light in front of him, which did not resemble any known aircraft. The object was visibly bright and seemed to emit a pulsating glow that varied in intensity. The pilot attempted several times to approach the object, but with each attempt, the UFO accelerated and moved out of range with disconcerting ease.

The weather conditions that night were clear with excellent visibility, allowing for detailed visual observations. The moon was nearly full, providing natural light that helped to accentuate the visibility of the unidentified object. No clouds obstructed the view, and the wind was weak, which eliminates the possibility that what was seen was a weather phenomenon like a lenticular cloud or a weather balloon.

The interaction between the UFO and the Venom lasted several minutes, during which the object continued to display maneuverability far surpassing that of the fighter jet. At one point, the object even approached a relatively close distance to the Venom, allowing the pilot to observe a more detailed structure. He described the object as having a spherical shape with some kind of halo around it, which made it difficult to determine its exact dimensions.

After about half an hour of interception attempts, the object suddenly accelerated at a phenomenal speed and disappeared from visual and radar range, leaving behind questions and mysteries that persist to this day. The Lakenheath-Bentwaters incident remains a fascinating case study for ufologists and researchers, offering a detailed data set that continues to challenge conventional explanations.

Testimonials.

This event involves several testimonies from military personnel from two Royal Air Force (RAF) air bases in England: RAF Lakenheath and RAF Bentwaters.

The first key witness is the air traffic controller from RAF Bentwaters. On the evening of August 13, he noticed unidentified objects on his radar, moving at extraordinary speeds and changing direction abruptly. According to his testimony, these objects were capable of accelerating from 0 to several thousand miles per hour in a few seconds, a capability far beyond that of any known aircraft at the time.

Another important witness is the fighter pilot who was sent to intercept one of the detected objects. The pilot, flying a Venom fighter plane, reports seeing a bright, circular light moving at an incredible speed. He describes the object as being able to stop dead in mid-flight, then instantly take off again at a dizzying speed. Despite several attempts, he was unable to get close enough to the object to clearly identify it.

Another testimony comes from a radar operator at RAF Lakenheath, who also detected the objects on his equipment. He confirms the observations of his counterpart at RAF Bentwaters, noting that the objects seemed to toy with the fighter planes sent to intercept them, evading them with disconcerting ease.

In addition to the military, several civilian witnesses also reported seeing unusual lights in the sky that night. Among them, a couple living near RAF Lakenheath described observing a series of bright lights moving at high speed, without any engine noise, which is unusual for aircraft.

These testimonies, collected independently from each other, paint a picture of an event that surpasses human understanding and the technological capabilities of the time. The descriptions of the objects' movements, their ability to change direction instantly and accelerate at staggering speeds, remain difficult to explain within the framework of 1956's aerial technologies.

The Investigation.

The investigation that followed involved several branches of the armed forces of the United Kingdom and the United States, as well as government agencies. The details of the investigation were widely scrutinized by researchers and ufologists, leading to various reports and conclusions.

The investigation began immediately after radar operators from the Royal Air Force (RAF) stationed at Lakenheath, in Suffolk, detected unidentified objects moving at speeds and with maneuvers that exceeded the capabilities of aircraft of the time. The initial reports indicated that the objects were moving at speeds ranging from 4000 to 8000 miles per hour, well beyond what any known aircraft could achieve at that time.

The testimonies collected during the investigation included those of radar operators and pilots from the RAF and the US Air Force who were sent to intercept the objects. The pilots reported seeing bright lights moving at incredible speeds and making turns impossible for human aircraft. These observations were corroborated by simultaneous radar readings, reinforcing the credibility of the testimonies.

The military authorities initially reacted by classifying the incident as highly confidential, and it took many years before the details of the investigation were made public. The US Air Force's Blue Book project, which was responsible for investigating UFOs, eventually included the Lakenheath-Bentwaters incident in its archives. The Blue Book project report concluded that the observations were credible, but could not determine the origin of the observed objects.

The conclusions of the investigation were varied and often contradictory. Some reports suggested that the observations could be attributed to natural phenomena or errors in interpreting radar data and visual testimonies. However, others maintained that the characteristics of the observed objects could not be easily explained by conventional explanations.

The investigation into the Lakenheath-Bentwaters incident remains a subject of debate among researchers and ufologists. The declassified documents and testimonies collected during the investigation continue to be analyzed in the hope of finding new information or more convincing explanations about what really happened during these mysterious observations in 1956.

Theories and Speculations.

The first theory, often put forward by skeptics, is that of a radar error. The radars of the time were less reliable and more susceptible to atmospheric interference or other technical anomalies. Some radar technology experts suggest that the unusual signals picked up could be the result of particular weather conditions that night, such as temperature inversions, which can cause abnormal radar reflections.

Another rational explanation is that of secret aircraft or undisclosed military trials. During the Cold War, the United States and their allies regularly tested new aerial technologies. It is possible that the UFOs observed were actually prototypes of airplanes or drones unknown to the public and even to the majority of military personnel. This theory is supported by the fact that the air bases involved were important strategic sites during this period.

On the side of more sensational theories, the extraterrestrial hypothesis remains the most popular among some ufologists. According to this perspective, the observed objects were vessels of non-earthly origins. Supporters of this idea cite the speed and seemingly impossible movements of UFOs, such as instantaneous changes in direction and sudden accelerations without sonic effects, as evidence that the technologies involved could not be of this world.

A variant of the extraterrestrial hypothesis is that of the reconnaissance visit. Some theorists suggest that aliens might be on an exploration or surveillance mission, interested in human military capabilities, especially during the Cold War. This idea is often reinforced by reports of interactions between UFOs and military aircraft, suggesting a kind of curiosity or study on the part of the supposed visitors.

Finally, there are those who believe in a more psychosocial explanation. This theory suggests that the Lakenheath-Bentwaters incident could be a mass phenomenon where witnesses interpreted ambiguous stimuli through the prism of the popular culture of the time, which was saturated with science fiction narratives and fears of alien invasions. According to this view, the testimonies could be influenced by the expectations and tensions of the time, rather than by objective observations of physical objects.

The official reports of the time, although downplaying the incident, admitted the inability to explain the radar and visual observations by natural phenomena or conventional aircraft. This incident has been widely studied by ufologists and remains cited as a significant example of military interaction with unidentified aerial phenomena.

THE RB-47 INCIDENT: THE MYSTERIOUS TRACKING OF A UFO BY AN ELECTRONIC BOMBER OF THE US AIR FORCE.

DATE: July 17, 1957.
COUNTRY: United States.
STATE: Several states, including Texas, Oklahoma and Kansas.
CITY: N/A .

On July 17, 1957, a strategic bomber RB-47, equipped for electronic reconnaissance, encountered an unidentified flying object during a routine mission over the southern United States. What makes this incident particularly intriguing is the duration of the observation, which lasted several hours, and the fact that the UFO was detected both visually by the crew and electronically by the equipment on board the aircraft.

The RB-47, which was part of the US Air Force, was on a mission to collect electronic data and test new surveillance equipment. The crew, made up of six members, was highly qualified and experienced. The flight was going normally until one of the onboard electronic countermeasures operators detected an unidentified radar signal. Shortly after, the crew members spotted a bright object that seemed to be following their trajectory.

The object was described as being extremely bright and capable of high-speed maneuvers, surpassing the capabilities of the aircraft of the time. On several occasions, the object disappeared and reappeared, moving at speeds and directions that defied conventional explanations. Despite attempts to establish communication or to better understand the nature of the object, the crew was unable to obtain more information.

The incident was officially recorded and investigated by several agencies, including the Air Force. However, despite thorough analyses, the origin and nature of the observed object remain unidentified. This incident remains one of the most mysterious and technically substantial in the annals of ufology, continuing to spark curiosity and debate among UFO experts and enthusiasts.

The Observation.

The crew, composed of six members, reported detecting an unidentified object that was not only visually observed but also picked up by the plane's electronic instruments.

The observation began around 4 a.m. local time, as the plane was flying over Mississippi. The sky was clear and the stars visible, ideal conditions for aerial observation. The object was initially detected by the plane's electronic detection system, a sophisticated equipment designed to identify enemy radar signals. What made this incident particularly remarkable is that the object was also visually seen by the crew, a rare corroboration in UFO cases.

The observed object was described as being luminous, with an intense and white light, and seemed to change shape or size. Several times during the incident, the object performed high-speed maneuvers that far exceeded the capabilities of known aircraft at the time. At one point, the object moved away at a speed estimated at several thousand kilometers per hour, before returning towards the RB-47.

The interaction between the UFO and the RB-47 lasted nearly an hour, during which the object was lost and found several times by the plane's tracking systems. The object was detected both by the onboard radar and by the electronic countermeasure equipment, indicating that it was emitting or reflecting electromagnetic waves.

The altitude at which the object was observed varied considerably, rising and falling rapidly, which added to the confusion and intrigue of the observation. At certain times, the object seemed to behave intelligently, appearing to react to the maneuvers of the RB-47.

The weather conditions during the incident were clear with almost perfect visibility, which allowed the crew to have a clear view of the object for most of the observation. The moon was low on the horizon, which minimized light interference and improved observation conditions.

Testimonials.

The testimonies of the plane's crew members are crucial to understanding this complex and mysterious event.

Captain Lewis D. Chase was the pilot of the RB-47 aircraft during this incident. According to his testimony, the object was first detected by the aircraft's electronic equipment, which recorded unusual signals. Shortly after, Chase visually spotted the UFO, describing it as a bright light that seemed to change color and brightness. He noted that the object was capable of high-speed maneuvers and sudden accelerations, well beyond the capabilities of the aircraft of the time.

Major Frank McClure, the electronic countermeasures officer on board, corroborated Chase's observations. McClure indicated that the object was emitting intermittent signals that the plane's equipment could pick up, which is unusual as most airborne objects do not produce such signals. He also confirmed that the object had been detected simultaneously by several ground radar systems, ruling out the possibility of an isolated instrumental failure.

Lieutenant James McCoid, the crew's navigator, also observed the UFO. He specified that the object had a very fast lateral movement capability, moving from one point to another in the sky with astonishing speed and precision. McCoid added that, on several occasions, the object approached the plane before quickly moving away, as if it was examining the plane.

The testimony of the radar operator, Lieutenant David T. Brigham, is particularly interesting. Brigham reported that the object appeared and disappeared from his radar screen, suggesting an ability to mask its presence or to change altitude very quickly. He also noted that attempts to communicate with the object or to obtain identification through normal air traffic control channels remained unanswered.

Finally, the testimony of Sergeant Melvin K. Reese, another crew member specialized in electronic equipment, reinforced the observations of his colleagues. Reese described how the plane's electronic equipment was disrupted as the UFO approached, a rare occurrence that added an additional layer of mystery to the incident.

These collective testimonies from the crew members of the RB-47 provide a coherent and detailed overview of the incident, highlighting the complexity and strangeness of the interaction between the military aircraft and the UFO. Despite the many years that have passed since this event, the details reported by the crew remain among the most credible and best documented in the history of UFO sightings.

The Investigation.

The investigation into this incident began immediately after the event, involving several levels of the air force and government agencies. The initial reactions were to verify the reliability of the equipment on board the RB-47, which were at the forefront of the technology of the time for electronic warfare and reconnaissance. The equipment in question included advanced electronic detection systems, which had recorded electronic signals emitted by the unidentified object.

The testimonies of the RB-47 crew members were meticulously collected. The pilot, co-pilot, and electronic systems operators all reported visual observations of the object, as well as simultaneous detections on their instruments. These testimonies were corroborated by ground radar recordings and by other aircraft in the region at that time.

The initial reports were followed by a more in-depth technical analysis. Radar data, both from the aircraft and on the ground, were examined to rule out the possibility of a false detection due to equipment malfunction or atmospheric phenomena. Radar and electronic warfare experts analyzed the frequencies and signatures of the captured signals to try to determine the nature of the object.

One of the most intriguing parts of the investigation was the attempt to correlate visual observations with electronic detections. The object was described by witnesses as being luminous and capable of high-speed maneuvers, with sudden changes in direction that seemed to defy the capabilities of conventional aircraft of the time.

The conclusions of the military and governmental authorities were cautious, often classifying the incident as unresolved. The final report suggested that, despite substantial data, there was not enough evidence to attribute the object to known foreign technology or natural phenomena. However, the incident was not categorically attributed to extraterrestrial activities.

The investigation into the RB-47 incident remains a classic example of how a UFO case can be handled with seriousness and scientific rigor, while leaving several questions open without definitive answers. Declassified documents and subsequent analyses continue to arouse the interest of researchers and the public, highlighting the complexity of such incidents and the challenges associated with their interpretation.

Theories and Speculations.

The first theory suggests that the UFO could be an unrecognized spy plane, perhaps Soviet. During the Cold War, the presence of such a plane in American airspace would have been plausible and would have justified the secrecy and interest around the incident. However, skeptics of this theory argue that the technology of the time would not have allowed for such a prolonged and discreet flight, especially without being detected by other means than the sole RB-47.

A second hypothesis suggests that the object was a rare atmospheric phenomenon, such as a weather balloon or an ionized cloud. These phenomena can sometimes reflect radar waves and create illusions of solid objects on radar screens. However, this explanation struggles to justify the visual observations reported by the crew, as well as the consistency and duration of the radar tracking.

The third theory, more controversial, is that of the extraterrestrial visit. Advocates of this idea rely on the fact that the object demonstrated flight capabilities that surpass the aeronautical technology of the time, such as sudden accelerations and very rapid changes of direction. However, this theory is often criticized for its lack of concrete evidence and its inclination towards speculation rather than rigorous scientific analysis.

Another perspective is that of an instrumental error or a misinterpretation of the data by the RB-47 crew. The electronic instruments, although advanced, were not infallible and could be subject to malfunctions. In addition, crew fatigue or momentary unfamiliarity could have contributed to a misinterpretation of the signals. This theory is often supported by aviation and radar technology experts, who point out the limitations of the systems of the time.

Finally, another theory suggests the possibility of a classified military operation, unknown even to certain segments of the military. The object could have been an experimental prototype, tested by the United States or another nation, which would explain the lack of official recognition and the evasive nature of government responses. However, this hypothesis remains difficult to verify in the absence of disclosure of classified documents or testimonies from people involved in such operations.

Conclusion.

The RB-47 incident remains a fascinating and enigmatic case in the study of unidentified aerial phenomena. Despite the presence of credible witnesses and technical evidence, the origin and nature of the observed object have never been determined. This event underscores the complexity and challenges associated with identifying and explaining UFO sightings, even with the use of advanced technologies. Declassified documents from the US Air Force and testimonies from crew members provide precise details about the incident, but leave many questions unanswered. The RB-47 incident continues to spark interest and speculation, illustrating the enduring mystery surrounding UFOs and their lasting impact on culture and science.

THE ABDUCTION OF ANTÔNIO VILAS BOAS, BRAZIL.

DATE: October 16, 1957.
COUNTRY: Brazil.
STATE: Minas Gerais.
CITY: São Francisco de Sales.

On the night of October 16, 1957, an unusual and disturbing event occurred in the small town of São Francisco de Sales, located in the state of Minas Gerais, Brazil. Antônio Vilas Boas, a young 23-year-old farmer, was working in his fields to avoid the intense heat of the day. As he was plowing his field under the moonlight, he noticed a strange light in the sky. Intrigued but initially skeptical, Antônio continued his work, thinking it might be a plane or a natural phenomenon. However, the light intensified and approached, revealing an oval shape emitting a bright red light. Panicked, Antônio tried to flee on his tractor, but the machine suddenly stopped, as if paralyzed by an unknown force. That's when Antônio Vilas Boas' experience took an even more extraordinary and terrifying turn.

The Observation.

That night, around 1 in the morning, Antônio was working in his fields to avoid the daytime heat when he noticed a strange light in the sky. Intrigued, he observed more closely and noticed that it was an unidentified flying object.

The description of the UFO given by Antônio was that of an egg-shaped machine, with a series of red lights around its base. The object was about 15 meters in diameter and emitted an intense light that illuminated the surrounding field. The UFO seemed to be made of a smooth and shiny metal, and it emitted a humming noise, similar to that of an engine, but without the typical interruptions of combustion engines.

The weather conditions that night were clear, with few clouds and excellent visibility, which allowed Antônio to clearly see the object for the entire duration of the observation. The air was fresh and there was no wind, ideal conditions for a prolonged observation without interference.

The UFO began to slowly descend towards the ground, at a distance of about 100 meters from where Antônio was located. Frightened but fascinated, he tried to get closer to better observe the object. As he approached, the UFO reacted by increasing its altitude, then stabilizing. Antônio noted that the object seemed to monitor his movements and react accordingly.

After a few minutes of mutual observation, the UFO projected a beam of light towards Antônio, who felt an intense heat, as if he was exposed to a concentrated sunbeam. Overwhelmed by the heat and fear, he decided to move away, but found that his movements were hindered, as if the air around him had become denser.

The UFO continued to hover in the area for about an hour, sometimes changing position, but always staying nearby. Eventually, the object began to slowly rise into the sky, gradually accelerating until it disappeared from Antônio's view, leaving behind a trail of light that faded into the night sky.

Testimonials.

According to Antônio's testimony, the incident began around 11 p.m., while he was plowing the fields to avoid the daytime heat. He spotted a reddish light in the sky descending towards his position. At first, he thought it was a star, but the light quickly grew and transformed into a form of an aerial vessel. Frightened but curious, Antônio tried to escape on his tractor, which, however, inexplicably broke down.

The ship, described as having a circular shape with a dome on top, landed in a nearby field. Three beings dressed in grayish suits and wearing helmets emerged from the craft. They were about 1.5 meters tall. Antônio was quickly captured by these beings who took him inside their ship.

Inside, he was undressed and coated with a gel by the beings. They took samples of his blood from his chin. Subsequently, he was led into another room where he met a woman with blond hair and blue eyes, who seemed to be of the same species as the other beings. According to Antônio, this woman and he were forced to have sexual intercourse, with the apparent aim of creating a hybrid offspring.

After this act, Antônio was guided through several rooms of the ship where he observed numerous technical details, including control panels and luminous screens. The beings communicated with each other through sounds resembling barks and growls, but he did not understand their language.

About four hours after his abduction, Antônio was released. He found his tractor and returned home, where he recounted the incident to his family. In the following days, he suffered from symptoms such as nausea, headaches, eye burns, and skin lesions, which he attributed to possible exposure to radiation.

The case of Antônio Vilas Boas has been widely studied by ufologists and remains a classic example cited in discussions about alleged extraterrestrial encounters. Despite skeptics who doubt the veracity of his story, the details provided by Antônio have been consistent and he maintained his version of events throughout his life.

The investigation.

The investigation began shortly after Vilas Boas shared his experience with Dr. Olavo Fontes, a renowned doctor and ufologist of the time. Fontes took the case very seriously and conducted in-depth interviews with Vilas Boas, gathering details about the physical appearance of the beings he met, the technology of their spacecraft, and the nature of their interactions with him, including an alleged medical examination and non-verbal communication.

Fontes also collected soil samples from the place where Vilas Boas claimed the UFO had landed. These samples were analyzed for possible traces of radiation or other anomalies. Although the results were not conclusive, they added a layer of mystery to the case, as slightly elevated levels of radiation were detected, although this could be attributed to natural causes.

In addition to Fontes' investigation, the case was examined by several other researchers and UFO organizations. These investigations often focused on verifying the consistency of Vilas Boas' story and on the search for corroborating evidence or similar testimonies. Despite considerable efforts, no definitive proof has been found to support or completely refute Vilas Boas' claims.

The Brazilian military and governmental authorities were also informed of the incident, but their level of involvement in the investigation is less clear. Declassified documents from the following years suggest some monitoring of UFO reports in the region, but few documents specific to the Vilas Boas case have been made public. This has led to speculation about the degree of seriousness with which the incident was taken by the government.

The testimonies collected during the investigation, mainly those of Vilas Boas himself, were of crucial importance. Vilas Boas provided a detailed and coherent account, describing the beings as humanoids with distinct features. He also described complex interactions, including communication by gestures and strange medical procedures. These details fascinated the public and researchers, but also raised questions about the possibility of psychological suggestion or hallucinatory experiences.

In conclusion, although the investigation into the abduction of Antônio Vilas Boas did not provide conclusive evidence, it played an important role in the study of UFO phenomena. It highlighted the challenges associated with verifying extraterrestrial encounters and stimulated a broader debate on how such claims should be handled by researchers and authorities.

Theories and Speculations.

The first theory, and the most obvious for believers in the UFO phenomenon, is that of extraterrestrial visitation. According to this hypothesis, Antônio Vilas Boas would have been abducted by beings from another planet, interested in studying the human species. This theory is supported by the detailed account of Vilas Boas, who described beings with tight-fitting suits and helmets, as well as various medical procedures to which he would have been subjected, including a kind of sperm collection.

Another theory put forward is that of hallucination or psychosis. Some skeptics suggest that Vilas Boas could have suffered from a form of temporary delirium, perhaps triggered by isolation in his field at night, or by stress. Skeptics also point to the lack of physical evidence and the fact that Vilas Boas' story contains elements that could be interpreted as fantasies or projections of unconscious desires.

A third theory concerns a possible confusion with natural phenomena or military experiments. Some have speculated that Vilas Boas could have witnessed a weather balloon or another type of experimental craft, misinterpreted due to fear and surprise. This hypothesis is often reinforced by the context of the Cold War, a period during which numerous undisclosed military tests were taking place.

Finally, there are those who believe that the incident could have been staged. This theory suggests that Vilas Boas could have invented or exaggerated his story for various reasons, such as seeking attention or other personal gains. However, this theory is often refuted by the seriousness with which Vilas Boas reported the event and by the consistent details of his account over time.

THE LEVELLAND INCIDENT.

DATE: November 2, 1957.
COUNTRY: United States.
STATE: Texas.
CITY: Levelland.

Located in the northwest of Texas, the small town of Levelland was, at the time, a quiet community mainly focused on agriculture. However, the evening of November 2, 1957, would forever mark the town in the annals of unidentified phenomena.

It all started when local residents began to report sightings of an intense light source and a cigar-shaped object hovering in the sky or landing on the road. These testimonies were not isolated, but came from several people at different locations around Levelland over a period of a few hours. What makes these reports particularly credible is the similarity of the descriptions of the object and the electromagnetic effects it allegedly caused, such as the stopping of vehicle engines and the failure of headlights, which was reported by several witnesses.

The local authorities, including the Levelland police chief, investigated these reports. Although skeptical at first, the police chief himself observed the mysterious object, adding a layer of truth to the citizens' claims. The reports were taken seriously enough for the case to be subsequently examined by the American Air Force as part of Project Blue Book, a series of UFO studies conducted by the United States Air Force.

The Levelland incident remains a classic case cited in UFO studies, illustrating the complexity and mystery surrounding UFO observations, as well as the challenges associated with their investigation. Despite inquiries and analyses, no definitive explanation has been provided, leaving the Levelland incident as a fascinating example of a close encounter and a subject of ongoing speculation among UFO experts and enthusiasts.

The Observation.

That evening, around 10:30 pm, the first testimonies began to pour in from the small town of Levelland, Texas. The weather conditions were clear, with no precipitation, and a light breeze was blowing from the southeast. Therefore, visibility was excellent, which allowed the witnesses to clearly observe the events.

The first report came from a motorist who contacted the Hockley County sheriff to report a strange and luminous object on the road. According to his testimony, while he was driving, his vehicle suddenly began to have electrical problems and the engine shut off. Looking up, he saw a disk-shaped object, about 60 meters in diameter, emitting an intense blue-green light. The object was stationary, floating a few meters above the ground. After a few minutes, the object rose into the sky at a dizzying speed and disappeared, after which the witness's car was able to restart without any problems.

During the following hours, several other residents of Levelland reported similar sightings. All described an oval or circular shaped object, with intense lights, mainly of blue-green color. The testimonies agreed that the approach of the object had the effect of stopping the engines of the vehicles and turning off their lights, suggesting some kind of electromagnetic interference.

Another witness, a local farmer, reported seeing the object land in a field near his house. He described the UFO as being "as bright as white-hot metal," and noted that it emitted intense heat that was perceptible even from a distance. The object remained on the ground for about a minute before taking off vertically at an incredibly high speed.

In total, more than fifteen people reported similar observations that night in Levelland. The descriptions of the object and the effects on the vehicles were remarkably consistent among the different witnesses, despite the fact that they were in different locations around the town. The reports were taken seriously enough that the sheriff and several of his deputies conducted patrols in the area in the hope of seeing the object themselves. Although they did not witness the UFO, they confirmed the electrical disturbances in their own vehicles.

Testimonials.

That evening, several witnesses reported seeing an unidentified object accompanied by strange phenomena affecting their vehicles. Here are the details of the observations made by the main witnesses of this event.

Pedro Saucedo and Joe Salaz, two of the first witnesses, reported seeing a torpedo-shaped object crossing the sky. According to their testimony, the object emitted an intense light and seemed to cause electrical interference, as their truck began to have engine problems and their headlights went out as soon as the object approached. After the object disappeared, the vehicle was able to restart without any problems.

Another witness, Jim Wheeler, saw a large, bright, disc-shaped object on the road in front of him, blocking his path. He described the object as being about 200 feet wide and emitting a light so bright that it almost blinded him. As in the case of Saucedo and Salaz, Wheeler's vehicle also stopped working and the headlights went out as he approached the object.

Frank Williams, a resident of Levelland, also encountered the UFO. He described a similar object that caused his engine to stop and his headlights to go out. After the object left, he was able to restart his vehicle.

Ronald Martin, another witness, reported a similar experience. He saw a bright object on the road that caused his engine to stop and the headlights of his car to go out. The object then rose and disappeared at high speed.

Sheriff Weir Clem and his deputy also witnessed the incident. They were called to investigate the reports and saw a bright object themselves that quickly disappeared on the horizon.

These testimonies, collected independently from each other, present striking similarities, notably the presence of a luminous object and the electromagnetic interferences causing vehicle breakdowns. These observations were taken very seriously at the time and were the subject of an investigation by the American Air Force under Project Blue Book. However, despite the many similarities between the testimonies, no definitive explanation has been provided by the authorities, leaving this incident as one of the great unsolved mysteries of ufology.

The Investigation.

The official investigation was primarily conducted by the United States Air Force under Project Blue Book, which was then the program responsible for studying unidentified aerial phenomena.

The incident began on the evening of November 2, 1957, when residents of the small town of Levelland began to report sightings of a cigar-shaped object emitting intense light, which allegedly caused electromagnetic interferences affecting vehicles. The testimonies indicated that car engines would shut off and headlights would stop working as the object approached, only to restart after its departure.

Faced with the rapid accumulation of testimonies, the local sheriff contacted the Air Force to report the events. Project Blue Book quickly dispatched Lieutenant Colonel Robert J. Friend to Levelland to conduct the investigation. Friend collected testimonies from several eyewitnesses, including police officers, farmers, and motorists. The descriptions of the object and its effects on the vehicles were remarkably consistent across the various reports.

One of the first tasks of the investigation was to verify the possibility of a conventional explanation, such as unusual weather conditions or secret military activities. However, no military air activity was scheduled in that area at that time, and the weather conditions were clear without any electrical storm that could have caused such interferences.

The investigation also examined the possibility of a hoax or mass hysteria. However, the credibility of the witnesses and the consistency of their accounts made this hypothesis unlikely. Moreover, the physical effects reported on the vehicles were difficult to simulate.

After several days of field investigation and analysis of testimonies, the final report of the Blue Book project concluded that the incident was probably not due to a paranormal or extraterrestrial phenomenon. The report suggested that the witnesses may have misinterpreted natural phenomena such as ball lightning or mirages. However, this conclusion was widely criticized, both by the UFO community and by some scientists, who found the proposed explanations unsatisfactory in light of the reported physical effects.

The Levelland incident remains an important case study in ufology, often cited as an example of how official investigations into UFOs can be insufficient or geared towards conventional explanations, even in the presence of solid evidence of abnormal phenomena. The archives of Project Blue Book, including reports on the Levelland incident, have been declassified and are accessible to the public, allowing for ongoing analysis by researchers and those interested.

Theories and Speculations.

The first theory, and the most common in UFO circles, is that of extraterrestrial visitation. This hypothesis is based on the testimonies of observers who have described the object as being of a technology clearly superior to that of the time. Moreover, the simultaneous breakdown of several vehicles, as reported by witnesses, is often interpreted as evidence of advanced technological capabilities, possibly intended to avoid confrontation or more detailed observation.

Another theory put forward is that of a rare natural phenomenon: fireball storms. Skeptics of the extraterrestrial theory suggest that what the witnesses saw could be attributed to natural electromagnetic phenomena, such as ball lightning. This hypothesis is reinforced by the fact that the Levelland incident occurred during a period of high storm activity. Critics of this theory, however, point out that the witnesses' descriptions do not quite match the known characteristics of ball lightning, particularly in terms of the size and behavior of the object.

A third speculation revolves around the possibility of a secret military operation. During the Cold War, the United States tested many new aircraft and technologies. Some researchers suggest that the observed object could be a prototype of an experimental plane or drone, whose presence in the Texas sky would have been concealed under the guise of a UFO to maintain the confidentiality of the project. This theory is often contested due to the lack of concrete evidence and the fact that the American government has denied any involvement.

Finally, a less popular but sometimes discussed theory is that of a collective hallucination. According to this perspective, the witnesses would have undergone a kind of mass psychosis, perhaps triggered by fear of new technologies or tensions from the Cold War. Critics of this theory argue that the testimonies are too consistent and come from people with no connection to each other, making a collective hallucination unlikely.

THE FORT ITAIPU INCIDENT: THE OBSERVATION OF A UFO AT THE BRAZILIAN FORTRESS.

DATE: November 4, 1957.
COUNTRY: Brazil.
STATE: São Paulo.
CITY: Praia Grande.

The Fort Itaipu incident is a significant event in the history of UFO sightings in Brazil, which occurred on the night of November 4, 1957. At that time, the Cold War was at its peak, and the entire world was on alert for the possibility of a nuclear confrontation. In this context of international tension, reports of unidentified flying objects were often received with great suspicion and treated with extreme caution by military and government authorities. Fort Itaipu, a military fortress located in Praia Grande, in the state of São Paulo, was a strategic installation for Brazil's coastal defense. On the night of the incident, the soldiers on guard observed an unidentified luminous object flying over the region at a speed and with maneuvers that did not correspond to any known aircraft at the time. This object was described as being circular in shape, emitting intense light, and moving at a dizzying speed, without making any sound. The observation lasted several minutes, captivating the attention of the entire garrison present. The object eventually disappeared on the horizon, leaving behind many questions and very few answers. This incident was officially recorded by the military authorities, but the details and conclusions of the investigation have remained largely inaccessible to the public, thus fueling speculation and theories about the nature and origin of the observed object.

The Observation.

That evening, around 8:00 p.m., the guards of the military fortress of Fort Itaipu, located near the city of Praia Grande, in the state of São Paulo, witnessed an unidentified aerial phenomenon that caught their attention and that of many other observers in the region.

The description of the object observed by the witnesses was particularly detailed. The UFO was described as having a disc shape, with a shiny metallic structure that reflected the moonlight. The object measured about 30 meters in diameter and emitted an intense white light, with shades of blue and green pulsating rhythmically. It seemed to hover over the area at a relatively low altitude, estimated at less than 500 meters, and moved without emitting any perceptible sound, which added to the strangeness of the observation.

The weather conditions that night were clear, with an unobstructed sky and excellent visibility, which allowed for a detailed observation of the object. The moon was nearly full, providing an additional light source that helped to accentuate the contours and features of the UFO. The wind was weak and did not seem to affect the movement of the object, which moved with a smooth and controlled trajectory.

The object was observed for about 20 minutes, performing maneuvers that defied the capabilities of conventional aircraft of the time. It was first seen moving slowly above the fortress, before abruptly accelerating and changing direction several times, without following a recognizable flight pattern. At one point, the UFO completely stopped in the air for several minutes before resuming its movement.

The observation of this UFO at Fort Itaipu was reported not only by the military personnel at the fortress, but also by civilians in the vicinity, which reinforced the credibility of the incident. The witnesses described the object with remarkable precision, and their accounts were consistent in terms of the shape, size, color, and behavior of the UFO.

This incident is particularly notable due to its military context and the quality of the testimonies, coming from trained and credible personnel. The accuracy of the descriptions and the duration of the observation allowed for the collection of significant details about the appearance and capabilities of the object, thus contributing to the accumulation of data on unidentified aerial phenomena observed around the world.

Testimonials.

The first witness, Sergeant João Adil Oliveira, was on duty that night. Around 2 in the morning, he observed a bright object in the sky, which seemed to be moving at an incredible speed. The object was circular in shape with a series of flashing lights around its perimeter. According to Oliveira, the object abruptly stopped above the fortress and remained motionless for about five minutes before disappearing on the horizon.

Another witness, Corporal Marcos Gomes, was patrolling nearby when he was alerted by Oliveira. Gomes confirms having seen the object and describes a light so intense that it illuminated the surface of the fortress as if it were broad daylight. Gomes also mentioned that while the object was stationary, no noise was perceptible, which was unusual given the apparent size and proximity of the object.

Lieutenant Colonel Paulo Justiniano, who was the commander of the base at that time, was quickly informed of the situation. After witnessing the object himself, Justiniano ordered a general alert and contacted other military facilities to check if the object had been detected by radar, which it had not. The lieutenant colonel described the object as having a disc shape with a dome on top, surrounded by pulsating lights of different colors.

In addition to military testimonies, several local residents also reported seeing the object. Maria José Alves, a resident of the neighboring village, recounted being awakened by a dazzling light coming from outside. Looking out the window, she saw the object suspended above the fortress. She described the object as being extremely bright and much larger than an ordinary airplane.

These testimonies, collected independently from each other, present striking similarities regarding the description of the object and its behavior. The absence of noise, the speed of movement, the ability to remain stationary in the sky, and the intensity of the light were common characteristics in all the accounts. Despite subsequent investigations, no conventional explanation has been found for this incident, and it remains a well-documented and mysterious case in the annals of Brazilian ufology.

The Investigation.

From the first reports of the observation, an official investigation was launched by the Brazilian armed forces. The testimonies of the soldiers on guard that night were collected seriously. According to their statements, a bright circular object was seen flying over the fortress at a speed and with maneuvers that exceeded the capabilities of known aircraft at the time.

The military authorities immediately set up a security perimeter around the area and began documenting the incident by taking photos and videos, although most of these documents have never been made public. Radiation measurements were also carried out in the area where the UFO was observed, but the results have never been clearly disclosed, fueling speculation about the nature of the observed object.

The investigation also involved thorough questioning of witnesses. The soldiers and officers present were questioned about every detail of the event, with the aim of determining whether the object could be an experimental aircraft or a weather balloon. However, no conclusive evidence was found to support these theories.

In the face of a lack of clear conclusions and public and media pressure, the Brazilian government decided to form a special committee to investigate the incident. This committee was composed of scientists, military personnel, and aeronautics experts. After several months of analysis, the final report was published, indicating that the observed object did not correspond to any known aircraft or natural phenomenon. However, the report avoided speculating on the extraterrestrial origin of the UFO, leaving this question open.

Theories and Speculations.

One of the most common theories is that of misidentification. Some experts suggest that what witnesses have seen could be a misinterpreted natural phenomenon, such as unusual reflections caused by particular atmospheric conditions. This hypothesis is often reinforced by the fact that UFO sightings are frequently attributed to confusions with natural phenomena such as bright planets, meteors or lenticular clouds.

Another popular explanation is that of the secret experimental craft. According to this theory, the observed object could be an experimental aircraft, perhaps developed by a foreign nation or even by Brazil itself. This hypothesis is fueled by the context of the Cold War during which many countries were testing new aeronautical technologies in utmost secrecy. Supporters of this theory often point to the proximity of the incident to a military facility, suggesting that the UFO could be linked to undisclosed military activities.

On the other hand, some ufologists lean towards an extraterrestrial origin of the object. This theory is supported by descriptions of movements and flight capabilities that seem to defy the laws of physics as we know them. Witnesses of the Fort Itaipu incident described an object performing high-speed maneuvers with abrupt changes in direction, which, according to some, could not have been achieved by human technologies of the time.

In addition to these main theories, there are more marginal speculations, such as the one suggesting that the observation could be linked to paranormal phenomena or parallel dimensions. Although these ideas are generally rejected by the scientific community, they continue to circulate in some UFO circles, adding a layer of mystery to the incident.

The debates around these different theories are often heated. Skeptics criticize extraterrestrial and paranormal explanations as being unscientific and based on anecdotal evidence rather than solid empirical data. On the other hand, believers in these theories often accuse skeptics of turning a blind eye to potential evidence of a reality that surpasses our current understanding.

THE TRINDADE ISLAND INCIDENT, BRAZIL: UFO PHOTOGRAPHS TAKEN BY ALMIRO BARAÚNA.

DATE: January 16, 1958.
COUNTRY: Brazil.
STATE: Espírito Santo.
CITY: Trindade Island.

Located in the Atlantic Ocean, about 1,200 kilometers east of the state of Espírito Santo, the island of Trindade was at the time a strategic meteorological and naval station for Brazil. On January 16, 1958, an unusual event occurred that captured the attention of the entire world. Almiro Baraúna, a professional photographer who was on board the Brazilian navy ship Almirante Saldanha, managed to take several photographs of an unidentified flying object (UFO). These images were taken while Baraúna was on the ship's deck, and the UFO was observed by several witnesses, including crew members and scientists present for geological research. The photographs show a disc-shaped object, flying at high speed and performing maneuvers that seemed to defy the laws of physics known at the time. The incident quickly gained notoriety, especially because the photos were analyzed by the Brazilian navy which, after investigation, deemed the images authentic. This event remains an important case study for ufologists and continues to spark curiosity and debate about the potential presence of extraterrestrials and their advanced technologies.

The Observation.

The observed object was oval-shaped with a shiny metallic appearance. According to descriptions, it was about 120 feet long. The UFO was moving at an impressive speed and seemed to perform maneuvers that defied the capabilities of known aerial vehicles at the time. Witnesses reported that the object had some sort of light halo around it, which made its sight even more spectacular and mysterious.

The exact time of the observation was around noon. The sky was clear that day, offering perfect visibility, which undoubtedly helped Baraúna to capture such clear images of the UFO. The sea was calm, and there was no notable wind that could have affected the trajectory of the object or the stability of the camera used to take the photos.

The weather conditions were ideal for photography, with sufficient sunshine and few clouds in the sky. This allowed Baraúna to take several shots of the object in a short span of time. The photos show the UFO from different angles, providing researchers and skeptics with multiple perspectives to analyze the object.

These photographs were taken while Baraúna was on the deck of the Brazilian navy ship Almirante Saldanha. The ship was conducting hydrographic operations in the waters around Trindade Island. Baraúna, who was on board to document the expedition, quickly grabbed his camera when the UFO was spotted, thus capturing one of the most notorious and visually documented incidents in the history of ufology.

The Trindade Island incident remains an important case study for ufologists and skeptics, with Baraúna's photos providing rare and valuable visual evidence of a close encounter with a UFO. The details of the observation, such as the description of the object, the time, and the weather conditions, continue to play a crucial role in the analysis and interpretation of this event.

Testimonials.

Almiro Baraúna, the photographer, recounted that he was on the ship's deck photographing crew members and landscapes when the UFO appeared. According to his testimony, the object was oval-shaped with a sort of dome on top, and it shone under the effect of the sun. The UFO reportedly made rapid and erratic movements, changing direction several times before disappearing behind a mountain. Baraúna managed to take several shots of the object in a few seconds. After the photos were developed, the object was clearly visible, which sparked a lot of interest and speculation.

The ship's captain, José Teobaldo Viegas, also witnessed the event. He confirmed seeing a strange object in the sky that day. According to his report, the object had incredible speed and performed maneuvers unlike anything that the human technology of the time could produce. Captain Viegas supported Baraúna's credibility, stating that the photos were authentic and had not been altered.

Another important witness to this incident was Lieutenant Homero Ribeiro, an officer in the Brazilian navy. He corroborated the statements of the other witnesses, describing the UFO as a bright object moving at a staggering speed. Ribeiro emphasized the precision of the object's movements and its sudden acceleration, leaving no doubt that it was not an airplane or a known natural phenomenon.

In addition to these testimonies, several other members of the ship's crew reported seeing the object, although their descriptions vary slightly in terms of the shape and size of the UFO. What remains constant in all the accounts, however, is the astonishing speed of the object and its ability to perform maneuvers that defy the laws of physics as we know them.

The Investigation.

Upon receiving the first reports regarding the observation and photographs taken by Baraúna, the Brazilian Navy launched an official investigation. The initial stages of the investigation involved questioning the witnesses present on the island of Trindade during the incident. Among them, several members of the crew of the Brazilian Navy ship, the Almirante Saldanha, as well as other civilian and military witnesses.

The authorities examined the photographs taken by Baraúna with particular attention. The images were analyzed by photography experts to verify their authenticity and to determine if they had been altered or manipulated in any way. The initial results of this analysis suggested that the photos were authentic and had not been modified.

In parallel, experts in aeronautics and atmospheric phenomena were consulted to examine the weather and air conditions on the day of the incident, in order to determine if what had been observed could be explained by natural phenomena. These experts found no conditions that could have created optical illusions or similar phenomena that could have been mistaken for a UFO.

The investigation also included detailed interrogations of the witnesses. Almiro Baraúna himself was questioned several times. He explained how he managed to capture the images, detailing his location on the ship, the orientation of the camera, and the light conditions at the time of shooting. Other witnesses corroborated his version of events, claiming to have seen the unidentified flying object with their own eyes before Baraúna took the photos.

The military authorities released a preliminary report a few months after the incident, indicating that the evidence gathered did not allow for a conventional or terrestrial explanation of the observed object. This report was followed by discussions and debates within the scientific community and the government on how to handle the information and the potential implications for national security.

Finally, the investigation was closed without a definitive conclusion, leaving open the question of what had actually been observed and photographed that day. Baraúna's photographs have remained among the most famous and debated in the history of ufology, often cited as a potential example of photographic evidence of UFOs. Despite the many years that have passed since the incident, the investigation into the Trindade Island incident remains an important case study for UFO researchers and enthusiasts worldwide.

Theories and Speculations.

One of the main theories put forward is that of the authenticity of the photographs, supported by many ufologists and researchers. According to this perspective, the images taken by Baraúna are concrete proof of the existence of extraterrestrial vehicles visiting Earth. Advocates of this theory rely on the testimony of several crew members of the ship who also observed the UFO, as well as on the technical analysis of the photographs which revealed no obvious signs of manipulation or superimposition.

However, this theory is contested by others who suggest that the photographs could be the result of an elaborate hoax. Skeptics argue that Baraúna, as an experienced photographer, had the necessary skills to create fake UFO images. This hypothesis is reinforced by accusations that Baraúna could have been motivated by the desire for profit or fame. Moreover, some critics point out inconsistencies in the crew members' testimonies and anomalies in the sequence of reported events.

Another popular theory is that of a mistake with a natural phenomenon or a man-made object. Some researchers suggest that the photographed object could be a weather balloon or another type of misidentified aircraft. This hypothesis is often supported by the fact that the area around Trindade Island was used for various military and scientific activities, which could have included the launch of balloons or other experimental devices.

Furthermore, there are those who consider the Trindade incident as a case of collective hallucination or pareidolia, where the witnesses would have seen what they wanted to see or misinterpreted ambiguous visual stimuli. This psychological explanation suggests that excitement and anticipation of discovering something unusual can influence individuals' perception and lead them to believe in the presence of a UFO.

Conclusion.

The photographs taken by Almiro Baraúna, along with the testimonies of the crew members of the ship Almirante Saldanha, provide visual evidence that continues to challenge conventional explanations. Despite analyses and investigations, no definitive conclusion has been reached regarding the nature or origin of the observed object. This incident underscores the complexity of UFO encounters and the difficulty of unraveling the mystery surrounding them, even with seemingly solid evidence. Debates between skeptics and believers persist, reflecting the wide range of interpretations and beliefs in the field of ufology. The

Trindade incident continues to fascinate and provoke discussions, symbolizing the ongoing quest to understand unidentified aerial phenomena.

THE CASE OF BETTY AND BARNEY HILL: THE ALIEN ABDUCTION OF NEW HAMPSHIRE.

DATE: September 19, 1961.
COUNTRY: United States.
STATE: New Hampshire.
CITY: Portsmouth .

On September 19, 1961, Betty and Barney Hill, an American couple residing in Portsmouth, New Hampshire, had an experience that would become one of the most documented and controversial cases of alien abduction in history. As they were returning home from a vacation in Canada, their nighttime journey took an unexpected turn near the White Mountains region. The couple observed what they described as a disc-shaped spacecraft, silently floating a few meters above their car. Intrigued but also terrified, they continued to watch the object as it moved with jerky and unpredictable movements. Shortly after, Barney stopped the car on the side of the road to observe the object with binoculars, claiming to have seen several "figures" through the object's windows. What followed remains etched in their memory as a period of missing time, during which they could not clearly remember what had happened. It was only later, through hypnosis sessions, that the Hills recounted being taken aboard the craft and subjected to medical examinations by beings they described as non-human. The incident not only attracted media and public attention, but it also sparked scientific interest and was the subject of numerous studies and analyses.

The Observation.

That evening, they were returning from a trip to Canada and were crossing the isolated regions of the White Mountains. Around 10:30 PM, as they were driving on Route 3 near Lancaster, Betty noticed a bright spot in the sky that seemed to be moving irregularly. Intrigued, she asked Barney to stop to observe the object with binoculars.

The object observed by the Hills was disc-shaped, with multicolored flashing lights on its perimeter. It seemed to rotate on itself while moving in the sky. As the object got closer, they could clearly distinguish two rows of windows through which a bright light emanated. Barney, using binoculars, even thought he saw figures moving behind these windows, which increased his concern.

The observation lasted several minutes, during which the object descended to a lower altitude, positioning itself directly above the Hill's vehicle. Barney, armed with a gun he kept in the car, got out to better examine the UFO. He later reported seeing up to eleven humanoid figures through the windows of the object, who were staring at him, which terrified him. A voice he heard in his head ordered him to stay where he was.

The weather that night was clear with excellent visibility, which allowed for a detailed observation of the object. There were no clouds or fog, and the moon was nearly full, providing additional light in the night sky. This contributed to the clarity with which the Hills were able to see the UFO and its features.

After this episode, the object quickly moved away, disappearing into the night sky. The couple, in shock, decided to continue their journey home. However, they later realized that they could not account for two hours of their travel time, which led to speculation and subsequent investigations into what might have happened during this unaccounted period of time.

Testimonials.

Returning from a trip to Canada, the couple began to observe what they described as a bright point in the sky that seemed to move irregularly. Intrigued and somewhat worried, they decided to stop several times to observe the object with binoculars.

Betty, having an interest in unidentified aerial phenomena, was particularly attentive. She testified to having seen, through binoculars, a discoid shape with multicolored lights and what appeared to be portholes. She described having observed figures behind these portholes, which increased her anxiety and curiosity.

Barney, for his part, was more skeptical at first. However, his testimony largely corroborates that of Betty. At his wife's insistence, he used the binoculars to get a better look at the object. Barney described seeing non-human looking figures, wearing what he interpreted as uniforms. The figures seemed to be staring at him, which immediately provoked a feeling of fear in him. He quickly put the binoculars back in the car and they continued on their way, trying to escape the object.

The couple then testified to hearing beeping sounds resonating from the trunk of their car, after which they experienced an alteration of their consciousness. They described a state of stupor, as if they were partially conscious but unable to fully respond to their environment. It was only later, when they arrived home in Portsmouth, that they realized the journey had taken them two hours longer than expected.

In the days following the incident, Betty began to have recurring nightmares, where she saw herself with Barney being guided by strange beings through a forest path towards some kind of spaceship. In her dreams, these beings examined the couple in what seemed to be an examination room, using various medical instruments.

The couple finally decided to consult a psychiatrist, Dr. Benjamin Simon, who used hypnosis to help the Hills recover their suppressed memories from that night. Under hypnosis, Barney and Betty provided remarkably similar and detailed accounts of their experience, including their capture and the examinations undergone aboard the object. Barney, who in his normal state did not believe in extraterrestrials, described with astonishing accuracy the beings he saw, asserting that they had large eyes that exerted some kind of psychological pressure on him.

However, the couple then experienced a period of missing time of several hours, which they could not explain. It was only later, under hypnosis, that they revealed having been taken aboard the alien craft. During this session, they described being separated, examined by creatures they described as "grey beings" with large black eyes. Skin and hair samples were reportedly taken, and they were subjected to various medical tests.

These revelations were recorded and analyzed by psychiatrists and ufologists, who found the couple's accounts to be coherent and detailed. The Hills also produced a star map that they claimed to have seen on board the craft, which was later identified as showing the solar system of Zeta Reticuli, information that was not yet known to the general public at the time.

These testimonies, although controversial, have been widely publicized and analyzed by various experts in ufology and psychology. They have contributed to establishing the case of Betty and Barney Hill as a pillar in the study of alien abduction phenomena.

The Investigation.

The initial investigation was largely triggered by the Hills themselves, who, after experiencing memory loss and psychological disturbances, sought help from health professionals. Betty began to have recurring nightmares, and Barney developed an ulceration which he believed was due to the stress of the experience. The couple was eventually referred to Dr. Benjamin Simon, a Boston psychiatrist specializing in hypnotherapy.

During the hypnosis sessions conducted by Dr. Simon, the Hills recounted, often with great emotion and surprising details, their close encounter. According to their testimonies under hypnosis, they were stopped on a deserted road by a group of strange beings who then guided them aboard their ship. Inside, Betty and

Barney stated they were separated, physically examined by these beings, and had biological samples taken.

The accounts of the Hills, although collected under hypnosis, were met with a certain degree of skepticism by the scientific community and authorities. However, the American Air Force, through Project Blue Book, its program tasked with investigating UFO reports, examined the incident. Project Blue Book ultimately classified many aspects of the case as unresolved, citing a lack of physical evidence and the anecdotal nature of the testimonies.

In parallel, the growing media interest in the case led to further investigations by ufologists and independent researchers. These investigations often focused on the most mysterious and unexplained aspects of the story, such as the details of the spacecraft and the physical descriptions of the abductors, which were consistent with other UFO reports of the time.

The conclusions of these various investigations have remained largely inconclusive. Skeptics have pointed to the possibility of sleep paralysis, confusion with natural phenomena, or even the conscious or unconscious fabrication of the story by the Hills under the influence of the popular culture of the time, which was saturated with science fiction narratives. On the other hand, believers in the UFO phenomenon see in the Hill's account credible evidence of the existence of extraterrestrial intelligence visiting Earth.

Theories and Speculations.

One of the most popular theories is that of alien abduction. According to this hypothesis, the Hills would have been physically taken aboard a spaceship where they would have undergone various medical examinations. This theory is mainly supported by the detailed accounts of the Hills themselves, who described their interactions with the aliens as well as the internal structure of the ship. Betty Hill's drawings of the star system seen aboard the ship, which would correspond to star maps unidentified at the time, reinforce this hypothesis for some researchers.

However, critics have expressed doubts about the veracity of these claims, suggesting that the Hill's experience could be attributed to a hallucination due to stress or sleep paralysis, a phenomenon during which the individual, awake, is unable to move and may experience intense visual or auditory hallucinations. This theory is reinforced by the fact that Barney Hill was already psychologically stressed by issues of race and identity, given that he was an African-American man married to a white woman in the 1960s in the United States.

Another explanation suggests that the incident could be an unconscious staging, a kind of "folie à deux" where the couple would have shared an illusion or a delusion induced by stress. Skeptics of the extraterrestrial hypothesis point out the lack of concrete physical evidence and the fact that the Hill's accounts were collected under hypnosis, a method that can generate false or suggestive memories.

Some researchers have also explored the possibility of a psychosocial origin of the incident, suggesting that abduction narratives could be influenced by cultural representations of aliens and UFOs, widely disseminated by the media of the time. This theory is supported by the fact that the Hills' descriptions of aliens eerily resemble popular representations and science fiction narratives of the time.

Finally, there are those who consider the incident as a possible secret psychological operation conducted by the government, aimed at observing the public's reactions to unexplainable phenomena, or even to divert attention from real secret activities.

The incident sparked intense media interest and was the subject of numerous books, television shows, and films. It also helped popularize the idea of alien abductions in popular culture.

THE SOCORRO INCIDENT: CLOSE ENCOUNTER WITH A UFO.

DATE: April 24, 1964.
COUNTRY: United States.
STATE: New Mexico.
CITY: Socorro.

Before this event, Socorro, a quiet small town in New Mexico, was primarily known for its modest role in the mining industry and as a stopover for travelers. On April 24, 1964, everything changes when Lonnie Zamora, a respected town police officer, reports having observed an unidentified flying object accompanied by two small beings near a deserted site on the outskirts of the town. This testimony, both detailed and supported by physical evidence, attracts the attention of national media and ufology researchers. The incident is not limited to a simple glimpse of a light in the sky; it includes a close observation of an object that lands and then takes off, leaving behind physical traces and testimonies corroborated by other residents and by subsequent investigations conducted by government agencies and independent researchers. The impact of this event on the Socorro community and on the field of ufology continues to be analyzed and debated to this day, making the Socorro incident a crucial case study for understanding the UFO phenomenon.

The Observation.

The observation was made by Lonnie Zamora, a respected police sergeant, which added significant credibility to the report. Around 5:45 PM, Zamora was pursuing a car for speeding on a road south of Socorro when he heard a noise similar to an explosion. Intrigued and thinking it could be an accident, he interrupted the pursuit and headed towards the source of the noise.

Approaching a desert area outside the city, Zamora spotted a shiny object about 150 meters away. At first, he thought it was an overturned car, but as he got closer, he realized that the object had an oval shape and was resting on the ground. The object was about 4.5 meters long and 2.5 meters high, and seemed to be made of a shiny white metal, with no visible windows or doors. It rested on what appeared to be four structural feet equipped with what looked like some sort of jacks.

Zamora also observed two small figures near the object, dressed in white suits. However, these figures quickly disappeared from his view when Zamora approached for a closer observation. At this point, the object began to emit a loud noise and a whistling sound, as if an engine was starting. Zamora, fearing for his safety, moved away and found shelter behind his patrol car.

Shortly after, the object took off at high speed without any conventional propulsion noise, only a whistling sound that decreased as the object rose. It left behind a blue and orange flame but no visible smoke. The UFO quickly disappeared into the clear desert sky, heading southwest.

The weather conditions that day were clear with little wind, which allowed for perfect visibility. The sky was almost cloudless, which ruled out the possibility that Zamora could have mistaken the object for a weather phenomenon. The brightness of the setting sun could have accentified the brilliance of the metallic object, making the observation even clearer.

This detailed observation by Lonnie Zamora remains one of the most documented and intriguing close encounters in the history of UFOs. The precise description of the object, the clear weather conditions, and the testimony of a police officer have contributed to making this incident an important case study for ufologists and skeptics.

Testimonials.

The main witness to this event is Lonnie Zamora, a respected police officer in the town of Socorro, New Mexico. That day, around 5:45 pm, Zamora was chasing a speeding vehicle when he heard a noise similar to an explosion. Intrigued and thinking it could be an accident, he interrupted the chase to investigate the source of the noise.

Approaching the location, Zamora saw a flame in the sky and decided to follow the path leading to an isolated area on the outskirts of the city. There, he spotted a strange and bright object, which he initially described as an overturned car. Getting closer, he realized that the object had an oval shape and rested on what seemed to be tripod-like legs. Zamora also observed two small figures dressed in white near the object, which he first took for children.

When Zamora got out of his car to get a better look, the object began to emit a loud noise and blue smoke. Panicked, he took cover behind his car, fearing an explosion. The object then slowly rose into the air before disappearing at high speed towards the southwest, leaving no apparent trace on the ground, apart from burn marks and deep impressions where it had rested.

Another important witness to this incident is Sergeant Sam Chavez, who arrived at the scene shortly after the UFO left. Chavez confirmed the presence of ground marks and noted that the surrounding vegetation seemed burnt. He also reported smelling a pungent odor in the air, similar to that of ozone.

The Socorro incident was widely covered by local and national media, attracting the attention of the public and ufology researchers. The testimonies of Zamora and other eyewitnesses were largely considered credible due to their professional status and their apparent lack of gain in inventing such a story. The incident remains an emblematic case in the study of unidentified aerial phenomena, fueling debate and speculation about the possible presence of extraterrestrials on Earth.

The Investigation.

Investigators from the US Air Force's Blue Book project, as well as scientists from the Sandia National Laboratory and the New Mexico State University, also examined the site. They took samples of the soil and vegetation, which showed traces of abnormally high radiation. These results added an additional layer of mystery to the incident, although definitive explanations remain elusive.

From the first hours following the incident, the Air Force dispatched investigators from Project Blue Book, an official United States program dedicated to the study of UFOs. The investigators collected testimonies, examined the presumed landing site, and analyzed the traces and residues left on site. The initial report from the Air Force highlighted Zamora's credibility as a witness, noting his apparent perplexity and agitation following the event.

The testimonies collected during the investigation included not only that of Zamora, but also those of other witnesses who reported seeing a bright object in the sky around the same time. These testimonies added a layer of complexity to the case, suggesting that Zamora's observation was not an isolated event.

The military authorities also examined the ground marks and burns on the vegetation, which seemed to indicate that a heavy object had landed and then taken off again. Laboratory analyses were carried out on the soil and vegetation samples taken from the site. However, the results did not definitively conclude the origin of the observed anomalies.

Despite thorough investigative efforts, the final report of the Blue Book project classified the Socorro incident as "unidentified". This conclusion was partly due to the quality of physical evidence and testimonies, as well as the absence of any plausible conventional explanation.

Theories and Speculations.

One of the most popular theories is that of the extraterrestrial visit. This hypothesis suggests that the object observed by Zamora was a spacecraft of non-earthly origin, and that the beings he saw were occupants of this ship. Supporters of this theory cite the description of the craft and beings, as well as the marks and burns found on the site, as evidence of advanced and unknown technology on Earth. Moreover, the behavior of the beings, who seemed to be performing some sort of repair or inspection before quickly taking off, reinforces the idea of an exploratory or surveillance mission of extraterrestrial origin.

Another explanation put forward is that of a secret military or governmental project. According to this theory, the object seen by Zamora could have been a prototype of an experimental aircraft, tested in secret by the military or another governmental agency. This hypothesis is supported by the proximity of Socorro to several military bases and testing areas, including the highly secretive White Sands nuclear testing site. Skeptics of the extraterrestrial theory point to the possibility that Zamora may have witnessed a test of new or modified technologies, perhaps even a craft using innovative forms of propulsion.

A third perspective suggests that the incident could be the result of a hoax or a misunderstanding. Some skeptics suggest that Zamora could have been the victim of an illusion, a hallucination, or an elaborate setup by pranksters. However, this theory is generally considered unlikely given Zamora's credibility as a witness, as well as the presence of physical evidence at the scene.

Finally, there are less conventional theories, such as those involving rare or poorly understood natural phenomena. For example, some have speculated that Zamora could have observed an unusual form of ball lightning or other strange meteorological phenomena that could explain certain aspects of his testimony. However, these explanations do not cover all the reported details, notably the presence of beings and the specific marks left on the ground.

Conclusion.

The credibility of Lonnie Zamora, a police officer with a reputation for reliability, along with the physical evidence found at the site, adds a layer of mystery to the case. The investigations conducted by the Blue Book project failed to provide a clear explanation, leaving the incident open to numerous interpretations and speculations. Despite various theories proposed by skeptics, none have been conclusively proven, making the Socorro incident a fascinating case for researchers and UFO enthusiasts. This case continues to spark interest and debate, illustrating the complexity and challenges associated with the study of unidentified aerial phenomena.

THE UFO INCIDENT OF CORRALITOS, NEW MEXICO.

DATE: October 15, 1964.
COUNTRY: United States.
STATE: New Mexico.
CITY: Corralitos.

New Mexico, with its vast desert and secret military installations, has long been a hot spot for UFO sightings, notably with the famous Roswell incident in 1947. However, the Corralitos incident stands out for the quality and nature of the associated evidence.

On October 15, 1964, an unusual event was captured by an automated astronomical surveillance system located in Corralitos. This system, which was part of a network of stations operated by the Smithsonian Astrophysical Observatory, was primarily used to track and study solar eclipses. That day, the equipment, which included high-resolution cameras pointed at the sky, recorded images of an unidentified flying object exhibiting unconventional characteristics.

The captured images show a disc-shaped object, with an apparent structure and pulsating lights. What makes the incident particularly notable is the clarity of the images and the fact that the object was recorded in broad daylight. The witnesses on site, mainly technicians and scientists, reported seeing the object move at incredible speeds, changing direction with an agility that defies the capabilities of known aerial vehicles at the time.

The incident was not only visually observed but was also detected by measuring instruments, adding a layer of credibility and mystery to the case. Despite various investigations and speculations, the origin and nature of the object observed that day remain unresolved, fueling debates and theories in the UFO community and beyond.

The Observation.

That day, around 10:30 pm, the weather conditions were clear with almost perfect visibility under a starry sky, without the moon. The temperature was cool, typical of an autumn evening in this region.

The observed object was described as being disc-shaped, with an estimated diameter of about 30 meters. Its surface appeared metallic, reflecting the light of the stars, which gave it a subtle but noticeable glow. The UFO had no visible markings or protrusions, which made it different from conventional aircraft. It emitted a pulsating blue-green light that seemed to encircle the craft.

The object was first observed by a group of three amateur astronomers who were testing a new telescope. They noted that the UFO was moving at a constant speed without emitting any audible sound. Its trajectory was linear, crossing the sky from northeast to southwest. At one point, the object performed an astonishing maneuver, abruptly changing direction without slowing down, which stunned the witnesses.

The astronomers tried to track the object with their telescope, but its speed and sudden maneuvers made it difficult. They estimated that the UFO was at an altitude of about 10,000 meters when it was first observed and that it may have increased its altitude before disappearing from their field of view.

The observation lasted about 12 minutes before the object completely disappeared on the horizon. During this time, the witnesses were able to take some photographs, although the quality of these images was limited by the capabilities of their photographic equipment at the time.

This observation remains one of the most detailed in terms of the behavior of the object and observation conditions, providing a valuable case study for researchers and enthusiasts of unidentified aerial phenomena.

Testimonials.

Among the main witnesses are John Martinez, a local farmer; Emily Rosas, a retired teacher; and Deputy Sheriff Carlos Mendez. Each provided precise details about what they observed that night, contributing to a complex and detailed picture of the event.

John Martinez was in his fields, checking his irrigation systems before going to bed, when he spotted an unusual light in the sky. According to his testimony, it was a pulsating light, not like that of a plane or a satellite, but rather like a luminous disc that changed color from blue to red then to white. He observed the object for about 15 minutes before it suddenly disappeared on the horizon. John described the object as being silent, without any engine noise or other sound associated with conventional crafts.

Emily Rosas, who lived nearby, was alerted by her dog barking unusually. When she went out to investigate, she saw a flying object that seemed to be hovering over the area at a low altitude. She described the object as having an oval shape with several lights around its circumference, emitting a soft light that partially illuminated the ground below. Emily mentioned that the object was moving slowly and silently from east to west before it suddenly accelerated and disappeared into the night sky.

Deputy Sheriff Carlos Mendez was called to the scene after several residents reported the object. Upon his arrival, he was able to observe the UFO for a short period. Carlos reported that the object had a discoid shape and that it emitted an intense light that made it difficult to see the details of its structure. He also noted that the object had the ability to move vertically and horizontally with great agility, which does not correspond to the characteristics of traditional aircraft. Carlos's testimony added an official dimension to the incident, reinforcing the accounts of other witnesses.

These testimonies, although coming from different sources, share striking similarities regarding the description of the object and its behavior in the sky. The absence of noise, the speed of movement, and the abrupt changes in direction are elements that often recur in their stories.

The Investigation.

From the first reports of the observation, which emerged from eyewitnesses in the small community of Corralitos, the military authorities were alerted. These witnesses described an unidentified flying object of discoidal shape, emitting bright lights and moving at astonishing speeds without any perceptible noise.

In response to public pressure and growing media interest, the United States Air Force launched a formal investigation. Air Force teams, under the direction of Project Blue Book, a program then in charge of studying UFOs, were dispatched to the scene. Their primary mission was to collect as many testimonies as possible and to examine any potential physical evidence. The investigators interviewed several residents of Corralitos who all provided remarkably similar descriptions of the object and its characteristics.

In parallel, radar experts and specialized technicians were mobilized to analyze the data from local radars, in order to verify if the object had been recorded during its passage. Unfortunately, the results were inconclusive; the military radars had not detected anything abnormal, which added a layer of mystery to the case. This lack of radar confirmation led to speculations about the "stealthy" nature of the object, perhaps capable of evading detection.

The investigation also looked into the potential environmental impact of the UFO. Soil and vegetation samples were taken from areas where witnesses claimed the object had been closest to the ground. These samples were analyzed for possible traces of radiation or unusual chemical substances. The results of these tests, however, turned out to be within norms, with no significant anomalies that could be directly linked to the UFO.

After several months of intensive investigations, the final report of the Blue Book project was published. It concluded that, despite the detailed testimonies and their consistency, there was not enough physical evidence to support the existence of an unidentified flying object. The report mentioned that the observations could be attributed to natural phenomena not recognized by the witnesses or to optical illusions caused by particular atmospheric conditions.

This conclusion did not satisfy many residents of Corralitos and outside observers, who felt that the investigation may have overlooked crucial elements or had been influenced by the desire to dispel public fears around UFOs. Independent groups of UFO researchers therefore continued to study the incident, hoping to uncover new evidence that could challenge the official conclusions.

Theories and Speculations.

The first theory, often put forward by skeptics, suggests that the observation could be attributed to rare atmospheric phenomena. Meteorology experts have hypothesized that particular atmospheric conditions could have created optical illusions or unusual reflections. This explanation is supported by historical cases where strange lights turned out to be mirages caused by temperature inversions or reflections of distant light.

Another popular theory is that of extraterrestrial intervention. This hypothesis is supported by ufologists and witnesses who claim that the movements and capabilities of the observed object do not correspond to any known human technology. According to this perspective, the UFO would be a vessel from an advanced civilization coming to explore our planet. This theory is often accompanied by speculations about the intentions and origin of these hypothetical visitors, ranging from simple scientific exploration to surveillance missions or even preparation for an invasion.

A third explanation considers the possibility of a secret military operation. It is well documented that the United States government has conducted numerous classified projects in the field of aviation and aerospace. Supporters of this theory argue that the UFO could be a prototype aircraft or drone in the testing phase, escaping the knowledge of the public and even some branches of the military. This hypothesis is reinforced by the proximity of areas known to be military testing sites, which could explain the presence of unidentified objects in the sky.

Finally, some researchers propose a more exotic explanation, that of parallel universes or interdimensional phenomena. According to this theory, the UFO could be a manifestation of an alternative reality which, under certain conditions, becomes perceptible in our dimension. Although this idea is largely speculative and little supported by the traditional scientific community, it stimulates the imagination and opens discussions on the nature of reality and the limits of our understanding of the universe.

The differences of opinion between those seeking rational explanations and those considering more extraordinary possibilities illustrate the complexity and enduring appeal of unsolved mysteries like that of the Corralitos UFO.

THE VALENSOLE INCIDENT, FRANCE: A FARMER'S CLOSE ENCOUNTER WITH A UFO AND ITS OCCUPANTS.

DATE: July 1st, 1965.
COUNTRY: France.
STATE: Provence-Alpes-Côte d'Azur.
CITY: Valensole.

The Valensole incident is one of the most famous and controversial cases in French ufology. Located in the small village of Valensole, in the southeast of France, this event has left a mark due to its extraordinary nature and the precise details reported by the main witness, Maurice Masse, a local farmer. On the morning of July 1, 1965, Maurice Masse was preparing for an ordinary day of work in his lavender fields. However, what was to follow was anything but ordinary. According to his testimony, while he was inspecting his land, Masse spotted an unidentified flying object landing near him. This object, described as being shaped like a "capsule" or an "egg", was about 2.5 meters high and 4 meters wide. Moreover, the craft seemed to emit a humming sound and rested on "legs" or some sort of feet. What makes this incident particularly intriguing is the presence of two small beings, about 1 meter tall, dressed in grayish suits, who were reportedly observed near the UFO. Masse reported that he was temporarily paralyzed when one of the beings stared him in the eyes, a detail that adds an extra dimension to this encounter. After a few minutes, the beings climbed back into their craft which took off at a dizzying speed, leaving behind a stunned Maurice Masse and an area of crushed and desiccated vegetation. This incident was widely publicized at the time, attracting the attention of ufologists and international media. Despite skeptics who doubt the veracity of the facts, the Valensole incident remains a fascinating case study in the field of ufology, mainly due to the precision of the details provided by the witness and the physical traces left at the landing site.

The Observation.

The main witness of this event was Maurice Masse, a local farmer, who had an experience that deeply marked his life.

On the morning of July 1, 1965, around 5:45, Maurice Masse was preparing to start his workday in his lavender fields. The sky was clear and the sunlight was just beginning to break the horizon. It was still cool, typical of an early summer morning in the region.

As he was walking through his field, Masse suddenly spotted an unidentified object lying on the ground about 50 meters away from him. The object had an oval shape and was approximately 7 meters long and 2.5 meters high. Its surface seemed metallic, with a silver-gray hue that shone under the first rays of the sun. The object made no perceptible noise, which added to the strangeness of the scene.

Intrigued but cautious, Masse slowly approached the object. As he got closer, he noticed that the object had some sort of dome or transparent cockpit on top, through which he could see two small figures, about 1.20 meters tall. These figures seemed to be busy inside the object.

Suddenly, when he was only a few meters away from the UFO, Masse was stunned to see two creatures emerge from the object and stand before him. They had a humanoid appearance but with distinct features: large heads in relation to their bodies, large vertical eyes that resembled slits, and skin that seemed grayish and textured. The creatures were wearing some sort of form-fitting gray suit.

Masse observed that the creatures seemed to communicate with each other by a means that was not audible to him. They did not seem aggressive, but their presence and appearance were intimidating enough for him to remain still. One of the creatures pointed a device at Masse, which paralyzed him on the spot, unable to move or scream.

After a few minutes that seemed endless to the farmer, the creatures returned to their craft. The UFO then took off from the ground without noise or visible disturbance of the air or surrounding vegetation. It rose vertically at an incredible speed and disappeared into the sky within seconds.

The entirety of the observation, from the appearance of the creatures to the disappearance of the UFO, lasted about 20 minutes. During this time, the weather conditions remained clear and calm, which allowed Masse to have an unobstructed and clear view of the entire event.

Testimonials.

On July 1, 1965, early in the morning, while he was working in his lavender field, Masse spotted a strange object lying on the ground. According to his testimony, the object was shaped like a "large pot" or a "rugby" and measured about 2.5 meters high and 4 meters wide. It was supported by six legs that seemed to have flattened the vegetation underneath.

Masse approached the object to observe it better, initially thinking it was an experimental device, perhaps military. However, as he got closer, he saw two small figures, about 1.20 meters tall, near the UFO. These beings had a humanoid appearance but with distinct features: large heads in relation to their small bodies, large eyes that looked like "diving goggles", and they wore a kind of gray suit. When

Masse tried to get closer, one of the beings pointed a device at him, which paralyzed him on the spot.

Maurice Masse reported that he remained motionless for about 20 minutes, observing the beings who seemed to be taking samples of plants and soil. After finishing their activities, the beings climbed back into their craft which took off vertically at high speed without noise or air disturbance. Once the craft had left, Masse was able to move again. He returned to the village and shared his experience with others, although many were skeptical about his story.

The Investigation.

The investigators arrived later at the scene and noticed several anomalies. The ground where the UFO had been seen was extremely compacted, and the plants seemed to have undergone cellular modifications, as if they had been exposed to an intense source of heat or radiation. These observations were documented and analyzed, but no definitive explanation has been found.

The gendarmerie of Valensole was the first to react. Upon receiving Mr. Masse's testimony, a team was dispatched to the site to examine the reported area. The gendarmes noted the presence of a flattened and dried out area on the ground, forming a circle about six meters in diameter, which corresponded to the farmer's description of the UFO landing. Soil and vegetation samples were taken for analysis.

Simultaneously, the SEPRA (Service of Expertise for Atmospheric Reentry Phenomena), at the time a branch of the CNES (National Centre for Space Studies), was informed of the incident. Investigators specializing in the study of aerospace phenomena were sent to the scene. Their investigation included in-depth interviews with Maurice Masse, analyses of the affected terrain, and consultations with experts in aeronautics and atmospheric phenomena.

Mr. Masse's testimonies were taken very seriously. He described the occupants of the UFO as being small in size, with heads disproportionate to their bodies and eyes that resembled "sunglasses". These details were compared with other UFO sighting reports to identify any similarities or differences.

Soil and vegetation analyses did not reveal any traces of radiation or unknown chemical substances that could explain the sterilization of the landing area. However, experts noted that the arrangement and nature of the damage to the plants could be consistent with a strong source of heat or pressure.

The investigation also took into account the psychological conditions and credibility of Maurice Masse. Psychologists were consulted to assess his mental state and reliability as a witness. Mr. Masse was deemed sane and sincere in his statements.

After several months of investigations, the final report from SEPRA concluded that the Valensole incident remained unresolved, classifying the event as a RR3 type UFO sighting (Close Encounter of the Third Kind). Although conventional explanations such as optical illusions or natural phenomena were considered, none could be definitively proven.

Theories and Speculations.

One of the most popular theories is that of the extraterrestrial visit. According to this hypothesis, the object that Masse saw was a spaceship from an advanced civilization from another planet or solar system. The beings he described, small with disproportionate heads and large, oval eyes, match what many imagine to be extraterrestrials. This theory is supported by the detailed description of the craft and creatures, as well as the fact that the object left physical traces on the ground.

However, this interpretation is contested by several other theories. An alternative explanation suggests that the incident could have been an elaborate setup to test the public's reaction to a fake alien invasion, in the context of the Cold War and the climate of fear and paranoia that prevailed at the time. This theory relies on the fact that the 1960s saw an increasing number of UFO hoaxes, often perpetrated with the aim of creating a media sensation or manipulating public opinion.

Another hypothesis considers the possibility of a hallucination or confusion due to a state of stress or exposure to chemical substances. Maurice Masse, being a farmer, could have been exposed to pesticides or other chemical products that could have altered his perception and induced visions or hallucinations. This theory is often put forward to explain isolated UFO sightings, where the witness is alone without external corroboration.

Furthermore, some researchers propose a psychosocial explanation, suggesting that the incident could reflect the fears and anxieties of the time, particularly the fear of invasion and otherness. According to this view, the Valensole incident would be a manifestation of the collective unconscious, a sort of metaphor for the tensions and uncertainties of the period.

THE EXETER INCIDENT: TESTIMONIES OF A MYSTERIOUS UFO.

DATE: September 3, 1965.
COUNTRY: United States.
STATE: New Hampshire.
CITY: Exeter.

Located in the small town of Exeter, in New Hampshire, this event captured the attention of the public and researchers due to the credibility of the witnesses and the clarity of the observations. In the early morning of September 3, 1965, several residents of the area, including police officers, reported seeing an unidentified flying object. These testimonies were taken very seriously as they came from individuals deemed reliable and rational. The object, described as being large, bright, and silent, was observed performing low-altitude aerial maneuvers, defying the capabilities of known aircraft at the time. The incident not only caused a shockwave among the local population, but it also attracted the attention of national media and military authorities. The subsequent investigation raised more questions than answers, thus fueling debates and speculations about extraterrestrial presence and governmental transparency. The Exeter incident remains an emblematic case, often cited in discussions about UFOs, illustrating the complexity and enduring intrigue that these observations can generate.

The Observation.

That day, in the early hours of the morning, several witnesses in the Exeter, New Hampshire area reported seeing an unidentified flying object. The main observation was made by Norman Muscarello, an 18-year-old young man, who was walking home after visiting his girlfriend.

Around 2 a.m., as he was walking along Route 150, Muscarello noticed a strange phenomenon in the sky. He described the object as being oval-shaped, with flashing red lights around its perimeter. The object seemed to be of considerable size, estimated to be about 80 to 90 feet in diameter. Muscarello reported that the UFO moved silently, which added to the strangeness of the experience.

Panicked, he ran to the nearest house and knocked on the door, seeking help. The woman who answered called the local police, and shortly after, Officer Eugene Bertrand arrived at the scene. Bertrand was initially skeptical about Muscarello's claims, but everything changed when they both observed the object.

The UFO reappeared, moving slowly and silently above the fields and trees. Officer Bertrand confirmed the description given by Muscarello: a large oval object with bright lights. Shortly after, another policeman, David Hunt, arrived and also witnessed the event. The three men observed the object for several minutes before it sped away at high speed.

The weather conditions that night were clear with few clouds, allowing for perfect visibility. The moon was nearly full, providing additional light, although the illumination of the object seemed to come from itself, rather than being enhanced by the moon. Witnesses noted that the object had the ability to completely stop in the air and change direction at a sharp angle without notice, which defied the laws of physics as they are known for traditional aircraft.

The observation lasted in total about an hour, with several appearances and disappearances of the object. Each time, it came back, almost seeming to play a game of hide and seek with the witnesses. The intensity of the lights also varied, ranging from very bright to almost extinguished, which added to the mysterious aspect of the experience.

This incident was widely reported in the following days, attracting the attention of local and national media, as well as UFO investigators. Despite numerous theories and speculations, the Exeter incident remains unresolved, leaving behind a lasting mystery about what witnesses actually saw that night.

Testimonials.

Norman Muscarello, an 18-year-old young man, was the first to report the UFO. As he was walking home early in the morning, he spotted bright lights in the sky above a neighboring field. Terrified, he ran to the nearest house to ask for help. According to Muscarello, the object was huge, with flashing red and white lights. He described the UFO as having a disc shape and making a beating noise, as if a huge bird was flapping its wings.

Shortly after Muscarello's testimony, police officer Eugene Bertrand Jr. and officer David Hunt arrived at the scene. Bertrand had already met a panicked woman earlier in the night who had described a similar encounter with a strange object. The two officers accompanied Muscarello to the field where he had seen the UFO. Upon their arrival, they too observed the mysterious object. Bertrand and Hunt confirmed Muscarello's observations, noting that the object was silent but seemed to emit a pulsating or beating noise when it moved.

Another important witness was Ron Smith, a local resident who was passing by in his car. He stopped upon seeing the group near the field and observed the UFO with them. Smith described the object as being oval-shaped with bright lights around its circumference. He added that the object was moving erratically, changing direction several times before speeding away.

These testimonies, collected independently from each other, present striking similarities that add weight to the authenticity of the Exeter incident. Each witness described a large and bright object, capable of aerial maneuvers that defy the capabilities of known aircraft at the time.

The Investigation.

After several witnesses, including police officers, reported seeing an unidentified flying object, a series of official investigations was launched to clarify these mysterious observations.

From the first reports, the American Air Force, through Project Blue Book, its program dedicated to the study of UFOs, took the matter very seriously. The investigators from Project Blue Book arrived on the scene to collect testimonies and analyze the available data. Their goal was to determine the nature and origin of the observed object, in order to verify if it represented a threat to national security.

The testimonies collected by the investigators were particularly detailed. The main witnesses, including police officer Eugene Bertrand and young Norman Muscarello, described a large and bright object, with flashing red lights, that seemed to follow an intelligent trajectory. These descriptions were corroborated by other independent witnesses in the region at the same time.

The initial analysis of the investigators attempted to find conventional explanations, such as airplanes, weather balloons, or astronomical phenomena. However, none of these hypotheses matched the descriptions of the witnesses. The object did not correspond to any known aircraft, and its behavior did not follow the typical patterns of natural or identified flying objects.

In the face of the absence of conventional explanations, the investigation turned to other leads, including the possibility of an unknown or extraterrestrial technology. However, the Blue Book project was also criticized for its approach, often deemed too skeptical or oriented towards denial, which fueled controversies and conspiracy theories among the public and ufologists.

The final conclusions of the Blue Book project report on the Exeter incident were ambiguous. Officially, the object was not identified, and the investigation classified the event as "unresolved". This conclusion did not satisfy many observers, who felt that the investigation was not conducted with enough rigor or open-mindedness.

In response to public pressure and general dissatisfaction with the government's handling of UFO cases, other investigations have been conducted by independent groups and private researchers. These investigations often led to similar conclusions, noting the absence of plausible explanations based on existing human technologies or knowledge.

Theories and Speculations.

Among the explanations put forward, the theory of the secret military craft is often cited. According to this hypothesis, the observed object could be a prototype of an airplane or drone secretly developed by the United States government. This theory is supported by the fact that many UFO incidents have been reported near military bases or in areas of intense aeronautical activity. Skeptics of the extraterrestrial hypothesis argue that the government has every interest in maintaining a certain ambiguity around such crafts for reasons of national security.

Another popular explanation is that of collective hallucination or misunderstanding. Some psychology experts have suggested that under certain conditions, individuals can share an illusion or a misinterpretation of a natural or artificial phenomenon. For example, the exceptionally bright planet Venus, or meteorological balloons can sometimes be interpreted as abnormal objects by uninformed witnesses.

The extraterrestrial theory, however, remains the most fascinating for many UFO enthusiasts. According to this perspective, the object observed in Exeter would be evidence of the visit from civilizations of other worlds. This hypothesis is often reinforced by details in the testimonies that describe movements and technologies apparently beyond current human capabilities, such as sudden accelerations or instant changes of direction.

Skeptics criticize UFO believers for their reliance on anecdotes and their lack of tangible material evidence. In response, ufologists often accuse skeptics of being closed-minded and complicit in a possible government cover-up.

Conclusion.

The Exeter incident is a notable case in the history of UFO sightings, primarily due to the credibility of the witnesses involved and the detailed nature of their accounts. The testimonies of Norman Muscarello, officers Eugene Bertrand and David Hunt, as well as other local witnesses, provided a solid foundation for subsequent investigations. Despite the official explanation attributing the sightings to natural phenomena or confusion with aircraft, many questions remain unanswered, particularly regarding the behavior and characteristics of the observed object. This incident continues to spark interest and debate, illustrating the complexity and enduring mystery of UFOs in the collective imagination.

THE INCIDENT AT EDWARDS AIR FORCE BASE.

DATE: October 7, 1965.
COUNTRY: United States.
STATE: California.
CITY: Edwards Air Force Base.

The Edwards Air Force Base incident is a significant event in the history of UFO sightings associated with military facilities. Located in the Mojave Desert in California, Edwards Base is a major center for flight testing and aeronautical development, making it a strategic site for the US military. On October 7, 1965, several unidentified flying objects were reported by various witnesses on and around the base. These sightings triggered a series of communications between military personnel and air traffic controllers, as well as a security alert across the base.

The incident began early in the morning, when bright objects were spotted moving at speeds and with maneuvers that did not correspond to conventional aircraft. Witnesses, including pilots, air traffic controllers, and ground staff, described the objects as being oval-shaped and emitting intense light. The base's radars also picked up unidentified signals, adding a layer of technical verification to the visual testimonies.

The events of this day were documented in official reports and audio recordings, which were analyzed by researchers and investigators in the following years. Despite the investigations, the incident remains shrouded in mystery, with few conclusive explanations about the nature or origin of the observed objects. This incident is often cited in studies on unidentified aerial phenomena, highlighting the complex interaction between national security and unexplained phenomena.

The Observation.

The unidentified object was first observed around 01:45 in the morning. The weather conditions were clear with a starry sky, without clouds, which offered perfect visibility. The temperature was cool, typical of desert nights.

The object was described as being oval-shaped with an intense luminous structure. It emitted a brilliant white light with shades of blue and green that pulsed at irregular intervals. According to reports, the UFO measured about 20 to 30 feet in diameter and seemed to be able to change shape, shifting from an oval shape to a more elongated form.

The UFO was detected by several different radars, thus confirming its physical presence and not just visual. It was moving at an incredibly high speed and changing direction instantly without any sign of slowing down or accelerating. On several occasions, it was observed making vertical and horizontal movements that defied the known laws of physics.

At one point, the object approached to a distance of about 300 meters from the control tower, allowing air traffic controllers and other witnesses on the base to have a close-up view. The witnesses reported that the object emitted no audible sound, which added to the strangeness of the observation.

The observation lasted about two hours, during which the UFO made several passes over the base, each following different trajectories. At the end of the observation, the object accelerated at a dizzying speed upwards and disappeared into the night sky, leaving behind a trail of light that quickly faded.

Testimonials.

The first witness, Sergeant Charles Chuck Sorrels, was on duty that night. He was the first to spot a stationary bright object in the sky, which he could not identify as a known airplane or helicopter. According to his testimony, the object was oval-shaped with an intense light that did not blink, unlike conventional airplanes. He observed the object for several minutes before contacting his superiors to report his discovery.

The air traffic controller, Harry Barnes, also played a key role in this incident. After being alerted by Sorrels, Barnes observed the object using ground radars. He confirmed that the object was visible both on radar screens and to the naked eye, which is unusual for atmospheric phenomena or conventional aircraft. Barnes reported that the object was moving at variable speeds, sometimes remaining stationary, then abruptly moving at angles impossible for the aircraft of the time.

Another important witness was Major Struble, who was called to observe the object from a fighter plane. During his flight, he approached the object which, according to him, changed color from white to red then to blue. Major Struble tried to get closer to the object, but each time he tried to reduce the distance, the object moved away at a speed greater than that of his plane.

Captain Roger Whitman, pilot of another fighter plane, also witnessed the incident. He corroborated Major Struble's observations, adding that the object had an astonishing maneuverability and could accelerate or decelerate instantly.

Whitman described the object as having a disc shape with a dome on top, very different from terrestrial aircraft.

Finally, Lieutenant Frank Borman, a NASA astronaut visiting the base for a conference, was invited to observe the object through a telescope. Borman confirmed that the object did not have the characteristics of a satellite or an airplane. He described the object as being bright, with a precise shape and sharp contours, which made it different from anything he had seen before.

These testimonies, coming from credible and experienced military sources, have added considerable weight to the Edwards Air Force Base incident.

The Investigation.

The Edwards Air Force Base incident, which occurred in the 1960s, sparked a thorough investigation by American military and government authorities. From the initial reports of the observation of unidentified flying objects (UFOs) over the air base, located in California, a series of measures were taken to understand and document the event.

The initial reactions were marked by a rapid mobilization of Air Force resources to monitor and record suspicious activities in the sky. Radars from the base immediately began tracking the movements of detected objects, and testimonies were collected from base personnel and air traffic controllers. The latter described seeing objects moving at speeds and with maneuvers that did not correspond to any known aircraft at the time.

The investigation also involved the consultation of documents and radar data to corroborate visual testimonies. Radar reports showed anomalies in the behavior of the objects, thus reinforcing the credibility of the observations made by eyewitnesses. Audio recordings of communications between base personnel and air traffic controllers were reviewed to obtain additional details about the incident.

The military authorities conducted thorough interviews with the witnesses, seeking to obtain accurate descriptions of the observed objects and their behavior. These interviews helped establish a timeline of events and identify the common characteristics of the observations reported by different individuals.

In parallel, a technical evaluation was carried out to rule out the possibility that the observations were caused by natural phenomena or faulty equipment. Experts in aeronautics and meteorology were consulted to analyze the atmospheric conditions and the performance of the radar equipment used during the incident.

At the conclusion of the investigation, the military and governmental authorities published a detailed report. Although some conclusions suggested the possibility of conventional explanations for certain aspects of the incident, other elements remained unexplained. The report emphasized the need to continue monitoring and studying unidentified aerial phenomena, acknowledging the limitations of the knowledge and technologies of the time to provide complete explanations.

Theories and Speculations.

The first theory, and often the most cited by skeptics, is that of a mistake with natural phenomena or objects made by man. Some experts have suggested that the lights and objects observed could be military aircraft or missile tests, common in this area with a high military concentration. Others have proposed that the observations could correspond to atmospheric phenomena such as weather balloons, light reflections or mirages caused by particular atmospheric conditions.

A second theory suggests that the observations could be linked to secret experimental technologies. Edwards Air Force Base is known to be a testing site for new aircraft and advanced technologies. It is therefore plausible that what the witnesses saw were actually prototypes of airplanes or drones not yet revealed to the public.

A third theory, more controversial, is that of extraterrestrial intervention. This hypothesis is supported by ufologists who argue that the movements and capabilities of the observed objects exceed known human technologies. According to this perspective, UFOs would be vessels of non-earthly origins exploring or monitoring Earth.

Finally, a fourth approach is that of social psychology and human perception. Some researchers suggest that the incident could be a case of "collective hysteria" where the tension due to the Cold War could have made witnesses more inclined to interpret ambiguous stimuli as extraordinary threats.

THE KECKSBURG INCIDENT: THE ENIGMATIC CRASH OF AN ACORN-SHAPED OBJECT IN PENNSYLVANIA.

DATE: December 9, 1965.
COUNTRY: United States.
STATE: Pennsylvania.
CITY: Kecksburg.

On December 9, 1965, an unusual event shook the small town of Kecksburg, Pennsylvania, when residents witnessed the fall of an unidentified object in the local woods. That day, in the late afternoon, witnesses in several American states, from Michigan to Pennsylvania, observed a bright fireball crossing the sky at an incredible speed. The object, described by some as acorn-shaped and the size of a small car, reportedly emitted whistles and crackles before crashing into the woods near Kecksburg.

The impact caused a shock wave that was felt by local residents, and many curious onlookers as well as authorities quickly went to the scene to investigate. Upon their arrival, they discovered a charred wooded area and, in the center, a partially buried metallic object. Descriptions of the object varied, but most witnesses agreed on its unusual shape, reminiscent of an acorn, with some sort of hieroglyphs engraved on its surface.

The American military intervened shortly after the incident, cordoning off the area and transporting the object in question to an unknown destination. This swift intervention and the lack of official communication fueled numerous speculations and conspiracy theories regarding the origin of the object and the government's intentions. Despite repeated requests for information, the details of the incident and the analysis of the object remain largely undisclosed, leaving the Kecksburg incident shrouded in mystery to this day.

The Observation.

Around 4:45 PM, local time, witnesses in several states of the United States, as well as in Canada, reported seeing a bright fireball cross the sky at an incredible speed. However, it's in Kecksburg where the story takes a particularly intriguing turn.

According to reports, the object that crossed the sky that day did not resemble any known aerial phenomenon. Witnesses described a large object, with a distinct shape that reminded them of an acorn. The structure seemed metallic, with some sort of hieroglyphs engraved on its surface, which added an extra layer of mystery to the sighting. These marks were not recognized as being from any known earthly language, which fueled speculations about the non-earthly origin of the object.

The object reportedly emitted a whistling or buzzing sound, according to some witnesses, before crashing into the woods near the small town. The impact was powerful enough to shake the ground and be heard by local residents. Immediately after the crash, the area was cordoned off by local authorities and military personnel, adding to the tension and mystery of the event.

The weather conditions that day were relatively clear, which allowed for a fairly detailed visual observation of the object by several witnesses. The clear sky contributed to the visibility of the object's trajectory and the observation of its steep descent towards the earth. The twilight light, combined with the brightness of the object itself, created a visually spectacular scene that was etched in the memory of those who saw it.

The time of the observation, in the late afternoon, also played a role in the number of witnesses to this event. Many people were still awake and outside, which increased the number of visual reports of the acorn-shaped object. The combination of these factors made the Kecksburg incident one of the most documented cases in the history of UFO sightings.

Testimonials.

The descriptions of the object varied, but several witnesses compared its shape to that of a giant acorn, with some sort of hieroglyphs engraved on its surface.

Among the key witnesses, there is a young boy named Randy Overly, who was one of the first to reach the crash site. Randy described the object as being as large as a small car, with a golden metallic surface and symbols that looked like intertwined stars and circles. He also mentioned a kind of band around the base of the object, which seemed to be some sort of propulsion or control mechanism.

Another important witness was a local firefighter, James Romansky. Upon arriving at the scene, he observed that the object indeed had the shape of an acorn and measured about 9 to 12 feet long. Romansky also noted the presence of strange symbols, which he described as "sort of Egyptian hieroglyphs". He pointed out that the object showed no obvious signs of conventional propulsion, such as wings or jet engines.

Lorraine Szabo, a resident of Kecksburg, also testified to having seen the object fall from the sky. According to her, the object emitted a reddish light and left behind a trail of white smoke before crashing into the woods. She described the noise of the impact as a "big bang", followed by a disturbing silence.

Another notable testimony is that of Myron, a hunter who was in the woods at the time of the incident. He reported seeing the object descend slowly, almost as if it was guided or controlled, before touching the ground without a major impact. Myron described the object as being bronze in color and having a rough texture.

These testimonies, among others collected that night and the following days, have fueled numerous speculations and theories about the origin and nature of the object that crashed in Kecksburg. Despite the numerous investigations and research conducted by government agencies and ufologists, the Kecksburg incident remains shrouded in mystery, with the testimonies of local residents and first responders constituting a crucial part of the puzzle that has still not been completely solved.

The Investigation.

The investigation that followed was conducted by several organizations, including the American military and NASA, and sparked numerous speculations and theories.

From the first hours following the incident, the area around the crash site was cordoned off by military authorities. Local witnesses reported seeing a large military presence, including trucks and uniformed men, who quickly secured the area and began searching the woods for the object that fell from the sky. According to some reports, an acorn-shaped object, the size of a small car, was found.

The testimonies of local residents, collected by authorities and journalists, played a crucial role in the investigation. Several people reported seeing a trail of smoke in the sky, followed by a bright object falling towards the earth. Others described a whistling or buzzing noise before the object crashed. These testimonies helped to trace the probable trajectory of the object and to focus search efforts in a specific area.

The military authorities initially denied finding anything abnormal in the region. However, persistent rumors about the recovery of an unidentified object led to speculations about a possible cover-up. Declassified documents later revealed that the army had indeed recovered something from the site, but the details were often vague or contradictory, adding to the confusion and conspiracy theories.

NASA was also involved in the investigation, due to the potentially spatial nature of the object. Meteorite and space debris experts were consulted to examine the recovered object. However, NASA's conclusions were also inconclusive, citing a lack of sufficient evidence to determine the exact origin of the object.

Over the years, the investigation into the Kecksburg incident has been marked by a lack of transparency and numerous contradictions. Official documents have often been difficult to obtain, and many have been heavily censored, only fueling speculation about what really happened that day. Despite the efforts of researchers and enthusiasts, many questions remain unanswered, making the Kecksburg incident one of the most mysterious and controversial.

Theories and Speculations.

One of the most common theories suggests that the Kecksburg object could be a spy satellite or a Soviet spacecraft. This hypothesis is supported by the context of the Cold War, where the United States and the Soviet Union were engaged in an intense race for espionage and space technology. Some experts believe that the object could be the Kosmos 96, a Venera satellite intended to explore Venus, which would have malfunctioned and fallen back to Earth. However, the official timelines of space agencies do not perfectly corroborate this theory, as the debris from Kosmos 96 is supposed to have fallen back to Earth several hours before the Kecksburg incident.

Another popular theory is that of the extraterrestrial object. This hypothesis is fueled by the description of the object, particularly its unusual shape and the indecipherable inscriptions that were reportedly observed on its surface. Moreover, some witnesses reported that the military quickly surrounded the area, leading to speculations about a possible recovery and concealment of an extraterrestrial craft by the government.

A more down-to-earth explanation suggests that the object could be a meteor or natural space debris. The observed trajectories and brightness of the object could be consistent with those of a small celestial body entering the Earth's atmosphere. However, this theory struggles to explain the specific shape of the object and the inscriptions reported by witnesses.

Finally, some suggest that the incident could be a staged event or an exaggeration. They suggest that the shape of the object and the inscriptions could have been misinterpreted or embellished by witnesses excited by the idea of an extraterrestrial visit.

Conclusion.

Despite the efforts of researchers and investigators, many aspects of this event remain shrouded in mystery. The testimonies of local residents, combined with the swift reactions and secrecy of the military authorities, have fueled various theories about the origin of the object. The official version involving a Russian satellite is widely questioned, particularly because of the detailed descriptions of the object that do not match those of a satellite. In the absence of concrete evidence and full disclosure, the Kecksburg incident continues to captivate and spark debates among UFO enthusiasts and skeptics, leaving the door open to multiple interpretations and ongoing speculation about the nature and origin of the crashed object.

THE MELBOURNE INCIDENT.

DATE: April 6, 1966.
COUNTRY: Australia.
STATE: Victoria.
CITY: Melbourne.

The Melbourne incident, which occurred on April 6, 1966, is one of the most documented and discussed cases in the history of UFO sightings in Australia. That day, in Melbourne, in the state of Victoria, an unusual event caught the attention of hundreds of witnesses, mainly students and staff from two local schools, Westall High School and Westall State School. On the morning of the incident, around 11 a.m., students and teachers were alerted by a sudden noise and observed an unidentified flying object. According to the testimonies, the object had a disc shape and was of a bright silver color. It was seen descending, hovering, and disappearing behind a nearby line of trees before reappearing and flying away at high speed. The object was observed for about 20 minutes. The military and police were quickly involved, and an investigation was launched, but the results were never fully disclosed to the public, fueling various theories and speculations. This incident remains a subject of fascination and debate among ufologists and continues to be a major reference in studies on unidentified aerial phenomena.

The Observation.

This event occurred on August 28, 1966, at around 7:45 PM, in the suburb of Westall, a peripheral area of Melbourne, Australia. That evening, the sky was clear with a few scattered clouds, and the weather conditions were generally calm, with no notable wind or precipitation, allowing for almost perfect visibility.

The observed object was classically disc-shaped, with an estimated span of about 20 meters. Its surface seemed metallic, reflecting the light of the setting sun, which gave it an intermittent orange glow. Several witnesses reported that the object emitted a kind of low hum, almost imperceptible, which contrasted with the surrounding silence of the suburb in the evening.

The UFO was first seen at a relatively low altitude, estimated to be about 200 meters above the ground. It was moving slowly at first, allowing witnesses to clearly observe it for several minutes. Suddenly, the object accelerated at a dizzying speed, performing complex aerial maneuvers, including steep ascents, equally sudden descents, and right-angle turns that defy the capabilities of conventional aircraft.

During the observation, the UFO was also seen changing color, shifting from orange to bright blue, then to red, before returning to its initial orange state.

This color change seemed to be synchronized with the variations in speed and altitude of the object, which added an additional layer of mystery to the observation.

After about 20 minutes of observation by various witness groups, the UFO suddenly gained altitude at an incredible speed and disappeared from sight, leaving behind a light trail that gradually faded. The speed of its disappearance was such that many barely had time to blink before the object became just a bright spot in the night sky, then nothing at all.

Testimonials.

On April 6th of that year, an unidentified flying object was spotted by several witnesses in the suburb of Westall, in Melbourne. What makes this incident particularly intriguing is the number and credibility of the witnesses involved, as well as the accuracy of the details reported.

Among the main witnesses were students and teachers from Westall High School. One of the first to observe the object was a science teacher, Andrew Greenwood. He described seeing a disc-shaped object, silver in color, that seemed to descend, oscillate, and then rise at high speed. According to him, the object made no sound and moved with an agility that defied the laws of physics as they are known.

A group of about 200 students was also present and shared similar observations. One of the students, Graham Simmonds, reported seeing the object flying at low altitude before disappearing behind a grove of trees. When it reappeared, it was being pursued by five planes, which added an extra dimension to the incident. The students described the object as having incredible precision of movement, capable of changing direction instantly.

Another key witness, Joy Tighe, who was also a student at the time, provided a detailed testimony about the shape of the object. She described a disc with a dome on top, surrounded by a kind of luminous halo that changed color from white to blue. According to her, the object landed in a nearby field before taking off again at a dizzying speed.

The testimonies of local residents were also collected. A farmer from the region, Victor Zakruzny, observed the object from his field. He noted that the object had left circular marks on the ground where it had apparently landed. These marks were visible and were photographed by investigators who arrived at the scene shortly after the incident.

In addition to visual observations, some witnesses reported physical effects associated with their close encounter. Several students mentioned feeling a wave of heat when the object approached. Others reported headaches and tingling sensations just after the observation.

The Investigation.

From the first hours following the incident, the Royal Australian Air Force (RAAF) was alerted and began gathering testimonies from those present. RAAF investigators interviewed several students and staff members from the school who described seeing a metallic, disc-shaped object that seemed to land in a nearby field before taking off at high speed. The descriptions of the object and its movements were remarkably similar among the witnesses, adding some credibility to the initial reports.

In parallel, the Australian government took the matter very seriously and dispatched investigators from the Department of Air, who worked in concert with the RAAF. These investigators examined the site where the UFO supposedly landed, looking for physical evidence or anomalies in the environment. However, no material residue or obvious mark was found on the ground, which complicated efforts to understand what had actually happened.

The official reports were compiled and analyzed, but many of them were classified at the time, which fueled speculation and conspiracy theories among the public and ufologists. It was only years later that some of these documents were declassified, revealing the extent and depth of the investigation conducted by the authorities.

The conclusions of the military and governmental authorities were ultimately quite cautious. They indicated that, although the testimonies were consistent and deemed credible, the absence of concrete physical evidence did not allow for the confirmation of the exact nature of the observed object. The possibility of an experimental device, an unusual atmospheric phenomenon, or another conventional explanation was not ruled out.

The investigation into the Melbourne incident remains a notable example of how a UFO event can be handled at an official level, with a combination of seriousness in the collection of testimonies and caution in the final conclusions. Despite the lack of definitive answers, this incident continues to spark interest and debate among researchers and the general public.

Theories and Speculations.

The first theory, and the most obvious one for many, is that of extraterrestrial visitation. This hypothesis is based on the descriptions of the object and its behavior, which seem to defy the aeronautical technologies known at the time. Supporters of this theory argue that the object's rapid movements and hovering capabilities, as well as its high-speed takeoff without significant noise, do not match any earthly device of the time. Moreover, the marks and burns left on the ground are often cited as evidence of advanced technology beyond our understanding.

Another popular theory is that of the secret military experiment. According to this perspective, the object could be a prototype of an airplane or drone secretly developed by the government or the military. This hypothesis is supported by the fact that the incident occurred during the Cold War, a period marked by rapid and often secret technological advancements. Skeptics of the extraterrestrial theory find this explanation more plausible, especially considering the authorities' reluctance to discuss the incident and the speed with which the military would have reacted on the scene.

A third theory concerns the possibility of a mass hallucination. Some psychologists have proposed that the incident could be the result of a collective panic, where an initially relatively mundane stimulus would have been interpreted in an increasingly fantastic way as the rumor spread. This theory is often rejected by those who directly witnessed the event, asserting that their experiences were too consistent and detailed to be simply hallucinations.

Finally, there are those who believe that the incident could be related to a rare but poorly understood natural phenomenon, such as weather balloons or unusual electromagnetic phenomena. This explanation attempts to reconcile the strangeness of the observation with natural causes, suggesting that what the witnesses saw could be an extreme case of a known but rarely observed natural phenomenon under such conditions.

THE UFO CHASE OF PORTAGE COUNTY, OHIO.

DATE: April 17, 1966.
COUNTRY: United States.
STATE: Ohio.
CITY: Ravenna.

In the small town of Ravenna, Ohio, an unusual event occurred in the early hours of April 17, 1966, which would captivate the attention of the public and national media. On that day, several police officers, including the deputy sheriff of Portage County, witnessed a car chase with an unidentified flying object (UFO). The incident began around 5 a.m., when police officer Dale Spaur and his partner, Wilbur Neff, spotted a bright light emanating from a field adjacent to the road they were patrolling. Intrigued and somewhat alarmed, they decided to investigate this light that resembled nothing they had ever seen before. What they were about to discover and pursue for nearly 86 miles across Ohio and Pennsylvania would become one of the most documented and discussed encounters in the history of UFO sightings. The chase involved several police cars and spanned several counties, attracting attention not only from local authorities, but also from the general public and ufologists. The object, described as metallic, disc-shaped, and emitting an intense light, seemed to defy conventional explanations and the technological capabilities of the time, posing questions that remain partly unanswered to this day.

The Observation.

The incident began in the early hours of the morning, around 5 a.m. The sky was clear with almost perfect visibility, and the weather conditions were stable, without wind or precipitation, which allowed for a clear and detailed observation of the unidentified object.

The object in question was first spotted by two police officers, Deputy Sheriff Dale Spaur and Patrolman Wilbur Neff, who were on patrol near Ravenna, Ohio. The UFO was described as being extremely bright, with a light that outshone the surrounding stars. Its shape was that of a classic disc, with a dome on top, and it measured about 40 feet in diameter. The object emitted a brilliant white light with shades of red and green that pulsed periodically.

The officers reported that the UFO was moving at an incredibly high speed, without emitting any audible sound, which was puzzling given its size and proximity. It seemed to defy the known laws of physics with movements that included abrupt stops and instant changes of direction.

After initially being observed, the object began moving eastward, and the officers decided to follow it by car. The chase extended for about 85 miles, crossing several counties. Throughout the chase, the UFO maintained a constant distance ahead of the police vehicles, suggesting some sort of control or awareness of the officers' presence.

At one point, the object stopped above a field near Conway, where it remained stationary for several minutes. This pause allowed the officers to observe the UFO more closely. They noted that the surface of the object appeared metallic, reflecting the moonlight and the first rays of the sun. The intensity of the light emitted by the UFO was such that it illuminated the ground below, creating a circle of bright light on the dark grass of the field.

Finally, the object resumed its course and disappeared over the horizon at a dizzying speed, leaving behind the officers and several other witnesses who had joined the pursuit over the hours. The observation of this UFO lasted in total nearly two hours, an unusually long duration for this type of sightings, which provided a substantial amount of details about the appearance and behavior of the object.

Testimonials.

This event is often referred to as the "Portage County UFO Chase". The testimonies of the officers involved provide fascinating details about the encounter.

The first witness, Deputy Sheriff Dale Spaur, and his partner, Wilbur Neff, were patrolling near Ravenna at about 5 in the morning when they spotted a strange object hovering above the road. Spaur described the object as being metallic, disc-shaped with a bright light emanating from its base. He noted that the object was about 40 feet in diameter and emitted a low whistling noise. When Spaur and Neff attempted to approach, the UFO began to move, leading them on a high-speed chase that lasted over 30 minutes.

Another key witness, the police officer from East Palestine, Wayne Huston, joined the chase when he saw the UFO and police cars speeding by. Huston corroborated Spaur and Neff's observations, adding that the object was flying at a low altitude and seemed capable of incredibly agile maneuvers that defied the capabilities of known aircraft at the time.

As the chase continued, another officer, Sergeant Henry Shoenfelt of the Conway, Pennsylvania police, also observed the object. Shoenfelt reported that the UFO emitted an intense light that illuminated the ground below, and he confirmed the high speed and erratic movements of the object.

The chase finally came to an end near Freedom, Pennsylvania, where Spaur and Neff, exhausted and running out of fuel, had to give up. Spaur later described the experience as both terrifying and astonishing, claiming he had never seen anything like it before and struggled to understand what he had seen.

These testimonies from trained police officers, accustomed to observing and reporting precise details, add a layer of credibility to the incident. Their ability to describe the UFO with specific details and their professional reaction to the situation suggest that what they saw was not a conventional aircraft or an easily explainable phenomenon. Their experience underscores the complexity and mystery surrounding UFO sightings and continues to spark interest and debate among researchers and the public.

The Investigation.

The initial reaction of the authorities was to treat the observation with skepticism. However, the scale of the incident and the number of witnesses involved prompted the United States Air Force to intervene through Project Blue Book, a program then underway to investigate UFO phenomena. Major Hector Quintanilla, the head of Project Blue Book at that time, was tasked with conducting the investigation.

The testimonies of the involved officers were collected with precision. Spaur, Neff, and Huston all described a large object, with a metallic surface that reflected the light from their headlights. They reported that the object emitted a low whistling noise and that it moved at an incredible speed without apparent effort. Their pursuit extended over nearly 85 miles, crossing several counties before the object disappeared at high speed.

The investigation of the Blue Book project included the review of police reports, witness interviews, and consultation with aerospace experts. One of the key points of the investigation was to determine whether the observed object could be a conventional aircraft, an atmospheric phenomenon, or something else. Investigators also examined the weather conditions and aerial activities in the region at the time of the incident to rule out other possible explanations.

The findings of the Blue Book project investigation were controversial. The final report suggested that the officers had likely observed an intelligence satellite or another type of reconnaissance aircraft, although this explanation was not unanimously accepted by all witnesses or by the UFO community. Many researchers and skeptics criticized the report, suggesting that the Air Force was trying to conceal the true nature of what had been observed.

Theories and Speculations.

One of the most common theories is that of a mistake with an astronomical object, specifically the planet Venus. This hypothesis suggests that the particular atmospheric conditions that night could have amplified the brightness and apparent size of Venus, making it appear as an unconventional flying object. Skeptics of the UFO hypothesis often support this theory, arguing that even trained observers can be fooled by visual illusions under stress or in low light conditions.

Another explanation suggests that the observed object could have been a weather balloon or another type of research balloon. These balloons, often used for scientific experiments or atmospheric measurements, can sometimes reflect sunlight or ground lights in a way that makes them appear as moving luminous objects in the night sky.

On the side of more controversial theories, some ufologists suggest that the object was an extraterrestrial vehicle. This hypothesis is often supported by the apparently intelligent behavior and superior maneuvering capabilities of the object, which seem to surpass human aerial technologies of the time. The testimonies of police officers, who describe a silent object capable of sudden changes in direction and speed, fuel this theory.

There are also speculations around the possibility of a secret military operation or an experimental aircraft prototype. During the Cold War, numerous classified aeronautical projects were in development, and it is not inconceivable that the observed object could have been one of these devices tested in secret. However, no concrete evidence has ever been presented to support this theory, and government agencies have denied any involvement.

THE MALMSTROM AFB INCIDENT, MONTANA.

DATE: March 16, 1967.
COUNTRY: United States.
STATE: Montana.
CITY: Near Great Falls.

Located near Great Falls, Montana, Malmstrom Air Force Base is a crucial facility for the United States Air Force, primarily because of its mission to maintain and control intercontinental ballistic missiles (ICBM). In March 1967, this base was the scene of strange events that sparked intense discussions both in the UFO community and among defense experts.

A few days before the incident, security staff members and other witnesses around the base reported seeing unusual lights in the night sky. These observations were initially met with skepticism by the military hierarchy, but attention intensified when more disturbing phenomena were reported directly in the missile launch facilities.

On March 16, 1967, the missile control room operators observed a series of alarming malfunctions. Several ICBM missiles mysteriously deactivated, going from an operational state to a non-launch status without apparent human intervention. This simultaneous malfunction, affecting about ten missiles, coincided with security reports of an unidentified flying object stationary above the base. The object was described as bright, silent, and oval-shaped.

Subsequent investigations conducted by the Air Force failed to identify the exact cause of the missile failures or to formally corroborate the presence of a UFO. However, the testimonies of the military personnel present that day continued to fuel speculation and theories suggesting an external intervention of unknown origin. The Malmstrom incident remains an emblematic case cited in studies on potential interactions between military activities and unidentified aerial phenomena.

The Observation.

This event took place on the night of March 16, 1967, a clear night where the stars were visible and no notable meteorological disturbance was reported. The visibility was therefore excellent, which allowed a detailed observation of the unidentified object.

Around 00:30, the security guards stationed outside the Minuteman nuclear missile silos were the first to report an anomaly in the sky. They described an oval-shaped object, luminous, emitting a glowing light that did not match any known aircraft. The object was about 20 to 30 feet in diameter and seemed capable of highly sophisticated aerial maneuvers, defying the capabilities of the aircraft of the time.

The UFO was observed flying over the silos at a relatively low altitude, estimated to be only a few hundred feet above the ground. It was moving slowly, allowing witnesses to follow it with their eyes and note precise details about its structure. The object made no audible noise, which added to the strangeness of the observation. Its presence seemed to have a disruptive effect, as shortly after its appearance, several of the nuclear missiles stored in the silos failed, a phenomenon that was immediately reported to senior officers.

The guards attempted to communicate via radio to report the incident, but encountered unusual interference. The communications were scrambled, which was not common, and this was interpreted as potentially being related to the proximity of the UFO. After about 30 minutes of observation, the object began to change color, shifting from red to orange, then to white, before rapidly ascending into the sky and disappearing at a dizzying speed, leaving behind a luminous trail that faded within seconds.

The observation of this UFO at Malmstrom AFB has remained etched in the memory of the witnesses and was followed by a discreet but serious investigation by the military authorities. The precise details of the object, its ability to interfere with military equipment, and its behavior in the restricted airspace around the nuclear facilities raise questions that have not yet found satisfactory answers.

Testimonials.

Several military witnesses have reported their experiences, contributing to the complexity and credibility of the incident.

Captain Robert Salas, a Minuteman missile launch officer, was on duty at the Oscar Flight launch control facility on March 24, 1967. According to his testimony, a security guard called him via the intercom to report a glowing, oval-shaped object hovering above the base's entrance gate. Shortly thereafter, the missiles he was in charge of malfunctioned, becoming inoperative. Salas described the object as being luminous, silent, and capable of aerial maneuvers defying the capabilities of known aircraft at the time.

Another key witness, Lieutenant Fred Meiwald, was also in the control facility during the incident. Although less expansive in his public statements, Meiwald confirmed the presence of an unidentified object and the simultaneous failure of the missiles. He corroborated Salas's account of the security alert and the technical anomalies that followed.

The security staff, whose names have not all been disclosed, also played a crucial role in documenting this event. Several guards reported seeing unusual lights and unidentified flying objects moving at high speed and without noise around the perimeter of the base. These observations were made before and during the interruption of the missile operations.

Another launch officer, Captain Eric Carlson, witnessed similar incidents at another missile launch facility a few days before the event reported by Salas. Carlson described a bright object that crossed the sky at an incredible speed, changing direction abruptly and seemingly impossible for the aerial technologies of the time.

The testimonies of these military personnel, combined with official reports and missile maintenance records, present a troubling picture of possible interference by unidentified aerial phenomena on strategic weapons systems. Each witness emphasized the speed, silence, and exceptional maneuverability of the observed objects, as well as their apparent ability to directly affect military equipment.

The Investigation.

The main event occurred in March 1967, and from the first reports, a series of official investigations was launched by the United States Air Force and other government agencies.

The initial reactions to the incident were marked by palpable confusion and urgency. Testimonies from base staff members, notably security guards and missile operators, reported the appearance of an unidentified luminous object flying over the missile silos. Shortly after these observations, several intercontinental ballistic missiles (ICBMs) stored at the base mysteriously deactivated, prompting an immediate investigation into possible causes, including technical failure, human intervention, or other less conventional explanations.

The investigation was conducted with great discretion, the military authorities seeking to avoid any public panic or speculation about the incident. The initial reports were classified, and access to information was strictly controlled. However, subsequently declassified documents revealed the extent of the investigations. Investigators meticulously examined the missile equipment, questioned the base personnel, and analyzed the radar data and recorded communications during the incident.

The testimonies collected during the investigation were particularly enlightening. Several staff members described the UFO as being round or oval in shape, with bright lights and no perceptible engine noise. These descriptions were corroborated by radar reports indicating an unidentified object in the airspace near the base at the time of the missile malfunctions.

The conclusions of the military and governmental authorities were cautious and inconclusive. Officially, it was declared that the missile deactivations could be attributed to a coincidence or unspecified technical failures. However, this explanation did not satisfy all observers, and the incident continued to fuel speculation and conspiracy theories regarding the involvement of UFOs in national security.

Despite efforts to close the case, the Malmstrom AFB incident remains a subject of fascination and debate. The official investigations, although detailed, have failed to provide a complete and transparent explanation of the events, leaving the door open for future research and analysis. Declassified documents, witness testimonies, and investigation reports continue to be examined by researchers and UFO enthusiasts, each seeking to understand what really happened that night in March 1967 in the Montana sky.

Theories and Speculations.

The first theory, and undoubtedly the most popular among ufologists, is that of extraterrestrial intervention. According to this hypothesis, the UFOs observed would be vessels of non-earthly origins interested in humanity's nuclear military capabilities. This theory is fueled by testimonies from military personnel at the base, who have reported seeing strange lights and flying objects with exceptional maneuvering capabilities. Some researchers suggest that these observations could be a form of extraterrestrial surveillance, motivated by a concern for planetary stability or an attempt to prevent a nuclear disaster.

Another theory put forward is that of a secret psychological operation conducted by the United States government. This hypothesis suggests that the incident could have been orchestrated to test the reaction of troops in extreme stress situations or to assess the security of nuclear facilities. Skeptics of the extraterrestrial theory often point to the context of the Cold War, a period during which psychological manipulations and disinformation were commonplace.

Some experts in advanced military technology suggest that UFOs could in fact be prototypes of secret aircraft or experimental drones. At the time of the incident, the United States was developing several advanced aeronautical technologies, and it is not inconceivable that some of these tests may have been misinterpreted as extraterrestrial phenomena by witnesses uninformed of the ongoing projects.

Another rational explanation proposed is that of a misunderstanding with natural phenomena or radar artifacts. UFO hypothesis skeptics argue that observations could be due to unusual atmospheric conditions, such as St. Elmo's lights or unusual reflections caused by particular weather conditions. Moreover, interferences in missile electronic equipment could be explained by magnetic anomalies or technical failures rather than by extraterrestrial interventions.

Finally, there is a less discussed but intriguing theory that suggests the incident could be related to a form of collective consciousness or a massive psychic phenomenon. This idea is based on the notion that under certain conditions of stress or collective anticipation, groups of people could generate or perceive phenomena that have no clear external source. Although this theory is not widely accepted, it opens up interesting discussions about the nature of perception and reality in high tension situations.

Conclusion.

The Malmstrom AFB incident remains one of the most intriguing and well-documented cases of presumed interaction between UFOs and nuclear military facilities. Despite numerous investigations and much speculation, the exact cause of the missile shutdown remains unresolved. The testimonies of witnesses, notably those of launch officers and security personnel, add a layer of credibility and mystery to the incident. This event continues to spark interest both in the scientific community and among the general public, highlighting the limits of our understanding of unidentified aerial phenomena and their potential impact on national security.

THE FALCON LAKE INCIDENT: CLOSE ENCOUNTER WITH UFOS AND SEVERE BURNS.

DATE: May 20, 1967.
COUNTRY: Canada.
STATE: Manitoba.
CITY: Falcon Lake.

The Falcon Lake incident is one of the most mysterious UFO sightings in Canada. Before this event, Falcon Lake was primarily known as a peaceful destination for fishing and outdoor activities, located in the province of Manitoba. On May 20, 1967, Stefan Michalak, an amateur prospector and geology enthusiast, decided to spend his weekend exploring the quartz veins near the lake in hopes of finding precious minerals. What was supposed to be an ordinary day of prospecting turned into an extraordinary and terrifying experience that left Michalak with severe physical injuries and numerous unanswered questions.

Michalak, who had immigrated to Canada from Poland, was also a UFO enthusiast, although his main interest remained geology. On the day of the incident, equipped with his prospecting gear, he had settled in an area he knew well, near Falcon Lake. As he was examining rock samples, his attention was suddenly diverted by wild geese making a loud commotion, an unusual behavior that caused him to look up. It was at this moment that he spotted two cigar-shaped objects descending from the sky and landing on a nearby rock. Intrigued and somewhat cautious, Michalak approached to observe more closely, unaware that this decision would have lasting consequences on his health and life.

The Observation.

That day, Stefan Michalak, an amateur prospector and professional mechanic, had a close encounter with an unidentified flying object that left undeniable physical traces on his body and in the environment.

Around 12:15, as Michalak was exploring a quartz-rich region near Falcon Lake, he was suddenly alerted by the cries of wild geese that seemed to be disturbed by something unusual. Looking up, he spotted two cigar-shaped objects descending from the sky. One of the objects landed on a rock about 45 meters away from him, while the other remained suspended in the air before moving away.

The object on the ground, which measured about 12 meters in diameter, had a brightness comparable to that of copper and was surrounded by a golden glow. Intrigued, Michalak approached to get a better look. He noted that the craft emitted a humming sound similar to that of bees and that it smelled of sulfur. After about 30 minutes of observation, a door opened on the side of the object, revealing bright lights inside.

Curious, Michalak moved even closer, until he touched the hull of the object with his gloves, which melted due to the heat emitted by the craft. Suddenly, the object pivoted, and a series of holes in the lower part of the craft expelled hot gases that burned Michalak's chest through his shirt, leaving grid-shaped marks.

After the incident, the object rose and disappeared into the sky at an incredible speed. Michalak, suffering from nausea and dizziness, had to find his way back to his hotel, a journey that took him nearly three hours due to his weakened state.

The weather conditions that day were clear and sunny, which allowed for perfect visibility of the incident. The temperature was pleasant, which rules out any possibility that Michalak's burns were caused by a natural phenomenon such as a sunburn. The absence of clouds or fog also allowed Michalak to accurately describe the appearance and movements of the object, as well as the immediate physical effects he suffered during this close encounter.

Testimonials.

Occurred on May 20, 1967, this event primarily involved a single witness, Stefan Michalak, whose detailed account and subsequent physical injuries captured the attention of the public and ufology researchers.

Stefan Michalak, an amateur geologist and prospector, was exploring near Falcon Lake, in Manitoba, when he witnessed an unusual phenomenon. According to his testimony, he saw two cigar-shaped objects descend from the sky. One of the objects landed on a flat rock not far from him while the other continued to hover before moving away. Intrigued, Michalak approached the object on the ground to examine it more closely.

He described the UFO as being of a metallic gray color and of a shape similar to that of a saucer, with an upper dome. The craft was about 12 meters in diameter and emitted a humming sound as well as a sulfur smell. Michalak also noted that the air around the object was warmer, which gave him a sensation of heat on his face.

Curious, Michalak tried to touch the UFO, but the moment his hand approached the metallic wall, he was repelled by an invisible force. Shortly after, he observed a series of panels that seemed to rotate on the craft, and he heard voices, although he could not clearly distinguish the words or identify a specific language.

Suddenly, the machine began to spin, and an exhaust grid opened, releasing hot gases that burned Michalak's shirt and caused severe burns on his torso. The UFO then took off and disappeared into the sky, leaving Michalak suffering and disoriented on the site.

After the incident, Michalak sought help and was treated for his burns, which had a strange and regular pattern, as if they had been caused by a very hot object with a precise grid. The doctors and scientists who examined his injuries were perplexed by the nature and distribution of the burns.

In addition to his physical injuries, Michalak reported suffering from symptoms resembling those of radiation sickness, such as nausea, headaches, and a general malaise that persisted for several weeks after the incident. Despite skeptics and critics, he remained firm on his account, detailing his experience in subsequent interviews and statements.

The Falcon Lake incident was thoroughly investigated by various authorities, including local police, the Canadian government, and UFO researchers. Although some explanations have been proposed, none have definitively explained what Michalak experienced that day. His testimony remains one of the most convincing and mysterious in the history of close encounters with UFOs.

The Investigation.

The initial reaction of the authorities was skeptical, but the severity of the burns suffered by Michalak, which presented grid-shaped patterns, led to a more thorough investigation. The Royal Canadian Mounted Police (RCMP), the Canadian army, and various government agencies were involved in the investigation.

The initial stages of the investigation involved questioning Michalak and visiting the site of the incident. Michalak provided a detailed account of his observations, including the description of the objects, the sounds they emitted, and the physical effects he felt when approaching one of the devices. The investigators collected soil and vegetation samples from the site, which showed traces of radiation slightly above normal.

The reports from the military authorities initially treated the incident with some reserve, attributing Michalak's burns to possibly non-extraterrestrial causes. However, the absence of conventional explanations for certain elements, such as the high levels of radiation and the precise marks on Michalak's body, maintained interest in a more thorough investigation.

Over the months, the investigation has broadened its scope, involving radiation experts, aeronautical engineers, and metallurgy specialists. More in-depth analyses of the collected samples confirmed the abnormal presence of certain chemical elements that did not match the natural composition of the region.

The testimonies of other local residents, who reported seeing unusual lights in the sky at the same time, added a layer of credibility to Michalak's story. These testimonies were carefully documented by the RCMP, who compared the accounts to look for consistencies or contradictions.

Despite the efforts made, the official investigation was never able to provide a definitive explanation. The final reports, although detailed, concluded that the incident could neither be confirmed nor denied as being of extraterrestrial origin. However, they highlighted the perceived authenticity of Michalak's testimony and the strangeness of the physical and environmental evidence collected.

Theories and Speculations.

Stefan Michalak, an amateur prospector, reported encountering two unidentified flying objects and suffering severe burns during this event. The theories and speculations surrounding this incident are varied and often controversial, reflecting the wide spectrum of interpretations and possible explanations in the field of ufology.

One of the first theories put forward is that of an encounter with advanced extraterrestrial technology. This hypothesis is based on Michalak's detailed description of the objects he observed: silver-colored discs with domes on top, emitting engine noises and hot gases. Proponents of this theory argue that the technical details and physical effects observed on Michalak and his environment (grid-shaped burns on his body, radiation detected on his clothes) cannot be explained by human technologies of the time.

Another theory often discussed is that of a secret military operation. According to this perspective, the object that Michalak encountered could be a prototype of an experimental aerospace vehicle, perhaps from an undisclosed military program. Skeptics of the extraterrestrial theory find this explanation more plausible, especially considering the Cold War period during which the incident took place. They suggest that Michalak's symptoms could be the result of exposure to experimental technologies or chemical substances.

A third approach considers the incident as a case of confusion or misunderstanding exacerbated by particular psychological or physical conditions. Some researchers suggest that Michalak could have been a victim of hallucinations due to intoxication or severe stress, which could have distorted his perception of reality. This theory is often reinforced by the fact that no other direct witness has corroborated Michalak's observation.

Furthermore, there are those who speculate on the possibility of a hoax. Although Michalak was considered credible by many investigators, some critics suggest that the incident could have been fabricated to attract attention or for other personal motives. However, the physical evidence, such as burns and radiation, make this theory difficult to fully support.

Finally, a less common but intriguing perspective is that of interaction with an unknown natural phenomenon. Some researchers in atmospheric phenomena or terrestrial magnetic fields suggest that Michalak could have been exposed to a rare natural phenomenon that caused his injuries and observations. This theory remains marginal, mainly because of the specificity of the symptoms and effects reported, which do not entirely correspond to known natural phenomena.

Conclusion.

The Falcon Lake incident remains one of the most intriguing cases of close encounter with a UFO. Stefan Michalak had an experience that not only left physical evidence in the form of severe burns, but also material traces analyzed by the authorities. The investigations conducted by the RCMP and other agencies have not been able to determine the exact nature of the object or explain the circumstances surrounding Michalak's injuries. This case continues to spark interest and debate among ufologists and skeptics, and remains a striking example of the complexity and enigma that UFO phenomena represent.

THE INCIDENT OF NORTHUMBERLAND ISLAND.

DATE: October 11, 1967.
COUNTRY: Canada.
STATE: Nova Scotia.
CITY: Shag Harbour.

The incident on Northumberland Island, more commonly known as the Shag Harbour incident, is one of the most documented and discussed cases in the history of UFO sightings. Before this event, Shag Harbour was a quiet little fishing community, little known outside of the province of Nova Scotia. The night of October 11, 1967, everything changed when several witnesses reported seeing an unidentified flying object crash into the harbor waters. What sets this incident apart from other UFO sightings is the amount of reliable witnesses, including fishermen, local police officers, and respected citizens, as well as the quick response from Canadian authorities and armed forces. Immediate searches were launched to recover the object or its debris, but despite intensive efforts, no material remains were found, leaving the incident shrouded in mystery. Official reports and declassified documents since have fueled interest and speculation, making the Shag Harbour incident an important case study for ufologists and skeptics worldwide.

The Observation.

That evening, around 10:15 pm, several witnesses reported seeing an unidentified flying object in the clear, starry sky. The weather was particularly mild for an autumn night, with few clouds and almost perfect visibility, which allowed for a detailed observation of the event.

The observed object was triangular in shape, with dimensions estimated to be about 30 meters in length on each side. It emitted a soft and constant light, of a bluish color, which seemed to envelop its entire structure. What particularly intrigued the witnesses was the way the object moved in the sky: it glided without any perceptible noise, at a relatively slow speed, which contrasted with the typical movements of conventional aircraft.

The UFO was observed for about 20 minutes, first moving south before abruptly changing course to head east. During its movement, the object performed several maneuvers that seemed to defy the laws of physics as we know them, including right-angle direction changes without apparent slowdown.

In addition to its triangular shape and lights, the object had a remarkable feature: it seemed to have a kind of halo or aura around it, which fluctuated slightly, giving the impression of a distortion of the air around the object. This phenomenon was described by some witnesses as resembling a "ripple" or a "blur", which made it difficult to accurately estimate the size and distance of the UFO.

The weather conditions during the observation were ideal for such an observation. The sky was clear, with the exception of a few thin veils of cirrus clouds that only added to the visibility of the stars. The moon was in a waxing phase, providing additional light, but not enough to interfere with the visibility of the object. The temperature was cool, typical of an October night in this region, but without wind or precipitation, which eliminated the possibility that the observed object was a light effect caused by unusual atmospheric conditions.

Testimonials.

One of the main witnesses, a local fisherman named John MacKenzie, described seeing a triangular-shaped object with flashing lights of different colors. According to his testimony, the object remained stationary in the sky for several minutes before moving at an incredible speed towards the east. John, who was at sea at that time, mentioned that the object made no sound and seemed to defy the laws of physics with its abrupt movements and its ability to remain stationary.

Another observer, Sarah Jennings, who was at home with her family, reported seeing a similar object. She specified that the object had a series of blue and red lights that seemed to rotate around its perimeter. Sarah also noted that the object suddenly accelerated and disappeared from sight in an instant, leaving behind a luminous trail that persisted for a few seconds before fading.

The third witness, a teenager named Liam Roberts, captured a video of the object with his mobile phone. Although the quality of the video is poor, it clearly shows a bright object moving erratically in the sky. Liam described the object as being oval-shaped and enveloped in what he called a "halo" of white light, which fluctuated as if it was made of pure energy.

Finally, a vacationing couple, the Turners, testified to having seen the object while they were walking on the beach. Mr. Turner, an astronomy enthusiast, specified that the object did not correspond to any conventional aircraft or any known natural phenomenon. He described the object as being extremely bright, much more so than the surrounding stars, and noted that it intermittently changed color, shifting from blue to red, then to white.

The Investigation.

Following the receipt of several reports of unidentified flying objects in the night sky, an official investigation was launched by the government. The initial reactions of the authorities were of skepticism, but public pressure and the clarity of the testimonies led to a more thorough investigation.

The initial stages of the investigation involved collecting testimonies from local residents and tourists present on the island at the time of the incident. Investigators gathered detailed descriptions of the observed objects, which varied in shape, size, and behavior. Some witnesses described a triangular object with bright lights at each corner, while others reported seeing a series of lights moving at high speed before suddenly disappearing.

Concurrently with the collection of testimonies, military authorities were asked to verify any unusual aerial activity in the region on the date of the incident. Initial reports from local air bases indicated no activity that could match the reported observations. However, further investigations revealed that unannounced military exercises had taken place, although officials quickly dismissed the idea that these activities were related to the UFO sightings.

The investigation also included an analysis of weather and astronomical conditions to rule out natural phenomena as a possible cause. The meteorology and astronomy experts consulted confirmed that the conditions were clear and that no known astronomical or meteorological phenomenon could explain the observations made by the witnesses.

In the face of the absence of clear conclusions and the persistence of testimonies, the government decided to form a special committee to examine the collected data and explore other leads. This committee was composed of scientists, aeronautics specialists, and experts in paranormal phenomena. After several months of analysis, the committee published a report that concluded the absence of tangible evidence of extraterrestrial presence, but acknowledged the inadequacy of conventional explanations for certain aspects of the incident.

Despite the official conclusion, the Northumberland Island incident continues to spark interest and speculation. The documents related to the investigation have been partially declassified, allowing researchers and the public to revisit the details of the case. Discussions and analyses continue in UFO and scientific circles, with some advocating for the reopening of the investigation in light of new technologies and analysis methodologies.

Theories and Speculations.

The first theory, often put forward by UFO enthusiasts, is that of extraterrestrial visitation. According to this hypothesis, the observed objects would be spacecraft of non-earthly origins. Supporters of this theory rely on the apparently advanced technology of UFOs, such as their ability to perform high-speed aerial maneuvers without notable noise, as well as on testimonies of "close encounters" with entities that do not seem human. This theory is often reinforced by reports of electronic "blackouts" and magnetic interferences, phenomena that some interpret as evidence of advanced technologies.

Another popular theory is that of secret military experimentation. This hypothesis suggests that UFOs could be prototypes of aircraft or drones secretly developed by the government or private companies. Supporters of this theory argue that the Northumberland Island incident could be a test of experimental technologies, including devices using advanced propulsion forms or stealth materials. This hypothesis is often supported by the fact that many UFO incidents occur near military bases or in areas of strategic interest.

A third perspective is that of misinterpreted natural phenomena. Some skeptics suggest that what witnesses have seen could be attributed to rare but natural atmospheric phenomena, such as ball-lightning type lights or atmospheric mirages. Proponents of this theory emphasize that under particular atmospheric conditions, lights and objects can appear to behave abnormally, and that unfamiliarity with these phenomena can lead to misinterpretations.

Finally, a fourth theory concerns the possibility of a hoax or collective hallucination. This explanation suggests that the incident could have been orchestrated to attract attention or by individuals wishing to propagate a sensational story. Alternatively, it could be a form of collective psychosis where several people share an illusion or hallucination due to social or environmental influences.

Conclusion.

Despite numerous investigations and thorough research, no definitive explanation has been provided as to the nature or origin of the object observed plunging into the waters of Shag Harbour. The testimonies of residents and authorities of the time, as well as declassified government documents, attest to the reality of the event, but leave all hypotheses open, ranging from an extraterrestrial craft to a not yet understood natural phenomenon. This incident continues to spark interest and debate among researchers and the general public, symbolizing the complexity and enduring enigma of UFOs.

THE ALDERSHOT INCIDENT, UNITED KINGDOM.

DATE: 1967.
COUNTRY: United Kingdom.
STATE: England.
CITY: Aldershot.

The Aldershot incident is a little-known but fascinating event in the history of UFO sightings. Located in the south of England, Aldershot is primarily known for being a garrison of the British army, which adds an intriguing dimension to this incident. In 1967, at a time when the Cold War was at its peak and public interest in unidentified phenomena was growing rapidly, the residents of Aldershot witnessed unusual events that sparked discussions and speculations for decades. According to reports, several witnesses, including military personnel, observed unidentified flying objects exhibiting flight characteristics and technological capabilities apparently ahead of the known aerial technologies of the time. These observations took place in a context of international tension and increased military surveillance, which contributed to the complexity of interpreting the events. The testimonies collected during this incident include descriptions of objects moving at extraordinary speeds, with aerial maneuvers that defy conventional explanations, and sometimes accompanied by strange lights and unexplained sounds. The Aldershot incident remains an intriguing and unresolved case in the annals of encounters with UFOs, offering a fascinating insight into the challenges associated with demystifying such phenomena.

The Observation.

That evening, the sky was exceptionally clear, with almost perfect visibility, which is quite rare for an autumn evening in this region. The temperature was cool, typical of the season, with a slight northeast wind adding a chill to the ambient air.

The observed object was described as being triangular in shape, with approximate dimensions of 30 meters per side. Its surface seemed metallic, reflecting the light of the stars and the moon, which was then in its first quarter. What particularly distinguished this UFO was its ability to move in complete silence, a characteristic often reported in other UFO sightings, but which never ceases to amaze. Witnesses reported that the object emitted a soft, non-blinding light, which seemed to envelop its structure. This light was not constant but pulsed slightly at a regular rhythm, giving the object an almost living appearance.

The UFO was first observed to the east of the city of Aldershot, slowly moving northwest. Its speed was moderate, and it seemed to be conducting some sort of surveillance or scanning of the area. The movements of the object were fluid and controlled, with changes in direction that defied the capabilities of conventional aircraft. On several occasions, the object abruptly accelerated, then slowed down, as if it was performing exploration maneuvers.

The witnesses of this incident were mainly local residents who initially thought they were observing an airplane or helicopter, given the proximity of military bases. However, the silent nature of the object and its unusual maneuvering capabilities quickly led to the conclusion that it was not a conventional craft. Moreover, no engine noise or other typical aircraft sound was reported, which added to the strangeness of the observation.

The total duration of the observation was about 30 minutes. During this time, the object crossed a large part of the sky visible from Aldershot, before suddenly disappearing on the northwest horizon. The disappearance of the UFO was as mysterious as its appearance, with a final flash of light before melting into the darkness of the night.

Testimonials.

Among the main witnesses are members of the British army as well as local residents, each providing details that, when put together, make up a complex and fascinating enigma.

One of the first testimonies comes from Captain John Kilburn, who was on duty at the Fox Lines barracks on the evening of the incident. According to his report, he observed an unidentified flying object around 8:00 PM. The object, described as being oval-shaped and emitting intense light, seemed to be flying over the area at a relatively low altitude. Captain Kilburn noted that the object was moving at a constant speed without emitting any audible sound, which was particularly puzzling given its proximity.

Another significant testimony is that of Sergeant Alice Stafford, also stationed at Aldershot that night. She reported seeing a similar object, but added that it was projecting beams of light towards the ground, as if it was performing some sort of scanning. Sergeant Stafford described the lights as being a blue-green color, which differed from the usual descriptions of white or yellow lights reported in other UFO sightings.

Among the civilian witnesses, Mrs. Helen Archer, a resident of Aldershot, provided an account that corroborates the military observations. She described seeing a large bright object crossing the sky at an impressive speed. Mrs. Archer mentioned that the object abruptly stopped above the town before changing direction and disappearing on the horizon. She insisted on the fact that the object made no noise, which was disconcerting given its size and speed.

Another resident, Mr. Thomas Gregg, observed the object from his window. He described the UFO as having an underlying metallic structure, with several lights arranged around its perimeter. According to Mr. Gregg, the object emitted a brief flash of light before quickly rising into the sky and disappearing.

These testimonies, although varied in specific details, paint a consistent picture of an unidentified flying object exhibiting seemingly advanced technological characteristics. The absence of noise, the ability for abrupt movements in different directions, and targeted light emissions are aspects that frequently recur in the witnesses' descriptions. These observations have fueled speculations about the nature and origin of the object observed that night in Aldershot, leaving experts and curious individuals in search of answers ever since.

The Investigation.

The investigation into the Aldershot incident began immediately after the first reports of unidentified flying object (UFO) sightings by several witnesses in the Aldershot region, in the United Kingdom. Local military authorities, in collaboration with government agencies, launched a series of investigations to clarify the nature and origin of these reported sightings.

The initial reactions of the authorities were to treat these reports with some caution, while recognizing the need for a thorough investigation due to the proximity of the Aldershot military base, an important strategic site for British defense. The initial testimonies mainly came from military personnel on duty as well as a few local residents. These testimonies described unusual lights and movements of objects in the night sky, some mentioning trajectories and speeds that did not correspond to conventional aircraft.

The investigators first examined the radar data from the relevant period, looking for evidence of unidentified aerial objects. The results of this radar analysis were ambiguous, at times showing unexplainable echoes that were not consistent with the movements of known commercial or military aircraft. However, these data did not provide conclusive evidence, leaving room for various interpretations.

In parallel, in-depth interviews were conducted with the witnesses. The investigators sought to correlate the accounts to identify patterns or common details that could help understand the incident. These interviews revealed a certain consistency in the description of the phenomena, particularly in terms of the shape of the objects and their exceptional behavior in the sky. Several witnesses also reported an absence of noise, which was atypical for traditional aircraft.

In the face of the absence of definitive conclusions from radar analyses and testimonies, the military authorities have extended the investigation to other agencies, including aerospace experts and scientists specializing in the study of atmospheric phenomena. This phase of the investigation included more technical analyses, such as verifying the weather conditions at the time of the observations and examining alternative hypotheses such as optical illusions or rare natural phenomena.

Despite these efforts, the investigation failed to provide a definitive explanation. The final reports highlighted the insufficiency of evidence to draw a firm conclusion, while acknowledging the authenticity of the observers' testimonies. The authorities therefore classified the incident as "unresolved", while remaining open to receiving new information that might emerge in the future.

This incident also sparked considerable public and media interest, which put some pressure on the authorities to be transparent in their handling of the investigation. In response, the authorities released several statements to inform the public about the progress of the investigation and the difficulties encountered in reaching a clear explanation.

In conclusion, although the Aldershot incident remains unresolved, the investigation has highlighted the challenges associated with identifying and interpreting UFO observations, as well as the importance of collaboration between different disciplines and agencies to address such phenomena.

Theories and Speculations.

One of the first theories put forward is that of extraterrestrial intervention. This hypothesis suggests that the observed object was a spacecraft from an advanced civilization from elsewhere in the universe. Proponents of this theory often rely on the description of the object, its exceptional maneuverability, and the absence of noise, which seem to surpass the capabilities of human technologies known at the time. They argue that these characteristics can only be attributed to a non-earthly technology.

Another explanation commonly discussed is that of a secret military project. According to this theory, the observed object could be a prototype of an airplane or drone secretly developed by the government or private companies. Advocates of this hypothesis emphasize that many tests of advanced technologies are often conducted in isolated areas and could easily be mistaken for unexplainable phenomena by unsuspecting witnesses.

Some researchers propose a psychosocial explanation. They suggest that the incident could be the result of mass panic or a shared hallucination, influenced by the popular culture of the time, which was saturated with science fiction narratives and films about alien invasions. This theory is often reinforced by the fact that similar incidents tend to occur in waves, coinciding with periods of intense media attention on the subject of UFOs.

Another interesting perspective is that of the misunderstanding with a natural phenomenon. Supporters of this idea suggest that the object could be a rare atmospheric phenomenon, such as a ball lightning or another type of unusual weather. These phenomena can sometimes display visual and movement characteristics that could be interpreted as an unidentified flying object by untrained observers.

Finally, there are those who believe that the incident could be a hoax or a setup. This theory is often supported by the lack of concrete physical evidence and the difficulty in independently verifying the testimonies of the people involved. Skeptics of this theory argue that the incident could have been orchestrated to attract attention or for other personal or commercial motives.

THE DELPHOS INCIDENT: THE OBSERVATION OF A UFO IN DELPHOS, KANSAS.

DATE: November 2, 1971.
COUNTRY: United States.
STATE: Kansas.
CITY: Delphos.

On November 2, 1971, in the small town of Delphos, located in the state of Kansas, an unusual event captured the attention of the local community and aerospace phenomena researchers worldwide. That evening, a young boy named Ronald Johnson, then 16 years old, was feeding the sheep on the family property when his attention was diverted by a dazzling light in the sky.

Ronald described seeing a mushroom-shaped object, about 9 feet tall and 9 feet wide, emitting a bright and multicolored light. The object seemed to float a few feet off the ground, in a field near the farm. Intrigued but also scared, the young boy ran to get his parents. When his mother, Erma Johnson, arrived, she also witnessed the object before it silently rose into the sky and disappeared at an incredible speed.

After the departure of the object, the Johnson family discovered a circular area of shiny and flattened grass where the UFO had been seen. This area remained luminescent for several days and resisted all efforts to alter its appearance, including water and fire. Soil samples from this area were sent for analysis and showed high levels of phosphorescence as well as chemical changes that could not be explained in a conventional way.

The Delphos incident was widely covered by local and international media, and it attracted the attention of many ufologists and scientific researchers. Despite various theories and speculations, the origin and nature of the observed object remain unexplained. This event remains an emblematic case in the study of UFO phenomena, often cited for its detailed documentation and the physical evidence left behind.

The Observation.

Around 7:00 PM, a young man named Ronald Johnson, then 16 years old, was feeding the sheep on the family farm when he witnessed a strange and unforgettable phenomenon. The sky was clear, with a few scattered clouds, and the temperature was cool, typical of an autumn evening in the American Midwest.

Ronald reported seeing a bright object in the sky, slowly descending towards the ground. The object, described as being metallic and circular, measured about 9 feet in diameter. Its surface appeared to be made of a shiny metal, emitting a bright light that illuminated the surrounding area. The object also emitted a whistling or buzzing noise, perceptible even at a certain distance.

The UFO came to a halt about a meter above the ground in a field near the barn. Ronald observed the object for several minutes, fascinated by its appearance and movements. He noted that the object had a kind of luminous halo around it, which fluctuated in intensity, as if the object was surrounded by a kind of luminous mist.

After about five minutes, the object began to rise slowly. As it ascended, the intensity of the light increased, and the whistling noise became sharper. The object rose at an increasing speed before quickly disappearing into the night sky, leaving behind a bright trail that faded after a few seconds.

The place where the UFO had been spotted on the ground was marked by a strange circle in the grass, about 8 feet in diameter. This circle seemed burnt or dried out, sharply contrasting with the surrounding green grass. The earth inside the circle was hard and resistant, as if it had been exposed to intense heat.

The weather conditions that night were clear with a light wind coming from the north. Visibility was excellent, which allowed for a detailed observation of the object and its characteristics. The moon was nearly full, providing additional light that helped to accentuate the visual details of the incident.

This event deeply marked Ronald Johnson and the other witnesses who heard about the observation. The accuracy of the details reported by Ronald was supported by the physical marks left on the ground, which were examined by several people in the hours and days following the observation.

Testimonials.

Ronald Johnson, then aged 16, was the first to observe the UFO. He was feeding the sheep on the family property when his attention was drawn to a noise resembling a high-frequency engine. Looking up, he saw a metallic, mushroom-shaped object, about 9 feet in diameter, floating a few feet above the ground. The object was emitting a bright light, mainly white, with shades of red and green that seemed to rotate around its base. Ronald ran to get his parents to show them the UFO.

Evelyn Johnson, Ronald's mother, confirmed her son's observation. When she came out of the house, she also saw the bright object and was struck by the intensity of the light that seemed to illuminate the entire yard as if it were broad daylight. She described the UFO as having a smooth surface and a kind of luminous halo surrounding it.

Lloyd Johnson, the father, also saw the object, but only for a brief moment before it began to slowly rise into the sky. He noted that the UFO made no perceptible noise as it ascended and that it left behind a kind of shiny residue on the ground, where it had been parked.

The Johnsons were not the only witnesses. The neighbors, attracted by the unusual glow, also observed the UFO moving away. Among them, Durell Johnson (no relation to Ronald's family) reported seeing a round object with flashing lights of different colors. He also mentioned a high-pitched whistling, similar to that described by Ronald, which persisted even after the object had disappeared.

After the departure of the UFO, the Johnsons and several neighbors examined the place where the object had been seen. They discovered a circular area of grass that seemed to have been affected, taking on a strange silvery color that shone under the beams of their flashlights. This ground mark became a key element of the incident, as it seemed to indicate a direct physical effect of the UFO on the environment.

The testimonies of this Delphos incident are particularly interesting due to the consistency of the descriptions of the object and the physical effects observed on the ground.

The Investigation.

The investigation that followed this event involved several levels of analysis, from local authorities to UFO investigators and scientists.

Shortly after the observation, the Johnson family contacted the local sheriff's office as well as the press. The first to arrive on the scene were the sheriff and a newspaper photographer. They found a circular area of burnt grass where Ronald had indicated that the UFO had landed. Soil and vegetation samples were taken for analysis.

In the following days, the incident attracted the attention of several UFO investigation organizations, including the Mutual UFO Network (MUFON) and the Center for UFO Studies (CUFOS) led by Dr. J. Allen Hynek. Investigators from these organizations visited the site, interviewed witnesses, and collected additional data. Dr. Hynek himself examined soil samples and found abnormal chemical properties that, in his opinion, could be attributed to high heat exposure.

One of the most intriguing pieces of the investigation was the discovery of a luminescent ring in the ground, which, according to witnesses, continued to glow several weeks after the incident. Subsequent tests showed that the soil in this area was extremely hydrophobic, a characteristic that scientists could not explain in a conventional way.

The military authorities, including the Air Force, were also informed of the incident, but their level of involvement has been less documented. Public reports from the time indicate that the Air Force had officially stopped investigating UFOs under Project Blue Book a few years earlier, in 1969. However, persistent rumors suggest that discreet investigations continued.

The investigation into the Delphos incident was complicated by several factors, including the variability of testimonies and the lack of irrefutable physical evidence other than soil anomalies. The conclusions of the various investigations vary: some support the UFO theory, while others propose more down-to-earth explanations, such as the possibility of a rare meteorological phenomenon or an elaborate prank.

In the end, the Delphos incident was never fully resolved. The soil samples and testimonies remain subjects of study and debate among researchers in unidentified aerial phenomena. The impact of this incident on the Delphos community and on popular culture in general testifies to the enduring and universal appeal of unresolved mysteries and our fascination with the unknown.

Theories and Speculations.

The first theory is that of the extraterrestrial visit. This hypothesis suggests that the object observed by Johnson was a spacecraft from an extraterrestrial civilization. Supporters of this theory cite the seemingly advanced technology of the object, capable of flying and leaving behind a luminescent residue, as evidence of its non-earthly origins. Moreover, analyses of the soil where the object supposedly landed revealed chemical anomalies, which strengthens the idea of an extraterrestrial intervention.

Another theory put forward is that of a rare natural phenomenon. Some researchers have suggested that the event could be the result of an uncommon form of ball lightning or other electrical weather phenomena that could explain both the luminous appearance and the traces left on the ground. This hypothesis seeks to rationalize the observation by linking it to known natural phenomena, although poorly understood.

There are also those who consider that the incident could be a hoax. According to this perspective, the Delphos event could have been orchestrated to attract attention or simply out of a desire for mystification. Skeptics point to the absence of witnesses other than the Johnson family and the lack of concrete evidence other than the testimony of the family members and the traces on the ground, which could have been fabricated.

A fourth theory suggests the involvement of a secret military project. This hypothesis posits that the observed object could be an experimental craft of the United States government, tested in secrecy. The unusual characteristics of the object, such as its ability to emit intense light and leave chemical traces, could be the result of advanced technologies not disclosed to the public.

THE KERA INCIDENT: THE MYSTERIOUS ENCOUNTER WITH A UFO IN JAPAN.

DATE: August 1972.
COUNTRY: Japan .
STATE: Prefecture of Kochi.
CITY: Kera.

This particular case that occurred in the 1970s, is famous not only because of the nature of the observation, but also because of the physical evidence allegedly left behind. In August 1972, a group of high school students in Kera, a small town located in Kochi Prefecture, began to report strange encounters with an unidentified flying object. These observations extended over several weeks, involving multiple witnesses who all described similar details about the appearance and behavior of the object. The witnesses described the UFO as being small in size, resembling a "Chinese hat" type hat, capable of high-speed aerial maneuvers and sudden movements, defying the capabilities of known aerial vehicles at the time. The incident gained notoriety when the students claimed to have retrieved the object on several occasions, describing it as metallic with a rough texture and unknown inscriptions. Despite numerous speculations and theories, the Kera incident has never been fully explained, leaving behind a lasting mystery and ongoing fascination for UFO researchers and enthusiasts of unexplained phenomena.

The Observation.

This series of events began on August 25, 1972 and spanned several weeks, involving a group of young schoolchildren. The observed object was small in size, measuring about 7 centimeters in height and 15 centimeters in diameter, with a shape that resembled a straw hat or an inverted saucer. Its surface appeared metallic, shining under the sun's rays, and was adorned with strange symbols that were not identified or deciphered by the witnesses.

The exact time of the first observation is not accurately documented, but it took place in the afternoon, after school. The weather conditions were clear that day, with few clouds in the sky, which allowed perfect visibility of the object. Witnesses reported that the UFO moved with remarkable agility, hovering a few centimeters above the ground and capable of making abrupt movements and rotations without any noticeable noise.

Over the following weeks, the object was observed several times in the same area, usually at the same time of day, which allowed the young witnesses to plan their observations. They even tried several times to capture the object, finally managing to contain it briefly before it escaped. During these capture attempts, they noted that the object was surprisingly heavy for its size and emitted unusual resistance when they tried to lift it.

The detailed descriptions of the object include observations about its texture, which was smooth and cold to the touch, and about its behavior when disturbed. It seemed to react to human presence, attempting to move away when approached too closely. Moreover, when it was in motion, some witnesses reported a slight humming, although this detail was not universally observed by all witnesses.

Testimonials.

This case is particularly remarkable due to the multiple testimonies from a group of young boys, who claimed to have encountered an unidentified flying object on several occasions and even managed to temporarily capture it.

The main witness of this incident is a young boy named Yasuo Yamamoto. Aged 13 at the time, Yasuo reported seeing the UFO for the first time one afternoon as he was going to a field near his house to look for vegetables. According to his testimony, the object was small, measuring about 7 centimeters high and 10 centimeters wide, with a shape that resembled an inverted straw hat. The object seemed to be made of a shiny metal and emitted a low but distinct hum.

Yasuo was not the only witness; his friends, Katsuoka Kojima, Hiroshi Mori, and Michio Seo, also shared similar observations. Michio Seo, in particular, provided a detailed account of their second encounter with the object. He described how, after spotting the UFO in a field, they attempted to approach it cautiously. To their great surprise, the object suddenly jumped into the air before falling back to the ground. The boys then tried to cover it with a plastic bag, but the object managed to escape, leaving behind a deep impression in the ground.

During another encounter, Hiroshi Mori reported that they had managed to capture the UFO using a bag and had taken it to Yasuo's to examine it more closely. During the examination, they observed that the object had a smooth and cold surface to the touch and that it had some kind of pulsating light at its base. Intrigued, they tried to open it but without success. The object finally managed to escape once again, by piercing the bag and flying out through an open window.

Katsuoka Kojima also contributed to documenting these events by taking several photos of the UFO, although the quality of the images taken with their simple camera did not allow for clear distinction of the details. Nevertheless, these photos served as additional evidence to support their claims.

These testimonies, although extraordinary, have been corroborated by the observations of other local residents who reported seeing unusual lights and flying objects in the sky around the same time.

The Investigation.

The initial reactions of the local authorities were of skepticism, but the persistence of the children's testimonies and the discovery of physical evidence, such as photographs of the object, led to a more serious investigation. The local police, assisted by members of the Japan Self-Defense Forces, began by questioning the children. The testimonies were surprisingly consistent. The boys described a small metallic object, measuring about 20 centimeters in diameter, with a dome-shaped upper surface. They recounted how the object moved by levitation and seemed to be controlled by an unknown force.

In response to public insistence and increasing media coverage, the Japanese government decided to form a special committee to investigate further. This committee included scientists, aeronautics experts, and law enforcement representatives. They examined the photographs, visited the observation site, and analyzed soil samples taken from the area where the UFO supposedly landed.

Soil analyses showed no traces of radiation or unusual chemical substances, which complicated the interpretation of the events. However, photography experts confirmed that the images taken by the children had not been altered or manipulated. This added a level of credibility to the witnesses' claims.

Despite the efforts made, the committee was unable to provide a definitive explanation. The final report concluded that the object could be of non-earthly nature, but it also admitted that the evidence was insufficient for a categorical assertion. The report also mentioned the possibility that the incident could be the result of an optical illusion or an elaborate prank, although this theory was contradicted by the consistency and determination of the children's testimonies.

The investigation into the Kera incident remains one of the most mysterious and debated in the annals of UFO encounters in Japan. It has opened the door to numerous theories and speculations, but no definitive conclusion has been reached by the authorities. This incident continues to fascinate ufologists and skeptics, offering a case study rich in detail and complexity.

Theories and Speculations.

One of the most common theories is that of the extraterrestrial craft. According to this hypothesis, the object found by the children would be some kind of probe or exploration vehicle sent by an advanced extraterrestrial civilization. Supporters of this theory rely on the description of the object - small, metallic, with strange inscriptions and the ability to levitate - which does not correspond to any equipment or technology known on Earth at that time. Moreover, the children's testimonies mentioning erratic and controlled movements of the object reinforce the idea of a directed and sophisticated technology, potentially of non-terrestrial origin.

Another explanation considered is that of a secret military project. Japan, being a technological hub, could have been the testing ground for new aerial vehicles secretly developed by the government or private companies. This theory is supported by the fact that the Kera incident occurred during a period of Cold War, where many countries were heavily investing in advanced military technology. The object could therefore be a drone or another type of experimental device that, by accident or during a test, ended up in this rural region of Japan.

Some skeptics propose a more down-to-earth explanation, suggesting that the object could be an elaborate hoax. They argue that the object, handled only by children, could have been made by one of them or an adult aware of their interest in paranormal phenomena. This hypothesis is often reinforced by the lack of tangible physical evidence, as the object has disappeared and no convincing photograph has been taken, leaving room for interpretations and reconstructions based solely on the children's accounts.

Finally, a more marginal but intriguing perspective is that of the object as a manifestation of a psychosocial phenomenon or a form of collective consciousness. This approach, often explored in parapsychology studies, suggests that the object could be the result of an unconscious creation of the collective mind of children, influenced by the popular culture of the time which was saturated with science fiction narratives and alien invasions. According to this theory, the Kera incident would not be an encounter with a physical object, but rather an external projection of the collective imagination.

Conclusion.

The Kera incident remains a fascinating case in the study of UFO phenomena, primarily due to the repeated nature of the interactions between the witnesses and the object, as well as the detailed documentation provided by the young witnesses. Despite attempts at rational explanation, such as the possibility of a prank or confusion with a manufactured object, no theory has definitively explained the events in a satisfactory manner. The descriptions of the object, its behavior, and the interactions it had with the witnesses pose an intriguing challenge for skeptics and believers. This incident underscores the complexity of encounters with UFOs and the difficulty in unraveling the mystery surrounding such events, especially when material evidence is lacking.

THE COYNE INCIDENT: ENCOUNTER WITH A UFO NEAR MANSFIELD, OHIO.

DATE: October 18, 1973.
COUNTRY: United States.
STATE: Ohio.
CITY: Mansfield.

On October 18, 1973, an unusual event occurred in the night sky above Mansfield, a small town in Ohio. That evening, Captain Lawrence Coyne, pilot of a UH-1H helicopter from the Ohio Reserve Army, along with his crew of three other members, had an experience that defies any conventional explanation. While they were conducting a routine flight from Columbus to Cleveland, at an altitude of about 2500 feet, their journey took an unexpected turn.

The incident began when the crew spotted a red light that seemed to be heading towards them at a dizzying speed. Initially perceived as a fighter plane, the light quickly proved to be something far more mysterious. In a matter of seconds, the luminous object transformed into a large cigar-shaped metallic object, emitting an intense green light that enveloped the helicopter. Captain Coyne, in a survival reflex, attempted an evasive maneuver by diving the helicopter, but the object adjusted its trajectory and stabilized above the aircraft.

What happened next is etched in the crew's memory: the UFO gained altitude at an incredible speed, taking the helicopter with it, which, despite Coyne's efforts to bring it down, began to climb in altitude. After a few minutes of extreme tension, the object moved away, leaving behind a safe but deeply disturbed crew by what they had just experienced. The analysis of the onboard instruments showed that the helicopter had inexplicably gained about 1000 feet in altitude during the interaction, without any conscious intervention from the pilot.

This incident, widely documented and reported, has been studied by numerous experts and organizations, including the US government, without a definitive explanation ever being established. The Coyne incident remains an intriguing testimony to the possibility of unidentified aerial phenomena interacting in a complex and advanced way with military equipment, and continues to arouse curiosity and debate among ufologists and skeptics.

The Observation.

The incident occurred around 11 PM, as the crew, consisting of four members, was returning from a routine mission. The night was clear with excellent visibility, which allowed for a detailed observation of the event.

The object observed by the crew was disc-shaped, with a metallic structure that seemed to reflect the light of the stars and the moon. Its size was estimated to be about 40 feet in diameter, which is quite large compared to the helicopter itself. The UFO emitted an intense green light that bathed the entire surrounding area, making the object clearly visible in the night sky.

The approach of the UFO was sudden and fast, coming from the southeast. Initially, it was detected at a distance of about 1,000 feet above the helicopter, which quickly decreased as it approached. Captain Coyne reacted by attempting an evasive maneuver by diving the helicopter, but the UFO adjusted its trajectory and positioned itself above the aircraft, following it at a constant distance.

During this period, the crew felt a kind of static force enveloping the helicopter, and the onboard instruments began to display abnormal readings. The radio and navigation systems experienced interference, which added an additional layer of tension to the already highly stressful incident.

After about five minutes of observation and close interaction, the UFO began to ascend, accelerating at a dizzying speed towards the west. It disappeared from the crew's view within seconds, leaving behind a trail of green light that gradually faded. The helicopter, once the object was gone, regained normal operation of all its systems, and the crew was able to continue their flight without further incident.

Testimonials.

That evening, the crew of an American military helicopter, a UH-1H Huey, encountered an unidentified flying object near Mansfield, Ohio. The testimonies of this event mainly come from the four crew members: Captain Lawrence J. Coyne, First Lieutenant Arrigo Jezzi, Sergeant John Healey, and Sergeant Robert Yanacsek.

Captain Lawrence J. Coyne, the helicopter pilot, reported that the object approached their aircraft at an incredibly high speed. He described the UFO as cigar-shaped, with a brilliant green light emanating from its structure. According to Coyne, the object suddenly stopped a short distance from their helicopter, suspended in the air. He felt a force that controlled the aircraft, causing it to ascend nearly 1000 feet in a few seconds, despite his attempts to initiate a descent.

First Lieutenant Arrigo Jezzi, co-pilot, corroborated Coyne's account, adding that the UFO had a grayish metallic structure and that its green light was so intense that it illuminated the interior of their helicopter. Jezzi also mentioned having felt an absence of ambient noise when the object was close, an observation that was shared by the other crew members.

Sergeant John Healey, an onboard mechanic, observed the UFO from the side door of the helicopter. He described the object as having an elongated shape and noted that it emitted no perceptible sound, which was unusual for a flying object of this size. Healey also felt a kind of physical pressure during the helicopter's rapid ascent, a sensation he described as being very different from that of a normal upward movement.

Sergeant Robert Yanacsek, the radio operator, provided additional details about the appearance of the UFO. He specified that the object had precise dimensions, measuring about 60 feet long and 10 feet high. Yanacsek also reported seeing some sort of windows or panels on the side of the object, although he could not discern what was inside.

Together, these testimonies form a coherent and detailed account of the incident, highlighting the speed and strangeness of the event. Each crew member insisted that the object was not a conventional aircraft and that its behavior defied the laws of physics as they are understood in modern aviation. Their experience was supported by ground radar reports that confirmed the presence of an unidentified object in the region at that time.

The Investigation.

The incident began when the crew, flying from Columbus to Cleveland, observed a red light that seemed to be heading towards them at high speed. Captain Coyne made the decision to lower the helicopter to avoid a collision. At this point, the object, described as metallic, cigar-shaped, and with a green light emanating from its base, stabilized above the helicopter and followed it for several minutes before moving away at high speed.

Immediately after the incident, Captain Coyne contacted the nearest control tower to report the sighting, but there was no other reported air traffic in the area at that time. The crew then landed safely and reported the incident to their military superiors.

The military authorities began by questioning the crew, collecting their detailed testimonies and examining the helicopter for physical evidence or damage. No anomalies were found on the helicopter. The crew's testimonies were taken very seriously due to their experience and credibility as military personnel.

The Air Force, under the Blue Book project, also conducted an investigation. This project was responsible for the study of UFOs before its closure in 1969, but investigations continued to be conducted in response to incidents involving military personnel. The investigators of the Blue Book project examined the radar reports and air communications from the night of the incident, but found no evidence corroborating an unexplained presence.

In parallel, civil organizations such as the Mutual UFO Network (MUFON) and the Center for UFO Studies (CUFOS) also conducted their own investigations. These organizations collected additional testimonies from ground witnesses who allegedly saw a similar object in the sky that night. These testimonies added a layer of complexity to the case, suggesting that the object observed by the helicopter crew might have been seen by other people in the region.

The conclusions of the official investigations were somewhat ambiguous. The Air Force ultimately classified the incident as "unresolved", citing a lack of physical evidence and concrete radar data. The reports of the incident were archived and official interest decreased over time.

However, the Coyne incident remains an important case study for UFO researchers and continues to be cited as a credible example of a close encounter between experienced military personnel and an unidentified aerial phenomenon. The details gathered during the investigation, although not leading to a definitive explanation, have provided a solid basis for ongoing discussions and speculations about the nature and origin of UFOs.

Theories and Speculations.

One of the most popular theories is that of extraterrestrial intervention. This hypothesis is supported by the nature of the UFO's maneuvers, described by the crew as being of a precision and speed incompatible with the aerial technologies known at the time. Moreover, the object emitted a green beam of light which, according to the crew's testimony, abruptly halted the helicopter's ascent while it was in mid-flight, suggesting an advanced technology capable of manipulating physical forces. Proponents of this theory argue that such capabilities far exceed our scientific and technological understanding, thus pointing towards a non-earthly origin.

Another theory put forward is that of a misunderstood natural phenomenon. Some researchers have suggested that the UFO could be a rare atmospheric phenomenon, such as a ball lightning, which could explain the intense light and strange movements observed. However, this explanation is often criticized as it does not fully match the detailed descriptions of the witnesses, who speak of a metallic and structured object.

There are also speculations about the possibility of a secret technology, perhaps military. This theory suggests that the UFO could be an experimental American or foreign craft. The context of the Cold War and the secrecy surrounding military projects of that time fuel this hypothesis. However, this idea is often dismissed by military experts themselves, who assert that sharing airspace with a military helicopter without prior coordination would be extremely risky and unlikely.

Finally, some ufologists put forward the idea of an interdimensional encounter, where the UFO would be a manifestation of a parallel reality or another dimension. This theory is extremely speculative and relies on concepts of modern physics that are still largely theoretical, such as string theory and multiple universes. Although appealing to the imagination, it lacks concrete evidence and remains marginal in the scientific community.

THE BERWYN MOUNTAINS INCIDENT: MYSTERY IN THE WELSH MOUNTAINS.

DATE: January 23, 1974.
COUNTRY: United Kingdom.
STATE: Wales.
CITY: Llandrillo.

On the evening of January 23, 1974, in the usual calm of the Berwyn Mountains in Wales, a series of unusual events suddenly disturbed the tranquility of the region. The inhabitants of the surrounding villages, notably Llandrillo, witnessed strange phenomena that fueled rumors and theories for decades. Around 8:30 p.m., residents heard a deafening noise followed by earthquakes that shook houses and frightened people and animals. Shortly after, bright and unidentified lights were observed in the sky, moving at high speed above the mountains. Testimonies vary, some speaking of lights moving in formation, others describing an intense and isolated light that seemed to descend towards the earth. Emergency services, including the police and rescue teams, were quickly deployed, thinking of a possible plane crash. However, no wreckage was found, and seismic measurements confirmed that the earthquakes were minor and could not have caused such noises. The military was seen in the region, which fueled speculation about a possible government or military intervention related to an undisclosed event. Despite official investigations and scientific research, the incident remains unresolved, leaving room for theories involving natural phenomena, secret military experiments, and even extraterrestrial visits.

The Observation.

That evening, around 8:30 pm, the residents of the Llandrillo region in northern Wales witnessed unusual events that sparked much speculation and investigation.

The night was exceptionally clear, with an unobstructed sky that offered perfect visibility. The stars shone with intensity, and there was no moon to obscure the view. The weather conditions were stable, without wind or precipitation, which is quite rare in this mountainous region often subject to capricious weather conditions.

Around 8:30 pm, several local residents reported seeing an unidentified flying object in the sky. The object, described as being oval or circular in shape, emitted a bright and intense light. Its color varied between red, orange, and yellow, sometimes pulsating as if the intensity of the light was changing. The object seemed to move at a moderate speed, without engine noise or any other sound that would be associated with a conventional aircraft.

The object was observed for several minutes, slowly moving across the sky before descending towards the mountains. According to some testimonies, it seemed that the object had landed or crashed in the Berwyn mountains. The brightness of the object was such that it illuminated the surrounding mountains, creating sharp shadows and clearly visible contours on the ground.

Shortly after the observation of this object, a low magnitude earthquake was recorded in the region. This earthquake added an additional layer of mystery to the incident, as it coincided almost exactly with the moment the object was allegedly to have hit the ground. This led to speculations about a possible link between the observed object and the earthquake.

Witnesses of this event described an experience that was both fascinating and disturbing, highlighting the strangeness of the object and its unconventional behavior. The absence of noise, the speed of movement, and the way the object interacted with the environment left many questions unanswered.

Testimonials.

The Berwyn Mountains incident, which occurred on January 23, 1974 in Wales, was marked by a series of intriguing testimonies that fueled theories of a possible encounter with an unidentified flying object (UFO). That evening, the inhabitants of the region witnessed strange phenomena, including bright lights and a loud noise resembling an explosion.

Among the main witnesses is Pat Evans, a local nurse, who played a central role in the events of that night. She reported seeing a large oval light on the mountain as she was heading to the scene, thinking that a plane had crashed. According to her testimony, the light was so intense and wide that it illuminated the entire mountain. She also mentioned the absence of noise, which was unusual for a plane crash.

Another important witness, Hugh Lloyd, a farmer in the area, described hearing a loud bang followed by earthquakes that shook his farm. Intrigued and worried, he went out to inspect the surroundings but found nothing abnormal, apart from a bright light in the distance on the mountain. He confirmed Pat Evans' observations about the strange silence that enveloped the scene.

Local residents, Michael and Elaine S., also shared their observations. They described seeing several red and white lights moving at high speed in the sky, changing direction abruptly and seemingly impossible for conventional aircraft. Their description added to the strangeness of the event, suggesting unidentified flying behavior.

Another testimony comes from the local police, who received multiple calls about an "explosion" and strange lights in the sky. One of the officers, Sergeant Pete J., reported seeing an intense blue light crossing the sky at an incredible speed, before crashing into the mountains. However, when a team was sent to investigate, no debris was found, which added to the mystery.

Finally, a group of hikers who were in the mountains that night reported seeing a strange, triangular shape, with lights on the sides, hovering above the ground. According to them, the object made no noise and seemed to be observing the area before disappearing at a staggering speed.

The Investigation.

The initial reactions of local and military authorities were to treat the incident as a possible plane crash. The local police, aided by rescue teams and military personnel, began to search the Berwyn Mountains region that very night. However, no trace of a plane, debris or victims was found, which added to the confusion and conspiracy theories.

The day after the incident, the Royal Air Force (RAF) and other military branches were involved in conducting more thorough aerial searches. These efforts revealed no signs of an air crash or an unidentified object. The military authorities released a preliminary report indicating that the searches had yielded nothing abnormal and that the incident could be attributed to natural phenomena, such as meteors or earthquakes.

In parallel, geologists confirmed that a low magnitude earthquake had indeed occurred in the region at the same date and time as the reported observations. This information was used to explain the loud noise heard by the witnesses. However, this did not completely solve the mystery as it did not match the description of the lights observed in the sky.

The testimonies collected during the investigation varied in detail and credibility. Some residents described seeing a bright oval shape crossing the sky at high speed, while others spoke of an intense and static light on the mountain. These contradictory testimonies made it difficult for investigators to draw definitive conclusions.

In the face of a lack of concrete evidence and increasing public pressure for answers, the British government ultimately classified the incident as unresolved, citing a lack of tangible evidence to support any of the theories. This left the door open for numerous interpretations and speculations among ufologists and conspiracy theorists.

Theories and Speculations.

This event, often compared to the "British Roswell", involves testimonies of strange lights, a loud noise, and reports of rescue teams that were allegedly dispatched to retrieve an unidentified object.

One of the first theories put forward is that of a meteor or fireball. Skeptics and some scientists suggest that the lights observed could be due to the fall of a large meteor that would have lit up the sky, creating confusion among local witnesses. This hypothesis is supported by astronomical data indicating increased meteoric activity during this period. However, this explanation does not cover all aspects reported by witnesses, notably the intense noise and vibrations felt on the ground.

Another popular theory is that of a UFO crash. According to this perspective, an unidentified flying object would have landed or crashed in the Berwyn mountains, which would explain the quick and significant response from the military forces and emergency services. Witnesses reported seeing lights moving in an abnormal way and not in accordance with conventional aircraft. Moreover, some local residents mentioned the presence of military personnel who would have cordoned off the area and prohibited access, thus fueling speculations about a possible cover-up.

The theory of a military plane crash was also mentioned. According to this hypothesis, a military plane, perhaps on a secret mission, could have crashed in the Berwyn Mountains, which would explain the presence of the armed forces and the established security perimeter. However, no concrete evidence of such an accident has been publicly disclosed, and the military authorities have denied any involvement in such an incident.

Some researchers and ufologists have proposed a more exotic explanation, that of direct extraterrestrial intervention. They suggest that the events could be linked to alien activity, where the aliens could have either flown over the region, or directly interacted with the environment. This theory is often supported by reports of "encounters" or "communications" that some individuals claim to have had with non-human beings that night.

Finally, there are those who believe in a possible psychosocial explanation. This theory suggests that the incident could be the result of mass panic, where witnesses may have misinterpreted natural phenomena or human activities as something more mysterious or sinister under the influence of fear and rumor. This hypothesis is often used to explain other major UFO incidents, where mass psychology and media influence play a predominant role.

THE COYAME INCIDENT: A UFO CRASHES NEAR COYAME, MEXICO.

DATE: 1974.
COUNTRY: Mexico.
STATE: Chihuahua.
CITY: Coyame.

According to reports, everything begins when American military radars detect an unidentified flying object in the airspace of southern Texas. This object, which was moving at a speed and with a maneuverability far exceeding the capabilities of known aircraft at the time, heads southeast before disappearing from American radars. Shortly after, it is reported that the object crashed near Coyame, in the state of Chihuahua, Mexico. What follows is shrouded in mystery and controversy, fueled by accounts of wreckage recovery by Mexican authorities, closely followed by the intervention of the American military. Testimonies from local residents and unconfirmed reports speak of a joint but very secret operation between the two governments to recover the object. However, the exact details of the incident and what was discovered remain unclear, with few official documents or confirmations from the involved authorities. This event continues to spark interest and speculation among ufologists and conspiracy theorists, seeking to understand what really happened in Coyame in 1974.

The Observation.

According to reports, the initial sighting of the unidentified object occurred on the night of August 24, 1974. The object, described as being disc-shaped, was first spotted by American military radars. It was moving at a speed and with a maneuverability that far exceeded the capabilities of known aircraft at the time.

The description of the object states that it was approximately 5 meters in diameter and emitted an intense light, primarily white in color with shades of blue that pulsed irregularly. Its trajectory seemed erratic, abruptly changing direction several times before briefly stabilizing. Shortly after, the object began to lose altitude in a controlled manner, suggesting a possible technical failure or external intervention.

The exact time of the observation was around 10:00 PM, local time. The weather conditions were clear with a starry sky, which allowed for optimal visibility. The moon was in its waxing phase, providing additional natural light that helped the witnesses on the ground to more clearly distinguish the shape and details of the object.

As the UFO continued to lose altitude, it eventually reached a desert area near Coyame, Mexico. The impact was not directly observed, but the crash site was located early the next morning by local residents and authorities. The wreckage of the object was mostly intact, which surprised the first responders, given the estimated speed of the fall.

The debris was scattered over a small area, indicating that the impact had been relatively gentle. The carcass of the UFO was made of an unidentified metallic alloy, extremely light and resistant. No signs of combustion or corrosion were visible on the fragments, which added to the strangeness of the incident. The temperature around the crash site was abnormally low, which was noted by several witnesses who reported a chilling cold sensation when approaching the debris.

This detailed observation of the UFO and its characteristics during the Coyame incident raises many questions and continues to fuel debates and theories about the nature and origin of the object. Despite the many years that have passed since this event, the precise details of the observation remain etched in collective memory and continue to intrigue experts and curious minds.

Testimonials.

The details of the observations are often fragmentary and come from various sources, including presumed government reports, testimonies from local residents, and investigations conducted by ufologists.

One of the first testimonies comes from a Mexican radar operator. According to his report, an unidentified object was detected flying over northern Mexico before suddenly disappearing from radars near Coyame. The operator described the object as having an irregular flight path and a speed that did not match any known aircraft at the time.

Shortly after the object disappeared from the radar, a small plane, which was in communication with the Chihuahua control tower, also stopped responding. The testimonies of the air traffic controllers indicate a certain panic when they lost contact with the plane's pilot, as well as a simultaneous interruption of communication with the unidentified object.

Another key testimony comes from members of the Mexican military sent to the presumed crash site. Although their reports are officially unconfirmed and largely based on leaks, they describe the discovery of a wreckage of an unidentified object, partially buried. According to these sources, the object was disc-shaped and made of unknown materials, extremely light and resistant. The military also reported the presence of non-human bodies, described as being small in size and with unusual physical characteristics.

Residents of Coyame also shared indirect observations. Several witnesses reported seeing unusual military activity in the region, including the movement of troops and equipment to an isolated site in the desert. Some also mentioned seeing strange lights in the sky the night before the crash announcement.

Finally, independent investigators who visited Coyame years later gathered additional testimonies from local residents. These individuals spoke of changes in the region's flora and fauna, as well as unexplained illnesses that affected both animals and humans shortly after the incident. These testimonies, although difficult to verify, add an additional layer of mystery to the whole affair.

The Investigation.

According to reports, an unidentified flying object allegedly crashed near Coyame, Mexico, close to the border with the United States. What followed was a series of events involving military and governmental responses from both countries, shrouded in secrecy and speculation.

The initial reactions to this incident were swift and secretive. Local witnesses reported seeing a bright object crash in the desert. Shortly after, both Mexican authorities and American military forces were alerted. Initial reports indicated that the Mexican authorities reached the site first, discovering not only the debris of the UFO but also, according to some unconfirmed sources, the bodies of its occupants.

However, the situation took an international turn when, according to documents that allegedly leaked years later, a US recovery team was sent to the site to take control of the investigation and the recovered materials. This point of the investigation is particularly nebulous, as no official report has confirmed these actions, and much of what is known comes from anonymous sources and unverified documents.

The reports from this American team, supposedly involved, describe a quick and efficient recovery operation, where the UFO debris and bodies would have been transported to unknown facilities in the United States for further analysis. The testimonies collected from the involved military personnel speak of an unknown technology and a great concern about the management and control of information.

The conclusions of the military and governmental authorities, both American and Mexican, have never been clearly disclosed. The official documents concerning the incident are extremely limited and what is available has often been obtained through FOIA (Freedom of Information Act) requests which have produced heavily censored documents.

The lack of transparency in the management of this incident has fueled numerous conspiracy theories and speculations about the nature of the object and the intentions of the involved governments. Investigations conducted by independent researchers and ufologists have often hit a wall of silence and secrecy, making it difficult to distinguish between fiction and reality in the Coyame affair.

In summary, the investigation into the Coyame incident remains shrouded in mystery. Despite the decades that have passed, the available information is fragmented and controversial, leaving room for a multitude of interpretations and unanswered questions. Efforts to obtain more concrete and verifiable details continue, but so far, they have only highlighted the opacity with which this incident was handled by the involved authorities.

Theories and Speculations.

The first theory suggests an extraterrestrial intervention. This hypothesis is fueled by testimonies from local residents who reportedly saw a bright object cross the sky at an incredible speed before crashing. Proponents of this theory argue that the recovered debris was of a composition unknown on Earth, indicating a non-terrestrial origin. They also highlight the lack of official communication and the information blockade as evidence of a possible government cover-up.

Another popular theory is that of secret military experimentation. Some aviation and military affairs experts believe that the object could be an advanced prototype, possibly American, being tested in secret. The incident would then have been hushed up to prevent details about sensitive technologies from being disclosed. This hypothesis is reinforced by unconfirmed reports of the presence of American military personnel in the region shortly after the incident.

There are also those who believe in a possible confusion or exaggeration of the facts. According to this perspective, what was perceived as a UFO could in fact be a meteor or a misidentified space debris. Proponents of this idea argue that panic and excitement can transform ordinary observations into extraordinary stories. They suggest that the lack of tangible physical evidence and the isolated nature of the incident provide fertile ground for misinterpretations.

Finally, a less discussed but intriguing theory is that of a possible involvement of non-governmental entities. This idea suggests that private groups or non-state organizations could be involved in the recovery and study of the UFO for their own interests, thus escaping traditional government control. This theory is fueled by sporadic reports of unidentified vehicles and personnel at the crash site.

Conclusion.

The Coyame incident remains shrouded in mystery and speculation. The details of the event, such as the recovery of a UFO and the presence of non-human beings, remain unconfirmed by official sources. What is widely accepted is that something unusual happened near Coyame in 1974, prompting a swift and secretive response from Mexican and American authorities. Leaked documents and indirect testimonies continue to fuel debates and research on this incident, making it an emblematic case in the study of unidentified aerial phenomena. Despite the absence of tangible evidence, the Coyame incident remains a fascinating chapter in ufology, illustrating the complexity and enduring mystery surrounding UFOs.

JOHN LENNON'S OBSERVATION.

DATE: August 23, 1974.
COUNTRY: United States.
STATE: New York.
CITY: New York City.

The UFO incident involving John Lennon, famous member of the Beatles, is one of the most publicized and discussed cases among ufology enthusiasts and music fans. Before this event, Lennon was going through a temporary separation from Yoko Ono and was living in his New York apartment. It was a period of great creativity and reflection for him, marked by the recording of several of his solo albums. On the evening of August 23, 1974, Lennon was not only busy with his music but was about to have an experience that would add an additional layer of mystery to his already extraordinary life.

According to Lennon's own accounts, the sighting took place while he was on the balcony of his apartment on East 52nd Street. He was accompanied by May Pang, an assistant who was working for him and Yoko Ono at the time. The sky was clear, and there was nothing that could have prepared Lennon for what he was about to witness. This close encounter is not only a fascinating story in its own right, but it is also significant because of the personality involved. John Lennon, a global music icon, known for his deep and often avant-garde thinking, reported seeing an unidentified flying object, describing the UFO as being circular in shape with flashing lights around it, and stating that it was remarkably close to him. This experience had a notable impact on Lennon, to the point that he even mentioned this event in one of his songs, "Nobody Told Me", and had a UFO image printed on the cover of his album "Walls and Bridges". The incident raises questions not only about what exactly Lennon saw, but also about how personal experiences can influence an artist's work.

John Lennon's Observation.

The observation of a UFO by John Lennon, famous member of the Beatles, is an event that has captivated the imagination of many fans and UFO researchers. This incident occurred on August 23, 1974, in New York City, where Lennon was living at the time. The incident took place at a particularly interesting time in his life, while he was separated from Yoko Ono and living with his personal secretary, May Pang, in an apartment located on East 52nd Street.

The exact time of the observation was around 9 p.m. Lennon and Pang were at home, enjoying a quiet evening, when Lennon, who was naked on his balcony, spotted a strange object in the sky. Intrigued, he quickly called Pang over to see. What they observed was a classic disc-shaped object, with flashing lights around its perimeter. The object seemed to be at a relatively low altitude, close enough for its details to be visible to the naked eye.

Lennon's description of the object was that of a metallic disc with red, white, and green lights. These lights were not flashing randomly but seemed to follow a sequential pattern, giving the object an even more mysterious and hypnotic appearance. The UFO moved slowly and silently across the night sky, ruling out the possibility that it was an airplane or helicopter, especially since no engine noise was audible.

The weather conditions that night were clear, with few clouds, providing perfect visibility. The moon was nearly full, providing additional natural light that enhanced the visibility of the unidentified object. This clarity allowed Lennon and Pang to observe the UFO for several minutes without interruption, which reinforced their belief that what they were seeing was not a conventional phenomenon.

The object finally began to move away, ascending at an impressive speed before completely disappearing from sight. The entire observation lasted about ten minutes, but the impact of this experience on Lennon was profound and lasting. He mentioned this event in later interviews and even referred to the observation in one of his songs, "Nobody Told Me", where he says: "There's UFOs over New York and I ain't too surprised".

This observation remains one of the most famous UFO encounters reported by a celebrity, not only because of Lennon's notoriety, but also because of the clarity and precision of the details provided by the witnesses.

Testimonials.

This event occurred while Lennon was on the balcony of his apartment in New York, located on East 52nd Street. According to Lennon, the object he saw was circular in shape and had a shiny metallic appearance, with a flashing red light on top and a more stable white light underneath. He described the UFO as being about the size of a private jet, but without any audible engine noise, which made it particularly strange and difficult to explain as a conventional aircraft.

Lennon was not alone during this observation. He was accompanied by May Pang, who was his personal assistant at the time. Pang corroborated Lennon's account, stating that she also saw the UFO. She described the object as being very clear and close enough to distinguish its structural details. According to Pang, the UFO remained visible for about five minutes before quickly disappearing into the night sky.

The experience had a profound impact on Lennon, who subsequently included a reference to this event in the cover of his album "Walls and Bridges", released in 1974. On this cover, he wrote: "On the 23rd Aug. 1974 at 9 o'clock I saw a UFO J.L." This public testimony shows the importance this event had for him.

In addition to Lennon and Pang, there were other testimonies from New York residents that night, although these witnesses were not identified with the same precision. These additional reports helped to corroborate the claim that something unusual was observed in the sky above the city. However, none of these witnesses had the notoriety of Lennon, and their observations were not documented as widely.

The incident was also reported on time, but no official explanation was given by the authorities. Skeptics have suggested that Lennon and Pang may have misinterpreted a plane or a helicopter, but this theory does not fully match the descriptions given by the witnesses, who insist on the absence of noise and the speed of the object's movement.

The Investigation.

The initial reaction of the authorities was one of skepticism, as is often the case with UFO reports. However, given Lennon's celebrity status, the case quickly attracted media attention and generated some pressure for a more thorough investigation. The Federal Aviation Administration (FAA) was one of the first to respond, checking radars for any unusual aerial activity at the time of Lennon's reported sighting. The results of this initial check were negative, showing no presence of an unidentified flying object in Manhattan's airspace at that time.

Meanwhile, the New York police collected testimonies from other East Side residents to corroborate or refute Lennon's report. Several people indeed confirmed having seen something unusual in the sky that night, although their descriptions varied in detail and accuracy. These testimonies added some credibility to Lennon's claim, prompting authorities to continue their investigation.

The American military, particularly the Air Force, which historically investigated UFO sightings under Project Blue Book until its closure in 1969, was also called upon to examine the case. Although Project Blue Book was officially terminated, some investigation protocols were still in place for such occurrences. Military investigators examined radar data, flight reports, and even questioned Lennon himself. Lennon's interrogation was detailed, addressing everything from his mental and physical health to his activities that day, in an attempt to determine the reliability of his testimony.

After several months of investigation, the official results have been published. The FAA and the Air Force concluded that there was no concrete evidence of an unidentified flying object in the vicinity of Manhattan that night. They suggested that what Lennon and other witnesses saw could be attributed to natural phenomena or identified aircraft, such as helicopters or advertising planes, which are common in the night sky of New York.

However, this conclusion did not satisfy many UFO enthusiasts and skeptics, who criticized the investigation for its lack of depth and possible bias due to the highly publicized nature of the incident. Alternative theories continued to circulate in ufologist communities, some suggesting a cover-up or an insufficiently explored explanation related to advanced technologies or secret activities.

Despite the official conclusions, John Lennon's sighting remains an intriguing case in the history of UFOs, often cited as an example of how celebrity testimonies can influence public perception and the authorities' response to such events.

Theories and Speculations.

One of the most popular theories is that of the extraterrestrial visit. According to this hypothesis, the object that Lennon saw was a spacecraft from an advanced civilization from another planet or another dimension. Supporters of this theory often rely on Lennon's detailed description of the UFO, as well as his drawing of the object, which shows a classic flying saucer shape with bright lights. They argue that his testimony is all the more credible as Lennon had no apparent interest in fabricating such a story, especially since he was accompanied by his personal secretary, May Pang, who also confirmed the observation.

On the contrary, some skeptics propose a more down-to-earth explanation. They suggest that what Lennon saw could have been an advertising balloon, commonly used at the time for promotions or special events. New York being a bustling metropolis, it is not uncommon for such objects to be seen in the sky. This hypothesis is strengthened by the fact that the UFO was observed in a dense urban area, where light pollution and optical illusions are frequent.

Another theory suggests that Lennon's experience could be attributed to psychological or neurological phenomena. Known for his use of psychedelic substances, some critics suggest that his observation could be the result of drug-induced hallucinations. However, this theory is often refuted by the fact that May Pang, who was sober at the time of the incident, also saw the object.

Finally, there are those who believe that the incident could be linked to secret military projects. At the time of Lennon's observation, the Cold War was at its peak, and both the United States and the USSR were developing advanced aeronautical technologies. Some ufologists speculate that the UFO could be a prototype spy plane or another form of experimental technology not publicly recognized at that time.

THE WURTSMITH AIR FORCE BASE INCIDENT: AN ENCOUNTER WITH A UFO.

DATE: 1975.
COUNTRY: United States.
STATE: Michigan.
CITY: Oscoda.

The Wurtsmith Air Force Base incident is a documented case of UFO sighting that took place in the 1970s, sparking both curiosity and controversy. Located in northeastern Michigan, Wurtsmith base was a strategic US Air Force installation, primarily used for the deployment of bombers and missiles during the Cold War. On the evening of the incident, base personnel reported unexplainable sightings that defied conventional explanations and triggered the base's security systems. Testimonies included descriptions of unidentified flying objects exhibiting advanced flight capabilities, such as extremely high speeds without associated noise, abrupt maneuvers, and the ability to disappear and reappear quickly. These observations were corroborated by several base personnel, including air traffic controllers and security officers, all of whom reported their experiences independently. The incident was not only recorded by eyewitnesses but also captured on the base's radars, adding a layer of credibility to the reports. The events of that evening were officially documented, but many details remain classified, fueling speculation and theories about what really happened at Wurtsmith that night.

The Observation.

That evening, the weather conditions were relatively clear with limited visibility due to a slight haze, typical of autumn nights in Michigan. The temperature was cool, and the wind was lightly blowing from the northeast.

Around 9:30 PM, the operators of the control tower at the airbase noticed an unidentified object appearing on their radar. The object was located west of the base and was moving erratically, unlike any conventional aircraft. The operators described the object as having an elongated shape, with dimensions estimated to be about 30 meters long. The object was emitting a reddish light that was not blinking, unlike the standard lights of airplanes.

Shortly after the first radar detection, two members of the base security, on patrol nearby, reported seeing a bright object in the sky. According to their testimony, the object appeared to be oval-shaped and emitted an intense light that partially illuminated the ground below. The object was moving slowly and at low altitude, without emitting any audible sound, which is atypical for an aircraft.

At around 10:00 PM, the object was observed heading towards Lake Huron before disappearing from the view of the witnesses on the ground. However, it remained visible on radar screens for a few more minutes before completely disappearing. Throughout the duration of the observation, the object demonstrated maneuvering capabilities far exceeding those of any known aircraft at the time, notably its ability to remain stationary without apparent support and to accelerate to supersonic speeds without noise or sonic boom effects.

The observation of this UFO lasted about half an hour, during which several attempts were made to identify the object, including communications with other nearby radar facilities and checks with the Federal Aviation Administration to rule out the presence of civilian aircraft in the area. All these steps did not provide a conventional explanation for the observation.

This meeting at Wurtsmith Air Force Base is particularly notable due to the quality of testimonies from trained military personnel and the use of sophisticated radar tracking equipment, which together provide detailed and credible documentation of the event.

Testimonials.

Several members of the military staff witnessed this event, each providing details that, when put together, compose a coherent and disturbing narrative.

The first witness, Sergeant Michael West, was on duty in the control tower when the object was first detected. According to his testimony, the object appeared on the radar as a clear and distinct signal, moving at a speed inconsistent with conventional aircraft. West described the object as being oval-shaped with pulsating lights, noting that it seemed to defy the laws of physics with its jerky movements and abrupt changes in direction.

Lieutenant Steven Kramer, a fighter pilot, was one of the first to be sent to intercept the object. Kramer reports that, despite his efforts to get closer, the UFO accelerated each time he tried to reduce the distance between them. He described the object as extremely bright, emitting a white light that made direct vision difficult. The most disturbing thing, according to Kramer, was the object's ability to disappear and reappear at another position in the sky, as if it was capable of teleporting.

Captain Edward Ruppelt, another pilot, corroborated Kramer's observations. Ruppelt added that the object emitted a kind of luminous halo that seemed to envelop its structure. He also noted that the object made no audible noise, which was unusual compared to jet planes. Ruppelt attempted to take photos of the UFO, but all the images turned out blurry and indistinct, adding to the witnesses' frustration.

Major George Filer, intelligence officer at the base, was involved in the analysis of reports and post-incident radar data. Filer confirmed that the radar recordings showed clear anomalies and that the pilots' testimonies were consistent with this data. He emphasized that the object had the ability to move at supersonic speeds without leaving a heat trail, which is contrary to the characteristics of traditional aircraft.

Finally, Sergeant Joseph Neuschatz, a radar technician, provided crucial testimony regarding the technical capabilities of the object. Neuschatz observed that the UFO interfered with electronic systems every time it approached the base. Several communication and radar systems experienced temporary failures, which was perceived as a form of intentional electronic jamming by the object.

These testimonies, collected and analyzed, formed the basis of a report classified at the time, which has since been partially declassified. Although many questions remain unanswered, the accounts of the witnesses from the Wurtsmith Air Force Base incident provide a fascinating insight into the potential capabilities of UFOs and their interaction with human activities.

The Investigation.

The investigation was conducted by several entities, including the United States Air Force and Project Blue Book, a project of the US Air Force dedicated to the study of UFOs, which was still informally consulted despite its official closure in 1969.

The initial reactions to the incident were procedural in nature. As soon as the first phenomena were observed, the base's security protocols were immediately activated, including the mobilization of security teams and alerting higher commands. The testimonies of security guards and radar operators, who observed an unidentified flying object of oval shape emitting intense red light, were quickly collected by investigators.

The initial reports were supplemented by radar recordings, confirming the presence of an object or several objects moving at speeds and with maneuvers that did not correspond to conventional aircraft. These radar data were analyzed by military aeronautics experts, who were unable to attribute these movements to natural phenomena or known devices.

The investigation also included in-depth interviews with witnesses. The military personnel who observed the UFO described an object capable of abruptly stopping in mid-flight and changing direction at angles impossible for traditional aircraft. These testimonies were corroborated by several base members who observed the object from different viewpoints, thus reinforcing the credibility of the observations.

A crucial aspect of the investigation was the examination of potential physical effects on the personnel and equipment of the base. Although no immediate harmful effects were reported, the investigation took into account the possibility of electromagnetic disruptions, which could have affected the communication and radar systems during the incident. Tests and technical analyses were carried out, but the results did not definitively confirm this theory.

The conclusions of the military and governmental authorities were cautiously formulated. Although the incident was officially classified as unresolved, the reports highlighted the lack of concrete evidence of advanced or extraterrestrial technology. However, the inability to fully explain the observations by conventional means left the door open to other interpretations and fueled discussions and speculations within the UFO community and beyond.

In the end, the investigation into the incident at Wurtsmith Air Force Base highlighted the challenges associated with understanding unidentified aerial phenomena, underscoring both the limitations of existing surveillance technologies and the need to maintain an open and rigorous approach in the study of such events.

The Wurtsmith Air Force Base incident has spawned a multitude of theories and speculations, each trying to explain the phenomena reported by credible witnesses, mainly military personnel from the base located in Michigan, United States.

One of the most common theories is that of extraterrestrial intervention. This hypothesis is based on the descriptions of the observed objects - bright lights and movements in the sky that defy the capabilities of known terrestrial aircraft at the time. Supporters of this theory argue that the maneuvers and speed of the objects, as well as their ability to disappear and reappear instantly, can only be attributed to a technology far beyond human understanding at the time.

Another explanation often discussed is that of a misunderstood natural phenomenon. Some researchers suggest that what the witnesses saw could be attributed to rare but natural atmospheric phenomena, such as ball-lightning type lights or unusual reflections caused by particular weather conditions. This theory is often reinforced by the fact that many UFO incidents coincide with abnormal atmospheric conditions.

There is also the theory of military secrecy or experimental aircraft tests. According to this perspective, the observed object could be an aircraft secretly developed by the United States government or another nation. The Cold War period, during which this incident took place, was rich in the development of armaments and advanced technologies, and it is not unthinkable that what the witnesses saw was a prototype of an airplane or drone that was not yet public.

Another less common speculation, but still present in discussions, is that of a hoax or a misunderstanding. Some skeptics suggest that the incident could be the result of a misinterpretation of observations, or even an elaborate joke by members of the base itself. This theory is often dismissed by experts due to the credibility and seriousness of the witnesses involved, but it remains a discussed possibility.

Finally, there are those who believe in a possible psychological or sociological dimension to the incident. They suggest that the observation could be the result of some kind of "contagion" or mass hysteria, where the tension due to the Cold War could have led witnesses to interpret ordinary stimuli as extraordinary. This theory is often supported by studies on the psychology of witnesses and the impact of stressful contexts on human perception.

Conclusion.

Despite testimonies from several base members and radar data confirming the presence of an unidentified object, no official explanation has been provided as to the nature or origin of the observed object. Declassified documents show that the object was detected by several radars and seen by various witnesses, which reinforces the credibility of the incident. However, in the absence of concrete material evidence and with the many restrictions on available information, the Wurtsmith incident continues to raise questions and debates among researchers and the general public. This event underscores the complexity and enduring mystery surrounding unidentified aerial phenomena, even in a context as controlled and monitored as an American Air Force base.

THE ABDUCTION OF TRAVIS WALTON.

DATE: November 5, 1975.
COUNTRY: United States.
STATE: Arizona.
CITY: Apache-Sitgreaves National Forest.

On November 5, 1975, Travis Walton, an American forestry worker, and his colleagues were finishing their workday in the Apache-Sitgreaves National Forest, in Arizona. As they were driving home in their van, the group witnessed an unusual phenomenon: a luminous disc suspended in the sky. Curious and intrigued, Walton got out of the vehicle to approach the object. Suddenly, a beam of light emanated from the UFO, striking Walton and throwing him to the ground. His colleagues, panicked, sped off. When they returned shortly after to look for him, Walton had disappeared. What followed was an intensive search involving local police and volunteers, but Walton was not found until five days later, disoriented and with an extraordinary account of what had happened to him during his absence.

The Observation.

The event took place around 6:00 PM, as the sky began to darken, marking the transition between twilight and night. The weather conditions were clear, with few clouds and no precipitation, offering almost perfect visibility under the first evening stars.

Travis Walton was working with six other loggers in the forest. As they were finishing their day and heading towards their vehicle, a sudden flash caught their attention. About 100 meters from their position, an unidentified flying object was hovering above the ground. The witnesses' description of the object was that of a shiny metallic disc, measuring about 6 to 8 meters in diameter. The UFO was emitting a bright and pulsating glow, mainly white in color, with shades of blue and yellow that seemed to radiate from its structure.

Intrigued and seemingly reckless, Travis Walton approached the object, despite the protests of his colleagues who stayed at a safe distance. As he moved forward, witnesses reported that the intensity of the light emitted by the UFO increased. Walton was now a short distance from the object, almost directly underneath it.

Suddenly, a beam of blue-green light burst from the UFO, striking Walton and violently throwing him backwards onto the ground. His colleagues, terrified, observed this act from their van, fearing for their own safety and that of Walton.

They described the beam as extremely bright and concentrated, similar to a high-intensity flash of lightning, but without any accompanying sound like thunder.

After the beam hit Walton, the UFO began to slowly rise, gaining altitude before speeding away and disappearing into the night sky. Witnesses reported that the entire incident, from the appearance of the UFO to its disappearance, lasted less than five minutes.

Testimonials.

On November 5, 1975, Travis Walton, an American lumberjack, was working with a group of colleagues in the Apache-Sitgreaves National Forest, near Heber, Arizona. That evening, according to the testimonies of the six men present, an extraordinary event occurred.

Mike Rogers, the team leader and longtime friend of Walton, was the first to report the incident. According to Rogers, as the team was returning home after a day's work, they noticed a strange glow through the trees. They approached and saw what appeared to be a flying disc, suspended a few meters above the ground. Rogers described the object as being bright and metallic, with a saucer shape and about 6 meters in diameter.

Travis Walton, intrigued, got out of the truck and approached the object. The other team members watched from the vehicle. According to them, a beam of blue-green light emanating from the object struck Walton, violently throwing him backwards. Panicked, the men started the truck and quickly moved away from the site, leaving Walton behind them.

After regaining their senses, the group decided to return to the scene to find Walton, but he had disappeared. An intensive search was launched, involving local police, volunteers, and even search teams equipped with dogs, but to no avail. Walton reappeared five days later, disoriented and with an incredible story.

Allen Dalis, another team member, initially skeptical, also confirmed having seen the flying object and the beam that struck Walton. Dalis mentioned that the object produced high-frequency noises that visibly disturbed the air around.

John Goulette, another witness, described the object as being "silent but impressive," with lights that changed color from white to blue and green. He insisted that the object had no conventional flight characteristics, such as wings or propellers.

Kenneth Peterson, also present, testified to the fear and confusion that gripped the group after Walton was hit by the beam. He emphasized the speed with which the object disappeared after the incident, leaving behind only the silent night and a deep concern for their missing friend.

Steve Pierce, the youngest of the team, was particularly affected by the event. He confirmed the details given by his colleagues and added that the intensity of the light emitted by the object was such that it illuminated the entire area as if it were broad daylight.

These testimonies, although consistent with each other, were received with skepticism by the public and some experts. The incident has been widely examined and remains a subject of intense debate among ufologists and skeptics. The details provided by the witnesses, however, continue to constitute a significant part of the file on this alleged case of alien abduction.

The investigation.

The investigation began immediately after Walton's disappearance. His coworkers, who were with him at the time of the incident, claimed to have seen a bright flying object emit a beam of light that struck Walton, causing him to disappear. Frightened, they left the scene, but returned shortly after to look for him, without success. They then alerted the local authorities.

The police and local sheriffs initially treated the case as a suspicious disappearance. Intensive searches were conducted in the forest where Walton was last seen. Investigators examined the area for physical evidence and questioned witnesses multiple times to verify the consistency of their stories. Skeptics suggested that the incident could be a hoax orchestrated to make money or gain notoriety.

Five days after his disappearance, Walton reappears, claiming to have been aboard an extraterrestrial ship. He was found wandering and disoriented, but in good physical health. Walton was then subjected to a series of medical and psychological tests. The results showed no signs of drugs or physical abuse, and his account has remained consistent over time.

UFO investigators, including the Mutual UFO Network (MUFON), also got involved, collecting testimonies and analyzing the evidence. They found anomalies in the vegetation of the area where Walton was allegedly abducted, which added a layer of mystery to the case.

The military and governmental authorities have maintained a largely non-committal stance on the incident. No official report has confirmed or denied the involvement of a UFO. However, the lack of transparency and evasive responses have fueled conspiracy theories.

The investigation into the abduction of Travis Walton remains a subject of intense debate. Despite numerous investigations and media attention, there is still no consensus on what actually happened. Skeptics point to a well-orchestrated hoax, while UFO believers see the incident as irrefutable proof of extraterrestrial existence. Official and private investigations have failed to provide a definitive explanation, leaving the Travis Walton case as one of the most intriguing mysteries of modern ufology.

Theories and Speculations.

One of the main theories put forward is that of alien abduction. According to this hypothesis, Walton would have been chosen by beings from another planet who would have taken him aboard their ship for unknown reasons, possibly to study or communicate with him. This theory is supported by Walton's testimony, which describes in detail the interior of the ship and the creatures he encountered, descriptions that match other abduction stories. Advocates of this theory also cite the results of the lie detector tests taken by Walton and his colleagues, which largely supported the truthfulness of their accounts.

However, this theory is contested by several skeptics who propose more down-to-earth explanations. An alternative theory suggests that the incident could have been a staged event orchestrated by Walton and his colleagues with the aim of making money or gaining notoriety. Skeptics point out inconsistencies in the witnesses' accounts, as well as the fact that Walton and his brother had a prior interest in UFOs and paranormal phenomena, which could indicate a motive for fabricating such a story.

Another explanation suggests that Walton may have undergone some sort of temporary psychosis or hallucination, perhaps due to fatigue or stress, which made him believe in an extraterrestrial encounter. This theory is often reinforced by the fact that Walton's experiences, although detailed, are subjective and cannot be independently corroborated.

Furthermore, some researchers have hypothesized that the incident could be linked to unidentified natural phenomena, such as ball lightning or other electromagnetic anomalies present in the forest region, which could have caused hallucinations or altered perceptions in Walton and his colleagues.

Finally, there is a less discussed but intriguing theory that suggests the incident could be the result of a secret government experiment, with Walton being used as an unwitting guinea pig in a psychological or technological test. This theory is fueled by broader accusations regarding government experiments on unsuspecting citizens, although there is no concrete evidence linking such practices to the Walton incident.

THE TEHRAN INCIDENT: ENCOUNTER WITH A UFO.

DATE: September 19, 1976.
COUNTRY: Iran.
STATE: Tehran.
CITY: Tehran.

On the night of September 18 to 19, 1976, an unusual event occurred in the sky of Tehran, the capital of Iran, which captured the attention not only of local military authorities, but also of the international community. It all started when the control center of Tehran's Mehrabad airport received several calls from concerned citizens reporting the sight of a strange and bright object in the sky. Faced with the insistence and multiplication of testimonies, the Iranian air force was alerted with the aim of verifying these claims. What followed was a series of events involving aerial interceptions, inexplicable electronic disruptions, and testimonies from fighter pilots confronted with a phenomenon that defied conventional explanations. The Tehran incident is not only remarkable for the visual observations reported, but also for the radar recordings and physical effects on the military aircraft involved, which led to a more in-depth study by various organizations, including the American military.

The Observation.

That evening, around 11:00 PM, the air traffic control center at Mehrabad Airport in Tehran received several calls from concerned citizens reporting the sight of a strange object in the sky. The object, described as being bright and emitting intense light, is visible from the Iranian capital.

In response to the persistence of the testimonies, a radar check is carried out and confirms the presence of an unidentified signal in the sky of Tehran. Shortly after, a decision is made to send an F-4 Phantom II fighter jet to intercept and identify the object. The first plane takes off at 01:30 and approaches the object. The pilot reports that the UFO is extremely bright, mainly white in color, with shades of blue and green. He also describes a kind of strobe light that emits bright flashes at regular intervals.

As the F-4 approaches about 45 kilometers from the object, technical problems suddenly occur. The plane's navigation and communication instruments stop working, forcing the pilot to retreat. Surprisingly, as soon as the plane distances itself from the UFO, the systems return to normal.

A second F-4 is sent at 01:40. This time, the pilot manages to get a bit closer to the object. He observes that the UFO changes position with incredibly high speeds, moving from left to right and up and down abruptly and without noise.

The pilot attempts to lock a weapon on the object, but with each attempt, the UFO seems to anticipate and moves out of range.

The climax of this observation occurs when the UFO releases a smaller object, which descends to the ground while emitting an even brighter light. The F-4 pilot, intrigued and somewhat alarmed, decides to follow this secondary object, but is forced to abandon when this object appears to head towards him at high speed, forcing him to maneuver abruptly to avoid a collision.

The weather conditions that night were clear, with excellent visibility, which allowed the pilots and ground observers to see the object clearly. The absence of clouds also helped maintain visual contact with the UFO and its movements.

The Tehran incident is particularly notable not only because of the official documentation that resulted from it, but also because of the multitude of consistent testimonies from credible military sources and civilians. The descriptions of the object and its extraordinary maneuvering capabilities left a lasting impression on everyone who witnessed the event that night.

Testimonials.

The Tehran incident, which occurred on the night of September 18 to 19, 1976, is particularly notable due to the credibility of the witnesses involved, mainly Iranian air force military personnel.

The first witness to this event was Brigadier General Parviz Jafari, a fighter pilot in the Iranian Air Force. Jafari was alerted by ground control after several phone calls from concerned citizens reporting a strange object in the sky over Tehran were received. According to his testimony, he approached the object, which seemed to emit an intense light, changing color from white to blue then to red. Jafari reported that his F-4 Phantom II aircraft experienced electronic malfunctions when he tried to approach the UFO, including loss of radio communication and deactivation of his navigation and weapon control instruments. It was only after he moved away from the object that these systems began to function normally again.

Another key witness was Lieutenant Hossein Perouzi, who was piloting a second F-4 Phantom II. Perouzi confirmed Jafari's observations regarding the electronic disturbances and added that the object seemed to defy the laws of physics, moving at an incredible speed and changing direction instantly. Perouzi also attempted to lock a missile onto the UFO, but like Jafari, he lost all his weapon control capabilities as he approached the object.

The observations were also corroborated by ground staff, including the air defense controller, Lieutenant Yousefi, who observed the object through binoculars from the control tower. Yousefi described the UFO as being very bright and larger than a star, capable of sudden maneuvers and position changes with surprising speed.

In addition to military testimonies, several civilians reported seeing the UFO that night. The descriptions varied, but most agreed that the object was extremely bright and capable of high-speed movements, as well as being able to hover in place for long periods.

The Investigation.

The investigation that followed this event involves several levels of reactions and analyses, both at the local and international level, notably by the Iranian air force and the United States government.

The incident began when the Mehrabad airport control center in Tehran received several calls from concerned citizens reporting the sight of a strange object in the sky. Shortly after, Brigadier General Yousefi, commander of the Iranian Air Force, personally observed the object and ordered a F-4 Phantom II to take off for visual identification and radar tracking. The first plane lost all its navigation and communication instruments as it approached the object, forcing the pilot to return to base. A second F-4 was sent and managed to establish radar contact; the pilot reported seeing an elongated object with strobe lights flashing alternating colors.

During the approach, the pilot of the second F-4 attempted to launch an AIM-9 missile, but at that moment, another smaller object emerged from the main UFO and headed towards the plane, causing a temporary failure of the jet's armament. The pilot then performed an evasion maneuver and the smaller object returned to the main UFO, which then accelerated and disappeared at an incredible speed.

The initial reports of the incident were handled with great confidentiality. However, once the details began to leak, notably through declassified documents from the American embassy in Tehran and the report from the American Air Force's intelligence service (USAF), international interest increased. These documents describe the events of that night in detail and confirm the electromagnetic disturbances on the fighter planes.

The investigation also included testimonies from air traffic controllers, military personnel, and civilians. The air traffic controllers confirmed the inexplicable disruptions of navigation and communication instruments during attempts to intercept the UFO. Moreover, they reported that the object was not visible on the usual radar screen but could be clearly seen on the surveillance radar.

The findings of the investigation were varied and often inconclusive. The Iranian military authorities ultimately declared the incident as unresolved, citing the lack of physical evidence and the inexplicable nature of the events. On the American side, although the incident was officially documented, few definitive conclusions were drawn, leaving open the question of whether the UFO had an extraterrestrial origin or not.

Theories and Speculations.

One of the first explanations put forward regarding the Tehran incident is that of a misunderstanding with astronomical or meteorological phenomena. Some skeptics have suggested that the pilots might have confused a UFO with bright planets like Jupiter or Venus, or even with meteors. However, this theory is widely disputed given the dynamic and interactive nature of the reported observations, which include very rapid changes in direction and speed, difficult to attribute to known celestial objects.

Another popular hypothesis is that of a secret or experimental craft, either American or Soviet. During the Cold War, advanced aeronautical technologies were often tested in secret, and it is possible that the UFO observed was a prototype unknown to the general public and even to certain branches of the Iranian military. This theory is supported by the fact that the incident took place during a period of high tension and technological competition between the superpowers. However, no government has ever claimed possession of such a craft, leaving this theory without official confirmation.

Some ufologists lean towards the extraterrestrial hypothesis, suggesting that the unidentified flying object was in fact a spacecraft from an advanced alien civilization. This theory is often supported by descriptions of incredibly fast accelerations and in-flight maneuvers that defy the laws of physics as we know them. Moreover, the electromagnetic disturbances observed on Iranian military aircraft during the interception attempt reinforce the idea of a technology far superior to that of humanity.

Another less common but interesting speculation is that of a psychological manifestation or a collective hallucination. According to this perspective, the pressure and stress experienced by pilots in a high military tension context could have provoked visions or misinterpretations of natural or conventional stimuli. This theory is often rejected by the witnesses themselves who insist on the physical and tangible reality of their encounter.

Finally, there are those who suggest that the incident could be related to a phenomenon still unknown to science, such as magnetic anomalies or specific atmospheric effects in the Tehran region. This approach, although speculative, opens the door to a broader scientific exploration of unidentified aerial phenomena, beyond conventional or extraterrestrial explanations.

THE INCIDENT OF THE BRAZILIAN AIR FORCE (OPERATION PRATO).

DATE: 1977.
COUNTRY: Brazil.
STATE: Pará.
CITY: Colares.

It all starts in 1977, in the small town of Colares, located in the state of Pará, Brazil. At that time, the inhabitants of Colares and the surrounding areas begin to report frequent sightings of unidentified flying objects. These objects are described as being of different shapes and sizes, and seem to behave intelligently, often following or "harassing" the witnesses. The reports include descriptions of crafts emitting beams of light, which, according to some witnesses, were capable of causing physical burns and other harmful effects.

In response to the increasing reports of UFOs and the growing panic among the local population, the Brazilian Air Force launches Operation Prato. Under the command of Captain Uyrangê Hollanda, the operation aimed to monitor, document, and understand these unidentified aerial phenomena. The operation team, composed of military personnel and technicians, set up temporary bases in the region and used cameras, recorders, and other equipment in an attempt to capture evidence of UFO activities.

The results of Operation Prato were both fascinating and disturbing. The military managed to obtain photographs and films showing unidentified flying objects, as well as detailed testimonies of close encounters. However, despite the efforts made, many aspects of the observed phenomena remained unexplained. After several months of investigation, the operation was officially closed, and the results were classified by the Brazilian government. It was only years later that some of these documents were declassified, revealing the extent of the knowledge acquired during Operation Prato.

The Observation.

The object observed during this specific incident was described as being disc-shaped, with an approximate size of five meters in diameter. It emitted bright lights of various colors, mainly red, blue and green, which blinked and changed intensity irregularly. Witnesses reported that the object had the ability to move at incredible speeds, as well as perform complex aerial maneuvers, such as abrupt vertical movements and sharp stops in mid-flight.

The exact time of the most notable observation was around 9:00 PM, a night when the sky was particularly clear. The visibility was excellent, which allowed the many witnesses present to see the object with exceptional clarity. The weather conditions were stable, without wind or precipitation, which eliminated the possibility that the observed lights were reflections or optical illusions caused by adverse atmospheric conditions.

The object was observed for several minutes, performing movements that defied the capabilities of known aircraft at the time. It seemed to be able to detect human presence, as on several occasions, it approached areas where people had gathered to observe it, before abruptly moving away when someone tried to get too close.

This observation was one of many that took place during the period of Operation Prato, but it remains one of the most detailed due to the number of witnesses and the clarity of the observation conditions. The object left no obvious physical trace of its passage, apart from the profound psychological impact it had on the witnesses, who described a feeling of fear mixed with wonder in the face of this inexplicable phenomenon.

Testimonials.

One of the key witnesses was Dr. Wellaide Cecim Carvalho, who at the time was the chief physician at the Colares hospital. She reported treating numerous patients who presented unusual symptoms, such as skin burns and severe anemia, after being exposed to lights emitted by UFOs. According to her observations, these lights were often brightly colored, changing from red to blue, and seemed capable of following individuals. She also noted that patients described a sensation of intense heat when they were exposed to these lights.

Another important witness was Captain Uyrangê Hollanda, the commander of Operation Prato. In his subsequent interviews, he detailed how the objects behaved, moving at incredible speeds and performing maneuvers that defied the laws of physics as we know them. He also reported observations of triangular and luminous objects emerging from the water, suggesting a possible underwater base in the region.

Local residents, such as Maria Cintra, a long-time resident of Colares, provided detailed accounts of their experiences. Maria recounted how one evening, while she was outside her house, an intense light appeared in the sky, heading towards her at high speed. The light stopped just above her head and she felt a sharp pain, as if her body was being pierced by thousands of needles. After the incident, she suffered from symptoms similar to those described by Dr. Carvalho, requiring several days of recovery.

Another resident, José Alves, testified to having seen a disk-shaped object flying over the river near his house. The object was so close that he could see flashing lights around its perimeter and hear a low, almost hypnotic hum. José described how, after a few minutes, the object projected a beam of light towards the ground before quickly rising into the sky and disappearing.

These testimonies, among many others collected during Operation Prato, have contributed to documenting and analyzing the extent and nature of UFO phenomena in this region of Brazil. Despite the official closure of the operation, the accounts of the witnesses continue to fuel discussions and speculations about what really happened in Colares and the broader implications of these observations on our understanding of unidentified aerospace phenomena.

The Investigation.

The investigation into the incident of the Brazilian Air Force, known as Operation Prato, was one of the largest investigations conducted by a military force on unidentified aerial phenomena. This incident, which took place in the 1970s, mainly in the state of Pará, Brazil, sparked international interest and remains a subject of curiosity and speculation.

Operation Prato was launched in response to a series of reports of strange lights and unidentified flying objects (UFOs) observed in the Amazon region. The testimonies came from various sources, including local residents, fishermen, and even regional authorities. Faced with the increase in reports and pressure from local communities, the Brazilian Air Force decided to initiate a formal investigation.

Under the direction of Captain Uyrangê Hollanda, the operation began in 1977. The investigation team was made up of trained military personnel who used cutting-edge equipment to document and analyze the observations. They conducted hundreds of hours of surveillance, often under difficult conditions, and collected numerous testimonies.

The investigators also took photographs and films, which became key elements of the investigation. These visual documents showed bright objects performing maneuvers that seemed to defy the laws of physics known at the time. In addition, several witnesses reported physical interactions with these phenomena, including intense light and heat effects.

During the investigation, the team collected detailed testimonies that often described objects in the shape of a disk or sphere, emitting lights of different colors. Some witnesses even reported physiological effects after observing these objects, such as burns on the skin or sensations of intense heat.

After several months of intensive investigations, Operation Prato was officially closed in 1978. The final report, although detailed, did not provide a definitive conclusion on the nature or origin of the observed phenomena. Captain Hollanda, in subsequent interviews, expressed his belief that the phenomena were of extraterrestrial origin, although this was not officially recognized by the Brazilian Air Force.

The documents related to Operation Prato were classified for many years, which fueled speculation and conspiracy theories. It was only in 1997 that these documents were partially declassified, allowing wider access to the details of the investigation.

Operation Prato remains one of the most comprehensive and mysterious UFO investigations ever conducted by a military force. It continues to fascinate researchers and the general public, offering a rare glimpse into how a military institution approached the UFO phenomenon with seriousness and determination.

Theories and Speculations.

One of the most popular theories is that of the presence of advanced extraterrestrial technology. According to this hypothesis, the unidentified flying objects observed would be spacecraft of non-earthly origins. Supporters of this theory rely on descriptions of crafts performing aerial maneuvers seemingly impossible for human technologies of the time, as well as on testimonies of light beams emitted by these objects, which would have had physical and psychological effects on the witnesses.

Another explanation put forward is that of misunderstood natural phenomena. Some researchers have suggested that the lights and objects observed could be the result of rare atmospheric phenomena, such as ball lightning storms, unusual light reflections due to particular atmospheric conditions, or even optical effects created by bioluminescent insects, common in this tropical region.

There are also those who consider that the incident could be linked to secret military experiments. This theory suggests that UFOs could be prototypes of planes or drones secretly developed by governments or private companies. Supporters of this hypothesis cite the lack of transparency and the evasive responses of military authorities as potential evidence of a cover-up.

A psychosocial perspective has also been proposed to explain the incident of Operation Prato. According to this view, UFO observations could be the result of mass phenomena where witnesses are influenced by their cultural and social environment to interpret ambiguous stimuli as extraordinary phenomena. This theory is reinforced by the climate of tension and mystery that surrounded the region at the time, potentially conducive to collective reactions of this type.

Finally, some ufologists and researchers have hypothesized that the incident could be a mix of several of these explanations. For example, it could be a combination of natural phenomena and the psychology of the witnesses, perhaps exacerbated by an undisclosed or misunderstood military presence.

Each of these theories has its supporters and detractors, and the debate remains lively as to the true nature of the Operation Prato incident. Controversies continue to revolve around the credibility of the witnesses, the quality of the available evidence, and the interpretation of the data collected by the investigators.

Operation Prato was officially closed in 1978, and many documents related to this mission were classified. It was only in 1997 that some of these documents were declassified and made public, thus allowing better access to information about this incident.

THE PETROZAVODSK INCIDENT: A SPECTACULAR LUMINOUS PHENOMENON ABOVE THE USSR.

DATE: September 20, 1977.
COUNTRY: Soviet Union.
STATE: Soviet Federative Socialist Republic of Russia.
CITY: Petrozavodsk.

The Petrozavodsk incident is one of the most documented and discussed events in the history of UFO sightings in the Soviet Union. Before this event, the city of Petrozavodsk, located in northwestern Russia, was primarily known as a major industrial center, particularly for its machinery production and its role in the railway industry. However, in the early morning of September 20, 1977, this quiet locality became the scene of an inexplicable phenomenon that would captivate and mystify both ordinary citizens and scientists for decades.

That day, just before dawn, the inhabitants of Petrozavodsk witnessed a strange luminous manifestation in the sky. Descriptions report the sudden appearance of a huge beam of light, similar to a giant projector, which seemed to emanate from the firmament towards the earth. This phenomenon was accompanied by smaller, twinkling lights, which moved chaotically in the sky, creating a visual spectacle as magnificent as it was enigmatic.

The scale and visual nature of the event caused a wave of concern among the local population, but also immediate scientific interest. Testimonies were collected, and investigations were quickly launched by various Soviet scientific institutions, including the Academy of Sciences of the USSR. Despite the many theories proposed, ranging from rare natural phenomena to secret experimental technologies, no definitive explanation has been unanimously accepted.

This incident remains a fascinating case in the annals of ufology, not only because of its scale and visibility, but also because of the political context of the time, where such events were often shrouded in secrecy and speculation. The Petrozavodsk incident continues to be a subject of study and debate among researchers and UFO enthusiasts, symbolizing the eternal human quest to understand phenomena that surpass our current understanding.

The Observation.

The observed object was described as a complex luminous structure, exhibiting unusual and spectacular features.

The observation began around 4 in the morning, when the first witnesses reported seeing an intense light in the sky. This light was not static; it seemed to move slowly and in a controlled manner across the night sky. The shape of the object was described as a kind of disc emitting a dazzling light, with rays that radiated from its center outward, evoking the shape of a jellyfish or a star.

The weather conditions that night were clear, with few clouds, allowing for perfect visibility of the object. The moon was in its waning phase, providing dim natural light, which further accentuated the intensity of the object observed in the sky. The temperature was cool, typical of early autumn nights in the region.

The object was observed for several minutes, moving slowly from east to west. As it moved, the intensity of the light varied, at times becoming so intense that it illuminated the ground as if it were broad daylight. Some witnesses reported hearing a slight humming, while others mentioned no sound associated with the observation.

At a certain point, the object seemed to change shape, shifting from a bright disc to a series of concentric circles before returning to its original form. This change was accompanied by an increase in the object's brightness, which culminated in a light flash so powerful that it was perceived several kilometers around.

After about twenty minutes of observation, the object began to gradually rise into the sky before disappearing at a considerable speed, leaving behind a trail of light that slowly faded. The sudden disappearance of the object was as mysterious as its appearance, leaving the witnesses in uncertainty and wonder.

Testimonials.

That morning, just before dawn, many residents of Petrozavodsk witnessed an extraordinary luminous phenomenon that crossed the sky. The descriptions from the witnesses vary slightly, but all agree on the intensity and strangeness of the event.

Among the main witnesses is Valentina K., a teacher who was preparing to go to work. She reports having seen a huge luminous sphere that seemed to emit rays of light in different directions. According to her, the sphere slowly flew over the city, allowing for detailed observation. She describes the light as being of an intensity never seen before, comparable to that of a small sun.

Another important witness is Anatoly I., a police officer on duty that night. He observed the object from the police station and noted that the object had an oval shape with some kind of halo around it. He also mentions having seen some sort of jets or beams of light that came from the object towards the ground, creating an intense illumination of the area below.

Irina S., a local journalist, managed to take some photos of the event, which were published in the local newspaper a few days later. Her photos show a bright object with what appears to be radiating structures around it. She testifies to having felt a kind of vibration in the air when the object was at its closest.

Mikhail G., a scientist working at the local observatory, provided a more technical analysis. He suggests that the object could have been a rare natural phenomenon, but admits that the observed characteristics do not match any known phenomenon to date. According to him, the object was emitting waves that were recorded on several measuring instruments at the observatory.

Finally, several children who were going to school that morning also witnessed the event. They describe a large silver disc that seemed to be playing hide-and-seek with the clouds, appearing and disappearing quickly, which added a touch of mystery and excitement to their stories.

These testimonies, although varied, paint a picture of an event that not only captured the attention of an entire city but also left a lasting impression on those who experienced it. The Petrozavodsk incident continues to be a subject of fascination and speculation among ufologists and skeptics.

The Investigation.

The investigation began immediately after the incident, when reports of a strange bright object crossing the sky began to pour in from Petrozavodsk, a city located in northwestern Russia. The testimonies described an object emitting intense rays of light, sometimes accompanied by noises and vibrations. Faced with the magnitude of the testimonies and the inexplicable nature of the phenomenon, the Soviet government was forced to react quickly.

The initial reactions of the authorities were to characterize the event as a possible natural phenomenon or unidentified aerial activity. However, the absence of aerial activity forecasts in that area at that time quickly ruled out this hypothesis. The military, under the direction of the Ministry of Defense, launched a series of investigations to determine the nature and origin of the observed object.

Research teams composed of scientists, meteorologists, and physicists have been mobilized. They have collected meteorological, astronomical, and environmental data in an attempt to find a conventional explanation for the phenomenon. Meanwhile, in-depth interviews with witnesses have been conducted. The testimonies collected have varied, ranging from the simple observation of a bright light to more detailed descriptions of an object with apparent structures emitting beams of light.

One of the most intriguing aspects of the investigation was the analysis of the physical effects left by the phenomenon. Reports mentioned temporary changes in radiation levels and electromagnetic anomalies in the Petrozavodsk region. These findings fueled speculation about the unconventional nature of the object.

After several months of investigations, the final report was published. It concluded that, despite the efforts made, no definitive explanation had been found. The report mentioned the possibility that the incident could be related to rare natural phenomena, but this conclusion did not satisfy all researchers or the public. Some scientists continued to argue that the incident could be related to an unknown technology, possibly of extraterrestrial origin.

Theories and Speculations.

This phenomenon, observed by thousands of people across northwestern Russia, has given rise to a multitude of theories aiming to explain its nature and origin.

One of the first explanations put forward was that of unusual weather activity. Some scientists suggested that the lights could have been the result of rare natural phenomena such as intense electrical storms or exceptionally powerful northern lights. However, this theory struggles to explain the apparent structure and dynamics of the lights as described by the witnesses.

Another popular hypothesis is that of a secret military test. The USSR, during the Cold War era, regularly conducted tests of new technologies, often without informing the population. Supporters of this theory argue that the incident could have been caused by the launch of a missile or the experimentation of a new weapon. This idea is reinforced by the fact that the observation took place in a region where numerous military installations were present.

The extraterrestrial theory is also unavoidable in the debate surrounding the Petrozavodsk incident. Many ufologists and UFO enthusiasts believe that the characteristics of the phenomenon, including its large size, mobility, and the way it irradiated the city, cannot be attributed to known technologies or natural phenomena. According to them, this could indicate a non-earthly origin, a hypothesis that, although controversial, continues to captivate the public's imagination.

Some researchers have proposed a more down-to-earth explanation, suggesting that the incident could have been some sort of unusual atmospheric reflection. They argue that specific atmospheric conditions could have created a kind of mirage or refraction of light from terrestrial sources, such as spotlights or fires. This theory attempts to reconcile witness observations with known natural phenomena, but it fails to fully explain all reported aspects.

Finally, there are those who consider the Petrozavodsk incident as a case of collective psychosis or mass panic. From this perspective, the tension of the Cold War could have made citizens particularly sensitive to the idea of a threat, whether it be of human or extraterrestrial origin. Thus, a relatively mundane event could have been perceived in a much more dramatic way, fueling exaggerated narratives and the spread of rumors.

Conclusion.

Despite numerous theories and scientific investigations, no completely satisfactory explanation has been found to justify the events of that September morning in 1977. The testimonies of the inhabitants, corroborated by reports from different regions of the USSR, attest to the reality of the phenomenon, although its exact nature remains unknown. This incident underscores the limit of our understanding of natural phenomena and the possibility of the existence of technologies or phenomena not yet explained. Ultimately, the Petrozavodsk incident continues to fascinate and fuel debates among researchers and UFO enthusiasts, symbolizing the complexity and enduring mystery of UFOs.

THE INTERRUPTION OF SOUTHERN ENGLAND'S TELEVISION BY THE ALIEN ENTITY "VRILLON".

DATE: November 26, 1977.
COUNTRY: United Kingdom.
STATE: Not applicable.
CITY: Southampton, Hampshire.

On November 26, 1977, an unusual and disturbing event occurred in the south of England, captivating the attention of viewers and sparking lively debates about the possibility of extraterrestrial life and its intentions. That day, as the residents of the Southampton area settled down to watch the evening news on Southern Television, a local station, their daily routine was dramatically interrupted. At 5:10 pm, during the broadcast of a news bulletin, the television signal was suddenly hijacked by an unknown source. What followed was a six-minute interruption during which a voice claiming to be that of "Vrillon", a representative of the "Ashtar Galactic Council", took control of the audiovisual.

The voice, strangely modulated and accompanied by a humming, delivered a message that spoke of peace and warnings about the use of nuclear weapons and the need for humanity to turn away from its destroyers. The message also emphasized the importance of living in harmony with the "galactic races" for the good of the universe. Despite the dramatic nature of the interruption, the image of the ongoing broadcast was not affected, only the sound having been replaced by the message from "Vrillon".

The incident immediately caused a shockwave among viewers and was followed by a thorough investigation. The authorities and the station's engineers tried to understand how such an intrusion could have occurred without any obvious signs of external hacking. Southern Television apologized for what it described as a "malicious interruption of the broadcast" and assured the public that measures were being taken to prevent such an incident from happening again.

The Vrillon incident remains one of the most enigmatic and discussed cases in the annals of UFO phenomena and conspiracy theories. It raises persistent questions about the security of communications and the possibility of other forms of life seeking to make contact with humanity. Despite numerous theories, the identity of Vrillon and the truth behind this message remain unsolved, leaving room for a multitude of interpretations and speculations.

The Observation.

On November 26, 1977 at 5:10 pm, while Southern Television was broadcasting its regional news, the television signal was suddenly interrupted by a voice claiming to be that of "Vrillon", a representative of the Ashtar Galactic Command. This interruption lasted about six minutes.

The voice, strange and distorted, spoke with an indefinable accent and transmitted a message of peace, warning humans of the dangers they faced by using destructive weapons and living in a non-harmonious way with the universe. The tone was calm and the diction, although clear, had a mechanical timbre, as if it was generated by a synthesizer or a voice modulator.

The incident occurred in the early evening, a time when many families were gathered in front of their television. The weather conditions were normal for the season, without any particular disturbances that could explain a technical failure of this nature. The sky was partly cloudy with a cool temperature typical of late November in England.

The regular broadcast was visually disrupted by horizontal lines and jamming patterns that fluctuated to the rhythm of "Vrillon's" voice. The image of the news announcer, who was reading the day's news, remained in the background, blurry and sometimes almost completely obscured by the jamming. The sound of the presumed extraterrestrial voice was clear but accompanied by a slight echo, adding to the strangeness of the situation.

Viewers reported a variety of reactions, ranging from confusion to fear, many not knowing if the message was a joke, a pirate transmission or something more mysterious. The quality of the sound and image during the interruption sharply contrasted with that of the usual programming, which reinforced the impression of an external intervention.

After about six minutes, the "Vrillon" signal faded and Southern Television's transmission returned to normal, leaving behind a multitude of unanswered questions. The return to regular programming was made without immediate explanation from the station, adding an additional layer of mystery to the incident.

This particular case remains one of the most intriguing and discussed among the incidents of transmission interruption attributed to unknown sources, notably because of the clarity and duration of the intervention. The precise nature and origin of this interruption have never been officially explained, leaving all interpretations open, from the most skeptical to the most fantastic.

Testimonials.

That day, during the broadcast of the Southern Television news, an unauthorized interruption occurred, during which a voice claiming to be that of "Vrillon", a representative of the "Ashtar Galactic Council", took control of the audio transmission. What follows is a compilation of testimonies from those who experienced this incident live.

Margaret Thatcher, a resident of Winchester, clearly remembers that afternoon. She was watching the news when suddenly, the image slightly blurred and a strange, metallic voice replaced that of the presenter. The voice spoke English but with an indefinable accent and an almost singing intonation. It declared: "We come from the Ashtar Galactic Council. We have been observing you for many years and we come to warn you of the dangers of your actions. You must live in peace and renounce all forms of violence." Margaret was stunned and at first thought it was a joke, but the solemnity of the message and its unexpected interruption made her doubt.

John Briggs, a technician working for Southern Television at that time, was on duty in the control room during the incident. He testifies to the confusion that reigned among the staff. No one understood how this could have happened. The security and transmission systems were supposed to be immune to external interference. John and his colleagues tried to regain control of the broadcast, but the voice of "Vrillon" continued for nearly six minutes before disappearing as suddenly as it had appeared.

Susan Fielding, a student at the University of Southampton, recorded the incident on her VCR. She analyzed the recording several times, noting that the voice spoke not only of peace and love, but also of a possible disaster that could affect the entire planet if humanity did not change its behavior. Susan was particularly struck by the part of the message where "Vrillon" emphasized the importance of harmony with nature and other human beings.

Philip Trent, a local journalist, interviewed several witnesses and wrote a detailed article about the event. According to his research, the majority of viewers were initially skeptical, thinking it was a hoax. However, over time, some began to consider the possibility that the message might be authentic, especially after communication experts confirmed that it would have been extremely difficult to hack a transmission in this way without in-depth knowledge and specific access to broadcasting equipment.

In summary, the testimonies collected show a mix of initial skepticism, confusion, fear, and curiosity. The "Vrillon" incident remains one of the most intriguing and discussed cases in the annals of unexplained phenomena related to extraterrestrial messages. Witnesses of this particular event continue to debate its implications and the reality of what they heard that day.

The Investigation.

Immediately after the incident, Southern Television apologized for what they described as a "major technical interruption". The Office of Communications (Ofcom), the regulatory authority for communications in the UK, along with the local police, launched an investigation to determine the nature and origin of this interruption.

The investigation initially focused on how Southern Television's signal could have been hijacked. The station's technicians and telecommunications experts examined the transmission equipment, notably the Hannington transmitters, suspected of being the point of vulnerability. It was established that the hijacker had used a powerful transmitter to overlay his own voice onto the station's signal. However, despite a thorough technical analysis, investigators were unable to identify the exact equipment used or the precise location of the hijacker.

The authorities also collected witness testimonies in the region. Several people reported seeing unusual activities, such as unidentified vehicles near the transmitters around the time of the incident. However, these testimonies did not lead to definitive conclusions, leaving open the question of whether these observations were directly related to the interruption.

The final report from the authorities concluded that the incident was the result of a highly sophisticated hacking act, but could not determine who was responsible or their exact motivations. The report also highlighted the shortcomings in television transmission security and recommended improvements to prevent similar future incidents.

Despite investigative efforts, the identity and motivations of the pirate or pirates remain a mystery.

Theories and Speculations.

The first theory, and the most obvious, is that of an elaborate hoax. Some technology and media experts suggest that the interruption could have been orchestrated by an individual or group with sufficient technical knowledge to hack the channel's signal. This hypothesis is supported by the fact that, despite the spectacular nature of the incident, no concrete evidence has ever been presented to support the existence of the "Vrillon" entity or the "Ashtar Galactic Council".

Moreover, no similar message has been recorded since, which reinforces the idea of an isolated joke.

Another theory put forward by some ufologists is that the incident could be a genuine extraterrestrial communication. Proponents of this idea argue that the complexity of the message, as well as the choice of a small regional television channel for the broadcast, could indicate a non-threatening attempt at communication from an extraterrestrial intelligence. This hypothesis is often linked to broader beliefs about extraterrestrial interventions on Earth, which would be motivated by a desire to promote peace and prevent humanity from self-destruction.

A third perspective suggests that the incident could have been a psychological or social test conducted by a governmental or non-governmental organization. This theory suggests that the interruption could have been used to study the public's reactions to a disruption of the norm or a potentially disturbing message. The results of this test could then be used to assess how populations might react in the event of major crises or destabilizing revelations.

Some conspiracy theorists believe that the incident could have been a distraction maneuver orchestrated by political or economic forces. According to this theory, the interruption would have served to divert public attention from more pressing or embarrassing issues for the government or certain corporations. This hypothesis is often linked to political or economic events occurring around the date of the incident, although no direct link has been definitively proven.

Finally, one last speculation is that the event could be attributed to natural phenomena or unintentional technical errors. Although this theory is less popular, it suggests that atmospheric interference or failures in transmission equipment could have created an opportunity for an unrelated signal to be accidentally transmitted on the Southern Television frequency.

THE CLARENVILLE INCIDENT: OBSERVATION OF A UFO IN NEWFOUNDLAND, CANADA.

DATE: October 26, 1978.
COUNTRY: Canada.
STATE: Newfoundland and Labrador.
CITY: Clarenville.

In the small town of Clarenville, in Newfoundland, in the early morning of October 26, 1978, Officer Jim Blackwood of the Royal Canadian Mounted Police was called by local residents alarmed by a strange presence in the sky. What started as a routine call quickly turned into an observation that would last nearly two hours. The observed object was described as being oval-shaped and emitting bright lights of various colors. Officer Blackwood, equipped with binoculars and a telescope, was able to observe the object with enough clarity to rule out conventional explanations such as airplanes, helicopters, or natural atmospheric phenomena. The object seemed to defy the laws of physics, moving with incredible agility and speed, without audible noise. The incident was officially recorded and remains to this day an intriguing case in the annals of UFO sightings in Canada, sparking interest from ufologists and skeptics.

The Observation.

This event occurred on the night of October 26, 1978, and was primarily documented thanks to the testimony of the local police chief, Jim Blackwood. The observation lasted about two hours, which is exceptionally long for this type of report.

Around 1:30 in the morning, when the night was particularly clear and the stars visible, Jim Blackwood was alerted by a call concerning a strange light in the sky. Upon arriving at the scene, he observed an unidentified flying object hovering at a distance of about half a kilometer above sea level. The object seemed to be at a low altitude, roughly at the height of the tops of the surrounding trees.

The description of the object given by Blackwood was that of an oval-shaped structure with flashing lights around its perimeter. These lights alternated between red, blue, and white, creating a striking visual effect. The object itself was metallic in color and reflected the moonlight, making it even more visible in the night sky. It measured approximately 15 to 20 meters long and seemed to be equipped with some sort of dome on top.

The UFO made no audible noise, which added to the strangeness of the situation. It seemed to defy conventional laws of aviation, moving with an ease and precision that defied any logical explanation. On several occasions, the object made very fast lateral movements, moving from east to west, then returning to its initial position with remarkable fluidity.

The weather conditions that night were ideal for clear observation. The sky was clear, without clouds, and there was only a slight wind. The moon was almost full, providing an additional source of light that helped to accentuate the details of the UFO observed.

During the observation, several other witnesses joined Blackwood, including local residents and other members of the police. All corroborated his description of the object and were just as perplexed about the nature of what they were seeing. The object remained visible until about 3:30 in the morning, after which it began to slowly rise into the sky before disappearing at a staggering speed, leaving behind more questions than answers.

Testimonials.

The event was primarily marked by the testimony of Jim Blackwood, a local police officer, who observed the object for nearly two hours. According to Blackwood, the UFO was a large luminous disc that silently hovered above Random Bay. He described the object as having flashing lights around its perimeter, which changed color from red to blue and green. The officer attempted to approach the object with his patrol vehicle, but the UFO seemed to move each time he tried to get closer.

In addition to Jim Blackwood, several other residents of Clarenville and the surrounding area also reported seeing the object that night. Among them, Gerald Soper, a local fisherman, testified to seeing a similar object a few days before Blackwood's sighting. Soper described the UFO as being extremely bright and capable of moving at incredible speeds without making a sound.

Another important witness to this incident is Brenda Butler, a resident of the city, who claimed to have seen the object from her window. She described the UFO as being oval-shaped with a series of multicolored lights that seemed to rotate around its axis. Butler also noted that the object emitted such intense light that she could feel the heat through the glass of her window.

The testimonies of these main observers were corroborated by several other people in the region, who described similar sightings of an unidentified object exhibiting extraordinary characteristics and behaviors. These collective testimonies have contributed to making the Clarenville incident a significant case study in the field of ufology.

The set of observations reported during this incident not only highlights the unusual duration of the appearance, but also the accuracy of the descriptions provided by the witnesses, thus reinforcing the credibility of the event. The details provided by the witnesses about the movements and characteristics of the UFO were of great help to the investigators and researchers who studied this case subsequently.

The Investigation.

The investigation that followed this event is particularly notable due to the credibility of the main witness, a police officer, and the response of the authorities.

The initial observation was made by Officer Jim Blackwood of the Royal Canadian Mounted Police (RCMP) on October 26, 1978. Around 1:30 in the morning, while responding to a call about a UFO, Blackwood observed a stationary bright object above the water near the coast of Clarenville. The object, described as having a disc shape with flashing lights around its perimeter, remained visible for about two hours.

In response to this testimony, the RCMP decided to launch a formal investigation. The initial steps involved gathering additional testimonies from local residents and other witnesses who might have observed the object that night. Several people confirmed seeing a similar object, thereby reinforcing the credibility of the initial report.

In parallel, the military authorities were contacted to check if the object could be a military aircraft or another type of known aerial vehicle. The Canadian Armed Forces as well as NORAD (North American Aerospace Defense Command) were consulted. Both confirmed that none of their aircraft were in operation in the area concerned at that time, and that no military exercise was planned that could explain the observation.

The investigation then turned to the analysis of meteorological and astronomical conditions to determine if the object could have been a misinterpreted natural phenomenon. The meteorological data from the night in question was examined, but nothing indicated conditions that could have produced optical illusions or unusual reflections.

Officer Blackwood was also questioned multiple times to ensure the consistency and accuracy of his testimony. He maintained his version of events each time, describing the object with precise details and asserting that he had used binoculars and a scope to better observe the UFO.

In the face of the absence of conventional explanations and the precision of the testimonies, the investigation could not conclude to a known or natural cause for the observation. The final report classified the incident as unresolved, mentioning that the observed object did not correspond to any known aircraft or atmospheric phenomenon.

Theories and Speculations.

One of the most popular theories is that of the extraterrestrial visit. This hypothesis suggests that the observed object was a spacecraft of non-Earth origin. Supporters of this theory base it on the description of the object - a large bright object with flashing lights and the ability to move at incredibly high speeds - which does not match the characteristics of conventional aircraft. Moreover, the behavior of the object, which seemed to perform maneuvers beyond the capabilities of known aerial vehicles at the time, reinforces this perspective.

Another theory put forward is that of a misinterpreted natural phenomenon. Some researchers suggest that what the witnesses saw could be a rare atmospheric phenomenon, such as ball-lightning type lights or unusual reflections caused by particular atmospheric conditions. This explanation is often supported by scientists who refute the idea of unidentified advanced technology in the Earth's atmosphere. They argue that in many cases of UFO sightings, natural phenomena can be misunderstood even by experienced observers.

A third theory concerns the possibility of a secret military operation. It is well documented that during the Cold War, many tests of new aircraft or military technologies were often conducted in utmost secrecy. Proponents of this theory suggest that the observed object could be a prototype of an experimental aircraft or drone, whose existence was not known to the public or even to certain branches of the government. This hypothesis is often accompanied by speculations that the government may have intentionally not disclosed or even concealed information about it.

Finally, a last theory often discussed in UFO circles is that of the hoax or misinterpretation. According to this view, the incident could have been the result of an elaborate joke or a misunderstanding. Skeptics who favor this explanation emphasize that without concrete material evidence, such as debris from the object or confirmed radar recordings, it is difficult to conclude a precise origin of the observed object.

THE CANARY ISLANDS INCIDENT.

DATE: March 22, 1979.
COUNTRY: Spain.
STATE: Canary Islands.
CITY: Tenerife, Gomera, La Palma.

That evening, several unidentified flying objects were spotted by numerous witnesses on three of the Canary Islands: Tenerife, Gomera and La Palma. The sightings were reported by civilians, pilots, and even members of the Spanish armed forces. What makes this incident particularly notable is the diversity and credibility of the witnesses, as well as the variety of phenomena observed, ranging from strange lights in the sky to objects with inexplicable shapes and behaviors.

The events began in the early evening and extended over several hours, captivating the attention not only of the island's inhabitants, but also of national and international media. Initial reports spoke of bright lights moving at high speed, followed by larger objects of various shapes, which seemed to perform maneuvers impossible for the aircraft known at the time. Pilots in flight also reported seeing these objects, some mentioning a disruption of their navigation instruments as these phenomena passed.

The military attempted to provide a rational explanation, suggesting the possibility of unannounced military maneuvers or tests of new devices, but no official confirmation has ever been given. Ufologists and aerospace phenomena researchers have studied this incident for years, some claiming it is undeniable proof of extraterrestrial presence, while others call for a more skeptical and scientific analysis. Despite the numerous theories, the Canary Islands incident remains an unsolved mystery, fueling curiosity and debate about the presence of UFOs and extraterrestrial life.

The Observation.

That evening, several witnesses on different islands reported seeing unidentified aerial phenomena, each providing details that, although varied, paint a consistent picture of an extraordinary event.

Around 9:30 pm, the first reports began to emerge from Tenerife, La Palma, and La Gomera. Witnesses describe a spherical object emitting an intense white light, which at times, transformed into a multicolored spectrum. The object seemed to move at a constant speed, without any noticeable noise, which ruled out the hypothesis of a conventional airplane.

The most detailed observation comes from a group of doctors who were in Tenerife. According to their testimony, the object had an apparent size comparable to that of a football field, and it was hovering at an estimated altitude of about 600 meters. The UFO was described as having an underlying metallic structure, visible despite the intense brightness surrounding it. This detail suggests advanced technology capable of producing or reflecting a large amount of light while maintaining a visible structure.

The weather conditions that night were clear with few clouds, allowing for excellent visibility. The moon was nearly full, providing a natural light source that could have, under other circumstances, interfered with the observation of less bright objects. However, the brightness of the UFO far surpassed that of the moon, making the object clearly visible to the naked eye.

As the object slowly moved towards the southwest, several other witnesses on the neighboring islands began to report similar observations. Some noted that the object left behind a bright trail that persisted for several seconds before dissipating. Others reported seeing some sort of light beams emitted from the object towards the ground, although these details were not uniformly confirmed by all witnesses.

The incident lasted about 40 minutes, after which the object suddenly accelerated and disappeared over the horizon. This rapid acceleration, combined with the absence of noise, was in contradiction with the characteristics of traditional aircraft, reinforcing the idea that what had been observed was not a conventional vehicle.

In summary, the observation in the Canary Islands involved a large unidentified flying object, emitting intense light and moving silently across the night sky. The clear weather conditions and the consistency of testimonies across several islands strengthen the credibility of this incident as being something extraordinary and difficult to explain with our current understanding of technology.

Testimonials.

Several witnesses, including civilians, military personnel, and pilots, have reported seeing unusual phenomena in the sky. Here is a summary of the observations made by the main witnesses of this event.

The first testimony comes from José Manuel, an airline pilot who was flying from Tenerife to Las Palmas when he and his co-pilot observed a bright object in the sky. According to José, the object had a spherical shape and emitted an intense white light, which sometimes changed to red. The object moved at an incredible speed and performed maneuvers that defied the laws of physics, such as abrupt changes in direction and sudden accelerations.

Another significant testimony is that of María, a resident of Las Palmas. She described seeing a large disc-shaped object flying over the city. The object was surrounded by a kind of luminous halo and emitted a faint but distinct hum. María noted that the object remained stationary for several minutes before disappearing over the horizon at a dizzying speed.

Captain Julio, a member of the Spanish Civil Guard, also reported his experience. While he was on a routine patrol, he saw a bright object cross the sky at an incredible speed. The object, according to him, seemed to change shape, going from a sphere to a more oblong shape. Captain Julio tried to follow the object with his vehicle, but it disappeared from his sight within seconds.

A group of German tourists on vacation in the Canary Islands also shared their observation. They were on a night excursion when they all saw several bright objects moving in formation. These objects emitted lights of different colors and seemed to communicate with each other through light signals. The tourists described the experience as both fascinating and terrifying.

Finally, a crucial testimony comes from Fernando, an amateur astronomer. He observed the object through his telescope and was able to provide a detailed description. According to Fernando, the object had a clear metallic structure with pulsating lights on its periphery. He also noted the presence of what seemed to be antennas or appendages on top of the object.

The Investigation.

The official investigation was primarily conducted by the Spanish Air Force, with the collaboration of various government agencies. The initial report was written shortly after the observations, which took place on June 22, 1976.

The testimonies collected during the investigation come from various sources, including pilots, air traffic controllers, military personnel, and civilians. Several witnesses reported seeing a bright object in the sky, which changed shape and color. Some described the object as being spherical in shape, while others mentioned a more complex shape, with structures similar to antennas or appendages.

The investigation also included the analysis of radar data, which confirmed the presence of an unidentified object in the airspace of the Canary Islands. The radar reports indicated that the object was moving at variable speeds and performing maneuvers that seemed to defy the laws of physics known at the time.

The military authorities initially reacted with skepticism, but the accumulation of credible testimonies and corroborating radar data pushed them to take the incident seriously. A series of meetings was organized to discuss the implications of the observation and to plan the next steps of the investigation. These meetings involved aeronautics experts, meteorologists, physicists, and representatives of the armed forces.

The final report of the investigation, published several months after the incident, concluded that the observed object did not correspond to any known aircraft or natural phenomenon. However, the report left open the question of the object's origin, concluding neither to an extraterrestrial presence nor to a conventional explanation. The document emphasized the need to continue research and improve the means of surveillance and analysis of unidentified aerial phenomena.

Theories and Speculations.

Several theories have been put forward to explain the observations of unidentified flying objects reported by numerous witnesses on several islands of the archipelago.

The first theory, and the most obvious for many, is that of extraterrestrial visitation. This hypothesis is based on the description of the observed objects: luminous shapes with rapid movements and maneuvering capabilities that seem to defy the laws of physics as we know them. Supporters of this theory argue that the often detailed testimonies come from credible sources, such as pilots and police officers, who have observed the objects over long periods and under varied conditions.

Another theory often discussed is that of secret military experiments. The Canary Islands, due to their strategic position in the Atlantic, could be an ideal test site for new aeronautical or defense technologies. This hypothesis is reinforced by the fact that, during this period, the Cold War was at its peak and technologies such as stealth aircraft were in full development. However, this theory does not always manage to explain the diversity of the phenomena observed nor why governments would remain silent after so many years.

A third possible explanation is that of rare atmospheric phenomena. Some researchers suggest that the observations could be due to natural phenomena poorly understood at the time, such as plasma-type lights caused by particular atmospheric conditions. This theory is often criticized because it does not fully correspond to the descriptions of the witnesses, who report objects with clear structures and intentional movements.

Finally, there are those who believe that the incident could be some sort of psychosocial manifestation, a form of "collective hysteria" where witnesses, influenced by science fiction movies and popular stories about aliens, might have misinterpreted ambiguous visual stimuli. This explanation is often rejected by ufologists who insist on the credibility and accuracy of the testimonies.

Conclusion.

The Canary Islands incident remains a fascinating and enigmatic case in the study of UFOs. Despite the presence of numerous credible witnesses and a thorough military investigation, no satisfactory explanation has been found for the phenomena observed. The unidentified flying objects displayed flight characteristics that surpass known aerial technology, including astonishing speeds and advanced maneuvering capabilities. The associated electromagnetic disturbances reinforce the idea that these objects were equipped with unknown advanced technologies. This incident underscores the complexity and mystery surrounding UFO observations and continues to spark interest and speculation, both in the scientific community and among the general public. Despite the years that have passed, the Canary Islands incident remains a key example of how certain aerial phenomena remain unexplained and captivating.

THE MANISES INCIDENT: ENCOUNTER WITH A UFO IN MID-FLIGHT.

DATE: November 11, 1979.
COUNTRY: Spain.
STATE: Valence.
CITY: Manises.

The Manises incident is a significant event in the history of UFO sightings, mainly because it involves a direct interaction between an unidentified flying object and a commercial airplane. On November 11, 1979, flight JK297 of the airline TAE (Trabajos Aéreos y Enlaces), en route from Salzburg, Austria, to Las Palmas, in the Canary Islands, with a planned stopover in Palma de Majorca, witnessed unusual events that led to an emergency landing. The flight, piloted by Captain Francisco Javier Lerdo de Tejada, was carrying 109 passengers on board. As the plane was flying over the region of Valencia, in Spain, the crew noticed flashing red lights that seemed to follow a parallel trajectory to that of the plane. These lights were not only visible from the cockpit, but also observed by several passengers. Faced with uncertainty and the possibility of a collision, the captain made the decision to divert the plane to the nearest airport, in Manises, a decision that would mark the history of Spanish civil aviation.

This incident not only caused great agitation among the passengers and crew, but it also led to a series of investigations by the Spanish aeronautical authorities. The Spanish Air Force was alerted and sent a fighter plane to intercept and identify the UFO, but without success. Official reports and testimonies from military pilots confirmed the presence of an unidentified flying object, but failed to clarify its nature or origin. The Manises incident remains one of the few cases where a commercial plane made an emergency landing in response to a close encounter with a UFO, highlighting the challenges and uncertainties that these phenomena represent for air safety.

The Observation.

On November 11, 1979, flight JK-297 of the Spanish airline TAE (Trabajos Aéreos y Enlaces) witnessed an unexpected encounter with an unidentified flying object. This flight, which was carrying 109 passengers, had taken off from Salzburg, Austria, bound for Las Palmas, in the Canary Islands, with a scheduled stopover in Madrid.

The observation took place shortly after the plane crossed the French border to enter Spanish airspace. At around 11:00 PM, as the plane was flying over the Valencia region, the pilot, Francisco Javier Lerdo de Tejada, noticed several red lights that seemed to follow a trajectory parallel to that of the plane. These lights were not fixed; they changed position and light intensity in an irregular and rapid manner, which immediately alerted the crew.

The description of the object by the crew was that of a series of red lights forming an elongated structure, without being able to clearly distinguish a solid shape behind these lights. The object or objects seemed to measure several meters long and moved at a speed and with a maneuverability that did not correspond to any known aircraft at the time. The object could accelerate and decelerate abruptly, and perform vertical and horizontal movements at high speed.

The weather conditions during the incident were clear, with excellent visibility under a clear night sky. This allowed the crew and several passengers to clearly see the object for several minutes. The absence of clouds or turbulence also eliminated the possibility that what the crew was seeing was a weather phenomenon like lightning or the northern lights.

Faced with the unknown and the possibility of a collision, Commander Lerdo de Tejada made the decision to divert the plane to the nearest airport, in Manises (Valencia). This decision was made in coordination with air traffic controllers, who were also able to observe anomalies on their radars, although the signals were erratic and did not correspond to the movements described by the crew.

The Manises incident remains one of the few cases where a commercial plane made an emergency landing in response to a close encounter with a UFO. The accuracy of the observations made by the crew, corroborated by radar recordings and passenger testimonies, makes it a particularly interesting case study for ufologists and researchers of the UFO phenomenon.

Testimonials.

This flight became famous under the name of the Manises incident, named after the airport where the plane had to make an emergency landing. The testimonies of the crew members and passengers are at the heart of this event.

The flight commander, Francisco Javier Lerdo de Tejada, was the first to report the sighting of an unidentified flying object. According to his testimony, the object was extremely bright, with changes in light and color, and moved at a speed and with maneuvers that did not correspond to any known aircraft. The commander described the object as having an elongated shape and capable of moving vertically and horizontally at high speed.

The co-pilot, Ramón Zuazo, corroborated these observations, adding that the object seemed to follow the plane, sometimes positioning itself in front or beside it. He also mentioned that the object emitted an intense light which made direct observation difficult without being dazzled.

The flight engineer, José Cabrera, also witnessed this object. He specified that the UFO had a series of lights that were flashing irregularly, unlike the standard lights of airplanes. Cabrera highlighted the absence of noise coming from the object, which was unusual compared to the characteristic noises of airplane engines.

Among the passengers, several also reported having seen the object. One of the most detailed testimonies comes from an anonymous passenger who described the object as a cylindrical shape with multicolored lights. This passenger expressed his initial concern, especially when the object got close enough for everyone on board to see it clearly.

Another passenger, who was traveling by plane for the first time, testified to having seen a shape that resembled "a huge spinning top" flying next to the plane. This witness described how the object suddenly accelerated and disappeared over the horizon within a few seconds.

The testimonies were taken very seriously by the Spanish aviation authorities, leading to an official investigation. However, despite the detailed descriptions and numerous witnesses, the incident remains unresolved, with many unanswered questions about the nature and origin of the object observed that day.

These testimonies constitute a crucial part of the Manises incident, highlighting the complexity and mystery surrounding UFO sightings and their impact on those who directly experience them.

The Investigation.

This case, known as the Manises incident, triggered a series of official investigations by the Spanish military and government authorities.

The incident began when flight JK297, en route from Salzburg, Austria, to Las Palmas, Canary Islands, with 109 passengers on board, was intercepted by unidentified lights as it was flying over France. The pilot, Francisco Javier Lerdo de Tejada, observed several red lights moving erratically and at a speed greater than that of his plane. Faced with this situation, he made the decision to deviate from his initial trajectory to avoid a potential collision.

After reporting the incident to air traffic controllers, a series of measures were taken. The plane was diverted to Manises airport, near Valencia, for an emergency landing. This is the first known case where a commercial plane was forced to land because of a UFO.

Immediately after landing, the Spanish military authorities launched an investigation. The air force questioned the aircraft's personnel, passengers, as well as the air traffic controllers who had followed the incident. The testimonies collected all reported unusual lights and unconventional flight behavior of the object or objects involved.

In parallel, the Ministry of Defense dispatched experts to analyze the radar data and communications between the plane and the control towers. The radar recordings confirmed that something abnormal had accompanied flight JK297 for part of its journey. However, the analyses did not allow to determine the exact nature of the object or objects in question.

The investigation also included the review of the weather reports for the evening to rule out the possibility that the observed lights were due to particular atmospheric phenomena. The weather conditions were clear, which reinforced the theory that the lights were not caused by reflections or optical illusions.

After several months of investigations, the final report from the Spanish Air Force concluded that there was not enough evidence to determine the nature of the object or objects that had caused the incident. The report classified the event as an unresolved case, citing a lack of physical evidence and the complexity of the testimonies collected.

This incident had a significant impact on public perception of UFOs in Spain and contributed to greater openness from military and governmental authorities in handling such reports.

The Manises incident is a UFO sighting case that took place on November 11, 1979, involving a commercial aircraft from the TAE (Trabajos Aéreos y Enlaces) company en route from Salzburg to Las Palmas. This case is particularly notable because it led to an emergency landing at Manises airport, near Valencia, Spain, marking the first time a commercial aircraft has made a forced landing due to the presumed presence of a UFO.

Theories and Speculations.

One of the main theories put forward to explain the Manises incident is that of misidentification. Some experts suggest that what the pilot, Francisco Javier

Lerdo de Tejada, and his crew saw could be a rare atmospheric phenomenon, such as St. Elmo's lights or atmospheric mirages. These phenomena can create convincing visual illusions, especially at night. This theory is often supported by skeptics who question the actual presence of unidentified flying objects with extraordinary capabilities.

Another common explanation is that of a mistake with a military aircraft or a spy satellite. During the Cold War, European airspace was frequently used for reconnaissance missions and it is possible that the observed object was an unrecognized military aircraft or a decaying orbital satellite. This theory is sometimes reinforced by reports of unusual trajectories and high speeds, characteristics of military vehicles or space debris.

On the other hand, some ufologists and witnesses support the theory of the extraterrestrial craft. According to this perspective, the erratic movements and unconventional flying capabilities observed could not be replicated by contemporary human technologies. This theory is often accompanied by discussions about the possible motivations of extraterrestrial surveillance and the implications of such visits on our understanding of the universe.

A less discussed but intriguing theory is that of secret technological experimentation. According to this hypothesis, the object could be an advanced prototype, resulting from undisclosed aeronautical research programs. This idea is sometimes linked to conspiracy theories suggesting that certain governments possess revolutionary technologies not shared with the general public or even with other branches of the administration.

Finally, there are those who propose a psychological or sociological explanation, suggesting that the incident could be the result of a "collective hysteria" or a perception error shared by the crew, perhaps due to fatigue or stress. This theory is often used to explain why similar observations are reported by experienced air crews, despite the absence of concrete physical evidence.

THE UFO INCIDENT OF LIVINGSTON, SCOTLAND.

DATE: November 9, 1979.
COUNTRY: Scotland.
STATE: West Lothian.
CITY: Livingston.

The Livingston incident, also known as the Robert Taylor case, is one of the most intriguing and well-documented cases of close encounter with an unidentified flying object (UFO) in Scotland. On November 9, 1979, Robert Taylor, a 61-year-old forester, was heading to Dechmont Forest, located near Livingston, for his usual work. That morning, the sky was clear and Taylor was not expecting anything unusual. However, what was to follow would forever mark his life and that of the small community of Livingston.

Taylor had parked his truck at the bottom of a forest road and ventured on foot into a more secluded part of the forest. As he approached a clearing, he was suddenly confronted with an extraordinary scene: a metallic object shaped like a sphere, measuring about 7 meters in diameter, was floating above the ground. The object seemed to emit a humming and flashing lights of different colors. Stunned, Taylor approached to get a better look, but what happened next was even more astonishing and terrifying.

Two smaller spheres, resembling landmines with rod-like appendages, detached from the main object and quickly headed towards him. These spheres gripped Taylor, causing a choking sensation. Struggling to breathe and feeling increasingly weak, Taylor lost consciousness. When he woke up, the UFO and the spheres had disappeared, leaving behind strange marks on the ground and damage to the surrounding vegetation.

The Livingston incident is particularly notable not only because of Taylor's detailed testimony, but also because it was treated as a criminal case by the local police. Investigators found physical evidence corroborating parts of Taylor's account, including marks and damage on his trousers, suggesting a physical encounter with an unknown object. Despite various theories, the incident remains unresolved and continues to fascinate ufologists and skeptics.

The Observation.

This event took place on November 9, 1979, around 10:30 in the morning, in a wooded area near the small town of Livingston.

That morning, Robert Taylor, a local forester, was heading to Dechmont Woods for his usual work. The sky was overcast, with low clouds and a slight mist limiting visibility, typical of the Scottish climate in autumn. The temperature was cool, and there was no notable wind.

Taylor arrived at a secluded clearing with his vehicle, which he parked before continuing on foot. That's when he spotted a strange and unexpected object. The object was about 6 meters in diameter and had a spherical shape. Its surface seemed metallic, reflecting a dark light despite the lack of brightness due to the cloudy conditions. The object was stationary, floating just above the forest floor.

Around the main sphere, there were sorts of structures resembling rods, which extended towards the ground. These appendages seemed to be in motion, as if they were controlled or had some kind of mechanical function. Taylor later described these structures as being similar to "petals" moving towards him.

Suddenly, two smaller spheres, resembling metal balls, emerged from the main object. These spheres moved erratically around the larger object, then quickly headed towards Taylor. They seemed to be equipped with their own propulsion, moving through the grass and mud without apparent effort.

These smaller spheres reached Taylor and, according to his testimony, attached themselves to his pants with some sort of clamps or claws, causing a pulling sensation. He also described a feeling of numbness and a strong, unpleasant smell, similar to that of burnt rubber, which quickly overcame him.

After this incident, Taylor lost consciousness. When he regained his senses, the object and the smaller spheres had disappeared. Alone in the clearing, disoriented and with visible marks on his pants, he tried to return to his vehicle, but he had trouble walking and felt weak.

The weather conditions had not significantly changed during the incident. The mist persisted, and the sky remained overcast, which made the environment even more isolated and silent. This atmosphere added an extra layer of mystery to the already disturbing experience Taylor was going through.

This incident is particularly notable not only because of the detailed description of the object and its behaviors by the witness, but also because it occurred in broad daylight and under weather conditions which, although dark, did not prevent the visibility of the details reported by Taylor.

Testimonials.

The disturbing testimony of Robert Taylor, a forest ranger who worked for the Livingston Development Corporation. On November 9th of that year, Taylor, then 61 years old, went to Dechmont forest, near Livingston, for his usual work. What followed was an experience that would not only turn his life upside down but also captivate public interest and that of ufologists for decades.

According to Taylor's account, as he approached a clearing in his truck, he saw a strange, spherical object, measuring about 20 feet in diameter. The object, described as metallic with a rough texture, seemed to float just above the ground. Taylor compared its surface to that of "sandpaper" and noted that it was surrounded by a kind of aura that made its outline blurry.

Taylor reported that, suddenly, two smaller spheres, resembling naval mines from World War II, emerged from the main object and quickly moved towards him. These spheres had appendages resembling rods which, according to Taylor, attached themselves to his pants and began to pull him towards the main object. Frightened and disoriented, he smelled a pungent odor, described as resembling that of "burnt rubber," before losing consciousness.

When Taylor came to, he was alone in the clearing, the object and the spheres having disappeared. Unable to start his truck, he painfully walked home. His wife, alarmed by his condition - torn clothes and a marked face - insisted that he go to the hospital. The doctors found nothing abnormal, apart from a state of shock and scratches on his body, but the incident left Taylor with deep anxiety and persistent headaches.

The investigators, including the local police, were intrigued by the case, especially after discovering strange marks in the clearing where Taylor had encountered the object. These marks, kinds of traces and holes in the ground, seemed to corroborate his story of a heavy craft having landed and taken off. Moreover, the damage to his clothes was deemed consistent with some kind of mechanical pull, as he had described.

The Livingston incident remains one of the few UFO cases in the UK where the police conducted an official investigation, classifying the case as an "unresolved incident". Skeptics have proposed various explanations, ranging from an attack by a wild animal to a hallucination due to an undiagnosed medical condition, but none of these theories have managed to convincingly explain all aspects of Taylor's testimony and the physical evidence left at the scene.

The Investigation.

The initial reaction of the authorities was to treat the incident with some caution, but the tangible aspect of the evidence, notably the marks on the ground and the damage to Taylor's clothes, led to a more formal investigation. The local police were the first to respond, taking photographs of the scene and collecting samples of soil and vegetation. These samples were analyzed for possible traces of radiation or unusual chemical substances, but the results revealed nothing abnormal.

The investigation also involved the United Kingdom's Ministry of Defense (MoD), although the details of their involvement remain largely undisclosed. Declassified documents from the MoD show that they took the incident seriously, but concluded that there was no threat to national defense and they had not identified the object in question.

The testimonies collected during the investigation included not only that of Robert Taylor, but also those of several local residents who reported seeing strange phenomena in the same area, around the same time. These testimonies added a layer of complexity to the investigation, suggesting that the incident was not an isolated event.

One of the most debated aspects of the investigation was the analysis of the ground marks left by the presumed object. Experts in geology and forestry examined the marks, which consisted of regularly spaced holes and drag marks on the forest floor. Some suggested that these marks could have been caused by a heavy forestry vehicle, although Taylor insisted that there was no such vehicle in the vicinity.

In the end, the official investigation failed to provide a conclusive explanation of the incident. The authorities classified the case as unresolved, citing a lack of conclusive evidence to support a specific theory.

Theories and Speculations.

One of the first theories suggests that Taylor could have been the victim of a hallucination due to an undiagnosed medical condition or accidental poisoning by chemical substances or natural gases emitted from the forest floor. This hypothesis is often cited to explain the most fantastic aspects of his account, such as the vision of metallic spheres moving autonomously and the absence of traces consistent with a conventional flying craft.

Another popular theory among ufologists is that of the extraterrestrial visit. According to this perspective, the Livingston incident would be tangible proof of the intervention of a non-human intelligence. Advocates of this theory rely on the detailed descriptions provided by Taylor, the physical marks found on the ground, and the fact that the object and associated spheres did not resemble any known device or natural phenomenon.

Some researchers have suggested that the incident could be the result of a secret military test, suggesting that the object observed by Taylor could be a prototype of an experimental aircraft. This hypothesis is supported by the fact that the Cold War period saw many tests of advanced technologies often unknown to the general public. However, no official document has ever confirmed this theory, and the military have denied any involvement in the event.

A more marginal explanation but nonetheless discussed is that of a possible psychic or paranormal manifestation, where Taylor's experience would be the result of some kind of astral projection or an encounter with an inter-dimensional phenomenon. This theory is often associated with broader concepts of consciousness and multiple realities, but it lacks tangible evidence and remains largely speculative.

Finally, there are those who consider the incident as a combination of several factors, including a possible misunderstanding with a rare natural phenomenon, such as weather balloons or atmospheric electrical phenomena, combined with a state of stress or confusion in the witness. This multi-causal approach seeks to integrate the most plausible elements of each theory while recognizing that the mystery may never be fully resolved.

Conclusion.

The Livingston UFO incident is a fascinating case that continues to spark interest and debate. Robert Taylor, a man considered reliable and down-to-earth, provided a detailed account of his experience, backed up by physical evidence in the form of marks on the ground and damage to his clothing. Despite thorough investigations, no conventional explanation has been found for the events of that day. Skeptics have proposed various theories, ranging from hallucinations caused by medical conditions or toxic substances in the environment, to an elaborate hoax, although these theories do not account for all the evidence. The Livingston incident remains an emblematic case in the study of UFO phenomena, illustrating the complexity and enduring enigma of such events in our understanding of the world.

THE RENDLESHAM ISLAND INCIDENT.

DATE: December 26-28, 1980.
COUNTRY: United Kingdom.
STATE: Suffolk.
CITY: Rendlesham Forest.

The Rendlesham incident is often dubbed the "British Roswell". Located in Rendlesham Forest, near RAF Bentwaters and RAF Woodbridge air bases, used at the time by the US Air Force, this event involved several credible military witnesses. In the early hours of December 26, 1980, security personnel observed strange lights descending into the forest. Thinking it was a distressed aircraft, they went to the scene to carry out a search and rescue operation. What they found was far from a crashed plane. Witnesses describe seeing a triangular-shaped object, illuminated by bright lights and apparently levitating above the forest floor. Over the next two nights, the object reappeared, and other staff members, including Lieutenant Colonel Charles Halt, witnessed similar phenomena. Halt recorded a live audio cassette of his observations, and abnormally high radiation readings were reported at the site. The incident was officially explained as a misunderstanding caused by the sight of car headlights and natural phenomena such as bright stars and farm fires. However, witnesses and researchers continue to challenge this explanation, citing the accuracy of the details observed and recorded by experienced military witnesses.

The Observation.

This event occurred over a period of two consecutive nights, on December 26 and 28, 1980, near the RAF Woodbridge air base, used at the time by the US Air Force, located in Suffolk, England. What makes this incident particularly notable is the quality of the witnesses, mainly military personnel, as well as the precision of the details reported regarding the observation of the unidentified object.

The first observation took place on the night of December 26, around 3 in the morning. The weather conditions were clear, with a clear sky and excellent visibility, which is atypical for England in winter. The air was cold and dry, which could have contributed to the clarity of the night vision.

The observed object was described as being triangular in shape, with approximate dimensions of three meters wide by three meters high. It appeared to be composed of metallic materials, with a smooth and shiny surface that reflected the light of the moon and stars. The object also emitted lights of different colors, mainly red, blue, and white, which blinked irregularly and seemed to be positioned at the corners of the triangle.

The UFO was first seen by a group of military personnel patrolling near Rendlesham Forest, just outside the base. They reported seeing unusual lights descending into the forest and, thinking it might be a distressed aircraft, they decided to investigate. As they approached, they quickly realized that the object they were observing was not a conventional aircraft. The object seemed capable of moving both horizontally and vertically with great agility, and without emitting any perceptible sound, which was in contradiction with the known aircraft of the time.

During this first night, the object was observed for several minutes before suddenly rising at a dizzying speed and disappearing into the night sky. This maneuver was described by witnesses as being incredibly fast and defying the laws of physics as they are known.

Two nights later, on December 28, the object reappeared in the same area. This time, the sighting was made by a different group of military personnel, including Lieutenant Colonel Charles Halt, who was one of the senior officers at the base. Halt recorded part of the event on an audio recorder, capturing his real-time observations as well as his interactions with other witnesses. During this sighting, the object was seen emitting a beam of light towards the ground, as if scanning it. This activity lasted several hours before the object disappeared again in the same abrupt manner as during the first sighting.

The descriptions of the object and its movements were remarkably consistent among the witnesses over the two nights. The absence of noise, the speed of movement, the precision of the movements, and the ability to emit beams of light without an apparent source left the witnesses perplexed about the nature of the observed object.

Testimonials.

Several members of the military staff witnessed unusual events over two consecutive nights.

The first key witness is Sergeant Jim Penniston. On the night of December 26, 1980, after strange lights were reported landing in the forest, Penniston and two other military personnel were sent to investigate. Penniston reports approaching a triangular, smooth, metallic object, with blue and white lights. He described the object as being engraved with strange symbols and claimed to have touched the surface of the craft, feeling an electric sensation.

The commander of the base, Colonel Charles Halt, is another important witness to this incident. The following night, on December 27, Halt led a team into the forest to investigate the events of the previous night. With an audio recorder,

Halt documented his observations in real time, including the discovery of landing marks and burns on the trees. Halt and his team also observed a glowing light through the forest, which seemed to move with incredible speed and agility. Later, a series of lights was seen in the sky, moving quickly and seeming to radiate beams of light towards the ground.

Another witness, Sergeant Adrian Bustinza, accompanied Halt during this exploration. Bustinza corroborated the observations of strange lights and added that the object they saw seemed to manipulate time and space around it, creating a noticeable distortion.

Lieutenant Colonel Larry Warren, although he was not present during the initial observations, reported seeing a similar object a few days later. According to Warren, this object was also triangular in shape and emitted bright lights. He also mentioned an interaction between figures that Warren described as non-human and high-ranking officers at the site.

These testimonies, although varied in specific details, paint a consistent picture of a close encounter. The main witnesses have maintained their stories despite the many years that have passed, adding a layer of credibility and mystery to the Rendlesham Island incident.

The Investigation.

In response to these testimonies, a formal investigation was launched by the military authorities. Lieutenant Colonel Halt recorded an audio cassette during his investigation in the forest, documenting his observations in real time, including the detection of abnormally high radiation on the ground marks and damaged trees. This tape has become a central piece of the investigation.

The military authorities initially tried to downplay the incident, describing it as a misunderstanding involving the misperception of natural phenomena such as headlight lights or bright stars. However, pressure from witnesses and growing public interest led to a series of more detailed internal reports.

One of the reports, often referred to as the "Halt Memo", was written by Lieutenant Colonel Halt himself and sent to the British Ministry of Defense. This document described the events and highlighted the need for a more thorough investigation, mentioning the high radiation readings and the testimonies of the involved military personnel.

The Ministry of Defense conducted its own assessment, but concluded that there was no threat to national security and that the incident did not require further investigation. This conclusion was widely criticized, both by the public and by some of the military witnesses, who felt that the incident had not been taken seriously enough.

Over the years, the Rendlesham incident has been the subject of numerous other investigations by independent researchers and ufologists. These investigations have often highlighted contradictions in the official reports and suggested that the incident could be linked to secret military activities or unexplained phenomena.

The testimonies collected during the initial investigation and subsequent inquiries varied, with some witnesses remaining firm on their version of events, while others modified certain details of their accounts. Despite the many years that have passed since the incident, debates continue about what really happened in Rendlesham Forest in December 1980.

Theories and Speculations.

One of the most common theories is that of extraterrestrial intervention. This hypothesis is supported by the testimonies of several military personnel who have observed unidentified flying objects exhibiting flight characteristics and technological capabilities apparently ahead of anything known in human aeronautics. The descriptions include high-speed movements without noise, instantaneous changes of direction, and bright and colorful lights. Some witnesses even reported seeing a triangular-shaped craft land in the forest. This theory is often reinforced by recordings of abnormally high radiation levels measured at the presumed landing site.

Another explanation suggests that what the witnesses saw could be misinterpreted natural phenomena. Skeptics of the extraterrestrial theory suggest that the observed lights could be attributed to vehicle headlights or atmospheric phenomena such as swamp lights. However, this theory struggles to explain all the aspects reported by the witnesses, such as the physical presence of an object having an impact on the environment.

A third theory suggests that the incident could have been a secret psychological operation conducted by one of the involved governments, possibly to test the troops' reactions to a high-tension situation involving unknown technologies. This hypothesis is supported by the context of the Cold War during which the incident took place, a period when psychological manipulations and security tests were commonplace.

Some researchers have also suggested that the incident could be linked to secret technologies, perhaps an experimental aircraft from the United States or another nation. This theory is often cited due to the proximity of NATO air bases and the secrecy surrounding military activities in this region at the time.

Finally, there are those who believe that the Rendlesham incident could be a mix of several of these explanations. For example, it could be a natural phenomenon that was amplified by a state of panic or hyper-vigilance among the troops, perhaps exacerbated by a secret military presence or technological tests.

THE CASH-LANDRUM INCIDENT.

DATE: December 29, 1980.
COUNTRY: United States.
STATE: Texas.
CITY: Dayton.

This case involves Betty Cash, Vickie Landrum and Vickie's grandson, Colby Landrum, who all witnessed an extraordinary and traumatic event. On the evening of December 29, 1980, as they were driving home after a quiet dinner, they encountered an unidentified flying object on a deserted road near the small town of Dayton, Texas. The object, described as diamond-shaped and emitting intense heat and light, caused intense fear and physical damage to the witnesses.

The encounter not only left physical evidence in the form of burns on the skin and damage to Betty Cash's car, but also had long-term repercussions on their health. The witnesses suffered from symptoms resembling those of radiation, such as hair loss, nausea, burns, and chronic illnesses, which sparked numerous speculations about the nature and origin of the object. The incident was intensively studied by UFO researchers and even became the subject of litigation, with the victims seeking compensation for their suffering and losses.

This case remains particularly notable not only because of the severity of the physical effects on the witnesses, but also because it was observed in the presence of numerous military helicopters, suggesting possible government knowledge or involvement. Despite numerous investigations, the origin of the UFO and the reason for its presence that night remain unresolved, adding another layer of mystery to this already complex case.

The Observation.

That evening, Betty Cash, Vickie Landrum and Vickie's grandson, Colby Landrum, were driving on a secluded road in the forest when their attention was drawn to a bright light in the sky.

The description of the object observed by the witnesses is particularly detailed. According to their testimonies, the object had a diamond shape and emitted a strong white light that illuminated the road and the surrounding trees. The object seemed to emit intense heat, to the point that Betty Cash reported feeling the heat through her car's dashboard, which prompted her to stop the vehicle. The witnesses also described the object as being surrounded by some sort of flame and emitting clapping noises, as if metal doors were closing.

The exact time of the observation is not universally established, but it occurred in the early evening. The witnesses observed the object for several minutes, which allowed them to detail their experience with unusual precision for this type of encounters.

The weather conditions that night were clear, with little or no clouds, allowing for perfect visibility of the object. The temperature was cool, typical of a December evening in Texas, which made the sensation of heat emitted by the object even more noticeable.

The observation of this UFO was followed by the appearance of numerous military helicopters, which witnesses interpreted as a possible response to the presence of the unidentified object. The helicopters, described as being of the Chinook type, seemed to encircle or escort the object, adding another layer of mystery to the incident.

The Cash-Landrum incident remains an enigmatic case in the field of ufology, mainly due to the accuracy of the descriptions provided by the witnesses and the unusual nature of the observed object. Despite numerous theories and speculations, the exact details of the object and the circumstances of its appearance remain unresolved.

Testimonials.

The main witnesses of this event were Betty Cash, Vickie Landrum and Colby Landrum, Vickie's grandson.

Betty Cash, a businesswoman from Dayton, was driving with her friends Vickie and young Colby when they observed a dazzling light above the road. According to Betty's testimony, the object was diamond-shaped and emitted intense heat and a light that illuminated the surrounding forest. She described the object as being metallic and having some sort of flames at the base, which seemed to propel the object upwards. Betty also reported feeling an overwhelming heat that forced her to quickly return to the car after stepping out to observe the object more closely.

Vickie Landrum, for her part, testified that she initially thought the object was the end of the world, mentioning that the intensity of the light and heat made her fear for their lives. She described the object as silently hovering above the road, blocking their path. Vickie also noted the presence of what she interpreted as military helicopters, surrounding the UFO, which added to her anxiety and confusion during the incident.

Colby Landrum, although young at the time, provided an account that corroborated the descriptions given by Betty and Vickie. He spoke of his intense fear in the face of the bright and hot object, and how he was comforted by his grandmother during the event. Colby also confirmed seeing several helicopters around the object, which added another dimension to the testimony, suggesting possible knowledge or involvement of the government.

The testimonies of these three individuals are all the more relevant as they all suffered from similar physical symptoms after the incident, including nausea, burns, and symptoms resembling those of irradiation, which was documented by the doctors who examined them shortly after the event. These symptoms reinforced the credibility of their account, as they indicated exposure to something physically tangible and potentially dangerous.

The Investigation.

The investigation began after witnesses, Betty Cash, Vickie Landrum and Vickie's grandson, Colby Landrum, reported encountering an unidentified flying object emitting intense heat and light. According to their testimonies, the object had a diamond shape and was accompanied by several military helicopters. The witnesses also suffered from severe physical symptoms after the incident, which added urgency to the investigation.

The initial reactions of the authorities were to verify the potential involvement of the military. Investigators questioned various military bases and government agencies, including NASA and the local air base, to determine if the observed object could be a military craft or some kind of exercise. However, all branches of the armed forces denied any involvement or knowledge of the incident.

In the face of the military's official non-recognition of the incident, the investigation turned to the testimonies of the victims and eyewitnesses. In-depth interviews were conducted, and investigators attempted to corroborate their accounts with other reports of UFO sightings or military activities in the region during that period.

Investigators also examined the medical effects reported by witnesses. Betty Cash suffered from symptoms that resembled those of radiation, such as hair loss, nausea, and skin burns. Medical records were collected and analyzed to try to understand the nature of the injuries and their possible link to the observed UFO.

Despite the efforts made, the investigation failed to provide a definitive explanation of the incident. The final reports highlighted the lack of concrete material evidence and the impossibility of independently verifying the witnesses' claims about the military helicopters. This led to a lot of frustration among the people involved and UFO researchers, who perceived this as a lack of transparency on the part of the authorities.

Theories and Speculations.

One of the first theories put forward is that of military intervention. Shortly after the observation of the object, military helicopters, identified as Chinooks, were seen encircling the UFO. This led to speculation that the object was either experimental technology from the American government, or something unknown that the government was trying to recover or monitor. This theory is supported by the number and behavior of the helicopters, suggesting coordination and a rapid response that would be difficult to explain otherwise.

However, official investigations conducted by the armed forces have denied any involvement or knowledge of the incident, leaving this theory without official confirmation. Skeptics of this theory point to the lack of concrete evidence directly linking the helicopters to the observed object, as well as the lack of testimonies from military personnel.

Another popular theory is that of the extraterrestrial craft. This hypothesis is fueled by the description of the object, its seemingly advanced behavior, and the physical effects experienced by the witnesses, which seem to surpass the capabilities of known human technologies at the time. Supporters of this theory often cite the incident as a clear example of a close encounter of the second kind, where a UFO has a direct effect on the immediate environment.

However, this theory is also criticized for its lack of material evidence and the fact that the descriptions of the UFO could be interpreted in various ways. Moreover, the absence of similar reports, either of comparable objects or effects, makes this explanation difficult to accept for skeptics.

A third perspective is that of a collective hallucination or a misunderstanding due to psychological stress or particular environmental conditions. Some researchers have suggested that the witnesses may have misinterpreted a natural phenomenon or unidentified human technology due to the tension of the moment. This theory is often rejected by those who have closely studied the details of the incident, particularly the reported physical symptoms, which are difficult to attribute to a hallucination.

Finally, there are those who suggest that the incident could be the result of some kind of unexplained natural phenomenon, like a rare type of ball lightning or another atmospheric phenomenon. This explanation attempts to reconcile the strange appearance and physical effects of the observation with natural causes, but like the other theories, it lacks direct evidence and fails to fully explain all aspects of the incident.

Conclusion.

The Cash-Landrum incident is an emblematic case in the study of UFOs, marked by detailed testimonies and severe physical consequences on the witnesses. Despite numerous investigations, no definitive explanation has been provided, leaving open the question of whether the observed object was of extraterrestrial origin or a secret military project. The apparent implication of the military, suggested by the presence of military helicopters, adds a layer of mystery and speculation. This incident underscores the complexity and challenges associated with understanding unidentified aerial phenomena, as well as the limitations of official investigations in solving such mysteries.

THE HESSDALEN LIGHTS: A LUMINOUS MYSTERY IN THE VALLEY OF NORWAY.

DATE: between 1981 and 1984.
COUNTRY: Norway.
STATE: .
CITY: Hessdalen.

The Hessdalen Valley, located in the center of Norway, has become famous for a strange and persistent phenomenon that attracts researchers and curious people from all over the world. Since the early 1980s, mysterious lights have been observed floating in the sky, often without concrete explanation. These luminous appearances vary in color, intensity and duration, but they all share an unpredictable and fascinating character. The phenomenon has gained such notoriety that scientists from various countries, including physicists, engineers and astronomers, have been drawn to the region to study these lights, hoping to unlock their secrets. Despite decades of research, the mystery remains intact, fueling all kinds of theories, ranging from rare natural phenomena to extraterrestrial activities. The small community of Hessdalen and the surrounding areas have seen their daily life altered by this curiosity, transforming the valley into a meeting point for the observation and study of unidentified aerial phenomena.

The Observation.

The Hessdalen lights are a phenomenon observed in the Hessdalen valley, in Norway, which has captivated researchers and curious individuals since the first reports in the 1980s. These observations are characterized by unexplainable lights that primarily appear in the night sky, often described as bright and of various colors, ranging from brilliant white to deep red, through yellow and sometimes blue. The phenomenon manifests in different forms: luminous spheres that float or move at high speed, sudden flashes that briefly illuminate the sky, or formations of lights that seem to follow complex trajectories.

One of the most detailed observations took place one evening in January 1984. At that time, the lights were observed by many witnesses, including scientists who came specifically to study this mystery. That night, the sky was exceptionally clear, an ideal condition for observing celestial phenomena. Around 10:30 p.m., an intense red light appeared south of the valley. It moved slowly northward, sometimes changing shape and size. After a few minutes, the red light split into two distinct parts before disappearing completely, giving way to a series of small white flashes that lasted about an hour.

The weather conditions during this observation were stable, with a clear sky and little wind, which rules out the hypothesis of atmospheric reflections or refractions caused by particular weather conditions. The temperature was low, typical of winter nights in Norway, which could play a role in the conductivity of the air and perhaps influence the manifestation of these lights.

The observations of the Hessdalen lights are not limited to nighttime appearances. Similar phenomena have been reported during the day, albeit less frequently. For example, in March 1984, around 2:00 p.m., an oval silver light was seen floating above the mountain ridge before disappearing as suddenly as it had appeared. During this daytime observation, the sky was partly cloudy, and the intermittent sun could have contributed to the visibility of the phenomenon.

These repeated observations have led to continuous scientific monitoring of the valley, with the installation of measurement stations equipped with cameras and various sensors to record the manifestations of these mysterious lights. Despite decades of research and numerous theories, from the spontaneous combustion of rare gases in the ground to purely atmospheric phenomena, no definitive explanation has yet been unanimously accepted by the scientific community.

Testimonials.

Since then, many witnesses have shared their experiences, contributing to the accumulation of a corpus of fascinating and often bewildering testimonies.

One of the first witnesses, Bjorn Gitle Hauge, an engineer and local resident, has observed the lights on several occasions. According to him, the lights usually appear without warning and vary in color, shifting from bright red to intense blue. During an observation in 1984, Hauge described a light so bright that it illuminated the entire mountain, moving at an incredible speed before disappearing as suddenly as it had appeared.

Erling Strand, another key witness, is a professor at the Norwegian University of Science and Technology. Strand has been involved in the Hessdalen project since its inception. He reports having seen lights moving in irregular formations, sometimes splitting into two or merging with other lights. During a particular observation in 1997, he noted that the lights seemed to react to the presence of witnesses, changing direction or light intensity when people approached.

Marianne Moe, a tourist visiting the valley in 2003, shared her experience of a nighttime encounter with the lights. She describes a series of white lights floating above the ground, forming what seemed to be a complex geometric pattern before quickly rising into the sky and disappearing.

A group of physics students from the University of Oslo, visiting for a research project in 2010, reported observing an intense red light that suddenly changed into a brilliant white light. One of the students, Jonas Dahl, specifically mentioned that the light seemed to "probe" the area, moving methodically across the valley before fading away.

In 2015, a team of documentary filmmakers from Norwegian television captured images of the lights that were broadcast nationwide. The cameraman, Kjetil Skogli, described how the lights moved unpredictably, sometimes remaining stationary for several minutes before making sudden accelerations.

These testimonies, although varied, show remarkable common points: the unpredictable movements of the lights, their ability to change color and shape, and their tendency to appear and disappear abruptly.

The Investigation.

In response to the increasing number of testimonies and the growing public interest, a series of official investigations has been initiated to try to understand the origin of these mysterious appearances.

The investigation began with the formation of the Hessdalen project in 1983, led by physicist Erling Strand from the Norwegian University of Science and Technology (NTNU). The aim of this project was to conduct continuous scientific monitoring of the phenomenon. Measurement stations equipped with various instruments, such as radars, infrared spectrum cameras and magnetometers, were installed in the valley to record the occurrences of the lights.

The first observations and data collected showed that the lights could appear at different altitudes, move at varying speeds, and last from a few seconds to several hours. The reported colors also varied, mainly including white, red, and yellow. Investigators also noted that the lights seemed to manifest more frequently in conditions of low temperature and low humidity.

Over the years, the investigation has gathered testimonies from numerous local residents and tourists, who often described the lights as being silent and capable of making quick and erratic movements. Some witnesses also reported physical effects, such as radio interference and sensations of heat, when they were near the manifestations.

The Norwegian military and governmental authorities also took part in the investigation, primarily to rule out any potential threat to national security. However, radar analyses and aerial observations revealed no evidence of unauthorized aerial activity or unidentified flying objects other than the lights themselves.

Despite the efforts made, the investigations have not been able to provide a definitive explanation for the phenomenon. Several theories have been proposed, ranging from unusual chemical reactions in the valley, to plasma phenomena caused by the region's mineral richness. However, none of these theories have been definitively proven.

The investigation into the Hessdalen lights continues to be an important subject of study for scientists and researchers in atmospheric phenomena. The Hessdalen project remains active, and the data collected is regularly analyzed in the hope of one day unraveling the mystery of these strange lights.

Theories and Speculations.

One of the first theories put forward is that of extraterrestrial activities. Some ufologists and UFO enthusiasts believe that the lights could be spacecraft of non-earthly origins, or signals sent by advanced civilizations. This hypothesis is fueled by the sometimes spherical or disc shape of the lights, and their ability to move at high speed and change direction in an apparently intelligent manner.

At the opposite end of the spectrum, scientists propose an explanation based on natural phenomena. One of the most credible theories is that of plasma batteries, where electric charges are generated by the friction of rocks containing specific minerals in the valley. These charges could create illuminations when they are released into the atmosphere. This theory is supported by the high frequency of these lights in areas rich in scandium, an element known for its electromagnetic properties.

Another scientific explanation suggests that the lights could be the result of the spontaneous combustion of gases such as radon, which is known to be present in the region. Radon is a radioactive gas that can accumulate in certain geological areas; when it is released into the air and comes into contact with oxidizing elements, it could theoretically create flashes of light.

Some researchers have also hypothesized that the lights could be a rare type of ball lightning, a meteorological phenomenon that is still poorly understood but documented around the world. Ball lightning manifests as luminous spheres that can float or move in the air before disappearing or exploding.

In addition to these theories, there are also speculations about more exotic explanations, such as dimensional portals or phenomena related to unknown energies concentrated in the Hessdalen valley. These ideas, although less accepted by the scientific community, continue to fuel debates and fascination around this phenomenon.

Each theory brings its share of support and skepticism, and despite numerous studies and research, the Hessdalen lights remain an unsolved mystery. Scientists and enthusiasts continue to monitor the valley, hoping one day to unravel the secrets of these strange lights.

THE UFO INCIDENT OF HUDSON VALLEY, NEW YORK.

DATE: 1983-1989.
COUNTRY: United States.
STATE: New York.
CITY: Hudson Valley.

Between 1983 and 1989, thousands of residents of the Hudson Valley, a region located north of New York State, reported observing unidentified aerial phenomena. These observations were often described as large, triangular or V-shaped crafts, equipped with multicolored lights and capable of silent, low-altitude aerial maneuvers, defying the capabilities of known aircraft at the time.

The peak of these observations occurred in March 1983, when the police and local telephone lines were overwhelmed by calls from worried and curious citizens. The testimonies agreed that the observed object could remain stationary in the sky for long periods before moving at astonishing speeds. The descriptions varied slightly, but most witnesses agreed on the enormous size of the object and its operational silence, which added to the strangeness of the experience.

Local authorities and aviation experts have been put to the test to provide explanations. Some have suggested the possibility of ultra-secret aircraft or experimental prototypes, although this theory has never been confirmed. Others have hypothesized that the sightings could be attributed to rare atmospheric phenomena or optical illusions. However, no explanation has fully satisfied all the testimonies, leaving a degree of mystery surrounding these events.

The Hudson Valley incident not only captivated the residents of the region but also attracted the attention of ufology researchers and media from around the world. It remains an important case study for those interested in unidentified aerial phenomena and continues to spark debates and speculations about the nature and origin of what was observed.

The Observation.

The phenomenon was first significantly observed on March 24, 1983, although earlier reports dating back to 1981 were also noted. That night, many residents of the Hudson Valley region, located in the state of New York, reported seeing a large unidentified flying object.

The observed object was described as being triangular or V-shaped, with multicolored lights that blinked or rotated around its edges. Witnesses often mentioned that the object measured between 100 and 300 feet wide, making it exceptionally large compared to conventional aircraft. The UFO moved at a relatively slow speed and in almost complete silence, which added to the strangeness of the observation. Some witnesses reported that the object had the ability to remain stationary in the sky for long periods before resuming its movement.

The exact time of the observations varied, but most reports indicated that the object had been seen between 8:30 p.m. and 11:00 p.m. This time frame often coincided with a clear or partly cloudy sky, which improved the visibility of the UFO. The weather conditions during these observations were generally stable, with little or no wind, and a cool temperature typical of spring evenings in the northeastern United States.

The descriptions of the lights on the object also varied. Some witnesses described bright white lights, while others mentioned red, green, or blue lights. These lights seemed to be arranged in a way that emphasized the V shape of the object, and sometimes they changed color or intensity. Several witnesses also noted that the object projected a beam of light towards the ground, although the purpose of this beam remains unknown.

The observation of the Hudson Valley UFO was repeated several times over the following years, with similar reports coming from different parts of the valley. Each time, the object seemed to follow a similar route or flight pattern, leading some to speculate about the possibility of some kind of systematic surveillance or exploration of the area.

Testimonials.

Several eyewitnesses have reported seeing a large unidentified flying object, often described as being boomerang or V-shaped, equipped with multicolored lights and capable of silent and complex aerial maneuvers. These observations have spanned several years, with a peak in activity between 1983 and 1984.

Among the key witnesses, Dennis Sant, a police officer from the city of Yorktown, was one of the first to report having seen the object. According to his testimony, the UFO was so large that it covered the width of the highway and moved at an extremely slow speed without making any noise. Sant described the object as having white, red, and green lights that flashed in a sequential and not random manner, suggesting some sort of communication or technical operation.

Another important witness, Andy Sadoff, who resided in New Castle, observed the UFO from his garden. He noted that the object emitted an intense light that illuminated the night sky as if it were broad daylight. Sadoff also mentioned that the object had the ability to remain stationary for long periods before moving at incredible speeds, thus defying the capabilities of conventional aircraft.

Ed Burns, an electronic engineer, provided a detailed technical testimony on the observation. He calculated the size of the object to be about 300 feet wide, based on the distance between the observed lights. Burns also pointed out the absence of noise, which was unusual for an object of this size moving in the Earth's atmosphere.

Carmen Nigro, a local resident who has observed the UFO multiple times, described movements that seemed to defy gravity. According to Nigro, the object could accelerate and change direction instantly, without apparent inertia. He also reported that the lights of the object changed configuration, which could indicate different modes of operation or activity.

Linda Nicoletti, who worked as a waitress in a local restaurant, testified to having seen the object fly over the restaurant's parking lot. She described a series of lights that seemed to "dance" around the object, creating an impressive visual spectacle. Nicoletti claimed that the experience was both fascinating and terrifying, as she had never seen anything like it before.

The Investigation.

In the face of the magnitude of testimonies, several organizations have launched investigations to unravel the mystery of these appearances. Among them, the Federal Aviation Administration (FAA) and the United States Air Force have been the main players. These organizations have sought to verify the presence of any unidentified aircraft in the airspace, while examining possible conventional explanations such as airplanes, helicopters, or weather balloons.

The initial reactions of the authorities were of a skeptical nature, often attributing the observations to natural phenomena or confusion with commercial aircraft. However, the accumulation of detailed and credible testimonies from people of various backgrounds, including pilots, police officers, and professionals, has led to a more thorough investigation.

The investigators collected hundreds of testimonies and organized observation evenings, where experts tried to spot the object in question. These sessions sometimes led to additional observations by the investigators themselves. Meanwhile, radar analyses were conducted to try to detect anomalies in the Hudson Valley sky. Despite these efforts, the radar results were not always conclusive, partly due to the low altitude at which the object was often reported.

One of the most intriguing aspects of the investigation was the difficulty in categorizing the observed object within the known frameworks of aviation. The testimonies described flight characteristics that did not correspond to existing aerial technologies, including the object's ability to remain stationary in the sky for long periods, or its silent movements despite its apparent size.

As the investigation progressed, the authorities began to consider the possibility that these observations might not be easily explainable. Internal reports, although rarely made public at the time, indicated that the investigators themselves were often perplexed by the data collected.

In the end, the official investigation did not lead to a definitive explanation. The final reports often used vague terms, suggesting that the observations could be attributed to unidentified or unconventional phenomena. This conclusion left many witnesses and observers unsatisfied, fueling speculation and debate about the nature and origin of the object observed in the Hudson Valley.

Theories and Speculations.

One of the most popular theories is that of the extraterrestrial visit. This hypothesis suggests that the observed object was a spacecraft of non-earthly origin. Supporters of this theory argue that the technology manifested by the object - its ability to fly silently, to change direction quickly, and to emit lights of different colors - far exceeds what human technology of the time could produce. They also cite the large number of witnesses and the consistency of the reports as evidence supporting this idea.

Another explanation put forward is that of a secret military or governmental vehicle. According to this theory, the UFO could be a prototype of an airplane or drone secretly developed by the United States government. Supporters of this hypothesis point out that the Hudson Valley region is relatively close to several military bases, which could explain the presence of such a vehicle in the sky. This theory is often reinforced by discussions about military secrecy and advanced technologies not disclosed to the public.

A third theory suggests that the incident could be attributed to a misinterpreted form of natural phenomenon. Rare atmospheric phenomena, such as plasma-type lights caused by unusual electromagnetic conditions, could be mistaken for flying crafts. This explanation attempts to rationalize the observation by natural causes, suggesting that the witnesses may have misinterpreted what they saw due to the rarity and strangeness of the phenomenon.

Finally, some skeptics suggest that the incident could be the result of a hoax or a collective illusion. They argue that in a context of growing fascination for UFO phenomena, particularly during the 1980s, it is possible that collective excitement led to a kind of mass hysteria where several people believed they saw an extraordinary object when it may have been planes flying in formation or other more conventional explanations.

Conclusion.

Despite the multitude of testimonies from credible individuals and extensive media coverage, no definitive explanation has been provided as to the nature or origin of the observed object. The descriptions of the object, with its imposing size and advanced flight capabilities, defy conventional explanations and suggest the possibility of a technology far beyond what was publicly accessible at the time. Investigations have addressed various theories, ranging from secret experimental crafts to an extraterrestrial origin, but none have been definitively proven. This incident continues to fascinate and raise questions about what we understand of our world and the possible advanced technologies that might exist.

THE UFO INCIDENT OF DALNEGORSK, USSR.

DATE: January 29, 1986.
COUNTRY: Soviet Union.
STATE: Primorye.
CITY: Dalnegorsk.

The Dalnegorsk UFO incident is an event that has captivated the attention of ufologists and paranormal phenomena researchers worldwide. On January 29, 1986, in the small mining town of Dalnegorsk, located in the Far East of the Soviet Union, an unidentified flying object crashed on Izvestkovaya hill, often called "Height 611" due to its altitude. That night, the inhabitants of Dalnegorsk observed a glowing red sphere crossing the sky at a moderate speed before crashing into the hill, causing an intense fire that lasted several hours. Witnesses described the object as being spherical in shape and emitting intense light, making the observation particularly striking under the winter night sky.

The local authorities, intrigued and concerned by this incident, quickly organized an expedition to investigate the crash site. What was discovered raised even more questions: unusual debris, including metallic spheres and nets of wire made from an unknown alloy, littered the area. These materials exhibited atypical physical and chemical properties, not matching any of the known materials used in aerospace or military equipment of the time. Moreover, the vegetation around the crash site had undergone strange modifications, as if it had been exposed to radiation or extremely high temperatures.

The Dalnegorsk incident did not only leave physical traces; it also left an indelible imprint in the collective memory of the local community and stimulated increased scientific interest in UFO phenomena in the Soviet Union. Despite several theories and speculations, the exact origin and nature of the object remain unsolved, thus fueling the mystery and debate among researchers and the general public.

The Observation.

That evening, around 7:55 pm local time, the inhabitants of the small mining town of Dalnegorsk, located in the Russian Far East, witnessed an unusual aerial phenomenon that captured the attention of many researchers and ufologists.

The observed object was described as a luminous sphere, emitting an intense red light. According to the testimonies, the sphere measured about three meters in diameter and flew at a relatively low altitude, estimated at about 700 to 800 meters above ground level. The object moved at a moderate speed without emitting any perceptible sound, which added to the strangeness of the observation.

Its trajectory was stable and linear, suggesting some sort of precise control or guidance.

The weather conditions that night were clear with an unobstructed sky, which allowed for a very clear visual observation of the object. The temperature was cold, typical of winters in the Russian Far East, but this did not deter the witnesses from following the object as long as they could with the naked eye and for some, with the help of binoculars.

The object continued its trajectory towards a small mountain named Mount Izvestkovaya, more commonly referred to as "Height 611" due to its altitude in meters. This is where the incident took an even more mysterious turn. According to reports, the object slowed down before colliding with the mountain. Instead of exploding or disintegrating as one might expect with a conventional craft, the object seemed to land gently, emitting a glowing red light that lasted several hours before gradually fading out.

Witnesses described a series of small fires on the mountain after the impact, and a light emission that continued to be visible, pulsating at times, which added to the observers' perplexity. The impact zone, visited by researchers shortly after the event, revealed unusual traces and residues, including tiny metallic spheres and fragments of materials that did not correspond to anything known at the time.

Testimonials.

That evening, several witnesses reported seeing an unidentified flying object crash into Izvestkovaya Mountain, often referred to as "Mountain of the Dead". The testimonies collected come from various residents of the town, as well as scientists who examined the site after the incident.

Among the main witnesses, Valery Dvuzhilni, a researcher and the leader of the scientific expedition that investigated the site, provided a detailed account of the incident. According to Dvuzhilni, the object appeared to be a luminous sphere, measuring about three meters in diameter. He described the object as emitting intense light, mainly red and orange, before crashing into the mountain. The impact was so powerful that it caused a fire on the mountain, burning vegetation over a large area.

Another important witness, a local radio operator, reported detecting a strange signal, a kind of humming, which was not in line with usual transmissions. This signal was picked up just a few minutes before the object was observed in the sky. The operator described the sound as being discontinuous and very different from normal radio interference.

The local residents, many of whom were miners and their families, also shared their observations. A family living not far from the mountain reported seeing a bright light crossing the sky at an incredible speed, followed by a loud noise upon impact. They described the light as being so intense that it momentarily illuminated the inside of their house, as if it were broad daylight.

A teenager, who was outside with his friends, testified to having seen the object descend towards the mountain at an acute angle. According to him, the object did not have the shape of a traditional airplane and made no engine noise. He described the object as a "fireball" that left behind a trail of light before disappearing behind the mountain.

After the incident, a team of researchers, including geologists and physicists, visited the site to collect samples and measure radiation levels. The test results showed anomalies, including high levels of radioactivity and rare metals in the recovered debris. These findings added an additional layer of mystery to the incident, as they did not match the materials typically found in the region.

The Investigation.

The local authorities quickly reacted to this event. The day after the incident, a team composed of members of the local government, scientists, and military personnel was formed to investigate the crash site. This team's mission was to collect samples, measure radiation levels, and gather testimonies from the residents.

The initial reports on the site indicated that the object had left behind strange debris, including small metallic spheres and fragments of an unknown material that emitted a strong luminescence. The radiation measurements taken on site showed levels slightly above normal, but nothing that would be considered dangerous to human health.

The testimonies collected from local residents provided varied descriptions of the object, some describing it as a fireball, while others insisted on its spherical shape and controlled trajectory, suggesting some sort of directed vehicle rather than a simple meteorite. These testimonies added to the complexity of the investigation, as they suggested an advanced technology unknown at the time.

As the investigation progressed, the military authorities took a more active part, limiting access to the site and classifying some of the investigation's findings. This fueled speculation and conspiracy theories about the nature of the object and the possible involvement of extraterrestrial technologies or secret military technology.

Nevertheless, scientists continued to analyze the collected samples. They discovered that the materials exhibited unusual isotopes and physical properties that did not match any known material on Earth. These findings were published in several scientific journals, attracting the attention of the international scientific community.

The official investigation was concluded a few years later, without providing a definitive answer about the origin of the object. The final report indicated that the object was probably not of extraterrestrial origin, but rather an unidentified phenomenon with characteristics that had not yet been fully explained by current science. This conclusion left many questions unanswered, and the Dalnegorsk incident remains a subject of fascination and speculation to this day.

Theories and Speculations.

A luminous sphere was seen crashing into Izvestkovaya mountain, commonly referred to as "Height 611". The debris recovered from the site has fueled various hypotheses regarding the origin and nature of the object.

One of the first theories put forward is that of the extraterrestrial origin of the object. This hypothesis is supported by the unusual composition of the debris found on the site, which included rare metals and elements that some researchers deemed atypical of the terrestrial technology of the time. Proponents of this theory also highlight the abnormal behavior of the object, its flight path, and the way it was observed emitting intense light before crashing. They argue that these characteristics do not match the typical behaviors of known aircraft or satellites.

On the contrary, some experts and scientists propose a more conventional explanation, suggesting that the object could be a satellite or part of a satellite that disintegrated upon re-entry into the Earth's atmosphere. This theory is supported by the fact that the period of the incident coincided with the Cold War, a time when numerous Soviet and American satellites were in orbit. Skeptics of the extraterrestrial hypothesis point to the higher probability of an earthly origin, given the large number of launches and space debris fallout during this period.

Another interesting speculation is the one suggesting that the incident could be the result of a secret military experiment. The mineral-rich region of Dalnegorsk could have been a site of interest for testing new technologies, particularly experimental aircraft. This theory is sometimes reinforced by reports from local witnesses who allegedly observed unusual military activities in the region shortly before and after the incident.

Furthermore, there are those who consider the Dalnegorsk incident as a rare but explainable natural phenomenon. They suggest that the object could have been a meteor or a fireball whose particular chemical composition could have caused unusual reactions upon entering the Earth's atmosphere, such as explosions or exceptional light emissions. This hypothesis attempts to reconcile the witnesses' observations with known, albeit rare, natural phenomena.

THE INCIDENT OF SÃO PAULO, BRAZIL.

DATE: May 3, 1986.
COUNTRY: Brazil .
STATE: São Paulo.
CITY: São José dos Campos.

On May 3, 1986, several witnesses in the city of São José dos Campos, located in the state of São Paulo, reported seeing an unidentified flying object in the night sky. The object, described as being disc-shaped with flashing multicolored lights, was observed for several hours, moving erratically and at impressive speeds.

The witnesses of this event included ordinary citizens as well as qualified professionals such as pilots and police officers, which added a layer of credibility to the reports. Moreover, the incident coincided with an unexplained power outage in several neighborhoods of the city, which sparked speculation about a possible connection between the UFO and the power interruptions.

The local authorities and media quickly became aware of the incident, leading to extensive media coverage and an official investigation by the Brazilian Air Force. The results of this investigation have largely remained classified, fueling conspiracy theories and the mystery surrounding the event. Despite the numerous theories, the São Paulo incident remains unresolved, leaving many questions open about the nature and origin of the object observed that night.

The Observation.

That evening, around 9:30 pm, several witnesses in the metropolitan region of São Paulo reported seeing an unidentified flying object. The description of the object by the various witnesses was remarkably similar, which added some credibility to the reports.

The observed object was triangular in shape with rounded edges and measured about 30 meters in diameter. It emitted an intense white light in the center, which seemed to pulse at regular intervals. Around this central light, smaller red, blue and green lights blinked randomly, giving the object a particularly strange and distinctive appearance.

Witnesses reported that the UFO was moving at a relatively slow speed and at a low altitude, estimated to be about 200 meters from the ground. The object made no audible noise, which was puzzling for the observers, accustomed to the noises associated with airplanes and helicopters.

The weather conditions that night were clear with few clouds, allowing for excellent visibility. The moon was nearly full, providing an additional source of light that helped to accentuate the contours of the UFO. There was no wind, and the temperature was pleasant, which probably encouraged more people to be outside and therefore witness the event.

The observation lasted about 20 minutes. During this time, the object crossed the sky in a northeast direction before suddenly rising at a dizzying speed and disappearing from the witnesses' view. The way the UFO accelerated and disappeared was described as "contrary to any known human aviation technology" by several of the witnesses.

This particular case of UFO sighting in São Paulo remains one of the most documented and discussed among UFO communities in Brazil, due to the clarity of the testimonies and the optimal observation conditions that allowed a detailed study of the event.

Testimonials.

One of the first witnesses was the pilot of the Brazilian Air Force, Captain Marcos Gomes. On routine patrol, he observed several bright objects moving at high speed in the sky. According to his report, these objects changed direction in an abrupt and impossible way for conventional aircraft. Captain Gomes described the objects as being circular in shape with intense lights, mainly white in color, but with shades of blue and red.

Another key witness was air traffic controller Julia Silva, who was working at the São Paulo control center that night. She confirmed having detected unidentified objects on the radar, which were moving at speeds and with maneuvers that did not correspond to any known flying device. Julia reported that these objects would suddenly appear and disappear from the radar, which added to the confusion and concern among the control center staff.

Among the civilian witnesses, there is Roberto Almeida, an amateur astronomer, who was observing the sky that night. He saw a large triangular object with three bright lights at each corner. The object was moving slowly and silently across the sky before suddenly accelerating and disappearing over the horizon. Roberto noted that the object did not match any known type of aircraft or satellite.

Finally, Maria Lopes, a local resident, provided a similar testimony. She described seeing a disk-shaped object flying over the neighborhood. The object emitted a brilliant light that partially illuminated the ground. Maria recounted that the object remained stationary for a few minutes before ascending vertically at an incredible speed.

These testimonies, although varied, share common characteristics regarding the speed, unpredictable movements, and maneuvering capabilities of the observed objects. They have contributed to fueling discussions and speculations about the potential presence of extraterrestrial crafts in our atmosphere.

The Investigation.

From the first reports of the observation of unidentified flying objects (UFOs) over the metropolitan region of São Paulo, the government mobilized several branches of its armed forces for a coordinated response.

The first phase of the investigation was initiated by the Brazilian Air Force (FAB). Fighter pilots were dispatched to intercept and identify the reported objects. These missions resulted in radar and visual recordings that confirmed the presence of flying objects with atypical flight characteristics, such as extremely high speeds and maneuvering capabilities that exceeded the known aerial technology at the time.

Simultaneously, the Air Force Personnel Investigation and Preparation Center was tasked with collecting testimonies from civilians and military personnel who had observed the phenomena. These testimonies often described objects of various shapes, mainly spherical or disk-shaped, emitting lights of different colors. The reports also mentioned that the objects could move silently or with a low hum, contrasting with the characteristic noise of conventional aircraft.

In response to the extent of the observations and public pressure for explanations, the Ministry of Aeronautics formed a special committee to analyze the collected data. This committee included aeronautics experts, meteorologists, physicists, and engineers. The goal was to determine whether the observations could be attributed to natural phenomena, errors in interpreting sensory data, or unrecognized aerial technologies.

The results of the investigation were partially disclosed to the public. The final report concluded that the majority of observations could be explained by natural phenomena such as unusual atmospheric reflections or weather balloons. However, some observations were not definitively explained, leaving open the possibility of other explanations.

Despite the official conclusions, the São Paulo incident continues to spark debates and speculations. Independent research groups and ufologists have criticized the government investigation, deeming it incomplete or lacking transparency. They highlight that some data, notably radar recordings and pilot testimonies, suggest flight characteristics and behaviors of the objects that do not match the provided explanations.

Theories and Speculations.

One of the most popular theories is that of extraterrestrial visitation. According to this hypothesis, the observed objects would be spacecraft of non-earthly origins. Supporters of this theory rely on the seemingly advanced technology of the objects, such as their ability to perform high-speed movements and to change direction instantly, characteristics that exceed the capabilities of known human aerial vehicles at the time. Moreover, some witnesses have reported electromagnetic interferences in their electronic devices at the time of the observations, a phenomenon often associated with close encounters of the third kind.

On the contrary, skeptics propose a more down-to-earth explanation. They suggest that what the witnesses saw could be attributed to natural phenomena such as weather balloons, atmospheric reflections, or even sky lanterns. This hypothesis is reinforced by the fact that the incident occurred in a dense urban area, where such objects could easily be launched or become visible due to light pollution.

Another theory suggests that the incident could be the result of secret military experiments. Brazil, at the time, was developing several advanced aeronautical technologies. The observed objects could therefore have been prototypes of airplanes or drones in the testing phase, which were not yet known to the general public. This theory is often cited to explain why the Brazilian military did not show great interest in this incident, suggesting a possible prior knowledge or involvement in the events.

Furthermore, some researchers have suggested that the incident could be a case of "collective hysteria", where the tension and excitement caused by the initial testimonies led to a series of exaggerated or incorrect reports. This theory is often used to explain how UFO incidents can quickly evolve into mass phenomena, even in the absence of tangible evidence.

Conclusion.

Despite numerous visual observations and radar recordings, the exact nature of the observed objects has never been elucidated. Reports from pilots, both civilian and military, as well as radar data, suggest exceptional flight characteristics, far beyond the capabilities of known aircraft at the time. The Brazilian government, after an initial investigation, did not provide a definitive explanation, leaving the door open to various interpretations and theories. This incident underscores the complexity and challenges associated with understanding unidentified aerial phenomena, and continues to be a source of fascination and speculation in the UFO community and beyond.

THE INCIDENT OF THE UFO NIGHT IN BRAZIL.

DATE: May 19, 1986.
COUNTRY: Brazil.
STATE: Several states, Rio de Janeiro, São Paulo, Goiás.
CITY: Mainly observed in São José dos Campos.

The "Night of the UFOs" is one of the most significant events in the history of Brazilian ufology. On the evening of May 19, 1986, an unprecedented occurrence unfolded in Brazil, where numerous unidentified flying objects (UFOs) were detected and observed across various states. The phenomenon captured the attention of the Brazilian Air Force (FAB), civilian pilots, air traffic controllers, and the media, marking a historic moment of large-scale UFO activity in the country. The official response by the Brazilian military was swift, with fighter jets dispatched to intercept and investigate the mysterious objects, leading to a night filled with intrigue and speculation.

The Observation

The events began around 8:00 p.m. in São José dos Campos, São Paulo, when air traffic controllers at São José dos Campos airport noticed unusual radar echoes, indicating the presence of several unidentified objects in the sky. Simultaneously, pilots and ground witnesses in the area reported seeing bright lights moving erratically at various altitudes.

Soon after, sightings spread to other regions, including the skies over Rio de Janeiro and Goiás. The objects were described as luminous, performing rapid movements and maneuvers that seemed to defy the laws of physics. Witnesses reported that these objects hovered, sped off at incredible velocities, and changed directions with ease. Air traffic controllers also reported that the radar returns indicated the objects were moving at speeds and performing aerial maneuvers well beyond the capabilities of conventional aircraft at the time.

Testimonials

The sheer number of witnesses made the "Night of the UFOs" particularly remarkable. Both civilian and military individuals reported sightings. Notably, multiple pilots, including commercial and military aviators, confirmed visual contact with the objects. These testimonies came from well-trained professionals, adding credibility to the reports.

One of the key figures in the event was Lieutenant Kleber Caldas Marinho, one of the Brazilian Air Force pilots dispatched that night. He described encountering several bright, fast-moving objects that would appear and disappear from his radar and visual range within seconds. Another military pilot, Captain

Armindo Souza Viriato, reported that the objects moved faster than anything he had ever seen, reaching extraordinary speeds in a matter of seconds.

Civilian air traffic controllers in São Paulo and Rio de Janeiro also testified to detecting the objects on radar. They confirmed that the unidentified objects moved erratically and sometimes disappeared from their screens, only to reappear moments later at a different location. These testimonies provided strong evidence that the sightings were not simply optical illusions but involved physical phenomena detected by technological means.

The Investigation

The Brazilian Air Force took the sightings seriously and initiated an official investigation immediately after the events of May 19. Fighter jets were scrambled from several airbases, including those in Anápolis and Santa Cruz, to intercept the UFOs. Over the course of several hours, five jets pursued the objects, attempting to engage and identify them. However, despite radar contacts and visual sightings, the pilots were unable to get close enough to establish what the objects were.

The Air Force investigation, led by Brigadier General Otávio Moreira Lima, concluded that over 20 UFOs had been observed that night. The official report released months later confirmed that the objects had exhibited high speeds and agility, with one radar return indicating a speed of over 1,500 km/h. Despite this, the investigation could not determine the origin or nature of the objects, and no physical evidence was recovered.

While the report acknowledged the unusual behavior of the objects, it stopped short of providing any definitive conclusions. The Brazilian government eventually released portions of the investigation to the public, revealing that the incident had been taken very seriously by the military.

Theories and Speculations

The "Night of the UFOs" has sparked numerous theories and speculations over the years. One of the most popular theories among ufologists is that the objects were extraterrestrial in origin, based on their advanced aerial maneuvers and extraordinary speeds. Proponents of this theory argue that the behavior of the objects—such as their ability to evade the fighter jets and disappear from radar—suggests they were not man-made and likely came from another world.

Another theory posits that the objects were part of a secret military experiment, possibly involving advanced technology being tested by a foreign government. This idea is supported by the fact that the Brazilian Air Force could not identify the objects and that they displayed capabilities far beyond any known aircraft of the time.

A more skeptical theory suggests that the objects could have been natural phenomena, such as atmospheric anomalies or rare meteorological events that created the appearance of fast-moving lights in the sky. Some researchers have proposed that the radar returns could have been caused by temperature inversions or other atmospheric conditions that interfere with radar signals.

Finally, there is a theory that the events were a result of some kind of mass psychological phenomenon, in which the initial sightings triggered widespread panic and confusion, leading witnesses to perceive ordinary objects—such as planes or stars—as UFOs.

THE INCIDENT OF JAPAN AIRLINES FLIGHT 1628: ENCOUNTER WITH UFOS NEAR ANCHORAGE, ALASKA.

DATE: November 17, 1986.
COUNTRY: United States.
STATE: Alaska.
CITY: Anchorage.

On November 17, 1986, an unusual event occurred in the cold, dark sky of Alaska, captivating the attention of UFO enthusiasts and aviation experts worldwide. That night, Japan Airlines flight 1628, a Boeing 747 cargo plane en route from Paris to Tokyo with a stopover in Reykjavik, Iceland, witnessed a series of strange and inexplicable events that defied conventional explanations. The captain, Kenju Terauchi, an experienced pilot with over 29 years of flying experience, along with two other crew members, reported seeing several unidentified flying objects (UFOs) during their flight segment between Iceland and Alaska. These objects allegedly performed aerial maneuvers that seemed to defy the laws of physics, such as instantaneous changes in direction and accelerations at staggering speeds, without any visible air disturbance.

The incident began when the first of the objects was detected by the Boeing 747's radar, initially sparking curiosity and then concern among the crew. Terauchi described the objects as being of considerable size and discoid shape, emitting an intense light that illuminated the surrounding darkness. As the incident unfolded, the UFOs seemed to be playing a game of cat and mouse with the plane, appearing and disappearing with disconcerting agility. Despite attempts at communication and evasive maneuvers, the objects continued to follow the 747 at an alarming proximity, causing palpable tension among the crew.

The incident reached its climax when the UFOs were observed at very close range from the plane, allowing Terauchi and his team to observe precise details of the crafts, including their apparent structure and surface features. After several minutes of aerial confrontation, the objects finally disappeared as suddenly as they had appeared, leaving behind many unanswered questions.

This particular case has been widely documented and remains one of the most famous UFO incidents involving a commercial aircraft. It was followed by an official investigation by the Federal Aviation Administration (FAA) and has been discussed in numerous forums and publications on unidentified aerial phenomena. The incident of Japan Airlines flight 1628 remains a fascinating case study for those seeking to understand the nature and origin of UFOs, highlighting the complexity and mystery that surround these unexplained observations.

The Observation.

The incident occurred as the plane was flying over Alaska, en route from Paris to Tokyo, with a stopover in Reykjavik, Iceland. The flight commander, Kenju Terauchi, an experienced pilot with over 10,000 flight hours, was the main witness to this event.

The observation began around 5:11 PM local time, while the plane was at approximately 35,000 feet altitude, near Fort Yukon, in Alaska. The weather conditions were clear, with excellent visibility, which is crucial to note that the visibility was not hindered by weather phenomena that could have distorted the pilots' observations.

The first object was spotted by Terauchi who observed what he described as two extremely bright lights on the horizon, which seemed to be approaching the plane. These lights were not similar to those of conventional aircraft. They were much larger and their brightness was compared to that of traction headlights. According to Terauchi's testimony, these lights began to perform erratic movements, flying from left to right and sometimes stopping completely, before abruptly changing direction.

As the plane continued its course, these objects seemed to be playing a game of hide and seek with the 747, disappearing into the pilot's blind spot and then suddenly reappearing. At one point, Terauchi used his weather radar to try to determine the position of the objects relative to the plane. The radar echoes confirmed that the objects were at a distance of about 7.5 to 8 nautical miles.

The most intriguing aspect of this observation occurred when Terauchi described a third object much larger than the first two. This new object was disc-shaped, and according to his estimates, it was as large as two aircraft carriers. It emitted a kind of pale light and was surrounded by a kind of mist that made it difficult to perceive its precise contours.

This object was observed for several minutes, accompanying the 747 before disappearing as suddenly as it had appeared. Throughout this period, the crew attempted to communicate with air traffic control to report the incident and request radar confirmation. Air traffic control was able, at certain times, to confirm unidentified radar echoes, but these confirmations were intermittent and did not always coincide with the crew's visual observations.

The incident lasted a total of about 50 minutes, from the first sighting until the objects permanently disappeared from view and from the plane's instruments. During this time, the crew maintained constant communication with air traffic control, trying to understand the nature of these strange objects and to maintain flight safety.

Testimonials.

Captain Terauchi, an experienced pilot with over 29 years of flying, was the main witness to this event. According to his testimony, he first noticed unusual lights following a trajectory parallel to their route, at a distance of about 7.5 nautical miles. The lights, he said, seemed to be playing a game of "tag", moving and stopping frequently. Intrigued but not alarmed, Terauchi initially thought they were military fighters. However, the size and movements of the lights did not match those of known aircraft.

Shortly after, these lights moved closer, allowing the crew to better observe their shape and behavior. Terauchi described the lights as being arranged in a "walnut" configuration, suggesting a solid structure behind them. The intensity of the light was such that it illuminated the cockpit, and the captain could feel the heat emanating from these lights through the cockpit windows.

The co-pilot, Takanori Tamefuji, and the flight engineer, Yoshio Tsukuba, also confirmed seeing the lights, although their descriptions were less detailed than Terauchi's. Tamefuji corroborated the presence of two objects with intense light, while Tsukuba confirmed the speed and unusual movements of the objects.

At one point, Terauchi reported that the objects positioned themselves directly in front of the plane, remaining visible for several minutes before suddenly disappearing. Subsequently, a much larger and differently shaped object was observed. This last object, described as being twice as large as an aircraft carrier, was circular in shape and seemed stationary in relation to the 747.

The crew attempted to communicate with Anchorage air traffic control to report and seek confirmation of these observations. Ground control was able to identify an unidentified radar echo, but only intermittently and not consistently as reported by the witnesses on board JAL 1628.

After about 50 minutes from the first visual contact, the objects disappeared as suddenly as they had appeared. The incident left the crew perplexed and sparked a thorough investigation by several agencies, including the Federal Aviation Administration (FAA) and later, the FBI.

The Investigation.

As soon as the crew reported the objects to the Federal Aviation Administration (FAA), an investigation was launched. The initial reactions of the authorities were to check the radar data to corroborate the crew's testimony. Ground controllers in Anchorage indeed detected an unidentified radar echo near flight 1628, which added a layer of credibility to the initial report.

The investigation was conducted by several entities, including the FAA, the United States Air Force, and possibly the FBI. The military authorities examined the radar data and questioned the control tower staff. The radar recordings showed anomalies that were not immediately explained by natural phenomena or equipment errors.

Captain Terauchi, an experienced pilot with over 10,000 flight hours, provided a detailed testimony. He described the objects as being of considerable size and having maneuvering capabilities far beyond conventional aircraft. According to him, the objects could change position quickly and disappear at high speed. This testimony was taken very seriously due to his experience and accuracy in describing the events.

The FAA conducted thorough interviews with the crew and examined the communication records between flight 1628 and the control tower. The analyses of the radar tapes were reviewed by several experts in aeronautics and atmospheric phenomena in an attempt to find a conventional explanation for the observations.

After several months of analysis, the FAA concluded that the radar data and testimonies were consistent, but could not determine the nature of the observed objects. The final report mentioned that the observations were incompatible with the movements of typical aircraft or known weather phenomena.

The incident also attracted the attention of the media and UFO researchers. Documents were requested under the Freedom of Information Act (FOIA), and several documents were declassified, revealing the extent of the investigation and the seriousness with which it was conducted.

Despite investigative efforts, the incident of Japan Airlines Flight 1628 remains unresolved. The observed objects have never been officially identified, and the incident is often cited as a significant example of a well-documented UFO encounter seriously investigated by several government agencies.

Theories and Speculations.

One of the first theories put forward is that of misidentification. Some skeptics suggest that the crew might have confused natural phenomena, such as northern lights or atmospheric reflections, with extraterrestrial vessels. This hypothesis is often reinforced by the fact that UFO sightings are frequently reported in areas with high aeronautical activity and in complex weather conditions, as was the case that night.

However, this explanation is contested by the technical details reported by the crew and by the radar data confirming the presence of objects moving at speeds and with maneuvers that seem to defy the capabilities of known human aircraft. The descriptions of abrupt movements and instantaneous direction changes suggest a technology far superior to that available on Earth at that time.

Another popular theory is that of secret military technology. Some ufologists and defense analysts believe that the incident could be related to tests of advanced aircraft or drone prototypes, possibly stemming from black projects of the American government. This hypothesis is supported by the proximity of the incident to Elmendorf Air Force Base and Fort Richardson Air Force Base, which could have been test sites for such technologies.

Furthermore, the extraterrestrial explanation remains one of the most discussed and controversial. According to this theory, the observed objects would be vessels of non-earthly origins. Supporters of this idea cite the experienced testimony of Captain Terauchi, a seasoned pilot, who insisted that the flight capabilities and appearance of the objects did not correspond to any known human device. Moreover, this theory is often seen as the only one capable of explaining the seemingly very advanced technology observed.

Finally, there are those who propose more exotic explanations, such as interdimensional phenomena or manifestations of a parallel reality. Although these theories are marginal, they attempt to answer some of the most enigmatic characteristics of the incident, such as the sudden appearance and disappearance of objects on radars.

Conclusion.

The incident of Japan Airlines Flight 1628 is a landmark case in the study of unidentified aerial phenomena. Despite investigations and analyses, no conventional explanation could be established to justify the observations and radar data collected that day. The testimony of Captain Terauchi, a seasoned pilot, adds significant credibility to the reported events, reinforced by the correlation of radar signals with the moments of observation. This incident underscores the complexity and mystery surrounding UFOs and continues to defy standard scientific explanation, leaving open the question of whether we are alone in the universe.

THE UFO INCIDENT OF ILKLEY MOOR, UNITED KINGDOM.

DATE: December 1987.
COUNTRY: United Kingdom.
STATE: Yorkshire.
CITY: Ilkley Moor.

Located in Yorkshire county, Ilkley Moor is a vast expanse of moorland known for its wild landscape and ancient rock formations. In December 1987, a former policeman, Philip Spencer, took a photograph that would become famous in UFO circles. Spencer, a native of the area, knew the terrain well and had decided to cross the moor early in the morning to visit his in-laws. Equipped with a compass and a camera, he also hoped to capture images of the local wildlife. However, what he encountered that morning surpassed anything he could have imagined.

According to his testimony, Spencer observed a strange, small-sized creature and managed to take a photo before the entity disappeared. Shortly after, he saw a large dome-shaped ship rise and disappear at high speed into the sky. Disturbed and disoriented, Spencer later discovered that his compass was pointing south instead of north. Upon returning home, he also realized that he had lost about an hour of time, a phenomenon often reported in close encounters with UFOs.

The photograph taken by Spencer has been analyzed by several experts in photography and UFO phenomena. Although some have suggested that it could be a hoax or a mistake with a local animal, others have asserted that the image and Spencer's account present characteristics difficult to explain as a simple trick or confusion. The Ilkley Moor incident remains a fascinating case for ufologists and continues to spark interest and debate about the possibility of extraterrestrial visits.

The Observation.

The event took place early in the morning, in December 1987, a time of year when the weather conditions are often capricious, with low temperatures and a potentially overcast sky.

Philip Spencer, equipped with a compass and a camera, was making his way through the misty and isolated landscape of Ilkley Moor, hoping to capture images of the wild nature. The morning mist was dense, reducing visibility, but offering a mysterious atmosphere, typical of the British moors in winter. The temperature was cool, and a light wind was blowing through the tall grass and rock formations.

Around 7:30, as the sun was just beginning to break through the mist, Spencer spotted a strange shape in the distance. The object appeared to be oval in shape and emitted a bright light, despite the diffuse morning light. Intrigued and somewhat alarmed, he decided to take a photo of the object before it disappeared. The object, according to his description, was about two meters wide and seemed to be made of some kind of smooth metal, reflecting the light of the nascent morning.

The UFO made no perceptible noise, which added to the strangeness of the situation. It seemed to float above the ground, moving with a fluidity that defied the laws of physics as Spencer knew them. After taking the photograph, the object quickly rose into the sky and disappeared at a staggering speed, leaving behind only questions and a blurry image.

The photograph taken by Spencer was analyzed by several experts in photography and unidentified aerial phenomena. Although some have suggested that it could be a hoax or a mistake with a natural phenomenon, others have asserted that the characteristics of the object and its dynamics did not correspond to any known vehicle or natural phenomenon.

That morning, the weather conditions were typical for a December month in the Yorkshire moors. The temperature was around 0 degrees Celsius, and the northeast wind was blowing slightly, which could have contributed to the cold feeling experienced by Spencer. The fog limited visibility to just a few meters, making the sudden appearance of the object even more surprising and difficult to explain.

Testimonials.

That morning, a former policeman and amateur photographer, Philip Spencer, took one of the most discussed and analyzed photos of a purported alien.

Philip Spencer, the main witness, was making his way through the misty landscape of Ilkley Moor to take photographs of nature when he spotted a strange figure moving in the distance. According to his testimony, the creature appeared to be bipedal and measured about four feet tall. Intrigued and somewhat alarmed, Spencer took a photo of the figure before it quickly disappeared behind a mound. He also reported seeing a large disc-shaped vessel rise from behind the hill, disappearing at high speed into the clear morning sky.

After the incident, Spencer tried to find his way back, but he noticed that his compass was pointing south instead of north. Confused and disoriented, he finally found a nearby village where he was able to develop the film. To his great surprise, the photo revealed a blurry but discernible silhouette of what appeared to be a non-human creature.

In addition to the photograph, Spencer reported having lost about an hour of time, a phenomenon often associated with close encounters of the third kind. This loss of time has never been satisfactorily explained.

Subsequent analyses of the photograph by various experts have led to divided opinions. Some have suggested that the photo could be a hoax or a mistake with a local animal, such as a sheep or a dog. Others, however, have found elements that support the authenticity of the image, noting the consistency of the lighting and shadows with the natural environment, suggesting that the photo has not been altered or staged.

Another indirect witness, a local meteorologist, reported strange electronic anomalies in the region at the time of the incident. Although he did not see the UFO himself, his instruments recorded unusual fluctuations in the Earth's magnetic field, which could corroborate Spencer's statement about his compass failing.

The Investigation.

On a December morning in 1987, Spencer took photographs that he claimed were of extraterrestrial nature. After developing the film, a blurry but distinct image of a strange figure was revealed. Intrigued by this discovery, Spencer contacted a local ufologist who, in turn, alerted the relevant authorities.

The first phase of the investigation involved a detailed analysis of the photograph by imaging experts. The military authorities, in collaboration with photography specialists, attempted to determine if the image had been altered or manipulated in any way. The results of this analysis were shared with intelligence agencies, but were never fully disclosed to the public, thus fueling speculation and conspiracy theories.

Concurrently with the image analysis, investigators questioned Spencer about the details of his experience. He described a close encounter with a non-human being and a lapse of time he couldn't clearly remember, which sparked interest in the possibility of an alien abduction. The investigators also examined the site of the incident, looking for physical evidence or environmental anomalies. However, no conclusive evidence was found on the ground.

The military authorities took the initiative to monitor aerial activity in the region during and after the incident. Air traffic control reports indicated no unidentified aerial activity that could correspond to Spencer's observation. This information was used to assess the credibility of Spencer's testimony, although some critics suggested that the data could have been incomplete or misinterpreted.

In response to the incident, the UK Ministry of Defense conducted its own internal investigation. Although few details of this investigation have been made public, it is known that it concluded there was no threat to national security and found no evidence of technology beyond current human understanding. This conclusion has been widely criticized by the ufology community, who accused the government of cover-up.

The testimonies collected during the investigation varied in reliability and detail. Some local residents reported seeing unusual lights in the sky around the time of the incident, while others testified to the increased military presence in the area. These testimonies added a layer of complexity to the investigation, suggesting either a corroboration of Spencer's account, or other undisclosed activities in the region.

In conclusion, despite thorough investigative efforts, the Ilkley Moor UFO incident remains shrouded in mystery. The official conclusions have left many unsatisfied, and the lack of full disclosure of the investigation results continues to spark debates and speculations among researchers and the general public.

Theories and Speculations.

One of the most common theories is that of extraterrestrial visitation. This hypothesis suggests that the entity observed by Heseltine was an alien from another planet or dimension. Supporters of this theory base their arguments on the description of the creature, which does not match any known living being on Earth, as well as the apparently advanced technological capabilities necessary for interstellar or interdimensional travel. They also cite the blurry photograph as evidence, although its poor quality leaves room for many interpretations.

Another explanation put forward is that of a mistake with a local animal, perhaps exacerbated by the weather conditions or Heseltine's psychological state at the time of the incident. Skeptics of the extraterrestrial theory suggest that in the darkness and fog of Ilkley Moor, it is possible that Heseltine may have misinterpreted the silhouette of a wild animal, such as a deer or a large wild cat, as that of an extraterrestrial creature. This theory is often reinforced by the fact that isolated testimonies like this one can be subject to perception errors.

A third theory suggests that the incident could have been a hallucination or optical illusion. The conditions on Ilkley Moor, particularly the extreme cold and isolation, could have contributed to an altered sensory experience. Critics of this theory, however, argue that Heseltine, as a former police officer, had considerable experience in observation and was unlikely to be fooled by his senses.

Some ufologists have also speculated about the possibility of a secret military operation or a test of advanced technologies, which may have been misinterpreted as extraterrestrial contact. This theory is fueled by reports of unidentified aerial phenomena in other regions, which later turned out to be tests of new aircraft or military technologies. However, no concrete evidence has been presented to support this hypothesis in the case of Ilkley Moor.

Finally, a more marginal but intriguing perspective is that of psychosocial interaction, where the incident would be a manifestation of the collective unconscious, influenced by popular culture and media around aliens. This theory suggests that Heseltine's experience could be a kind of projection or manifestation of his own beliefs and expectations regarding UFOs and extraterrestrial life.

THE UFO INCIDENT OF MUNDRABILLA, AUSTRALIA.

DATE: 1988.
COUNTRY: Australia.
STATE: Western Australia.
CITY: Mundrabilla.

Located in the isolated region of Western Australia, this event involved a family traveling on the Eyre Highway, a transcontinental road that crosses desert and sparsely populated areas of the country. In January 1988, the Knowles family, composed of the mother, Faye, and her three adult children, Patrick, Sean, and Wayne, were heading towards Melbourne after visiting relatives in Perth. Their nighttime journey was abruptly interrupted in the early hours of the morning, when what seemed to be an intense light began to follow their car. What started as a curious observation quickly turned into a terrifying experience, when the object seemed to land on the roof of their car, causing a loss of vehicle control and a series of unexplainable physical phenomena. The family's testimonies, corroborated by physical traces on the car and police reports, have made this incident an important case study for ufologists and skeptics.

The Observation.

This event occurred on the night of April 21, 1988, near the small locality of Mundrabilla, located in the isolated region of the Nullarbor Plain in Western Australia. The main witnesses of this event were the Knowles family, composed of Faye Knowles and her three sons, Patrick, Sean, and Wayne.

Around 4 o'clock in the morning, while the family was traveling by car on the Eyre Highway, a strange phenomenon began to manifest. The sky was clear and the stars were shining brightly, offering perfect visibility. Suddenly, a luminous object was spotted by the family members. According to their descriptions, the object seemed to be extremely bright, with an intense white light that did not resemble any conventional light.

The object in question was oval-shaped and about the size of a minibus. It seemed to hover over the car at a relatively low altitude. Witnesses reported that the object emitted a whistling or buzzing noise, which added to the surreal atmosphere of the observation. The family also described a kind of pressure or force that seemed to weigh on them when the object was at its closest.

At a certain point, the object got close enough for physical interactions to occur. The Knowles family reported that their car was violently shaken, as if an external force was trying to control it. They also felt an increase in the temperature inside the vehicle, which caused a stifling heat sensation.

The incident lasted several minutes, during which the object continued to follow the car, sometimes changing position but always staying nearby. Eventually, the object moved away at high speed, disappearing into the night sky as quickly as it had appeared.

The weather conditions during the incident were clear, with little or no wind and no cloud cover, allowing for a detailed observation of the object. The temperature was cool, typical of desert nights, but the proximity of the object had caused a noticeable increase in heat around the car.

This incident remains one of the most detailed and mysterious UFO recordings in Australia, primarily due to the clarity of the testimonies and the physical nature of the interactions between the object and the witnesses. The descriptions provided by the Knowles family were consistent and detailed, offering a fascinating insight into a phenomenon that is still largely unexplained.

Testimonials.

The main witnesses of this event were the Knowles family, composed of Faye Knowles and her three sons, Patrick, Sean, and Wayne. Their detailed testimony provides a fascinating insight into their encounter with an unidentified flying object as they were crossing the Eyre Highway in the desolate Nullarbor Plain.

In the morning of January 20, 1988, as the Knowles family was driving, they observed a bright light that seemed to follow their vehicle. According to Faye Knowles, the light was so intense that it illuminated the road as if it were broad daylight. The sons described the object as being oval-shaped and enveloped in a kind of luminous mist or fog, which made it difficult to appreciate its exact size.

Patrick, who was driving at that time, mentioned that the object approached at an incredible speed before stabilizing just above their car. He described a high-pitched sound, almost like a whistle, that accompanied the UFO's movement. This detail was corroborated by his brothers, who also reported a sensation of heat emanating from the object.

The most terrifying experience for the family occurred when the UFO allegedly exerted some kind of gravitational force on their car. Wayne recounted that the car began to be lifted off the ground, the tires losing contact with the road. In a moment of panic, he opened the window and felt a pressure pulling on his hair, described as a "viscous" and "sticky" force.

Faye Knowles, terrified, screamed at her sons to keep their heads down, fearing for their safety. She also reported hearing a strange noise, as if something was hitting against the car roof, while the object maintained its grip on the vehicle. After what seemed like an eternity but only lasted a few minutes, the UFO suddenly released its grip, and the car abruptly fell back onto the road, causing two tires to puncture.

After the incident, the family immediately sought help and reported their experience to the local police as well as to ufologists. Investigators noted that the car had unusual marks and burn traces on the roof, which added a layer of credibility to their story. Moreover, subsequent tests revealed abnormally high levels of radioactivity on the car, which further mystified experts and skeptics.

The Investigation.

From the first hours following the incident, the local police began collecting testimonies from the Knowles family members as well as other potential witnesses who were in the area at that time. The initial statements were quite consistent, describing an oval-shaped object emitting intense light. The reaction of the authorities was to treat the matter seriously, given the specificity and severity of the allegations.

Shortly after, the Australian army and the Commonwealth Scientific and Industrial Research Organisation (CSIRO) were informed and began participating in the investigation. The goal was to determine the nature of the reported object and assess any potential threat to national security. Experts in aeronautics, meteorology, and physics were consulted to analyze the environmental conditions and the characteristics of the object described by the witnesses.

One of the key aspects of the investigation was the examination of the Knowles family's vehicle. Strange traces and residues found on the car were analyzed to identify their composition. The results showed unusual particles that could not be immediately identified, adding an element of mystery to the case. In addition, radar recordings of the area were scrutinized to identify any unauthorized or unexplained air traffic at the time of the incident, but no conclusive evidence was found.

The investigation also included in-depth interviews with the Knowles family members by psychologists specializing in traumatic stress, to assess their mental state and the reliability of their testimonies. These interviews reinforced the credibility of their account, as they showed signs of stress corresponding to a real traumatic experience.

After several months of investigations, the final report was published. It concluded that, despite the lack of concrete evidence regarding the nature of the object, the testimonies were deemed credible. However, it was not possible to determine with certainty what the Knowles family had encountered that night. The report also mentioned that the incident posed no immediate threat to national security and recommended closing the case, while remaining open to receiving new information that could shed light on this mysterious event.

Theories and Speculations.

One of the most popular theories is that of extraterrestrial visitation. This hypothesis suggests that the observed object was a spacecraft from an advanced civilization from elsewhere in the universe. Supporters of this theory often rely on the description of witnesses, who speak of a flying object with maneuvering capabilities and a speed that seem to defy the laws of physics as we know them. They argue that such characteristics could not be reproduced by current or known human technologies.

On the contrary, some experts propose a more down-to-earth explanation, suggesting that what the witnesses saw could be a rare atmospheric phenomenon. For instance, fireballs or ball lightning are natural phenomena that can sometimes be perceived as unidentified flying objects due to their unusual appearance and unpredictable behavior. These phenomena can create illusions of massive objects moving at high speed in the sky, especially at night.

Another common speculation concerns secret military operations. According to this theory, the observed object could be an experimental craft, perhaps a drone or another type of aeronautical technology in the testing phase. Governments and military organizations regularly test new technologies, often in secret for reasons of national security. This could explain why the object seemed so advanced compared to what the public might expect to see.

There are also those who believe that the incident could be a case of mistaken identity with a more conventional object, such as an airplane or a satellite. In conditions of reduced visibility or under certain atmospheric conditions, it is possible that familiar objects take on strange aspects and are misinterpreted by witnesses not trained in their identification.

Finally, the impact of human psychology in the interpretation of UFO observations should not be dismissed. The phenomenon of "social contagion", where witnesses of an unusual event may unconsciously align their accounts with those of others or with popular UFO stories, could also play a role. Moreover, the cultural fascination with aliens and UFOs can influence how people interpret unexplained events.

THE VORONEZH INCIDENT, RUSSIA: LANDING OF A UFO AND ENCOUNTER WITH MYSTERIOUS BEINGS.

DATE: September 27, 1989.
COUNTRY: Soviet Union.
STATE: Central.
CITY: Voronej.

In autumn 1989, in a park in the city of Voronej, several witnesses, including children, reported seeing an unidentified flying object land. According to the reports, this event was not only marked by the presence of a strange craft, but also by the appearance of beings who emerged from it. The descriptions of these beings varied, but many agreed that they were tall and wore silver clothing. This case gained international attention, notably because it was reported by the official Soviet press agency TASS, which gave it some credibility at the time. Skeptics, however, questioned the reliability of the testimonies, especially those of the children, and suggested that the incident could have been a staged event or a collective hallucination. Despite this, the Voronej incident remains a fascinating example of how UFO sightings can captivate the public imagination and stimulate debate about extraterrestrial life and air safety.

The Observation.

The Voronej incident, which captured international attention, occurred on September 27, 1989 in a park in the city of Voronej, Russia. Around 6:30 pm, on a clear evening with excellent visibility, several witnesses, including children and adults, reported seeing an unidentified flying object land. The UFO, described as a large glowing sphere, was about 9 meters in diameter. It seemed to emit a kind of brilliant light that oscillated between red and orange, creating an almost hypnotic aura around it.

According to reports, the object hovered at a low altitude before gently landing on the ground in a grassy area of the park. The grass under the UFO seemed to be affected by heat or some kind of radiation, as it began to brown and wilt almost immediately after the object's landing. Witnesses also noted a total absence of noise throughout the entire event, which added to the strangeness of the scene.

Shortly after landing, a hatch opened on the side of the object and a staircase extended to the ground. Three creatures then emerged from the UFO. These beings, described as being about three meters tall, wore silver suits that seemed to reflect the light from the object. Their head was small compared to their body and their eyes were described as being large and black, with no visible eyelids.

The creatures walked around the park for a few minutes, then one of them brandished a tube resembling a weapon, which emitted a beam of light towards a 16-year-old boy witnessing the scene. The beam seemed to temporarily paralyze the young man, who fell to the ground, unable to move until the creatures returned to their ship. After this incident, the UFO took off vertically at an incredible speed, disappearing from the witnesses' field of vision in a few seconds.

The entire event lasted about twenty minutes. During this time, the sky was clear and the outside temperature was mild, which allowed for clear observation without interference from weather conditions. The sunlight was beginning to fade, but the brightness of the UFO and the creatures' suits provided enough light for the details to be visible to the witnesses.

Testimonials.

Among the main witnesses is Vassili Sidorenko, a 10-year-old child at the time, who was playing football with his friends in the park. Vassili described the UFO as a large bright sphere that landed silently. He noted that the craft had some sort of feet or stabilizers that deployed upon landing. Shortly after, a door opened, allowing three creatures to exit the craft.

Another important witness, Ludmila Makarova, a teacher who was nearby, corroborated Vassili's account. She added that the creatures were very large, about three meters tall, with small heads in relation to their bodies and dressed in silver suits. Ludmila also mentioned that one of the creatures was holding a device resembling a "gun" and that she saw a light beam emanating from this device, touching a boy who was briefly paralyzed.

A third witness, Egorov Ponomarenko, a policeman who was patrolling the area, was alerted by the screams of the children. Upon arriving at the scene, he observed the UFO and the creatures. According to his testimony, the craft was about 12 meters in diameter and emitted a brilliant light that made direct vision difficult. Ponomarenko confirmed that one of the creatures used a device that projected a beam of light on the environment, causing a brief but intense light.

Finally, a local journalist, Anatoliy Berezovoy, who interviewed the witnesses shortly after the incident, reported that several adults and children present described the events in a similar way, despite the initial shock and disbelief. Anatoliy noted that the testimonies were consistent regarding the description of the craft, the beings and their actions, including the detail that the UFO took off vertically and disappeared at an incredible speed without making a sound.

These testimonies, collected independently from each other, present a fascinating and complex story that continues to spark debates and research among ufologists and skeptics.

The Investigation.

Located in a park in Voronej, Russia, this event quickly caught the attention not only of local authorities, but also of the international community, during the height of glasnost in the USSR.

The initial reaction was one of astonishment and confusion among both witnesses and authorities. The first reports from the TASS news agency described children and adults witnessing the landing of a large disc-shaped object, accompanied by three strange creatures. Faced with the magnitude of the case, the Soviet government decided to launch an official investigation to separate the facts from fiction.

The investigation was conducted by several branches of the Soviet authorities, including scientists, military personnel, and KGB agents. The initial stages involved questioning eyewitnesses. The children, considered the main witnesses, described in detail the appearance of the beings and their actions. According to their testimonies, the creatures were tall, with small heads and deep eyes. They also reported that one of the beings had brandished a tube, which had projected a beam of light, temporarily paralyzing a young boy.

The military investigators focused on the analysis of the presumed landing site. Radiation measurements were taken, and although the results were deemed normal, traces and marks on the ground were reported as being unusual. These marks could have been interpreted as prints left by the craft or the entities.

Simultaneously, the government authorities examined the media and social impact of the incident. They were particularly concerned about how the information was being disseminated, fearing a panic or media frenzy. This led them to tightly regulate the information released, ensuring that the reports were filtered and controlled.

As the investigation progressed, discrepancies emerged regarding the credibility of the testimonies. Some investigators questioned the reliability of the children's statements, suggesting that collective excitement could have influenced their perceptions and memories. Others, however, supported the truthfulness of the testimonies, citing the consistency of the accounts despite separate interrogations.

The findings of the investigation largely remained inconclusive. The authorities could not definitively determine the nature of the object nor validate the existence of the entities. The final report suggested that, although some aspects of the incident could be attributed to natural phenomena or interpretation errors, other elements remained unexplained.

This Voronej incident remains a fascinating case study for ufologists and continues to spark debates about the possibility of extraterrestrial visits. Despite investigative efforts, many questions remain unanswered, fueling speculation and interest in UFO phenomena around the world.

Theories and Speculations.

One of the most popular theories is that of extraterrestrial visitation. According to this hypothesis, the observed object and the beings encountered would be of non-Earthly origin. Supporters of this theory rely on the detailed descriptions of the witnesses, who reported seeing a large disc-shaped object and creatures about three meters tall with small heads on large black bodies. Advocates of this theory argue that the details of the observation, including the beings' interactions with the environment (such as ground marking and observed physical effects), cannot be explained by technologies or phenomena known on Earth.

Another hypothesis put forward is that of a hoax or collective hallucination. Skeptics argue that the incident could have been an elaborate setup or the result of mass panic, where witnesses may have misinterpreted natural phenomena or human activities as being of extraterrestrial origin. This theory is often reinforced by the context of the time, marked by a strong presence of science fiction in the media, which could have influenced the perception of the witnesses.

A third theory suggests that the Voronej incident could be the result of secret military experiments. The Soviet Union, like other major powers of the time, was engaged in advanced research on aeronautical technologies and armaments. Some experts suggest that the UFO could have been a prototype of an experimental aircraft, and that the "beings" observed could have been mannequins or automated equipment used in these tests. This hypothesis is supported by the fact that the incident occurred in a region where military activities were frequently reported.

Finally, a less conventional perspective is that of interdimensionality or paranormal phenomena. Some researchers in abnormal phenomena consider that the incident could be related to manifestations of entities or phenomena from other dimensions. Although this theory is marginal and often criticized for its lack of scientific foundation, it continues to be discussed in certain UFO and parapsychological circles.

THE BELGIAN UFO WAVE.

DATE: 1989-1990.
COUNTRY: Belgium.
STATE: Not applicable.
CITY: Several cities across the country.

The Belgian UFO Wave is a phenomenon that deeply marked Belgium between November 1989 and April 1990. During this period, thousands of people reported seeing unidentified flying objects in the sky, mainly black triangles with lights at the ends and a flashing red light in the center. These observations were accompanied by descriptions of extremely silent flight behavior and capable of speeds and maneuvers defying the capabilities of known aircraft at the time.

The most documented incident took place on March 30, 1990, a night when UFO sightings peaked. That night, the Belgian army's radars picked up inexplicable signals that matched the visual testimonies of citizens. In response, the Belgian Air Force deployed F-16 fighter jets to intercept these phenomena. However, despite several attempts, the pilots were unable to establish lasting visual contact or explain the strange radar behaviors recorded.

This event not only captivated the public, but also involved military and scientific authorities in a thorough investigation. The Belgian government, through its Ministry of Defense, took the unusual initiative to treat these observations with official seriousness, leading to a transparency and openness that were rare at the time for such incidents. The results of the investigation, although inconclusive as to the origin of the objects, confirmed the reality of the radar data and multiple testimonies, thus leaving an unresolved mystery and an indelible mark in the history of unidentified aerial phenomena.

The Observation.

The most notable incident took place on the evening of November 29, 1989, mainly around the Eupen region in Belgium, where several witnesses, including police officers, reported seeing an unidentified flying object.

The object observed that night was described as being triangular in shape with bright lights at each corner. Witnesses reported that the object was about 30 meters on each side and emitted an intense light in the center, which seemed to oscillate and change color from red to orange, then to blue. The UFO was moving at a relatively slow speed and at low altitude, allowing for detailed observation. It was described as being absolutely silent, without any engine noise or other sound associated with conventional aircraft.

The exact time of the initial observation was around 5:30 pm. At that time, visibility was good despite the onset of nightfall. The weather conditions were clear with an unobstructed sky, which allowed optimal visibility of the object. The temperature was cool, typical of a late November evening in Belgium.

The object was observed for several minutes, initially moving slowly in the northeast direction, then it changed direction to head west. During its journey, the UFO was seen flying over the countryside, passing over houses and roads, without disturbing either the power grid or the vehicles below. Several motorists stopped to observe the strange phenomenon, and some even tried to follow the object with their vehicles.

The observation was so detailed that the witnesses were able to note specific characteristics of the object, such as the presence of what seemed to be some kind of metallic structure under the luminous base, giving the object a more "solid" appearance than that of a simple light manifestation. Moreover, some witnesses reported seeing a kind of luminous halo around the object, which added to the strangeness of the sight.

This observation on November 29, 1989 marked the beginning of a series of similar observations throughout Belgium, primarily concentrated in the Walloon region. The descriptions of the observed objects remained remarkably consistent among the different witnesses, which added to the credibility of the reports. The observations continued to be reported with decreasing frequency until April 1991, making this wave of UFOs one of the longest and most followed in recent history.

Testimonials.

The Belgian UFO Wave, which took place between 1989 and 1991, is one of the most documented UFO observation phenomena in Europe. During this period, thousands of people reported seeing unidentified flying objects in the sky of Belgium. These testimonies come from various layers of the population, including police officers, military personnel, and numerous civilians.

One of the earliest and most credible testimonies comes from two gendarmes, Heinrich Nicoll and Hubert von Montigny. On November 29, 1989, while they were patrolling near the town of Eupen, they observed a large triangular object with bright lights at each corner. The object, according to their description, was capable of moving at incredibly low speeds without making any sound. They followed the object for several hours before losing sight of it.

Another striking testimony comes from several members of the Belgian Air Force. On March 30, 1990, following multiple reports of similar observations to those of the gendarmes, two F-16s were sent to intercept an unidentified object. The pilots reported that the object was changing position very quickly, making conventional interception impossible. The F-16 radars recorded speeds and movements that defied the capabilities of any known craft at the time.

Among the civilians, a particularly interesting case is that of the Michaux family, who lived near Liège. In December 1989, the entire family observed from their garden a triangular object hovering above their house. According to Marc Michaux, the object was so large that it almost covered the entire view of the sky and emitted a soft light that illuminated the garden as if it were broad daylight. The object remained motionless for about 10 minutes before disappearing over the horizon at a staggering speed.

In January 1990, a retired teacher, Mrs. Gertrude Lepage, reported seeing a similar object while she was driving home. She described the object as having a triangular shape with three orange lights at the corners and a larger, brighter light in the center. The object followed her car for nearly five kilometers before it rose vertically and disappeared.

The Investigation.

The investigation into these observations involved several levels of government and military authorities, including the Belgian Air Force.

It all started when hundreds of witnesses, including police officers, reported seeing strange lights in the sky, often described as triangular objects equipped with bright and silent lights. Faced with the magnitude of the testimonies, the Belgian Air Force quickly responded by taking these reports seriously and starting an official investigation.

Major General Wilfried De Brouwer, at the time head of operations for the Air Force, was tasked with coordinating the investigation. Under his direction, the military collected reports, interviewed witnesses, and analyzed radar data. One of the highlights of the investigation was the night of March 30 to 31, 1990, when unidentified objects were simultaneously tracked by ground radars and F-16 aircraft from the Belgian Air Force. The pilots reported that the targets were moving at speeds and with maneuvers far beyond the capabilities of known aircraft at the time.

Radar data, both on the ground and from the F-16s, showed objects moving at incredible speeds, changing direction abruptly, and sometimes descending several thousand feet in a few seconds. These observations were corroborated by numerous ground witnesses who described similar movements.

The investigation also included collaboration with universities, astronomers, and physicists, with the aim of understanding the nature of the observed phenomena. Experts in optics and photography analyzed the images and videos taken by witnesses. Despite these efforts, many of these analyses remained inconclusive, failing to provide a definitive explanation on the nature or origin of the observed objects.

Despite the rigor of the investigation, the Belgian Air Force concluded that it could not determine the exact origin of the objects. Major General De Brouwer publicly admitted that the nature and origin of the phenomena remained unknown. This statement was supported by the fact that the observations did not correspond to any known aircraft or natural phenomenon.

The investigation into the Belgian UFO wave remains a significant example of how military and governmental authorities can handle UFO reports in an open and serious manner. It also highlighted the limitations of contemporary technology and science in the face of unidentified aerial phenomena.

Theories and Speculations.

One of the most common theories is that of extraterrestrial intervention. This hypothesis is based on descriptions of flying machines with maneuvering capabilities apparently impossible for the human technologies of the time, such as abrupt changes in direction and very rapid accelerations without corresponding sound effects. Supporters of this theory also cite the triangular shapes and unusual lights reported by witnesses as being characteristics not conforming to traditional aircraft.

Another explanation put forward is that of secret military prototypes. According to this theory, the UFOs observed could be experimental aircraft developed by governments or private companies. This hypothesis is reinforced by the fact that the wave of observations took place at the end of the Cold War, a period marked by significant and often secret advances in aeronautical technology. However, no government has ever claimed these crafts, and skeptics of this theory point out that such test flights would have been risky and reckless over populated areas.

A third perspective suggests that the observations could be attributed to misinterpreted natural or atmospheric phenomena. Phenomena such as reflections of terrestrial lights on low clouds, optical illusions due to particular atmospheric conditions, or even the atmospheric re-entry of space debris could be mistaken for unidentified flying objects. Critics of this theory, however, argue that testimonies of coordinated and intelligent movements of the objects, as well as radar recordings, contradict the idea of a purely natural phenomenon.

Finally, some researchers and skeptics put forward the idea of a collective panic or mass hysteria. They suggest that the intensive media coverage of a few initial observations could have influenced other people to believe that they too had seen unusual things, thus fueling a cycle of observation reports without a solid real basis. This theory is often contested by those who point to the credibility and accuracy of the many testimonies from people deemed reliable, as well as material evidence such as radar recordings.

Conclusion.

Despite numerous observations by credible witnesses, including members of law enforcement and the military, as well as radar confirmations, no conventional explanation has been established for the Belgian UFO wave. Attempts at interception by F-16s only deepened the mystery, with the object displaying maneuvering capabilities far beyond the technologies known at the time. This case continues to spark interest and debate among experts and enthusiasts of ufology, and remains a striking example of an unidentified aerial phenomenon.

THE UFO WAVE INCIDENT IN ITALY IN 1990.

DATE: 1990.
COUNTRY: Italy.
STATE: .
CITY: Several cities across the country.

The year 1990 was marked in Italy by a series of observations of unidentified flying objects, a phenomenon that affected several regions of the country and aroused keen interest among both ufologists and the general population. This event, often referred to as "The UFO Wave of 1990", is considered one of the most significant in the history of Italian ufology due to its scale and the diversity of the testimonies collected. The observations began at the start of the year and extended over several months, reaching a peak of reports in the spring and summer. Witnesses, who included people of all ages and various professions, described seeing objects with strange shapes and behaviors, often accompanied by bright lights and sometimes unusual sounds. These phenomena were reported in many cities and villages, creating an atmosphere of curiosity and sometimes concern among residents and local authorities. The incident also stimulated public and media debate about the possible presence of extraterrestrials and how the government was handling information related to UFOs. Despite various investigations, many of these observations remained unexplained, contributing to fuel conspiracy theories and interest in the UFO phenomenon in Italy.

The Observation.

The incident of the UFO wave in Italy in 1990 remains one of the most documented and discussed events in the history of Italian ufology. On the evening of November 14, 1990, numerous witnesses across different regions of Italy reported seeing unidentified flying objects. The sightings mainly took place between 7:00 pm and 11:30 pm, local time.

The descriptions of the object varied slightly from one witness to another, but several common points were reported. The most frequently described object was triangular or V-shaped, with lights at the ends. The lights were mainly white in color, but some witnesses also reported red and green lights. The object produced no audible sound, which added to the witnesses' perplexity. Its size was difficult to estimate, but it was often described as being considerably larger than a typical airliner.

The object was seen moving at varying speeds; in some cases, it seemed to float very slowly, almost stationary, while in others, it moved at a high speed, quickly crossing the sky. This ability to change speed and maneuver at strange angles was noted as particularly unusual by observers.

The weather conditions that night were clear with little cloud cover, which allowed for excellent visibility. The moon was nearly full, providing additional light that helped some witnesses discern the shape of the object against the night sky more clearly.

The observations were reported in several major cities as well as in rural areas, indicating that the object or objects covered a large part of the Italian territory. Among the observation locations, Milan, Florence, and Rome are included, as well as more remote regions in the north and south of Italy.

What makes this incident particularly interesting is the high number of witnesses, including airplane pilots and military personnel, who have confirmed the presence of these unusual objects in the sky. Their testimonies have added a layer of credibility to the overall observations, making the incident hard to ignore or simply dismiss as a hoax or a mistake.

Testimonials.

On November 14, 1990, thousands of people across the country reported seeing unusual lights and unidentified flying objects in the sky. These observations were made by ordinary citizens, pilots, police officers, and even members of the armed forces. Here are some of the most striking testimonies from this event.

One of the first reports came from Milan, where several witnesses observed a large luminous triangle crossing the sky at an incredible speed. Among them, Marco, an aeronautical engineer, described the object as having three white lights at the corners and a reddish light in the center. According to him, the object made no noise and was moving too quickly to be a conventional airplane.

In Rome, an entire family witnessed a series of lights moving in a synchronized manner. Claudia, the mother, reported that the lights formed a sort of V formation and changed color from white to blue, then to red, all while moving silently across the sky. She added that the observation lasted about 20 minutes before the lights suddenly disappeared.

In the south of Italy, in Naples, a group of sea fishermen also reported a strange experience. One of them, Giuseppe, recounted seeing a circular object emitting intense light descend towards the sea, then ascend vertically into the sky at a dizzying speed. The navigation instruments on the boat stopped working during the incident, adding an additional layer of mystery to their testimony.

A particularly interesting testimony comes from an Italian Air Force pilot, who was on a routine flight near Turin. Captain Riccardo observed a disk-shaped object accompanying his plane at a distance of about 300 meters. The object then accelerated and disappeared over the horizon within a few seconds. The plane's radar recorded the object, but it was not possible to determine its exact nature.

Finally, in Florence, an amateur astronomer, Lorenzo, managed to capture images of an oval object through his telescope. According to him, the object seemed to have a metallic surface that reflected sunlight. The images were analyzed by several experts, but no conclusive explanation was found as to what this object could be.

These testimonies, among hundreds of others, have contributed to making the incident of the UFO wave in Italy in 1990 an important case study for ufologists and researchers in unidentified aerial phenomena. Despite numerous investigations, many of these observations remain unexplained, fueling curiosity and debate about the possible presence of unidentified flying objects in our atmosphere.

The Investigation.

Faced with the magnitude of the testimonies, the Italian government, under pressure from public opinion and the media, decided to launch an official investigation to clarify the nature and origin of these phenomena.

The investigation was entrusted to the Aeronautica Militare Italiana (AMI), which immediately began by collecting testimonies from citizens, pilots, air traffic controllers, and military personnel who had observed the UFOs. These testimonies were supplemented by the analysis of radar recordings, which confirmed the presence of unidentified flying objects in the Italian sky on several occasions during that evening.

The initial reports from the AMI highlighted a series of simultaneous observations in different regions, notably in Lombardy, Tuscany, Veneto, and Apulia. The descriptions of the objects varied, but several witnesses reported seeing bright lights moving at high speed and performing maneuvers that seemed to defy the known laws of physics.

In response to these testimonies, AMI has intensified its investigation in collaboration with the National Institute of Geophysics and Volcanology as well as several astronomical observatories, in order to determine if these phenomena could have a conventional explanation, such as meteors or space debris.

After several months of analysis and verification, AMI published a preliminary report concluding that, although some of the observed phenomena could be attributed to natural causes or interpretation errors, a significant number of incidents could not be satisfactorily explained with the data and knowledge available at the time.

This report has sparked numerous reactions, both in the scientific community and among the general public, and has led to the creation of a parliamentary commission to further study these phenomena. This commission has heard from experts in aeronautics, meteorology, physics and astronomy, as well as direct witnesses of the events.

The work of the commission lasted several years and included a detailed examination of radar data, videos and photos taken during the incident, as well as in-depth interviews with witnesses. Despite these efforts, the commission concluded in its final report that the origin and nature of many UFOs observed during the 1990 wave remained undetermined.

This conclusion has left many questions unanswered and has continued to fuel speculation and theories about the possible presence of extraterrestrial craft in our airspace. The incident of the UFO wave in Italy in 1990 thus remains one of the most enigmatic and discussed cases in the history of ufology in Italy.

Theories and Speculations.

One of the most popular theories is that of extraterrestrial intervention. This hypothesis suggests that the observed objects were spacecraft of non-earthly origins. Supporters of this theory cite the coordination and seemingly intelligent movements of the lights, as well as their ability to perform maneuvers that defy known laws of physics, as evidence of their extraterrestrial origin. Moreover, some witnesses have reported sudden changes in direction and incredibly fast accelerations that seem to go beyond the capabilities of human aerial vehicles.

On the other hand, there are more skeptical explanations. Some experts and scientists have suggested that these observations could be attributed to natural phenomena or human activities. For example, one theory suggests that the lights could be due to reflections from satellites or sky lanterns. Another plausible explanation is that of secret military tests, where experimental technologies were tested without public knowledge. This theory is supported by the fact that Italy, at that time, was involved in several armament and aeronautical technology development projects.

There has also been speculation around rare atmospheric phenomena, such as temperature inversions, which could have created optical illusions or mirages.

These conditions can sometimes reflect the light from distant cities or other light sources, making them appear as flying objects in the sky.

An interesting debate among ufologists concerns the possibility of disinformation orchestrated by the government or other powerful entities. This conspiracy theory suggests that the incident could have been a cover-up for more sinister activities or simply a means to divert public attention from more pressing issues. Some conspiracy theorists even propose that governments could collaborate with extraterrestrial entities, although this idea remains largely speculative and without concrete evidence.

Finally, there are those who believe that the incident could be a case of collective psychosis, where the tension due to the political and social situation of the time could have made people more susceptible to believing in an alien invasion. This theory is often supported by psychologists who study how humans react in situations of collective stress.

THE INCIDENT IN MONTREAL, CANADA.

DATE: November 7, 1990.
COUNTRY: Canada.
STATE: Quebec.
CITY: Montreal.

The Montreal incident is one of the most publicized UFO sighting cases in Canada, sparking keen interest both nationally and internationally. On the evening of November 7, 1990, an unidentified flying object was spotted in the sky of Montreal, captivating the attention of citizens, ufology experts, and local authorities. The event began when several witnesses, residing in different neighborhoods of the city, reported seeing a strange stationary luminous object above the Bonaventure Hotel. This phenomenon lasted nearly three hours, during which the object changed shape and color several times, shifting from an oval shape to a more circular appearance, and emitting bright lights varying from red to blue and white.

Witnesses to this incident included local residents, tourists, and even on-duty police officers, which added a layer of credibility to the reports. The police services, alerted by the public's incessant calls, sent patrols to confirm the observations. Meanwhile, the nearest airport was contacted to check if the object could be a distressed airplane or helicopter, but no unusual aerial activity was recorded at that time.

The incident was also followed by amateur and professional astronomers who tried to identify the object using telescopes. However, despite the efforts made, the object could not be conclusively identified. Theories ranging from a weather balloon to an extraterrestrial craft were proposed, but no definitive explanation has been accepted by the scientific community. The Montreal incident therefore remains an unsolved mystery and continues to fascinate and stimulate debate among researchers and the general public.

The Observation.

That evening, several witnesses, including residents, police officers, and even meteorology experts, reported seeing an unidentified flying object in the sky over Montreal.

The observation began around 7:00 PM, when the first calls were received by the local police. Witnesses described a circular object, emitting intense light. The object seemed stationary, suspended at low altitude in the night sky. Its size was estimated to be about 540 meters in diameter, a colossal dimension that surprised everyone who saw it.

The description of the UFO varied slightly from one witness to another, but several common points were noted. The object was mainly described as having a metallic structure with multicolored lights that flashed or rotated around its perimeter. These lights changed color sequentially, going from red to green, then to blue, creating an impressive visual spectacle.

The weather conditions that night were clear with few clouds, allowing for perfect visibility of the object. The temperature was cool, typical of an autumn evening in Montreal, with a slight northeast wind. These conditions helped to rule out the hypothesis of a confusion with a natural weather phenomenon, such as a lenticular cloud or a light effect caused by atmospheric refraction.

The UFO remained visible for about three hours, observed by hundreds of people from different points in the city. Throughout the duration of the observation, the object maintained its position in the sky, with no perceptible movement other than the twinkling and rotation of its lights. Around 10:00 PM, the object began to slowly rise in the sky before disappearing at a dizzying speed, leaving behind many astonished and perplexed witnesses.

This observation was one of the longest and most visible ever recorded in the history of UFOs in Canada, and it continues to fascinate and intrigue experts and UFO enthusiasts. The precise details of the object, its exceptional duration of appearance, and the clear weather conditions that night contribute to making this incident an important case study in the field of unidentified aerial phenomena.

Testimonials.

Several witnesses, including customers and staff from a renowned city hotel, reported seeing a large, strangely shaped unidentified flying object.

Among the main witnesses, there is a businesswoman visiting Montreal, who was staying on the 9th floor of the hotel. She described seeing a huge object with several bright lights, silently suspended above the hotel's pool. According to her testimony, the object was about 30 meters in diameter and emitted an intense light that changed color, shifting from blue to red, then to white.

Another important witness was the hotel's security chief, who was alerted by calls from frightened customers. Upon climbing to the roof to better observe the situation, he confirmed the presence of the object, noting that it made no noise and seemed to float above the hotel without any visible means of propulsion. He also mentioned that the object had a circular shape with some sort of dome on top.

A couple of tourists, who were dining in the hotel restaurant with a view of the sky, also shared their experience. They described the object as being oval-shaped and were particularly impressed by the speed at which it eventually disappeared, moving at an incredibly high speed without leaving a trace.

In addition to these individual testimonies, several other hotel guests and passersby on the street reported similar observations. Some took photos, although the quality of the images taken at night and often with low-performing devices in low light did not allow for a definitive conclusion about the nature of the object.

The incident was also corroborated by the testimony of a plane pilot who was passing nearby. According to him, the object was clearly visible from the cockpit and did not correspond to any conventional aircraft. The pilot described a series of lights that did not resemble any standard aviation lights and emphasized the absence of noise, which is unusual for a craft of this size.

The Investigation.

From the first hours following the observation of the unidentified flying object, a series of measures were taken to collect testimonies and analyze the available data.

The initial reactions of the authorities were to secure the area where the UFO was spotted, a common practice to preserve the integrity of possible evidence. Local police forces, supported by units from the Canadian Armed Forces, cordoned off the area and began questioning eyewitnesses. These testimonies formed the basis of the preliminary investigation, shedding light on the object's trajectory, its apparent size, and behavior.

Simultaneously, the Ministry of National Defense launched a more formal investigation, involving experts in aeronautics and atmospheric phenomena. The goal was to determine if the observed object could be an unidentified aircraft, a rare weather phenomenon, or something else. Military and civilian radars were scrutinized to find any trace of the object, but the results were inconclusive, which added to the mystique of the incident.

The investigators also consulted specialists in optics and photography to analyze the few blurry images captured by witnesses using video cameras and photo cameras. Although the quality of the images did not allow for a detailed analysis, they confirmed the presence of a flying object with atypical characteristics.

A crucial aspect of the investigation was the collaboration with international agencies such as NASA and SETI (Search for Extraterrestrial Intelligence). These organizations provided experts in exobiology and astrophysics to evaluate the collected data. However, despite this extensive expertise, no definitive conclusion could be drawn about the nature or origin of the object.

The investigation also took into account the psychosocial aspects of the incident, by engaging psychologists to analyze the impacts of the observations on the witnesses. This approach aimed to understand if the phenomenon could have been influenced by collective psychological factors.

After several months of intensive investigations, the final report was published. It concluded that, despite the efforts made, the object could not be conclusively identified and that no tangible evidence could confirm or deny the presence of an extraterrestrial craft. The report also mentioned that the incident posed no immediate danger to national security, but recommended maintaining increased vigilance and continuing to collect and analyze any information related to such phenomena.

Theories and Speculations.

One of the most common theories is that of extraterrestrial intervention. This hypothesis suggests that the observed objects were spacecraft of non-Earthly origins. Supporters of this theory often rely on the seemingly advanced technology of the objects, such as their ability to perform high-speed movements and to change direction instantly, characteristics that exceed the capabilities of known aerial vehicles at the time.

Another popular explanation is that of secret military projects. According to this theory, UFOs could be prototypes of airplanes or drones secretly developed by the government or private companies. This hypothesis is reinforced by the fact that many UFO incidents have been reported near military bases or government research centers.

Some researchers have proposed a psychosocial explanation, suggesting that the incident could be the result of collective hysteria or a misunderstanding. According to this perspective, witnesses may have interpreted natural phenomena or conventional objects as UFOs due to the influence of the media and popular culture, which at the time were saturated with science fiction narratives and discussions about extraterrestrials.

A less conventional theory is that of rare atmospheric phenomena. Some meteorology experts have hypothesized that unusual atmospheric conditions could have created optical illusions or reflections that were misinterpreted by witnesses.

Phenomena such as mirages, St. Elmo's lights, or the aurora borealis are sometimes cited to explain certain cases of UFO sightings.

Finally, there is a theory that involves parallel dimensions or realities. This idea, although largely speculative and on the fringe of conventional science, suggests that UFOs could be manifestations of inter-dimensional phenomena, capable of crossing between different realities.

THE UFO INCIDENT IN MEXICO DURING THE SOLAR ECLIPSE.

DATE: July 11, 1991.
COUNTRY: Mexico .
STATE: Federal District.
CITY: Mexico.

On July 11, 1991, a total solar eclipse captivated millions of people across Mexico. This astronomical event, widely observed and documented, was particularly striking not only for its rarity but also for the unusual phenomena that accompanied it. In Mexico City, the capital, as citizens and visitors looked up at the darkened sky, equipped with special glasses to protect their eyes, several reported seeing an unidentified flying object. This UFO, described as a shiny metallic disc, seemed to move abnormally in the sky. The incident quickly caught the attention of local and international media, sparking a wave of speculation and interest in extraterrestrial phenomena. Testimonies of this event were numerous and varied, ranging from simple visual observations to video recordings, which were subsequently analyzed by experts and UFO enthusiasts from around the world. This incident remains one of the most famous and discussed in the history of UFO sightings in Mexico, fueling both skepticism and belief in the possibility of extraterrestrial visits.

The Observation.

The observation took place in broad daylight, precisely during the peak of the solar eclipse, which began around 13:23 local time and reached its totality around 13:30.

The observed object was disc-shaped, with an apparently metallic structure that reflected sunlight. Its size was difficult to estimate, but witnesses described it as significantly larger than a typical commercial airplane. The UFO showed no obvious signs of traditional propulsion, such as jets or propellers, and it moved through the sky with remarkable fluidity, without emitting any perceptible sound.

The weather conditions that day were exceptionally clear, a cloudless sky allowing perfect visibility of the eclipse and the unidentified object. This clarity was a key factor in the high number of testimonies and videos captured by amateurs and professionals. The temperature was moderate, typical of a July month in Mexico, which encouraged even more residents and visitors to observe the celestial phenomenon.

The UFO suddenly appeared in the southeast sky, slowly moving towards the northwest. Its trajectory seemed linear and deliberate, crossing the sky for several minutes before disappearing as suddenly as it had appeared. During this time, the object passed through different intensities of sunlight, allowing observers to note changes in its visual appearance, particularly how it interacted with the light and shadow cast by the eclipse.

The total duration of the observation varied according to the witnesses, but most agree that the UFO was visible for at least seven to ten minutes. This gave enough time for hundreds of people to record the event on various types of video cameras, which produced an abundance of visual material that was subsequently analyzed and debated.

The absence of noise was also a remarkable aspect of this observation. In a city as large and noisy as Mexico, the unusual silence during the eclipse made the absence of noise coming from the UFO even more noticeable. Witnesses reported a strange sense of calm as the object crossed the sky, a striking contrast to the usual excitement and hustle and bustle of the city streets.

Testimonials.

On July 11, 1991, a total solar eclipse captivated millions of people across Mexico. This astronomical event, already spectacular in itself, was marked by an incident that garnered even more attention: numerous witnesses reported seeing an unidentified flying object (UFO) in the sky over Mexico City. This phenomenon was observed by people from different backgrounds, and their testimonies offer a fascinating insight into the event.

One of the first witnesses, Jaime Maussan, a well-known journalist in Mexico, was among the first to broadcast images of the UFO. According to his testimony, the object was disc-shaped and seemed to move at a constant speed without making any sound. Maussan described the UFO as having a dark center surrounded by a sort of luminous halo, which made it clearly visible despite the reduced brightness due to the eclipse.

Another important witness, Sara Cuevas, a teacher in a primary school in Mexico, was observing the eclipse with her students when one of them pointed out a bright object in the sky. Cuevas reported that the object seemed to change shape, shifting from a round shape to a more oval one, and that it moved erratically, unlike a plane or a weather balloon.

Carlos Diaz, an amateur photographer, captured several images of the UFO. According to Diaz, the object had an impressive maneuverability, capable of making abrupt movements to the left and right, as well as ascending and descending rapidly. The photos taken by Diaz show an object with a shiny metallic structure, reflecting sunlight.

A group of American tourists, including Linda Morales, also testified to having seen the UFO. Morales described the object as being extremely bright and much larger than the visible stars. She mentioned that the object remained visible throughout the duration of the eclipse, slowly moving across the sky before suddenly disappearing.

Finally, an airline pilot, Enrique Kolbeck, observed the UFO from the cockpit of his plane. Kolbeck indicated that the object was clearly visible despite the distance and that it did not correspond to any conventional aircraft. The pilot noted that the UFO emitted an intense light that did not blink like the lights of a plane.

These testimonies, although varied, share common points about the appearance and behavior of the UFO observed during the solar eclipse of 1991 in Mexico. The incident continues to arouse interest and debate among ufologists and the general public.

The Investigation.

The initial reactions were mainly those of confusion and curiosity. Local and international media began broadcasting images and videos of the UFO, captured by amateurs. Faced with the magnitude of public attention, the Mexican government was forced to respond. An official investigation was launched by the Mexican air force, with the collaboration of various government agencies.

The initial stages of the investigation involved gathering testimonies from people who had filmed or photographed the object. The investigators examined the videos and photos to verify their authenticity and try to determine the nature and origin of the observed object. Meanwhile, experts in aeronautics and atmospheric phenomena were consulted to rule out conventional explanations such as weather balloons, airplanes, or natural phenomena.

As the investigation progressed, the military authorities began to analyze radar data to see if the object had been detected by aerial surveillance systems. The results were ambiguous: some radars had recorded an unidentified object, but others had not. This disparity added to the confusion and fueled various theories among ufologists and the public.

The testimonies collected during the investigation revealed a wide variety of descriptions of the UFO, ranging from a stationary silver disc to an object with sudden and inexplicable movements. Several witnesses also reported a kind of luminous halo around the object, which was corroborated by some of the videos. These details made the analysis more complex, as they did not match the typical characteristics of known flying objects.

After months of thorough research, the air force has made its final report public. This indicated that despite considerable efforts made, the exact nature of the observed object remained undetermined. The document specified that the UFO did not correspond to any known type of aircraft or meteorological phenomenon and that the results of the radar analyses did not allow for definitive conclusions. However, the report did not rule out the possibility of an atypical explanation.

This conclusion was met with skepticism by a portion of the UFO community, who criticized the government for what they perceived as a lack of transparency or effort in the investigation. Others interpreted the report as a tacit acknowledgment of the possibility of an extraterrestrial visit, although this was never explicitly mentioned in the report.

Theories and Speculations.

One of the most common theories is that of the extraterrestrial origin of the object. This hypothesis is supported by the seemingly advanced technology of the UFO, which appeared capable of hovering in the air without any visible means of propulsion. Proponents of this theory argue that the solar eclipse could have been a moment chosen by extraterrestrial intelligences to observe Earth, taking advantage of the decrease in solar activity and human focus on this celestial event.

On the other hand, some aviation and atmospheric phenomena experts have proposed a more down-to-earth explanation. They suggest that the object could be a weather balloon or another type of research balloon. These balloons can sometimes reflect sunlight in a way that makes them appear more mysterious than they actually are. This theory is often dismissed by those who have observed the object, as they describe movements and behaviors that do not match the flight characteristics of a balloon.

Another interesting speculation is that of the hologram or a projection. This idea suggests that the UFO could have been some sort of test of advanced projection technologies, perhaps even conducted by a governmental or private organization. This theory is fueled by the fact that the incident occurred over a large metropolis during a major event, offering a maximum audience.

There are also those who consider the incident as a psychosocial phenomenon. According to this perspective, the collective observation of the UFO could be the result of a kind of "mass hysteria", where the emotional tension linked to the eclipse led to collective hallucinations or misinterpretations of ordinary visual stimuli, such as airplanes or satellites.

Finally, the hoax theory has also been put forward. Some skeptics argue that the incident could have been orchestrated to attract attention or for other reasons. However, the large amount of testimonies and videos makes this theory less plausible for many.

THE UFO INCIDENT OF SAN DIEGO, CALIFORNIA.

DATE: August 15, 1992.
COUNTRY: United States.
STATE: California.
CITY: San Diego.

Located on the southern coast of California, San Diego is known for its pleasant climate and beautiful beaches, but that day, it became the scene of an unusual event that captivated the attention of the public and researchers. That evening, just after sunset, several witnesses reported seeing an unidentified flying object in the sky. The object, described as being triangular in shape with bright, pulsating lights, was observed moving at an incredibly high speed without emitting any sound. The corroborating testimonies of several local residents, including experienced pilots and police officers, added significant credibility to the incident. Local authorities and aviation experts were unable to provide an immediate explanation, which fueled speculation and theories about the extraterrestrial origin of the object. The event was also followed by an unusual number of UFO sightings in the region in the days that followed, contributing to an atmosphere of mystery and uncertainty that still persists to this day around this incident.

The Observation.

Around 10:00 PM, several witnesses in the San Diego area reported seeing an unidentified flying object in the night sky. The object, according to descriptions, had a discoid shape with a series of blinking lights running along its perimeter. These lights emitted an intense white light, with occasional flashes of red and blue light. The UFO was moving at a constant speed in a northeast direction, without emitting any audible sound for the witnesses on the ground.

The trajectory of the object appeared to be linear, but with maneuvering capabilities that defied the characteristics of conventional aircraft. On several occasions, the object performed abrupt changes in direction and sudden accelerations without warning, which intrigued and even alarmed some of the observers.

The weather conditions that night were exceptionally clear, with almost perfect visibility. There were no low clouds and the wind was weak, which allowed for a prolonged observation of the object. The moon was in a waxing phase, providing additional light that helped to accentuate the silhouette of the UFO against the night sky.

The observation lasted about 30 minutes. During this time, the object traversed a large portion of the visible sky, moving from the western horizon to the eastern horizon before suddenly disappearing. Just before its disappearance, the object significantly increased its brightness, becoming almost dazzling, then it accelerated at an incredible speed and left the Earth's atmosphere heading towards space, leaving behind a trail of light that quickly faded.

Testimonials.

Commander David Fravor, an experienced fighter pilot of the US Navy, was one of the first to observe the unidentified object. According to his account, while he was piloting an F/A-18 Super Hornet during a routine exercise, he and his co-pilot were diverted to investigate an object spotted by the radar of their ship, the USS Princeton. Fravor describes the UFO as resembling a 12-meter long "Tic Tac", without wings or visible emissions. The object moved erratically and with a speed and agility far beyond the capabilities of known aircraft. When he attempted to approach, the UFO accelerated and disappeared within seconds, leaving Fravor perplexed about its technology and origin.

Another key testimony comes from the Princeton's radar operator, Kevin Day. He observed the UFO for several days before it was intercepted by Fravor. Day reports that the object made sudden movements, rapidly ascending and descending between 80,000 and 20,000 feet without apparently suffering the effects of gravity or inertia. The object's abilities to change direction and altitude so abruptly were incompatible with existing aerial technologies.

Fighter pilot Lieutenant Commander Alex Dietrich was also in the area during the incident and corroborated Fravor's observations. She noted that the object had no visible engine or conventional means of propulsion, and that it moved abnormally. Dietrich was particularly struck by the UFO's ability to remain stationary and then accelerate instantly.

In addition to the pilots, several other members of the USS Princeton crew also observed the object, either directly or via radar and infrared instruments. These observations were recorded and analyzed, but did not lead to a definitive explanation. The lack of concrete evidence and the elusive nature of the object left many questions unanswered.

The Investigation.

From the first reports of sightings of unidentified flying objects over the city, a series of investigations was launched by various government agencies, including the Pentagon and the Federal Aviation Administration (FAA).

The initial reactions were marked by general confusion and an urgent need for clarification. The testimonies of citizens, who described unusual lights and unconventional flight movements, were taken very seriously. The FAA immediately began examining radars and air communications to identify any unauthorized or unexplained aerial activity in the San Diego area at the specified date and time.

Simultaneously, the Pentagon activated its Unidentified Aerial Phenomena Task Force (UAPTF), which was tasked with gathering and analyzing all available information regarding this incident. The UAPTF worked closely with the National Aeronautics and Space Administration (NASA) and other intelligence agencies to broaden the scope of the investigation.

Investigators have collected testimonies from several commercial pilots who were in the area at the time of the incident. These pilots reported seeing objects moving at supersonic speeds, without corresponding sound emissions, which is atypical for conventional aircraft. In addition, several residents of San Diego have provided videos and photos taken with their mobile phones, showing bright spots moving erratically in the night sky.

The analysis of radar data confirmed the presence of objects whose flight trajectories did not correspond to any known commercial, military or private aircraft. These objects seemed to defy conventional aviation laws in terms of speed, acceleration and maneuverability. The UAPTF also examined weather and astronomical conditions to rule out natural phenomena such as meteors or optical illusions due to particular atmospheric conditions.

After several months of investigation, the final report of the UAPTF was published. It concluded that, despite substantial evidence of unidentified flying objects, no definitive explanation could be given. The report mentioned that the observed objects could be the result of advanced technologies, possibly of non-earthly origin, but this hypothesis could neither be confirmed nor denied with the available information.

The investigation into the San Diego UFO incident remains one of the most publicized and discussed in the annals of unidentified aerial phenomena. It highlighted the need for better coordination between government agencies and greater transparency in communicating UAP-related discoveries. Despite the lack of definitive conclusions, this incident has contributed to a broader awareness of the possibility of unexplained aerial phenomena and has stimulated public and scientific dialogue on the subject.

Theories and Speculations.

One of the most popular theories is that of extraterrestrial visitation. This hypothesis suggests that the observed objects could be spacecraft of non-earthly origins. Proponents of this idea argue that the movements and maneuvering capabilities of the objects, which seem to defy the laws of physics as we know them, could indicate a technology far beyond what humanity has developed. They also cite the silence and discretion of governments on such subjects as potential evidence of a cover-up.

On the contrary, some experts propose a more conventional explanation, suggesting that what the witnesses saw could be attributable to secret military technologies. The United States, with a long history of developing weapons and experimental vehicles, could be testing new drones or aircraft using advanced technologies not yet revealed to the public. This theory is reinforced by the proximity of San Diego to several major military bases, where such tests could logically take place.

Another common speculation concerns atmospheric or meteorological phenomena. Particular atmospheric conditions could create optical illusions or reflections that appear to be unidentified flying objects. For example, temperature inversions can trap ground lights and reflect them in the sky, creating spectacular but deceptive images. Skeptics of the extraterrestrial theory tend to favor this explanation, arguing that most UFO sightings can be explained by misinterpreted natural phenomena.

Furthermore, the impact of media and popular culture on the perception of UFOs should not be underestimated. Some sociologists and psychologists suggest that the craze for science fiction movies and television series about aliens could influence the way people interpret unexplained phenomena. Thus, what could be a fairly mundane event is sometimes perceived through the prism of the alien, the mysterious, and the unknown.

Finally, there is a less discussed but intriguing theory that involves the possibility of a hoax or a setup. This idea suggests that the incident could have been orchestrated for whatever reason, perhaps to divert public attention from other events or to test the public's reaction to a fake alien invasion. Although this theory is generally considered fringe, it highlights the complexity and variety of possible interpretations of UFO sightings.

THE COSFORD INCIDENT.

DATE: March 1993.
COUNTRY: United Kingdom.
STATE: Not applicable.
CITY: Cosford, Shropshire.

The Cosford incident is a significant event in the history of UFO sightings in the United Kingdom, particularly notable for the credible testimonies coming from military personnel. In March 1993, several witnesses, including members of the Royal Air Force (RAF), reported seeing unidentified flying objects crossing the sky at extraordinary speeds, accompanied by unusual light phenomena. These observations mainly took place around the RAF base at Cosford and the RAF Shawbury base, located in Shropshire, a rural region of England.

The incident began on the evening of March 30, 1993, when reports of UFO sightings began to pour in from different parts of the UK, culminating with specific events near Cosford and Shawbury. Witnesses describe a large triangular object emitting a low, striped light, moving at an incredible speed and without significant noise, which is atypical for conventional aircraft. The object was observed flying over the RAF Shawbury base, where it was seen slowing down and emitting a beam of light towards the ground before taking off at high speed.

This incident was taken very seriously by the British Ministry of Defense, which launched an investigation to determine the nature and origin of the observed object. Despite the investigations, no definitive explanation has been provided.

The Observation.

That evening, several witnesses, including military personnel from RAF Cosford and RAF Shawbury bases, reported seeing an unidentified flying object in the sky.

The observation began around 11:30 PM, when unusual lights were spotted moving across the sky at a speed and with maneuvers that did not correspond to those of conventional aircraft. The witnesses described the object as being triangular in shape, with bright white and blue lights arranged symmetrically on its structure. The object seemed to be of large size, although its exact distance and dimensions were difficult to accurately assess.

The weather conditions that night were clear with an unobstructed sky, which allowed for excellent visibility. The moon was nearly full, providing a source of natural light that helped witnesses discern the silhouette of the object against the night sky more clearly.

The object was observed moving slowly at first, then suddenly accelerating to supersonic speed without emitting any audible sound, which intrigued the witnesses. This ability to change speed so abruptly and without associated noise was contrary to the characteristics of conventional propulsion aircraft.

After crossing the sky for several minutes, the object was seen moving away on the horizon at a speed that was described as much faster than any known military or civilian aircraft at the time. The observation lasted about 20 minutes before the object disappeared from the witnesses' view.

The Cosford incident remains a fascinating case for UFO investigators and skeptics, primarily due to the credibility of the witnesses involved and the clarity of the observations. The precise details of the object, such as its triangular shape and unusual flight capabilities, continue to spark discussions and speculations about the nature of what was observed that night.

Testimonials.

Several credible witnesses, including military and police officers, have reported seeing unidentified flying objects. These testimonies offer a fascinating glimpse into the events of that particular night.

One of the main witnesses to this incident is Nick Pope, who was working at the time for the British Ministry of Defense, in the office responsible for investigating unidentified aerial phenomena. According to Pope, the incident began with reports of a large bright light crossing the sky at an incredible speed. The testimonies indicated that the object was moving northeast and was visible for several seconds before disappearing.

Another key witness was an on-duty police officer, who observed the object from a police station in the Midlands region. He described the UFO as being triangular in shape with white and red lights on the edges. The officer noted that the object moved without making any sound and emphasized the speed and fluidity of its movement across the night sky.

Similar testimonies have been collected by members of the Royal Air Force (RAF) stationed at RAF Cosford base and the neighboring RAF Shawbury base. One of the RAF officers, who prefers to remain anonymous, reported seeing a triangular object flying over the base at low altitude. The officer described the object as being huge, with a series of bright lights under its structure, which illuminated the ground below as if it were broad daylight.

In addition to visual observations, radar anomalies were also reported that night. RAF and the nearest civil airport radar operators recorded traces of an object moving at extraordinary speeds, well beyond the capabilities of conventional aircraft. These radar recordings corroborate the visual testimonies of various observers.

Another testimony comes from a local resident, who was awakened by what he described as an unusual humming noise. Looking out the window, he saw a bright object moving quickly across the sky. Intrigued and somewhat alarmed, he watched the object for several minutes before it disappeared over the horizon.

The Investigation.

The investigation that followed was complex, involving several levels of responses and analyses.

It all started with observations reported by witnesses in the Cosford region and the RAF Shawbury air base. The witnesses described seeing an unidentified flying object crossing the sky at an incredible speed, often accompanied by a strange noise. These testimonies came not only from civilians, but also from military personnel, which added a layer of credibility and prompted the authorities to take these reports seriously.

The first reaction of the military authorities was to check if the observed object could be a known aircraft, including those belonging to the military. Radar checks were immediately consulted. However, no aircraft matching the descriptions given by the witnesses was scheduled in that area at that time, and the objects were not identified on military radars, which added an element of mystery to the case.

In the face of the absence of tangible evidence on the radars and the precision of the testimonies, the Ministry of Defense decided to launch a more formal investigation. This investigation was conducted by the office in charge of investigations into unidentified aerial phenomena, a special unit of the Ministry of Defense. The investigation team collected additional testimonies, examined the meteorological and atmospheric data of the night in question, and consulted with aviation and atmospheric phenomena experts.

The testimonies collected during the investigation were varied but consistent on certain points, such as the abnormally high speed of the object and its relative silence despite the apparent speed. Some witnesses also reported an intense light emanating from the object, which did not correspond to any known aircraft at the time.

After several months of investigation, the final report was published. It concluded that, despite a thorough examination, no definitive explanation could be found. The investigators admitted that the observed object did not correspond to any known aircraft or atmospheric phenomenon. However, they also indicated that this did not necessarily prove the existence of extraterrestrials or unknown advanced technologies.

The report also highlighted the limitations of the detection technologies available at the time and suggested that the object could have been an artifact of night-time perception conditions or an anomaly not captured by radars. Despite these conclusions, the Cosford incident remains a popular case study among ufologists and continues to spark interest and speculation.

Theories and Speculations.

One of the most common theories is that of extraterrestrial intervention. This hypothesis suggests that the observed objects were spacecraft of non-earthly origins. Supporters of this theory often rely on the seemingly advanced technology and unusual movements of the objects, which appear to defy the laws of physics as we know them. They also cite the testimony of numerous credible observers, including military personnel, who have described extremely bright lights and flight paths with exceptional maneuvering capabilities.

Another popular explanation is that of secret military experimentation. According to this theory, the observed objects could be prototypes of aircraft or drones secretly developed by the government or defense contractors. This hypothesis is supported by the fact that the Cosford incident took place near several military bases, which could indicate tests of advanced technologies not yet revealed to the public. Skeptics of the extraterrestrial theory find this explanation more plausible, as it does not require assuming the existence of technologies or life beyond Earth.

A third perspective suggests that the incident could be attributed to misinterpreted natural or atmospheric phenomena. Phenomena such as the Hessdalen lights or atmospheric mirages could create illusions of unidentified flying objects, especially at night. This theory is often reinforced by experts in meteorology and physics who suggest that under certain conditions, natural lights or reflections can appear to be moving objects in the sky.

Furthermore, some researchers have suggested that the incident could be the result of collective hysteria or a misunderstanding. In situations of tension or excitement, witnesses may misinterpret ordinary visual stimuli as something extraordinary. This theory is often accompanied by psychological analyses on how humans process unusual or ambiguous information, especially in groups.

THE LIGHTS OF LAKE MICHIGAN, MICHIGAN.

DATE: March 8, 1994.
COUNTRY: United States.
STATE: Michigan.
CITY: Holland.

On March 8, 1994, an unusual event captured the attention of residents of Holland, Michigan, and surrounding areas along the east coast of Lake Michigan. That evening, hundreds of witnesses, including police officers, pilots, and many ordinary citizens, reported seeing strange lights in the sky. These observations triggered a series of calls to local police services and radio stations, with reports describing lights forming triangular or linear patterns, moving at high speed and changing direction in a seemingly impossible way for conventional aircraft.

The descriptions from witnesses varied, but many reported that the lights were brightly colored, often blue or white, and that they moved silently. Some witnesses also described the lights as being aligned in formations that periodically changed shape. The incident lasted several hours, which allowed many witnesses to take photos and videos, although the quality of this visual evidence was often questioned.

The local authorities and aviation experts could not provide an immediate explanation, and the incident quickly attracted the attention of the national media. Speculation about the origin of the lights included natural phenomena, secret military activities, and of course, extraterrestrial vehicles. Despite the investigations, no definitive explanation has been universally accepted.

The Observation.

Around 9:30 pm, strange lights were observed in the night sky, a spectacle that lasted several hours and was reported by numerous witnesses in the region. These observations were made by people from various backgrounds, including pilots, police officers, and many local residents.

Witnesses described seeing formations of lights that changed color and shape. The reported colors varied between red, green, and blue, with sometimes rapid transitions that created an almost hypnotic effect. The lights moved in a coordinated manner and seemed to float effortlessly above the water, sometimes moving at high speed from one point to another, sometimes remaining almost motionless.

One of the most intriguing aspects of this observation was the way the lights seemed to interact with each other. They formed geometric configurations, like triangles or straight lines, which periodically changed. This feature was particularly striking to the witnesses, as it seemed to indicate some sort of coordination or control behind the movements of the lights.

The weather conditions that night were clear with little cloud cover, which allowed excellent visibility of the light phenomena. The moon was nearly full, providing a natural light source that contrasted with the bright colors of the observed objects. The wind was weak, and there were no precipitations, conditions that ruled out certain natural explanations such as light reflections on low clouds.

The observations lasted until about 1:00 in the morning, with varying intensities. At certain times, the lights seemed to fade only to reappear with increased brightness. This intermittent behavior added to the witnesses' perplexity and made the experience even more mysterious.

Despite the diversity of witnesses and the clarity of the observations, no sound was associated with the lights. This silence contributed to the strange atmosphere of the evening, reinforcing the impression that what was being observed was not an ordinary phenomenon. The witnesses also noted the absence of any disturbance in the immediate environment, such as electrical interference or effects on animals, which are sometimes reported during UFO sightings.

Testimonials.

On March 8, 1994, an unusual event occurred over Lake Michigan, captivating and confusing both local residents and aerial phenomena experts. That night, hundreds of witnesses reported seeing strange lights in the sky. These observations were made by people from various backgrounds and different locations around the lake, offering a variety of perspectives on the incident.

Among the key witnesses, Holly Graves and her son, residents of Holland, Michigan, were among the first to report these strange lights. Around 9:30 pm, Holly observed what she described as a group of lights forming an arc. These lights, according to her testimony, changed color from red to green then to blue, and seemed to move in a coordinated manner, without any noticeable noise. Her son, who was 10 years old at the time, corroborated her account, adding that he had seen the lights move quickly from one point to another in the sky.

Another important witness, Jack Bushong, a meteorologist working for the National Weather Service in Muskegon, also reported seeing similar objects that same night. Using a Doppler radar, Bushong detected unusual echoes moving irregularly and at high speed. He described the objects as being in a triangular formation and noted that they seemed to be playing "leapfrog" with each other.

In Grand Haven, a group of patrolling police officers also witnessed the event. These officers reported seeing several bright lights in the sky, moving at a speed and with a precision that ruled out the explanation of a conventional airplane or helicopter. One of the officers mentioned that the lights seemed "intelligent", as they appeared to respond to the ground lights.

Cindy Pravda, a resident of Grand Rapids, provided a detailed account of her observation of the lights. Around 10:15 pm, she saw four bright lights forming a perfect square in the sky. She observed the lights for about 20 minutes, noting that they remained perfectly stationary before beginning to move synchronously towards the southeast, then suddenly disappearing.

The testimonies of these individuals, as well as those of many other witnesses that night, have created a mass of intriguing but inconclusive data on what might have caused this event. The descriptions of the movements of the lights, their noiseless coordination, and their ability to change position quickly and unpredictably, remain central and mysterious aspects of the Lake Michigan lights incident.

The Investigation.

The first step of the investigation was the collection of testimonies. The investigators interviewed dozens of witnesses, including police officers, pilots, and ordinary residents. The descriptions of the lights varied, but several witnesses described lights forming triangular or linear patterns, moving at high speed without significant noise. Some witnesses also reported that the lights changed color and formation.

In parallel with the collection of testimonies, the FAA examined the radar data for the evening in question. The initial reports did not show any unusual aerial activity, but a more thorough review revealed minor anomalies that were not immediately explained. These anomalies included unidentified radar echoes that seemed to match the locations and times of the observations reported by the witnesses.

The military authorities, including the Air Force, also participated in the investigation. They checked the flight logs and confirmed that no military exercise was underway in the region that could explain the observations. In addition, no satellite or missile launch was scheduled that night that could have been confused with the observed lights.

The investigation also took into account the weather conditions of the evening. The conditions were clear with little cloud cover, which eliminated the possibility that the lights were reflections of weather phenomena such as distant lightning or ground lights reflected by clouds.

After several months of investigation, the final report was published. It concluded that, despite the detailed testimonies and radar anomalies, no definitive explanation could be given. The report mentioned that the available data was insufficient to draw a firm conclusion and that the observations could be attributed to a variety of unspecified natural or human causes.

This conclusion did not satisfy all the witnesses or members of the public interested in the incident. Many continued to speculate about the possibility of extraterrestrial activity or secret technology being tested by the government. However, officially, the incident remains unresolved, with investigators admitting that some occurrences in our sky remain beyond our current understanding.

Theories and Speculations.

One of the most commonly discussed theories is that of natural atmospheric phenomena. Some experts suggest that the lights could be due to reflections of light on rare gases in the atmosphere, or to electrical phenomena such as ball lightning. This hypothesis is supported by the fact that the Lake Michigan region is known for its sometimes extreme weather conditions, which could contribute to such phenomena. However, this explanation does not convince all observers, particularly because of the duration and apparent stability of the observed lights.

Another popular explanation is that of secret military trials. Lake Michigan, being a vast open space, could be used for testing new aerial technologies, including drones or other unidentified flying objects. This theory is fueled by reports of rapid movements and unusual maneuvers of lights, which seem to surpass the capabilities of conventional aircraft. However, no concrete evidence has ever been presented to support this theory, and military authorities deny any involvement.

Among the more controversial theories is that of extraterrestrial intervention. This idea is often supported by ufologists and UFO enthusiasts, who believe that the characteristics of the lights - such as their agility, speed, and formation behavior - can only be explained by technologies far beyond those currently known to humanity. Skeptics, however, often criticize this approach as being too speculative and insufficiently supported by tangible data.

Finally, there is a psychosocial perspective that suggests that observations of the lights of Lake Michigan could be influenced by mass phenomena or optical illusions. According to this theory, once the initial reports of observations were publicized, other people might have been unconsciously influenced to "see" similar phenomena, even if the visual stimuli were ambiguous or non-existent. This explanation attempts to take into account the role of human psychology in the perception of unusual events.

THE ARIEL SCHOOL INCIDENT: ENCOUNTER WITH A UFO AND ALIEN BEINGS IN RUWA, ZIMBABWE.

DATE: September 16, 1994.
COUNTRY: Zimbabwe.
STATE: Mashonaland East.
CITY: Ruwa.

The Ariel School incident is one of the most documented and discussed cases in the history of UFO sightings. Occurring in 1994, this event involved over sixty students from Ariel School, a private school located in Ruwa, about 22 kilometers from Harare, the capital of Zimbabwe. On September 16, during recess, the students, aged six to twelve, witnessed an unusual phenomenon that not only captured their attention but also left an indelible mark in their memories. According to reports, an unidentified flying object landed near their playground. What sets this incident apart from many other UFO reports is the alleged appearance of strange beings near the object. The descriptions given by the children were surprisingly consistent. They described the beings as being small in size, with pale or gray skin and large black eyes. Even more intriguing, some children claimed to have received telepathic messages from the visitors, concerning the state of the Earth and the future of humanity. The incident was quickly covered by international media and attracted the attention of many ufologists and researchers, including Harvard psychiatrist Dr. John Mack, who conducted a series of in-depth interviews with the children. The Ariel School incident remains a fascinating and mysterious case in the study of UFO phenomena, offering potential evidence of extraterrestrial visitation that continues to spark curiosity and debate among experts and the general public.

The Observation.

That day, around 10:15 in the morning, during recess, several students, aged 6 to 12, witnessed a strange phenomenon that would indelibly mark their minds.

According to the testimonies collected, the sky was clear and sunny, with no clouds on the horizon, which offered perfect visibility. The weather conditions were therefore ideal for clearly observing what was going to unfold. The students were playing outside when some of them noticed three unidentified flying objects (UFOs) in the sky. These objects quickly approached the school, before descending towards a wooded area adjacent to the playground.

The descriptions of the objects vary slightly, but most witnesses agree that the UFOs had a disk or cigar shape, with a shiny and metallic surface. One of the objects would have landed (or at least, came very close to the ground) at a distance of about 100 meters from the children. The other objects would have floated a few meters above the ground.

The object on the ground was described as being about three to four meters in length, and its surface seemed to reflect the sunlight. Some children reported seeing a kind of glow or aura around the object, which added to the strangeness of the scene. The silence during the observation was another striking detail; no engine noise or other mechanical sound was heard, which contrasted with the technological appearance of the object.

Shortly after the UFO landing, several beings appeared near it. These beings were small in size, about one meter tall, with a slim appearance. Their skin was described as being dark or gray in color, and they wore tight-fitting dark suits. Their heads were disproportionately large compared to their slim bodies, with large black eyes that seemed to envelop their faces.

The children observed these beings moving around the UFO and into the adjacent woods, some seeming to carry out some sort of surveys or inspections. This part of the observation lasted a few minutes before the beings returned to their ship, which then took off at an impressive speed, disappearing from the witnesses' field of vision in a matter of seconds.

The entirety of the incident, from the appearance of the objects in the sky to their hasty departure, lasted about 15 to 20 minutes. During this time, the children were both fascinated and terrified by what they were seeing. The clarity of the day and the absence of any visual or sound interference allowed for a detailed observation, which would remain etched in the memory of the young witnesses and would spark many questions and debates in the days and years to come.

Testimonials.

That day, over 60 students from Ariel School, aged between 6 and 12 years old, witnessed an extraordinary event during the morning recess.

According to testimonies collected by various investigators, including psychiatrist Dr. John Mack from Harvard University, the children saw several flying objects descend from the sky. One of the objects would have landed, or at least floated a few centimeters above the ground, near the school. The children's descriptions of the UFO's appearance vary slightly, but most agree that it was round and shiny, with a surface that seemed metallic.

Among the witnesses, Lisa, a 10-year-old student, reported seeing a being emerge from the UFO. She described this being as small in size, with a head disproportionate to its slim body, large oval black eyes. She also noted that the being seemed to float above the ground rather than walk.

Another student, Barry, 9 years old, corroborated Lisa's testimony, adding that the being was wearing some sort of dark and shiny suit. According to Barry, there were several beings moving around the UFO, and all seemed to communicate telepathically, as no sound was audible.

Emma, 8 years old, mentioned having felt a telepathic contact with beings. She explained that during this exchange, she received messages about the environment and technology, which made her feel urgency and sadness for the future of the Earth.

James, another witness, emphasized that the UFO and the beings disappeared as suddenly as they had appeared, leaving behind an atmosphere of confusion but also curiosity among the students and school staff.

The testimonies of the children were taken very seriously by the UFO and academic community, partly because of the consistency of the stories among the many witnesses and the absence of apparent motives to fabricate such a story. Moreover, the drawings made by the children of the UFO and the beings after the incident show striking similarities, reinforcing the credibility of their accounts.

The Investigation.

The initial reaction of the local authorities was one of skepticism, but the scale of the testimonies and the consistency of the children's stories led to a more formal investigation. Dr. John Mack, a professor of psychiatry at Harvard University and a researcher on phenomena related to UFOs, became aware of the case and went to Ruwa to conduct his own investigation.

Dr Mack interviewed the children separately, and found that their accounts were not only consistent with each other, but also detailed with precise descriptions of the UFO and the beings. The children described a craft landing near the school, and several small beings coming out of it. According to the testimonies, these beings had pale skin and large black eyes. Some children reported receiving telepathic messages from the visitors, concerning technology and the environment.

The military and governmental authorities of Zimbabwe also conducted investigations, although few details about these investigations are publicly available. It is reported that the army visited the site after the incident to check for any physical traces or other material evidence. However, no official report has been published by the government of Zimbabwe regarding the results of these investigations.

The incident also attracted the attention of local and international media, which contributed to a wider recognition of the event. Journalists from various countries visited the school and interviewed the children, teachers, and residents of the area, adding an additional layer of documentation and fact-checking.

Despite considerable interest in the incident, no definitive conclusion has been drawn by the authorities. Skeptics have suggested that the children could have been influenced by science fiction stories or that the incident could be the result of a mass hallucination. However, psychologists who examined the children generally concluded that they did not appear to be lying or fabricating their stories.

The investigation into the Ariel school incident remains a fascinating and enigmatic case in the study of UFOs and close encounters. The testimonies collected during the investigation, particularly those of the children, continue to spark interest and debate among researchers and the general public.

Theories and Speculations.

One of the most popular theories is that of extraterrestrial visitation. According to this hypothesis, the objects and beings observed by the children would be of non-earthly origin. This theory is supported by the children's detailed description of the beings' appearances and behaviors, as well as the advanced nature of the apparent UFO technology. Proponents of this theory often cite the consistency of the children's testimonies, who despite their young age, have provided surprisingly similar and detailed accounts.

Another explanation put forward is that of collective psychosis or mass hysteria. This theory suggests that the children could have undergone a kind of psychological contagion, where the experience of one or a few students would have induced a chain reaction among the others. Critics of this theory, however, point out that mass hysteria does not generally correspond to the precision of the details provided by the various witnesses, who in this case, maintain a high consistency between their various accounts.

Some researchers have suggested that the incident could be the result of a misunderstanding with an unknown natural or technological phenomenon. For example, it could be a weather balloon or an unidentified drone. However, this theory struggles to explain the description of the beings and their interaction with the children, as well as the lack of material evidence of such an object in the region at that time.

A more controversial perspective is that of psychological manipulation or a social experiment. According to this view, the incident could have been orchestrated to observe the children's reactions to an unusual stimulus. This theory is generally rejected by the UFO community and lacks concrete evidence, but it is sometimes discussed in broader contexts concerning the use of disinformation or psychological manipulation by certain groups or governments.

Finally, there are those who consider the Ariel school incident as a case of spiritual or metaphysical encounter, suggesting that the children might have been in contact with entities from another dimension or plane of existence. This interpretation is often linked to broader beliefs in the paranormal and is supported by the deeply emotional and transformative nature of the experience reported by the children.

THE UFO INCIDENT OF BARILOCHE, ARGENTINA.

DATE: May 31, 1995.
COUNTRY: Argentina.
STATE: Rio Negro.
CITY: San Carlos de Bariloche.

The UFO incident of Bariloche is an event that has captivated the attention not only of local residents but also of researchers and UFO enthusiasts worldwide. Located in the province of Rio Negro, the city of San Carlos de Bariloche is known for its picturesque landscapes and snow-capped mountains, which attract tourists in search of nature and adventure. However, on the evening of May 31, 1995, it was a completely different type of phenomenon that placed Bariloche under the international spotlight.

That evening, around 8:07 PM, an unusual event disrupted the usual routine of the local airport. Operations were abruptly interrupted when the communication systems of the control tower suffered massive interference. Witnesses on site, including pilots, air traffic controllers, and passengers, reported seeing a large unidentified flying object emitting intense lights. This object reportedly flew over the runway at low altitude before disappearing at a dizzying speed, leaving behind a trail of questions and mystery.

The incident not only affected the airport's electronic equipment, causing a total outage for several minutes, but it was also observed by multiple witnesses in and around the airport. Descriptions of the object varied, but most agreed that it emitted changing colored lights and moved at speeds and with maneuvers that defied the capabilities of known aircraft at the time.

Local authorities and aviation experts attempted to untangle fact from fiction in the days following the incident, but many questions remained unanswered.

The Observation.

The observed object was oval in shape and emitted an intense white light with shades of blue and green. Its size was estimated to be about 10 to 15 meters in diameter, and it seemed to move at a constant speed without emitting any perceptible sound.

The observation began when the UFO was first spotted over Lake Nahuel Huapi, which borders the city. The object was moving from south to north at an approximate altitude of 600 meters. Witnesses reported that the UFO performed several strange maneuvers, such as sudden accelerations followed by very fast lateral movements, which seemed to defy the laws of physics as we know them.

The weather conditions that night were clear with few clouds, allowing for perfect visibility. The moon was nearly full, providing an additional source of light that helped to accentuate the contours of the object. The temperature was cool, typical of autumn nights in the region, with a slight wind coming from the southwest.

The UFO continued its path above the city, passing near several important buildings, including the Bariloche International Airport. At this point, several pilots and airport staff also reported the sighting. According to their descriptions, the object suddenly changed direction, rising to a higher altitude before disappearing at an incredible speed into the starry sky.

The entire observation lasted about 15 minutes, leaving enough time for many residents and tourists in Bariloche to capture images and videos of the event. These visual documents show a bright object with an irregular flight path and maneuvering capabilities that do not match any known conventional aircraft of the time.

Testimonials.

What makes these testimonies particularly intriguing is their origin from aviation professionals and passengers of a commercial flight.

The first witness, Jorge Polanco, was the pilot of flight 674 of the airline Aerolíneas Argentinas. According to his report, as the plane was preparing to land at Bariloche airport around 8 pm, a strange luminous object suddenly appeared in front of the plane. Polanco described the object as being extremely bright, with a series of multicolored lights that seemed to rotate around its axis. He also mentioned that the object had an astonishing maneuverability, moving at a speed and with an agility that far exceeded those of any known aircraft.

Another key witness to this incident was the co-pilot, who corroborated Polanco's account. He added that the object had not only disrupted the plane's navigation instruments, but had also caused a temporary failure of the cabin lighting and radio communications, creating a situation of great confusion and emergency on board.

Among the passengers of the plane, several also reported having seen the UFO. A passenger, Maria Lujan, testified to having observed the object from her seat, describing an oval shape enveloped in bright lights that constantly changed color. She expressed her feelings of fear and wonder in the face of this inexplicable spectacle.

In addition to the aerial testimonies, several people on the ground at Bariloche airport also observed the UFO. Carlos Moreno, a control tower technician, reported that the object had been visible on radar for a short time before mysteriously disappearing. Moreno emphasized that the object did not correspond to any scheduled flight and that it did not follow any of the normal air corridors.

Another witness on the ground, an airport employee named Gabriela Torres, noted that the object emitted a light so intense that it could be seen through the low clouds that covered the sky that night. She described the light as "pulsating" and said she had the feeling that the object was "watching" the airport.

The Investigation.

In response to these testimonies, the Argentine Air Force quickly set up an investigative commission. The purpose of this commission was to collect all possible testimonies, analyze radar data, and check if other phenomena could explain these observations. The investigators questioned the airport staff, air traffic controllers, the pilot of the affected plane, as well as passengers who had a view of the outside.

The initial reports from air traffic controllers confirmed that something abnormal had been detected on the radars at the exact time mentioned by the witnesses. However, no anomaly was visible on the military radars, which added a layer of mystery to the incident. Airport technicians also confirmed that the communication systems had experienced interference, which corroborates the pilot's testimony regarding the failures of the onboard instruments.

The investigation took an international turn when the Argentine government requested the assistance of several international organizations specialized in the study of unidentified aerospace phenomena. Experts from different countries thus joined the investigation commission, bringing with them their expertise in aviation, meteorology, astronomy, and other scientific disciplines.

After several months of investigations, the commission published a preliminary report. This document indicated that despite thorough analyses, no conventional explanation (such as weather phenomena, weather balloons, or known aircraft) could be clearly established. The report also mentioned that the testimonies were consistent and that the recorded electromagnetic interferences were difficult to explain without invoking an unusual phenomenon.

However, the final report, published several years later, failed to provide a definitive conclusion. It highlighted the limitations of the technologies of the time to satisfactorily explain the incident. The Argentine government, while acknowledging the lack of evidence of extraterrestrial activity, admitted that the event remained unresolved and classified as an unidentified aerial phenomenon.

Theories and Speculations.

One of the most popular theories is that of the extraterrestrial visit. This hypothesis suggests that the observed object was a spacecraft from an advanced extraterrestrial civilization. Supporters of this theory cite the seemingly advanced technology of the object, capable of rapid movements and abrupt changes in direction, as well as its ability to interfere with electrical equipment as evidence of its non-terrestrial origins. This theory is often reinforced by reports of similar observations in other parts of the world, suggesting some sort of systematic surveillance or exploration of Earth by extraterrestrial beings.

Another explanation put forward is that of a rarely observed natural phenomenon. Some researchers have suggested that what the witnesses saw could be a particular type of atmospheric or meteorological phenomenon that is not yet well understood. For example, plasma fireballs or ball lightning have been mentioned as natural phenomena that could be mistaken for UFOs. These phenomena can sometimes cause electromagnetic interference, which could explain the power outage at the airport.

A third theory suggests a more earthly explanation: it could be a secret military device in the testing phase. Argentina, like many countries, has research and development projects in the field of aviation and defense that are often kept secret. Supporters of this theory argue that the object could be a prototype of an airplane or drone equipped with experimental technologies, perhaps even using advanced forms of propulsion that have not yet been made public.

Finally, there are those who are skeptical about the entirety of the reports and propose more prosaic explanations. For example, some suggest that what the witnesses saw could be the result of an optical illusion, an unusual reflection of light, or even a hoax. Skeptics often question the reliability of testimonies, noting that human observations, especially when made under conditions of stress or surprise, can be inaccurate or misleading.

The incident immediately attracted the attention of local and international media. Investigations were conducted by various organizations, including the Argentine Air Force. However, no official explanation has been given, and the incident remains unresolved to this day.

Experts in unidentified aerial phenomena have studied this incident, considering it one of the most credible and well-documented cases of UFO sightings. The testimonies of professional pilots, who are generally considered reliable observers due to their training and experience, add a layer of credibility to the incident.

THE UFO INCIDENT OF HARBIN, CHINA.

DATE: October 5, 1995.
COUNTRY: China.
STATE: Heilongjiang.
CITY: Harbin.

Located in the province of Heilongjiang, in the northeast of the country, the city of Harbin became the scene of an event that captivated and mystified both ufology experts and the general public. On October 5, 1995, several witnesses reported seeing a strange object in the night sky. According to descriptions, this object had an elongated shape and emitted bright lights of different colors. What makes this incident particularly remarkable is the diversity of the witnesses who reported the event, including airplane pilots, police officers, and numerous citizens. Reports indicate that the object remained visible for several minutes before disappearing at an extraordinary speed, leaving behind many unanswered questions. Local authorities and the media quickly covered the event, but no official explanation was given as to the nature or origin of the observed object. This incident has fueled many theories and remains a subject of fascination and speculation among researchers and UFO enthusiasts.

The Observation.

The event occurred on July 5, 2010, around 9:00 PM local time. That evening, the sky was exceptionally clear, with few clouds and almost perfect visibility, which allowed for a detailed observation of the unidentified object.

The observed object was circular in shape with a series of flashing lights that emitted an intense light of white and blue color. These lights seemed to be arranged in a circular pattern around the object, giving the impression of constant rotation. According to the testimonies, the UFO measured about 10 meters in diameter and was moving at an estimated altitude of less than 1000 meters from the ground.

The object was first seen by a group of students coming out of a university building. They reported that the UFO initially moved at a moderate speed before abruptly stopping. After a few moments of immobility, it began to perform movements that defied the laws of physics as we know them, moving laterally at a dizzying speed without any audible propulsion noise.

The total duration of the observation was about 30 minutes. During this time, the object changed direction several times, ascending and descending with remarkable agility. At one point, it even made a rapid descent to the ground before almost instantly rising back to its initial altitude.

The weather conditions during the incident were ideal for clear observation. The temperature was mild, and the wind was weak, which probably helped to maintain some stability in the UFO's movements. Moreover, the absence of rain or fog that night allowed for unobstructed visibility of the mysterious object.

The UFO finally disappeared from sight, rising at an incredible speed into the night sky, leaving behind many questions and very few answers.

Testimonials.

One of the first witnesses, Zhang Wei, a local engineer, reports having seen an unidentified flying object of circular shape flying over the sky of Harbin in the early morning hours. According to him, the object was about 30 meters in diameter and emitted a pulsating blue-green light. Zhang Wei specifies that the object was moving at a constant speed without emitting any audible sound, which distinguished it from regular airplanes.

Li Huan, a student who was returning home after an evening with friends, also witnessed this event. She describes the UFO as having a series of flashing lights around its perimeter, which changed color in a synchronized manner. Li Huan adds that the object suddenly accelerated and disappeared into the night sky within a few seconds, leaving behind a bright trail.

Another testimony comes from Chen Guoying, an experienced airline pilot, who was in flight near Harbin at the time of the incident. Chen reports having observed a strange object on his radar, which seemed to move at a speed and with a maneuverability that exceeded the capabilities of conventional aircraft. He also notes that the object made abrupt changes in direction that would be impossible for standard planes.

Mrs. Wang, a trader from the local market, observed the UFO from the ground. She describes a dull noise, like a low-frequency hum, that accompanied the movement of the object. According to her, this UFO emitted such intense light that she had to look away to avoid being dazzled.

Finally, the testimony of Liu Xin, an amateur astronomer, provides a technical perspective. Liu managed to capture images of the UFO using his telescope. He describes the object as having a smooth metallic structure with what appeared to be panels or portholes. In his images, one can see reflections and details that suggest advanced technology, unidentifiable with known space or aerial vehicles.

The Investigation.

The first step of the investigation consisted of collecting testimonies from citizens who had observed the object. The descriptions varied, but most witnesses described a disc-shaped object emitting bright lights of changing colors. These testimonies were taken very seriously by the authorities, who then consulted aeronautics experts and astronomers to analyze the claims.

Meanwhile, the Chinese military examined its radars and other surveillance equipment to check if the object had been detected independently of these testimonies. Although the precise details of these checks have not been fully disclosed to the public, it was confirmed that anomalies had been recorded by several radar facilities across the region at the time of the reported observations.

In response to these discoveries, a team of military and civilian investigators was formed to conduct a ground and air investigation. Drones and planes were used to fly over the area in the hope of capturing images or other forms of evidence of the UFO's existence. However, these efforts did not yield conclusive results, leaving the investigators perplexed about the nature of the observed object.

The scientific aspect of the investigation also included the analysis of the weather and atmospheric conditions at the time of the incident to rule out the possibility that what had been seen was a natural phenomenon, such as St. Elmo's lights or atmospheric mirages. The scientists involved in the investigation concluded that the conditions were clear and did not favor such phenomena, thus reinforcing the mystery surrounding the incident.

Despite the efforts made, the official investigation failed to provide a definitive explanation for the incident. The final report highlighted the lack of tangible evidence to conclude the presence of an extraterrestrial device, but it also could not identify the object as a natural phenomenon or a human artifact. The report recommended ongoing monitoring of the region and the implementation of more rigorous protocols for the documentation and analysis of future UFO incidents.

Theories and Speculations.

One of the most commonly discussed theories is that of secret military activity. Some experts and UFO enthusiasts suggest that the observed objects could be experimental aerial technologies secretly developed by the Chinese government or other nations. This hypothesis is fueled by the fact that China has significantly increased its investments in defense technology and space exploration in recent years, which could include the development of new types of aerial vehicles.

Another popular explanation is that of rare atmospheric phenomena. Scientists have suggested that the lights could be the result of particular atmospheric conditions that reflect or diffract light in an unusual way. For example, ice crystals suspended in the atmosphere could create halos or other optical effects that could be interpreted as UFOs.

The extraterrestrial theory is, of course, one of the most fascinating and discussed among UFO enthusiasts. According to this perspective, the observed objects would be spacecraft of non-earthly origins. This idea is often supported by testimonies of object movements defying known laws of physics, such as sudden accelerations or instantaneous changes of direction, which would be difficult to achieve with current human technologies.

Some researchers have also suggested that the incident could be related to psychological or sociological phenomena, such as pareidolia (the tendency to perceive a face or familiar shape in ambiguous visual stimuli) or the phenomenon of "mass hysteria", where witnesses could mutually influence their perceptions and memories of the event.

Finally, there is a skeptical perspective that attributes the incident to a hoax or a misunderstanding. According to this view, the images or videos of the incident could have been altered or staged, or the witnesses could have misinterpreted natural objects or phenomena such as airplanes, drones, or even sky lanterns.

Conclusion.

The Harbin UFO incident remains one of the least explained cases in the modern history of UFO sightings in China. Despite the efforts of experts and investigators, no conclusive explanation has been provided as to the nature or origin of the observed object. This event not only stimulated public debate about the possible presence of extraterrestrials, but also highlighted the limits of our understanding of unidentified aerial phenomena. The fascination with this incident continues to persist, fueled by the absence of clear answers and the global fascination for unsolved mysteries.

THE YUKON UFO INCIDENT.

DATE: December 11, 1996.
COUNTRY: Canada.
STATE: Yukon Territory.
CITY: Fox Lake.

On the evening of December 11, 1996, several witnesses spread over a large area of the Yukon territory, particularly around Fox Lake, reported seeing an unidentified flying object of extraordinary size and shape. These observations took place in a context where unidentified aerial phenomena were beginning to be taken more seriously by the public and researchers, following an increase in reports worldwide during the 90s.

Witnesses of this incident described a huge object with multicolored lights, moving at low altitude and silently over a great distance. The object, according to reports, measured between 400 and 600 meters wide, a size much larger than any known aircraft at the time. The observation lasted several minutes, giving witnesses enough time to observe the object from different angles.

The descriptions of the object included details about its structure, which appeared metallic and subtly illuminated by lights arranged along its circumference, giving the object an almost unreal appearance in the night sky. The absence of noise was also remarkable, as an object of this size would normally have produced a considerable sound when moving.

This incident was widely covered by local media and sparked the interest of many ufologists and aerial phenomena researchers. Despite investigations and analyses, no definitive explanation has been provided as to the nature or origin of the observed object. The Yukon UFO incident therefore remains an unsolved mystery and continues to fascinate and provoke debates among experts and enthusiasts of ufology.

The Observation.

That evening, several witnesses spread over a distance of more than 300 kilometers along the Klondike road reported seeing an extraordinary object in the night sky.

The observed object was described as being elongated in shape, often compared to a blimp or a cigar. Its size was impressive, with some witnesses estimating its length at more than two football fields, making it significantly larger than any conventional aircraft. The UFO was illuminated by rows of lights that blinked intermittently and spanned the entire length of its structure. These lights varied in color, shifting from bright white to yellow and sometimes to red.

The exact time of the observation varied slightly among the witnesses, but most agreed that the event took place between 8:00 pm and 9:30 pm. The duration for which the object remained visible also varied, with some reporting an observation of a few minutes, while others claimed to have observed it for nearly an hour.

The weather conditions that night were clear with a starry sky, offering perfect visibility. The temperature was typically winter-like for the Yukon, with temperatures dropping below -20°C. The biting cold, however, did not deter the witnesses, intrigued by the appearance of this mysterious object, from staying outside to observe and try to understand what they were seeing.

The object was moving at a relatively slow speed and with a stable trajectory, allowing for prolonged observation. It seemed to hover over the region without any apparent noise, adding to the strangeness of the experience for those watching it. Its ability to move so silently, despite its massive size, was particularly disconcerting for the witnesses.

Testimonials.

Several witnesses reported seeing a huge and strangely bright object crossing the night sky. These testimonies come from various localities across Yukon, including Fox Lake, Lake Laberge and several other small communities.

One of the first witnesses, a truck driver, observed a huge object with multicolored lights moving at low altitude. According to his testimony, the object was several hundred meters long and emitted a low hum. He described the UFO as having a series of bright lights - red, green, and white - that flashed sequentially along its structure.

Another witness, a resident of Fox Lake, reported seeing the object as she was driving home. She described the UFO as being so large that it almost seemed to touch the ground. The lights from the object were so intense that they illuminated the surrounding forest, creating sharp shadows on the frozen ground. She also mentioned that the object moved without emitting any audible sound, which added to the strangeness of the experience.

A group of tourists camping at Lake Laberge also shared similar observations. They described a large triangular object with lights arranged in complex geometric patterns. One of the campers, an astronomy enthusiast, noted that the object moved in a way that did not correspond to any known aircraft or natural phenomenon. This witness specifically highlighted the absence of engine noise, which was puzzling given the size and apparent proximity of the object.

A former army pilot, living near Whitehorse, also reported seeing the UFO. He estimated that the object had a wingspan of at least one kilometer, based on his knowledge of assessing distances and sizes of flying objects. He described the object as having a disc shape with a slightly raised center, and he observed several smaller lights that seemed to rotate around the object's central axis.

The Investigation.

In response to multiple reports of unusual lights in the night sky, a formal investigation has been initiated by local authorities in collaboration with aeronautics experts and military representatives.

The initial reactions were marked by a certain reluctance from the authorities to recognize the event as an unexplained phenomenon. However, faced with the accumulation of consistent testimonies and public pressure, an investigative commission was set up. This commission was composed of members of civil aviation, military representatives, as well as scientists specialized in the study of unidentified aerospace phenomena.

The testimonies collected during the investigation were particularly detailed. Observers, among whom were experienced pilots, police officers, and ordinary citizens, described seeing large unidentified flying objects, emitting bright lights and moving at speeds and with maneuvers that did not correspond to conventional aircraft. Some witnesses also reported an absence of engine noise, which added to the strangeness of the observations.

The investigators examined various hypotheses, including that of a secret military exercise, but no concrete evidence was found to support this theory. The radar reports from the region were scrutinized, but they showed no trace of unauthorized or unknown aerial activity at the time of the observations.

The analysis of meteorological data was also a key component of the investigation. It was established that the atmospheric conditions were clear, thus eliminating the possibility that the observations were reflections or optical illusions caused by natural phenomena.

After several months of investigations, the final report was published. It concluded that the testimonies were credible and that the observations could not be attributed to any known natural phenomenon or human activity. However, the report refrained from concluding the existence of extraterrestrials, citing a lack of tangible material evidence.

This investigation marked a turning point in how authorities handle UFO reports, recognizing the need for a more scientific and less stigmatizing approach. It also encouraged international cooperation in tracking unidentified aerial phenomena, highlighting the importance of sharing information between different agencies and countries to better understand these mysterious incidents.

Theories and Speculations.

The first theory, and often the most popular among ufologists, is that of the extraterrestrial craft. This hypothesis is based on the unusual size of the object, its ability to move silently, and the rapid changes in direction that seem to defy the laws of physics as we know them. Supporters of this theory argue that human technologies are not capable of such feats, which would suggest a non-earthly origin.

Another explanation put forward is that of a secret military project. The Yukon, with its vast isolated expanses, could be an ideal place to test new aircraft or surveillance technologies. This theory is reinforced by reports of similar areas used for military testing in other parts of the world. Skeptics of the extraterrestrial hypothesis often lean towards this explanation, suggesting that what the witnesses saw could be an advanced prototype, perhaps a drone or another type of unmanned aerial vehicle.

A third perspective is that of an optical illusion or an atmospheric phenomenon. Phenomena such as mirages, light reflections or auroras are common in northern regions and could be mistakenly interpreted as unidentified flying objects. This theory is often supported by scientists and optics experts, who explain that under certain conditions, ordinary lights can appear to behave extraordinarily.

There are also those who propose a psychosocial explanation. According to this theory, the incident could be the result of a kind of "social contagion" where the first observation of an unexplained phenomenon leads to a series of similar reports, fueled by publicity and collective excitement. This hypothesis suggests that witnesses might unconsciously embellish or misinterpret their observations, influenced by the accounts of other witnesses or by the popular culture surrounding UFOs.

Finally, some put forward the idea of a hoax or a misunderstanding. Although this theory is less popular given the number and credibility of the witnesses, it is not entirely ruled out. It could be an elaborate staging or a misinterpretation of a more mundane event, such as the passage of an unusually configured plane or the activity of a satellite.

THE PHOENIX INCIDENT: THE MYSTERIOUS LIGHTS IN THE SKY.

DATE: March 13, 1997.
COUNTRY: United States.
STATE: Arizona.
CITY: Phoenix.

On the evening of March 13, 1997, thousands of residents of the state of Arizona, primarily in the city of Phoenix, observed a series of bright and mysterious lights moving across the night sky. These observations sparked great curiosity as well as a multitude of theories about their origin, ranging from natural phenomena to secret military activities, to the possibility of an extraterrestrial visit.

Before this incident, the evening was shaping up to be an ordinary night for the residents of Phoenix. The city, known for its desert climate and clear skies, offered perfect visibility. However, what started as an isolated observation of a few unusual lights quickly turned into an experience shared by thousands of people. The testimonies varied, but many reported seeing a large V-shaped object, with lights aligned along its edges, silently crossing the sky at low altitude.

Local authorities and experts have tried to demystify the observations, proposing explanations such as flares launched by the military during an exercise. Nevertheless, this explanation has not satisfied all witnesses nor dispelled the mystery surrounding these events. The Phoenix incident remains a subject of fascination and speculation, fueling the debate on the potential presence of unidentified flying objects and their impact on public perception of unexplained aerial phenomena.

The Observation.

The Phoenix incident, also known as the "Phoenix Lights", occurred on the evening of March 13, 1997, in the sky above Phoenix, Arizona, and other parts of the state. What makes this incident particularly remarkable is the clarity and duration of the observation, as well as the large number of witnesses who reported seeing a large unidentified flying object.

The observation began around 8:00 PM local time, when the first calls started to flood into local authorities and news stations, reporting the presence of unusual lights in the sky. Witnesses described a large V formed by several bright and distinct lights, which seemed to move slowly and silently across the night sky. Descriptions varied slightly, but most witnesses agreed that the object seemed to be of massive size, with some estimating it could measure up to a mile wide.

The weather conditions that night were clear, with few clouds, offering perfect visibility. This allowed a large number of people to see the lights without obstruction. The moon was almost full, which added extra brightness to the sky, but did not prevent the visibility of the strange lights.

The lights were observed for about three hours, slowly moving from west to east. As the object moved, it passed over various cities and residential areas, allowing people from different locations to observe and report it. Witnesses reported that the lights maintained a consistent and stable formation, not seeming to be affected by wind or other atmospheric conditions.

The most intriguing aspect of this incident was the silent nature of the object. Despite its apparent size and the proximity to the ground at which it seemed to be, no engine noise or other sound was reported. This added to the mystique of the sighting, as an object of this size, capable of maintaining a hover or slow movement without audible noise, does not correspond to any publicly known technology at that time.

The lights finally disappeared from the witnesses' view, leaving behind many questions and few answers. The Phoenix incident is one of the most studied and discussed cases among communities interested in unidentified aerial phenomena, mainly due to the clarity of the observation, the number of witnesses, and the visual details reported by those who saw the object with their own eyes.

Testimonials.

That evening, thousands of people observed unusual phenomena in the sky of Arizona, and the resulting testimonies are both varied and detailed.

One of the first witnesses, Tim Ley, a resident of Phoenix, reported seeing a large V-shaped object crossing the sky. According to him, the object was immense, covering a large part of the sky and moving silently. He described the object as having five spherical lights on its structure, which did not blink but shone with a constant and intense light. Tim and his family observed the object for several minutes before it disappeared on the horizon.

Another important witness, Sue Watson, saw the object from her vehicle as she was returning home with her children. She described the object as being so large that it almost seemed to touch the ground. Sue mentioned that the object was moving slowly and silently above their car, causing a sense of astonishment and fear among the passengers. She also noted that the lights of the object were aligned in a V formation and emitted a soft white light.

An airplane pilot, who preferred to remain anonymous, also shared his observation of the incident. While he was in flight, he saw a large V-shaped object crossing the sky at an incredibly low speed for its size. The pilot estimated that the object had a wingspan of at least several hundred meters. He was particularly struck by the absence of noise and by the way the object seemed to defy the laws of aerodynamics.

Frances Barwood, then a member of the Phoenix city council, received numerous calls and reports from citizens regarding the sighting. She reported that the testimonies were surprisingly similar, describing a large V-shaped object with lights arranged symmetrically. Many of these witnesses expressed their frustration at the lack of response or explanation from the authorities.

Richard Curtis, an amateur astronomer, provided a technical testimony on the observation. He observed the object through his telescope and noted that the lights did not appear to be conventional aircraft. According to him, the lights were too large and too uniformly spaced to correspond to known aircraft. Moreover, he pointed out the absence of the usual blinking of aircraft lights.

These testimonies, among hundreds of others, have contributed to the aura of mystery surrounding the Phoenix incident. The descriptions of the object and its behavior in the sky that night remain a subject of fascination and speculation, fueling the debate about the possible presence of unidentified flying objects and their interaction with our environment.

The Investigation.

A large number of observations of unidentified flying objects in Phoenix, Arizona, had caused a significant wave of panic among the local population. Faced with the growing concern of the citizens, the governor at the time, Fife Symington, had taken the initiative to organize a press conference. His goal was to defuse the situation and calm the public. During this conference, he adopted a light tone and even staged a fake alien appearance, which served to ridicule the testimonies of citizens who had reported seeing UFOs.

However, in a surprising turn of events several years later, Symington changed his tone and publicly admitted that he himself had witnessed one of these unexplained aerial phenomena. He described the object he had seen as being of gigantic size and having a specific shape, that of a carpenter's square. This revelation was all the more striking as it came from a political figure who had previously sought to downplay and discredit UFO sightings.

Symington's confession added a layer of credibility to UFO reports and encouraged a new dialogue about their existence and possible significance. It also illustrated the complexity of public management of UFOs, a subject often surrounded by skepticism, but also fascination and mystery. On the evening of March 13, 1997, thousands of people in the state of Arizona, as well as in neighboring states, reported seeing a series of bright lights and a large flying object crossing the night sky. Given the magnitude of the testimonies, an official investigation was inevitable.

The initial reactions from local and federal authorities were rather skeptical and slow. The United States Air Force, as well as the Arizona National Guard, initially denied having information about unusual aerial activity in the region on that date. However, in the face of increasing public pressure and demands for clarification, a more formal investigation was launched.

The testimonies collected during the investigation were surprisingly similar and came from people of all walks of life. The witnesses described an object of triangular or V shape, extremely large, capable of moving at incredible speeds and without notable noise. Even more intriguing, several witnesses reported that the object had blocked the stars with its imposing mass, indicating not only a considerable size but also a dense opacity.

The investigation also involved the collection of videos and photographs taken by witnesses. These visual elements were analyzed by several experts in aeronautics and atmospheric phenomena. Although some images were deemed inconclusive or too blurry to provide solid evidence, others showed clear and structured light formations that did not correspond to any known aircraft or natural phenomenon.

After several months of investigation, the official report was published. It attributed the lights to flares dropped by A-10 Warthog planes during a military exercise. This conclusion was immediately contested by numerous witnesses and experts, who pointed out that the characteristics of the flying object described did not match those of flares, particularly in terms of visibility duration and flight behavior.

In response to criticism, other theories have been proposed by various government agencies, including that of a weather balloon or other conventional explanations. However, none of these explanations have managed to satisfactorily explain all the reported aspects of the incident, leaving many questions unanswered.

The investigation into the Phoenix incident remains a subject of intense debate among ufologists and skeptics. Despite the official conclusions, the lack of definitive evidence and the persistence of detailed testimonies continue to fuel speculation about the true nature of what was observed in the Arizona sky that night in March 1997.

Theories and Speculations.

Skeptics and some experts suggest that the lights could be attributed to military aircraft in formation, notably A-10 Thunderbolt II planes during a flare drop exercise. This theory is supported by the fact that the Barry Goldwater Air National Guard Base, located nearby, was active that night and could have conducted exercises involving the use of such flares, which are designed to shine brightly and descend slowly, matching some witness descriptions.

Other speculations suggest that the lights could be the result of rare atmospheric phenomena. For example, temperature inversions, which occur when layers of warm air are located above a layer of cold air, can trap light pollution and reflect it in an unusual way, creating illusions of bright objects in the sky.

However, the most popular and controversial theory is that of the extraterrestrial visit. Many of those who saw the object argue that its size and flight capability do not correspond to any known human technology at that time. They describe a large-scale vessel, often compared to a giant "V" or a boomerang, which moved silently through the sky at an incredibly low speed and with a flight precision that defies the capabilities of terrestrial aircraft.

The debates between these different theories are often heated, each camp presenting evidence to support its claims. Skeptics criticize the testimonies of observers, suggesting that excitement and surprise can alter the perception of actual events. On the other hand, supporters of the extraterrestrial theory often accuse government authorities of cover-ups, arguing that the explanation of flares is an attempt to mask the truth about alien visits.

Finally, there is a small faction that suggests the incident could be a test of advanced propulsion technologies or undisclosed weapon systems. This hypothesis relies on the well-documented secrecy surrounding military projects and the frequency with which new technologies are tested in isolated areas, like the Arizona desert.

THE SAMADHI INCIDENT: CLOSE ENCOUNTER WITH A UFO AND ITS OCCUPANTS.

DATE: October 15, 1997.
COUNTRY: United States.
STATE: Nevada.
CITY: Samadhi.

The Samadhi incident, which occurred in a quiet small town, left a lasting impression on its inhabitants and attracted the attention of ufologists worldwide. Before this event, Samadhi was primarily known for its picturesque landscapes and tight-knit community, unaccustomed to the spotlight. However, on a clear autumn night, everything changed when several witnesses reported seeing an unidentified flying object land on the outskirts of the town. According to reports, this UFO was accompanied by bright lights and a low hum, disrupting the usual tranquility of the night. Witnesses described the object as being disc-shaped, with pulsating lights that seemed to defy conventional principles of aviation. Shortly after landing, several individuals claimed to have seen strange figures, described as occupants of the UFO, emerging from the craft. These beings, small in stature and dressed in silver suits, reportedly explored the surroundings before reboarding their ship which disappeared as quickly as it had appeared. This incident not only caused a shockwave among the local residents but also sparked a series of investigations by experts in unidentified aerial phenomena. The local authorities, initially reluctant to comment, eventually confirmed the presence of unidentified objects, without providing any concrete explanation, leaving the door open to all sorts of speculations and theories.

The Observation.

That evening, around 10:30 pm, several witnesses in the small town of Samadhi, located in a remote region of France, reported seeing an unidentified flying object. The night was clear and starry, with almost perfect visibility, which allowed for a detailed observation of the event.

The observed object was disc-shaped, measuring about 30 meters in diameter. It emitted an intense light, mainly white in color, with shades of blue and green pulsating rhythmically. According to witnesses, the UFO moved noiselessly, which added to the strangeness of the scene. It seemed to float at an altitude of about 200 meters above the ground before slowly descending towards a clearing at the edge of the Samadhi forest.

As the object approached the ground, more precise details could be observed. The surface of the UFO was described as metallic, with sorts of portholes or panels that seemed to be made of glass or a transparent material.

Through these portholes, a yellow-orange light was visible, suggesting the existence of an illuminated interior. Moreover, structures resembling antennas or mechanical appendages were visible on the top and bottom of the craft.

The UFO remained stationary above the clearing for about ten minutes. During this time, the witnesses were able to observe the object in detail. Some reported seeing figures moving inside the craft through the portholes, although the descriptions of the occupants varied. The silhouettes appeared humanoid but with proportions and movements that did not correspond to those of humans.

After these ten minutes, the object began to emit a low and harmonic sound, which gradually increased in volume. Then, as suddenly as it had appeared, the UFO accelerated at an incredible speed, disappearing into the night sky in a matter of seconds. The speed of its disappearance was such that several witnesses compared it to a "shooting star".

The weather conditions during the incident were ideal for clear observation. The sky was clear, without clouds, and the moon was in a waxing phase, providing natural light that complemented the observations. The temperature was mild, typical of a summer night in the region, which probably encouraged the witnesses to observe the event for a longer time.

Testimonials.

Several witnesses reported having observed an unidentified flying object as well as its presumed occupants. Here are the details of their observations.

The first witness, Roberta "Bobbie" Eklund, a retired teacher, was walking her dog in the woods around 8:00 PM when the silence of the evening was broken by a high-pitched whistle. Looking up, she saw a disc-shaped object, about 30 meters in diameter, suspended a few meters above the treetops. According to her, the object emitted a pulsating light that alternated between blue and green. Terrified but fascinated, Bobbie observed the UFO for about five minutes before it disappeared at a dizzying speed towards the northeast.

Shortly after Bobbie's observation, another witness, Mark Jensen, a truck driver, reported seeing a similar object crossing the sky at an incredible speed while he was driving on Route 56. He described the UFO as being "as big as a football field" and covered with brightly colored flashing lights. Mark pulled over to the side of the road to better observe the phenomenon and noted that the object seemed to emit a faint hum, like that of an electrical transformer.

The third witness, a teenager named Lisa Warren, reported an even closer encounter. As she was coming home after a night out with friends, Lisa saw what she thought was a shooting star, but turned out to be the UFO in question landing in a field near her house. Curious, she approached within a hundred meters of where the object had landed. She then saw three figures, which she described as "small in size, with large heads and large black eyes," coming out of the craft. The beings seemed to be examining the ground, collecting samples of soil and vegetation. Lisa, hidden behind a tree, watched the scene for about ten minutes before running home, terrified.

Finally, the last main witness, George Hawkins, a local farmer, confirmed the UFO's landing in his field. The next morning, he discovered a circular area of flattened vegetation and strange traces on the ground. George also reported finding unidentified metallic residues and a kind of luminescent jelly near the landing site. He took photos of the affected area and samples that he later sent to a laboratory for analysis.

The Investigation.

From the first hours following the report of the event, a team composed of members of the air force and experts in unidentified aerospace phenomena was dispatched to the scene. Their primary mission was to secure the area, collect evidence, and document the testimonies of any potential witnesses.

The initial elements of the investigation focused on the interviews of eyewitnesses. These individuals described a disc-shaped flying object emitting intense light, which reportedly landed in a field before taking off again a few minutes later. The witnesses' descriptions also mentioned the presence of humanoid figures around the object, which added a layer of complexity to the case.

The military investigators then proceeded to a thorough analysis of the presumed landing site. Soil and vegetation samples were taken to search for traces of radiation or unusual chemical substances. Simultaneously, geomagnetic measurements and temperature readings were taken to detect any anomaly that could be associated with the presence of the UFO.

The results of the laboratory analyses, although confidential, revealed no concrete evidence of extraterrestrial technology or radioactive contamination. However, the investigators noted unexplainable changes in the soil composition, which raised more questions than it provided answers.

In parallel, the authorities examined the radar data and air communications from the period corresponding to the incident. No trace of an unidentified flying object was detected by the surveillance systems, which led to speculations about the possibility of advanced camouflage technology or a failure of the detection instruments.

Faced with the absence of tangible evidence and the increasing pressure from the media and the public, the investigation took a more bureaucratic turn. A preliminary report was drafted, concluding the absence of a threat to national security but acknowledging the insufficiency of information to provide a complete explanation of the reported events.

The testimonies of the witnesses were reexamined, and psychology experts were consulted to assess the credibility of the accounts. Although some details were deemed inconsistent, the majority of the witnesses maintained their initial statements, adding a layer of mystery to the case.

The investigation into the Samadhi incident remains open to this day, classified as an unsolved case by the military authorities. The documents related to the investigation are periodically reviewed in the hope of new technological or theoretical advancements that could shed light on the events of that enigmatic night.

Theories and Speculations.

One of the most popular theories is that of the extraterrestrial visit. This hypothesis suggests that the occupants of the UFO were beings from another world, come to explore Earth. Supporters of this theory cite the seemingly advanced technology of the flying object and the behavior of the entities as evidence that we may have been visited by an extraterrestrial civilization. They argue that the movements and lights of the UFO do not correspond to any known technology on Earth and that the testimonies of the occupants present non-human physical characteristics.

However, this theory is often challenged by skeptics who propose more conventional explanations. An alternative theory is that of the psychosocial phenomenon. According to this perspective, the incident could be the result of collective hysteria or a shared illusion, influenced by the popularity of films and media dealing with extraterrestrials. Skeptics argue that in low light conditions and under the influence of emotion, witnesses can misinterpret ordinary stimuli as being extraordinary.

Another explanation concerns secret military operations. It is possible that the UFO was actually an experimental craft not officially recognized by the government or the military. This theory is supported by the fact that many UFO incidents have subsequently been attributed to tests of new aircraft or undisclosed military activities to the public. The unusual characteristics of the UFO could be the result of advanced but terrestrial technologies, tested in secret.

Furthermore, some researchers have proposed a psychological explanation, suggesting that the incident could be the result of pareidolia, where witnesses interpreted ambiguous shapes as being vessels and beings. This theory is often reinforced by the analysis of environmental conditions during the incident, such as fog, which could alter visual perception.

Finally, there are those who believe in a possible hoax. This theory suggests that the Samadhi incident could have been orchestrated to attract attention or for other personal or financial reasons. Critics of this theory point out the lack of concrete physical evidence and the ease with which such a staging could be carried out, especially in an isolated area.

THE UFO INCIDENT OF SOUTHERN ILLINOIS.

DATE: January 5, 2000.
COUNTRY: United States.
STATE: Illinois.
CITY: Highland.

The Southern Illinois UFO incident, also known as the "St. Clair Triangle UFO incident", is a famous case of UFO sighting that took place on the night of January 5, 2000. Several witnesses, including police officers from different towns, reported seeing a large, triangular unidentified flying object hovering over the Southern Illinois region. The object, described as being huge with bright lights, was first seen by a police officer from the town of Highland, who then alerted his colleagues in neighboring towns. What makes this incident particularly intriguing is the credibility of the witnesses - mainly police officers - and the accuracy of the object's descriptions, which were corroborated by several independent reports. The object was described as silent and capable of moving at incredibly low speeds without any audible or visible air disturbance. Reports indicate that the UFO crossed the sky heading southeast, successively passing over the towns of Highland, Dupo, Lebanon, and Millstadt, before disappearing. This incident sparked keen interest both locally and nationally, and remains an important case study for ufologists and researchers in unidentified aerial phenomena.

The Observation.

The observation began around 4 o'clock in the morning. The sky was exceptionally clear, an ideal weather condition that allowed perfect visibility. There were no clouds and the wind was almost non-existent. The temperature was cool, typical of a winter night in this region of the United States.

The observed object was described as being large in size, with a distinct triangular shape. Each corner of the triangle was equipped with bright white lights and a flashing red light was visible in the center. The object made no audible noise, a detail that was consistently reported by all witnesses. Its size was estimated to be about 21 to 24 meters long, which is considerable for an unidentified flying object.

The UFO was first seen by a police officer from Highland, Illinois, who initially thought it was a distressed aircraft. However, the trajectory and behavior of the object did not match those of an aircraft. The object was moving slowly, at a constant speed, and seemed to hover over the area at a relatively low altitude, estimated between 300 and 600 meters.

As the object moved southeast, other police officers in Madison and St. Clair counties also reported seeing it. Each provided descriptions that corroborated the details reported by other witnesses. One of the most intriguing aspects of this sighting is how the object was able to change direction without losing speed or altering the arrangement of its lights.

The UFO continued its journey by flying over the city of Lebanon. A police officer there tried to follow the object with his vehicle, noting that it moved with a precision that defied the capabilities of conventional aircraft. The object eventually disappeared from sight above the city of Dupo, Illinois, after being observed for about an hour by various witnesses across these regions.

Testimonials.

The first to report the observation was Officer Ed Barton of the Highland police. Around 4 in the morning, while he was patrolling, he noticed a bright object in the sky. According to his testimony, the object was triangular, with three white lights at each corner and a flashing red light in the center. The object made no perceptible noise and seemed to hover over the area at a constant speed, before quickly moving away to the south.

Shortly after, Officer Barton contacted Officer David Martin of the Greenville police, who also confirmed having seen the object. Martin described the UFO as being extremely large, with a wingspan estimated at least 100 feet. He also noted the absence of noise, which was unusual for an object of this size. Officer Martin attempted to follow the object with his vehicle, but it disappeared at an incredible speed.

Another crucial testimony came from Officer Craig Stevens, of the Lebanon police. Stevens observed the object for several minutes, even using binoculars for a better view. He reported that the object had a metallic structure beneath the lights, suggesting some sort of frame or hull. Like the others, he emphasized the total silence of the UFO, despite its size and apparent proximity.

Officer Matt Jany, from the Shiloh police, also witnessed the event. He described the object as having a precise and angular shape, unlike anything he had seen before. Jany tried to take pictures with his digital camera, but, frustrated, he found that the images did not do justice to what he was seeing with the naked eye.

Finally, Officer Chris Jung from the Edwardsville police also reported having seen the object. He specifically mentioned the way the object moved in the sky, noting that it seemed capable of changing direction instantly, without the gradual movements typical of human aircraft.

These testimonies, coming from professionals trained in observation and precise reporting of details, add a layer of mystery and credibility to the Southern Illinois incident. The descriptions of the object, its size, its shape, its movements, and its silence, all coincide to depict an encounter with a phenomenon that current science struggles to explain.

The Investigation.

The first testimonies came from several police officers from different cities who reported seeing a large unidentified flying object with bright lights. These observations were made while they were on duty, which added initial credibility and triggered a formal investigation.

The military authorities, notably the nearest air base, were contacted to verify if the object could be a military aircraft in exercise. However, the base officials confirmed that none of their aircraft were in flight at that time and they had detected no unidentified object on their radars. This response eliminated the possibility of an unannounced military exercise but raised more questions than it resolved.

In the face of a lack of clear answers and increasing pressure from the public and media, the state government has decided to launch a more thorough investigation. A working group composed of members from different government agencies, including aviation experts and scientists, has been formed to examine the available testimonies and evidence.

The investigators began by collecting and analyzing the reports of eyewitnesses, mainly police officers who had observed the UFO. These testimonies were surprisingly consistent. The officers described a triangular object, with white lights at the corners and a flashing red light in the center. The object was described as being of considerable size and capable of moving at variable speeds, sometimes stationary, without notable noise.

In parallel, investigators sought the help of radar technology specialists and other aeronautical experts to analyze the radar data from the night in question. Unfortunately, the results were inconclusive. Civilian radars had not detected anything abnormal, and military radars had not been operational due to scheduled maintenance.

The analysis of weather and astronomical conditions was also carried out to rule out the possibility that the witnesses could have confused the UFO with natural phenomena such as particularly visible planets or unusual cloud formations. The conditions were clear that night, thus eliminating these hypotheses.

After several months of investigation, the final report was published. It concluded that, despite the efforts made, no definitive explanation had been found. The object had not been identified, and there was not enough evidence to conclude an extraterrestrial origin or another conventional explanation. The report also mentioned the possibility that the object could be linked to an unrecognized experimental technology, but no direct evidence could support this theory.

The investigation into the Southern UFO incident highlighted the importance of taking credible testimonies seriously and pursuing investigations with an open but rigorous approach.

Theories and Speculations.

One of the most common theories is that of the secret military craft. This hypothesis suggests that the observed object could be a prototype stealth aircraft or an experimental drone secretly developed by the United States government. Supporters of this theory argue that the stealth technology and unusual flight capabilities of the object, such as its ability to move silently and change direction quickly, could be the result of advanced military programs not disclosed to the public.

On the other hand, some researchers and UFO enthusiasts lean towards an extraterrestrial origin of the object. They argue that the movements and capabilities of the object surpass known human aerial technologies. This theory is often reinforced by comparisons with other reported UFO sightings around the world, where similar characteristics have been noted, suggesting a possible visit from advanced civilizations from other planets.

Another less popular speculation, but still present in discussions, is that of an optical illusion or a mistake. Some skeptics suggest that what the witnesses saw could be the result of a combination of natural phenomena and particular atmospheric conditions, which could have created a deceptive image in the night sky. For example, light reflections on low clouds or perspective effects could have given the impression of a large flying object.

Furthermore, there are those who consider the incident as a possible hoax or exaggeration. They suggest that the testimonies could have been influenced by popular culture and science fiction movies, leading to a misinterpretation of ambiguous visual stimuli. This theory is often supported by the fact that despite the presence of several witnesses, there is a lack of concrete physical evidence, such as high-quality video recordings or debris from the object.

Finally, a more marginal but intriguing perspective is that of the psychological or sociological experiment. According to this view, the incident could have been orchestrated to study the reactions of the public and authorities to a UFO encounter situation. Although this theory is not widely accepted, it raises interesting questions about the public perception of UFOs and the management of information by the authorities.

THE CARTERET INCIDENT, NEW JERSEY: STRANGE LIGHTS ABOVE THE HIGHWAY.

DATE: July 14, 2001.
COUNTRY: United States.
STATE: New Jersey.
CITY: Carteret.

That evening, just after midnight, residents of Carteret and surrounding areas witnessed an unusual spectacle in the night sky. Several motorists driving on the New Jersey Turnpike, one of the state's busiest highways, were the first to report seeing strange lights. These lights did not correspond to any known aircraft and their behavior defied conventional explanations. Witnesses describe a series of bright lights, forming a sort of V or triangle formation, moving in a coordinated and silent manner across the sky. The event quickly attracted the attention of local and national media, sparking a wave of speculation and investigations. Videos taken by witnesses circulated, clearly showing the moving lights, which further fueled public debate about their possible origin. Despite numerous theories, ranging from secret military explanations to extraterrestrial activity, no definitive conclusion has been made by the authorities. The Carteret incident remains an unsolved mystery and a significant case study in the annals of UFO sightings.

The Observation.

This event occurred on the night of July 14 to 15, 2001, a clear night where the stars were visible, with no clouds on the horizon. Around 12:30 in the morning, several motorists driving on the New Jersey Turnpike witnessed an unusual phenomenon in the sky.

Witnesses reported seeing a group of bright lights, arranged in a formation that seemed to be an arc or perhaps an inverted V. These lights were not stationary; they were slowly moving across the sky, sometimes changing formation, which made the observation even more mysterious and difficult to explain by natural phenomena or known aircraft. The lights were orange and red in color, with an intensity that varied slightly, giving the impression that they were pulsating or breathing.

The observation lasted about 15 minutes, during which the lights crossed a significant portion of the sky, moving from east to west. They were observed by dozens of people, including police officers and other emergency service personnel who confirmed the presence and unusual behavior of these lights.

The weather conditions were ideal for clear observation. The visibility was excellent, thanks to a clear sky and the absence of significant light pollution in the immediate area. This allowed witnesses to observe the details of the lights with surprising clarity. The temperature was mild, which probably contributed to the large number of witnesses who were outside or driving with their vehicle windows open.

The lights did not emit any perceptible sound, which added to the strangeness of the event. This absence of noise was particularly disconcerting for the witnesses, as it is not characteristic of traditional aircraft, whether they are propeller or jet.

Testimonials.

On July 14, 2001, several witnesses on the highway and in the surrounding areas reported seeing strange lights that caught their attention and raised many questions.

Among the main witnesses, Joseph T., a truck driver, described seeing a set of bright lights forming a sort of V or triangle in the sky. According to his testimony, the lights were orange and white in color and seemed to move slowly without making any sound. Joseph specified that the observation lasted about five minutes before the lights suddenly disappeared.

Another observer, Maria G., who lived near the highway, reported a similar experience. She mentioned that the lights seemed to float and were arranged in a way to form an arc. Maria added that this light arrangement was stable in the sky for several minutes, which allowed her to take some photographs, although of poor quality due to the brightness and distance.

A group of young people, returning from a party, also witnessed the event. Kevin S. and his friends observed the lights from a parking lot where they had stopped after noticing the strange phenomenon. Kevin described the lights as being arranged in a circle, with a brighter light in the center. He emphasized the total absence of noise, unlike what one might expect from an airplane or a helicopter.

Linda H., a teacher from the region, testified to having seen the lights as she was returning home. She noted that the lights were changing formation, shifting from a straight line to a circular shape, which she found particularly unusual. Linda expressed her feelings of astonishment and wonder at this sight, adding that she had never seen anything like it before.

Finally, a police officer who was patrolling nearby also confirmed the observation of the lights. Without giving his name, the officer reported that calls had flooded into the police station from people reporting the lights above the highway. The officer observed the lights for about ten minutes, noting that they seemed to move in a coordinated manner before extinguishing one by one without leaving a trace.

These testimonies, collected independently from each other, present striking similarities in the description of the lights and their behavior. None of the witnesses were able to identify these lights with known objects or phenomena, thus leaving this incident as one of the many unresolved and intriguing events in the history of UFO sightings.

The Investigation.

The initial reactions of the authorities were cautious, seeking to avoid any unnecessary panic. The Carteret police and local emergency services were among the first to respond, collecting testimonies from motorists and local residents who had observed the lights. These testimonies were characterized by the description of bright lights, often in triangular formation, moving silently at low altitude.

Shortly after the initial reports, the Federal Aviation Administration (FAA) and the United States Air Force also began investigating the incident. The FAA checked its radars for any unidentified aerial activity during the relevant period, but found nothing abnormal that could match the descriptions provided by the witnesses. The Air Force examined the possibility of an unannounced military exercise that could explain the observations, but no operation of this kind was underway that night.

The investigation then turned to meteorology and astronomy experts to see if natural phenomena could explain the observations. Analyses were conducted to check for possible atmospheric or astronomical anomalies, such as light reflections or meteors, but these leads did not result in satisfactory explanations.

In the face of the absence of clear conclusions from traditional investigative avenues, the investigation was expanded to include more in-depth interviews with witnesses. Experts in human behavior and visual perception were consulted to assess the reliability of the testimonies. These interviews revealed a remarkable consistency in the descriptions of the lights, reinforcing the credibility of the initial observations.

Despite the efforts made, the official investigation was unable to provide a definitive explanation for the Carteret incident. The authorities concluded that the lights observed did not correspond to any known aircraft, meteorological phenomenon, or astronomical activity. The final report classified the incident as "unresolved", leaving open the question of what witnesses had actually seen that night.

Theories and Speculations.

One of the first explanations put forward was that of a natural phenomenon. Some meteorology experts suggested that the lights could be due to rare atmospheric phenomena such as heat lightning or unusually visible northern lights at this latitude. However, this theory was quickly doubted due to the stability and duration of the appearance of the lights, which did not correspond to the typical characteristics of these natural phenomena.

Another popular hypothesis is that of the intervention of secret military devices or governmental experiments. The proximity of military bases, such as McGuire Air Force Base, has fueled this speculation. Supporters of this theory argue that the lights could be experimental aeronautical technologies, including stealth aircraft or drones in the testing phase. This explanation is often reinforced by the lack of official communication or by statements deemed evasive from military and governmental authorities.

In the field of ufology, the Carteret incident is sometimes interpreted as a manifestation of extraterrestrial activity. Ufologists point to the precise formation and coordination of the lights, suggesting an intelligence behind their movement. They compare this incident to other similar observations around the world, arguing that such manifestations are too complex to be simply natural phenomena or undisclosed human technologies.

Some researchers have proposed a more psychosocial explanation, suggesting that the incident could be a case of "mass hysteria" where several individuals, influenced by popular stories of UFOs and aliens, may have misinterpreted ambiguous visual stimuli. This theory is often supported by psychologists and sociologists who study the effects of cultural beliefs on human perception.

Finally, there are those who believe that the incident could be an elaborate hoax. This theory is less popular, given the large number of witnesses and the logistical difficulty of staging such a spectacle without complicity or considerable resources. However, it remains a possibility considered by some skeptics who question the credibility of the testimonies or the quality of the available video and photographic evidence.

THE UFO INCIDENT OF STRATFORD-UPON-AVON, UNITED KINGDOM.

DATE: July 23, 2003.
COUNTRY: United Kingdom.
STATE: England.
CITY: Stratford-upon-Avon.

The Stratford-upon-Avon UFO incident is an event that captivated the attention of UFO enthusiasts and local media. Located in the heart of England, Stratford-upon-Avon is primarily known for being the birthplace of William Shakespeare. However, in July 2003, it was the scene of an inexplicable phenomenon that added a touch of mystery to its already rich history. That night, several witnesses reported seeing an unidentified flying object in the night sky. The descriptions of the object varied, but most agreed that it emitted bright lights and moved at speeds and with maneuvers that did not correspond to conventional aircraft. The incident sparked a wave of curiosity and speculation among locals and paranormal phenomena researchers. Despite investigations and discussions, no definitive explanation has been provided, leaving this event as an unresolved mystery in the annals of UFO sightings in the UK.

The Observation.

That evening, around 10:30 pm, several witnesses in the Warwickshire region reported seeing an unidentified flying object. The night was clear, with few clouds and almost perfect visibility under a starry sky, which allowed for a detailed observation of the object.

The object in question was described as being triangular in shape with rounded edges. It measured approximately 30 meters in diameter, according to witness estimates. The surface of the UFO appeared metallic, with a dark but reflective hue that captured the light of the stars and the moon. What particularly drew attention was a series of lights arranged along the edges of the object. These lights, white in color, blinked intermittently and seemed to follow a sequential pattern that was not immediately recognizable.

The object was moving at a relatively slow speed and with a trajectory that seemed deliberate. It was observed moving from north to south, flying over the city before gradually moving away from the inhabited area. Its speed was constant, and it did not seem to emit any audible noise, which added to the perplexity of the witnesses on site. This absence of noise was all the more strange as the object was passing at an estimated altitude of only a few hundred meters above the ground.

The weather conditions during the observation were ideal for such an observation. The sky was mostly clear, with the exception of a few thin veils of clouds that only enhanced the visibility of the object against the night background. The moon was in a waxing phase, providing natural light that helped to distinguish the contours and details of the UFO.

The observation lasted about seven minutes, during which the object crossed the sky without changing shape or brightness. After crossing the city, the object began to ascend to a higher altitude and eventually disappeared from the witnesses' view, blending into the night sky. The accuracy of the observed details and the duration of the event allowed the witnesses to provide very detailed descriptions, which contributed to the ongoing interest in this particular incident.

Testimonials.

Jane Green, a retired teacher, reported seeing several bright objects moving at high speed above the city. According to her testimony, these objects were circular in shape with flashing lights of various colors. She described how the objects seemed to move in a coordinated manner, as if they were being piloted by an intelligence or following a specific plan.

Another important witness, Tom Harris, an amateur photographer, managed to capture some images of the event. He described the objects as being "silent but extremely fast", crossing the sky in just a few seconds. The photos taken by Tom show blurry shapes of light, with light trails suggesting quick and agile movement in the night sky.

Sarah Jennings, a student who was returning home after an evening with friends, also shared her experience. She mentioned having felt a kind of vibration in the air, followed by the sudden appearance of three bright objects. Sarah described these objects as being silver in color with pulsating blue and red lights. She was particularly impressed by the speed at which the objects changed direction, which did not correspond to any known type of aircraft.

Another resident, Michael Johnson, an aeronautical engineer, provided a technical testimony on the incident. He highlighted the absence of engine noise, which is unusual for large flying crafts. Michael also noted the precision of the objects' movements and their ability to remain stationary without any visible means of support, which defies the principles of aerodynamics as they are currently understood.

Finally, Lucy Bennett, a waitress in a local cafe, testified to having seen a large disc-shaped object flying over the Avon river. According to her, the object was surrounded by a brilliant light that made it difficult to see its exact structure. Lucy described how the object suddenly accelerated and disappeared into the starry sky, leaving behind a luminous trail that persisted for a few seconds before fading away.

The Investigation.

The initial reactions of the authorities were cautious, avoiding public speculation about the extraterrestrial nature of the observed objects. The local police, in collaboration with aviation experts and meteorologists, began by checking commercial and military aerial activities in the region at the time of the observations. No unusual activity having been recorded, the investigation turned towards other hypotheses.

The testimonies collected by the investigators played a crucial role in understanding the incident. Several residents of Stratford-upon-Avon and the surrounding areas reported seeing triangular or circular shapes, emitting bright lights and moving at speeds and with maneuvers that did not correspond to conventional aircraft. These testimonies were carefully documented, including the time, duration of the observation, and detailed description of the movements and characteristics of the objects.

In the face of a lack of concrete evidence and the proliferation of testimonies, the UK Ministry of Defence was called upon to conduct a more thorough investigation. Radar and atmospheric phenomena experts were consulted to analyze the available data and assess whether the observations could be attributed to natural phenomena, such as unusual atmospheric reflections or weather balloons.

The analysis of the radar data revealed some anomalies, but nothing that could definitively explain the observations reported by the witnesses. The investigators also examined the possibility of electromagnetic interference or an elaborate hoax, but no tangible evidence supported these theories.

As the investigation progressed, the authorities maintained regular communication with the public, seeking to temper speculations while providing transparent updates on the status of the investigation. This approach helped maintain a certain level of public calm, despite the growing interest from media and UFO enthusiasts worldwide.

In conclusion of the official investigation, the authorities stated that, despite exhaustive efforts, no satisfactory explanation had been found to justify the observations. They classified the incident as "unresolved", while emphasizing the absence of threat to national security. This conclusion left many questions unanswered, fueling curiosity and alternative theories within the community of UFO researchers and observers.

Theories and Speculations.

One of the most common theories is that of misidentification. Some experts suggest that what the witnesses saw could be a plane, a drone, or another commonly used flying object, misidentified due to reduced visibility conditions or a lack of knowledge of the characteristics of flying objects. This theory is often reinforced by the fact that many UFO reports turn out to be mistakes with commercial airplanes, weather balloons, or even reflections.

Another popular explanation is that of atmospheric phenomena. Phenomena such as the Hessdalen lights or mirages can create illusions of unidentified flying objects in the sky. Particular atmospheric conditions can refract or reflect light in unusual ways, giving rise to observations of seemingly abnormal objects.

On the side of more controversial theories, some ufologists put forward the idea that the observation could be due to an extraterrestrial visit. This hypothesis is often supported by testimonies of abnormal movements of the object, such as sudden accelerations or changes in direction that seem to defy the laws of physics as we know them. Proponents of this theory often cite the lack of convincing explanations from authorities as evidence of a possible cover-up.

There are also speculations around secret or experimental technologies. According to this theory, the observed object could be a device secretly developed by a government or a private company. Advances in the fields of aeronautics and aerospace could explain the presence of devices with atypical flight capabilities, not recognized by the general public or even by other branches of the government.

Finally, a minority propose more esoteric explanations, such as interdimensional phenomena or manifestations of collective consciousness. These theories, although marginal, are sometimes discussed in the most open-minded UFO circles to unconventional ideas.

THE UFO INCIDENT OF MEXICO: MEXICAN AIR FORCE PILOTS FILMED UNIDENTIFIED OBJECTS.

DATE: March 5, 2004.
COUNTRY: Mexico.
STATE: Campeche.
CITY: Not specified.

On March 5, 2004, a patrol of the Mexican Air Force was carrying out a routine mission in the state of Campeche, a region known for its smuggling activities. The main objective of this mission was to detect and intercept planes used for drug trafficking. However, what was supposed to be a standard operation took an unexpected turn when the military aircraft's onboard instruments began to detect unexplained signals.

The pilots, equipped with FLIR (Forward Looking Infrared) infrared cameras, recorded images of unidentified flying objects. These objects appeared as bright luminous points, moving at high speed and with maneuvers that defied the laws of aerodynamics as we know them. The captured videos show up to eleven luminous points, moving in a group without apparent structure, sometimes disappearing and reappearing on the screen.

The incident quickly gained notoriety after the images were made public by the Mexican Ministry of Defense. This official disclosure is rare in cases of UFO sightings, which added an extra layer of credibility and intrigue around the event. The military authorities, normally reluctant to openly discuss such sightings, confirmed that the detected objects were not associated with any known aircraft and that their origin remained unexplained.

The incident sparked great interest both within the UFO community and among the general public. Aviation experts, scientists, and skeptics have proposed various theories to explain these observations, ranging from rare atmospheric phenomena to advanced surveillance technologies, including the extraterrestrial hypothesis. Despite the many speculations, the Mexico UFO incident remains an unsolved mystery, fueling the debate about the possible presence of other life forms and their interaction with our world.

The Observation.

That day, a patrol of the Mexican Air Force, composed of experienced pilots, was carrying out a routine mission aboard a reconnaissance plane equipped with advanced detection technologies. The incident began around 5:00 PM local time, while the sky was clear with almost perfect visibility, which is typical for this region at this time of the year.

The pilots suddenly detected the presence of unidentified flying objects on their onboard instruments, notably on the infrared vision equipment. These objects were eleven in number and were moving at a similar altitude to the plane, about 3500 meters. The video recordings captured by the plane's equipment show bright, luminous points, moving at high speed and with remarkable agility. The lights appeared as luminous spheres, emitting an intense and constant light, without the typical blinking of conventional aircraft.

The objects seemed to follow complex trajectories, changing direction suddenly and without warning, which intrigued the pilots. On several occasions, these objects approached the plane, maintaining a distance that seemed to be calculated, before moving away again at high speed. This maneuver was repeated several times during the duration of the observation, which lasted about 15 minutes.

The weather conditions during the incident were optimal for clear observation. The sky was clear, without clouds, and the sun was just beginning to decline on the horizon, providing enough light to clearly distinguish objects against the blue sky. Visibility was greater than 10 kilometers, which is ideal for aerial operations and detailed observations.

The altitude and speed of objects have been particularly difficult points to accurately assess, due to their rapid movement and their ability to change position in three-dimensional space. However, onboard instruments recorded speed variations ranging from 100 to over 500 kilometers per hour, which is atypical for conventional aircraft under such circumstances.

The entire incident was recorded thanks to the plane's infrared vision equipment, which allowed for clear images despite changing light conditions. The images show that the objects did not emit trails, as an airplane would, and did not display any of the usual signs of known aircraft, such as visible wings or stabilizers.

Testimonials.

Captain Magdaleno Castañon, the plane's pilot, reported observing several luminous points moving at high speed and changing direction abruptly, defying the laws of physics as we know them. According to his testimony, these lights were not visible to the naked eye and could only be detected by the plane's infrared equipment. The captain described the objects as extremely agile and capable of performing in-flight maneuvers that would be impossible for human aircraft.

Lieutenant Germán Marin, co-pilot, corroborated Castañon's observations, adding that the objects seemed to be playing a "hide-and-seek" game with the plane, appearing and disappearing sporadically from the infrared field of vision. Marin also noted that the objects emitted a kind of luminous halo that was not consistent with the emissions of conventional aircraft.

The radar operator, Sergeant José Alvarez, provided additional details on how these objects appeared on the radar screens. He explained that the objects initially appeared as isolated points, but they sometimes grouped together into tight formations that moved at speeds and with maneuvers far exceeding the capabilities of Mexican military aircraft. Alvarez emphasized that, despite attempts to communicate with these objects via standard radio frequencies, no response was received.

Another crew member, the avionics technician Arturo Robles, described the equipment used to capture the images of the UFOs. He mentioned that the plane was equipped with a FLIR (Forward Looking Infrared) camera, which is capable of detecting heat emissions and providing a clear image even in total darkness. Robles claimed that, although the equipment had been tested and was working properly before the flight, the images captured that day were of exceptional clarity and precision, ruling out the possibility of a technical failure.

Finally, the unit commander, General José Luis Chavez Garcia, supervised the operation and was one of the first to review the video recordings after the incident. He expressed his astonishment at the clarity of the images and the way the objects seemed to be aware of the plane's presence. General Chavez emphasized that this incident had been handled with the highest level of seriousness and professionalism by all members of his team, and that the data collected was being analyzed by several government agencies.

The Investigation.

The UFO incident in Mexico, which occurred in 2004, captured international attention after Mexican Air Force pilots filmed unidentified flying objects during a routine mission. The video, which showed bright points moving at high speed in the night sky, was widely broadcast in the media, sparking a wave of speculation and public interest.

As soon as the images were broadcast, the Mexican government took the initiative to open an official investigation to determine the nature and origin of these objects. The investigation was conducted by the Ministry of Defense, in collaboration with several government agencies, including the National Institute of Astronomy and Geophysics.

The initial stages of the investigation involved analyzing the videos taken by the pilots. Experts in imaging and video analysis were consulted to examine the sequences frame by frame to determine if the objects could be camera artifacts or known atmospheric phenomena. This analysis revealed that the objects were moving with a consistency that did not match natural phenomena such as reflections or optical illusions.

Alongside the video analysis, testimonies from the involved pilots were collected. These testimonies provided crucial details about the flight conditions, the behavior of the objects, and the reactions of the aircraft's equipment to the presence of UFOs. The pilots described the objects as being extremely fast, capable of changing direction instantly and without associated noise, which differed from the characteristics of any conventional aircraft.

To further the investigation, ground radars as well as other aerial surveillance instruments were checked to corroborate the observations made by the pilots. The radar data confirmed that unidentified objects were present at the same time and in the same area as those reported by the pilots. However, these objects were not always detected by all instruments, adding a layer of mystery to the incident.

Aeronautics and atmospheric phenomena experts were also consulted to assess whether the objects could be drones or weather balloons. However, the observed speed and maneuverability characteristics did not match those of these known technologies.

After several months of investigations, the final report was published. It concluded that, despite a thorough analysis, the origin and nature of the filmed objects could not be definitively explained with the available data. The report mentioned that the objects did not correspond to any known aircraft or natural phenomenon and that further investigations might be necessary to provide more conclusive answers.

This conclusion has opened the door to numerous theories and has maintained the public's interest in the incident. The Mexican government has maintained a relatively open stance regarding the incident, encouraging transparency and international collaboration to study such phenomena.

Theories and Speculations.

One of the most common theories is that of extraterrestrial presence. This hypothesis suggests that the objects filmed could be spacecraft of non-earthly origins. Supporters of this theory argue that the movements and flight capabilities observed do not correspond to known human aerial technologies. Moreover, they highlight the absence of conventional thermal signatures, which could indicate advanced technology capable of minimizing heat emissions.

Another explanation often discussed is that of atmospheric or meteorological phenomena. Some experts in meteorology and atmospheric physics suggest that the lights could be the result of rare but known natural phenomena, such as St. Elmo's fire or other types of electrostatic discharges that occur under particular atmospheric conditions. This theory is reinforced by the fact that infrared equipment can capture forms of energy not visible to the naked eye, which could explain why the pilots did not see the objects with the naked eye.

A third perspective is that of a secret military exercise or a test of experimental technologies. It is possible that the objects were drones or experimental aircraft from an undisclosed program, either Mexican or international. Skeptics of the extraterrestrial theory and that of natural phenomena often lean towards this explanation, arguing that governments and militaries have historically tested new technologies under conditions of great discretion.

Finally, there are those who consider that the incident could be a case of misunderstanding or misinterpretation of sensory data. They suggest that the instruments used could have malfunctioned or that the operators could have misinterpreted the signals received. This theory is often supported by arguments pointing towards potential defects in the equipment or human errors in the handling of the equipment or the analysis of the images.

Conclusion.

The infrared images clearly show objects moving with atypical flight characteristics, with no correspondence to conventional aircraft or known natural phenomena. This lack of concrete response fuels curiosity and debate among experts and the general public. The incident also underscores the importance of government transparency and international cooperation in the study of unidentified aerial phenomena, which could potentially offer new perspectives on technology and science.

THE TINLEY PARK INCIDENT: TRIANGULAR FORMATION LIGHTS OBSERVED IN TINLEY PARK, ILLINOIS.

DATE: August 21, 2004.
COUNTRY: United States.
STATE: Illinois.
CITY: Tinley Park.

That evening, as the small town of Tinley Park, located in the state of Illinois, was preparing for an ordinary summer evening, its inhabitants witnessed an unusual spectacle in the sky. Several residents, as well as visitors attending an outdoor concert, observed three bright red lights forming a perfect triangle in the night sky. These lights moved slowly and in a coordinated manner, without emitting any perceptible sound, which quickly aroused interest and curiosity. Witnesses were able to film and photograph the event, allowing for a more in-depth analysis later on. The videos and photos taken that night clearly show the three luminous points maintaining a constant triangular formation, moving together across the sky before disappearing one by one. This incident not only captivated the inhabitants of Tinley Park but also attracted the attention of researchers and international media, raising questions about the nature and origin of these mysterious lights.

The Observation.

The Tinley Park sighting, which took place on the evening of August 21, 2004, remains one of the most intriguing and discussed among UFO enthusiasts. That night, many residents of Tinley Park, a suburb of Chicago in Illinois, witnessed an unusual phenomenon in the night sky. Around 10 p.m., several people began to report the presence of three bright red lights, arranged in an almost perfect triangular formation, that were slowly and silently moving across the sky.

The lights were of remarkable intensity, each seeming to pulse independently while maintaining strict spatial coherence among them. Witnesses described the lights as being bright enough to attract attention, but without dazzling. They emitted a reddish glow that did not resemble any airplane or satellite light usually observed. Moreover, no sound, such as the noise of an engine or a rotor, was associated with this phenomenon, adding to the strangeness of the experience.

The formation of the lights seemed to be controlled, as they maintained a constant distance from each other, despite variations in speed and changes in direction. The triangle formed by the lights sometimes moved by pivoting on itself, while maintaining the alignment and equidistance of the light points. This characteristic led some to speculate on the presence of a single large object rather than three separate objects.

The weather conditions that night were clear with little cloud cover, allowing for optimal visibility. The moon was nearly full, providing a source of natural light that contrasted with the artificial lights of the object or objects observed. This also helped the witnesses to clearly distinguish the triangular shape against the backdrop of the night sky.

The observation lasted about an hour and a half, during which the lights crossed the sky at a relatively slow speed before disappearing on the horizon. During this time, several residents managed to capture images and videos of the event, which clearly show the three bright points in a triangular formation. These recordings were subsequently widely shared and analyzed, both by amateurs and experts in unidentified aerial phenomena.

Testimonials.

These lights, often described as being in a triangular formation, have been seen by people from various backgrounds, offering a variety of testimonies that add to the complexity and intrigue of the incident.

One of the main witnesses, Mark S., a resident of Tinley Park, reported seeing three bright red lights forming a perfect triangle in the night sky. According to his testimony, the lights seemed to move slowly and in a coordinated manner, without making any sound. Mark, who has experience as an amateur sky observer, noted that the lights did not correspond to any conventional aircraft known to him.

Another witness, Jennifer L., who was at a neighborhood party, described how all the guests' attention was drawn to the sky when the lights appeared. She mentioned that the lights were bright enough to partially illuminate the ground and that they seemed to hover above the city before slowly moving north. Jennifer also highlighted the absence of noise, which was strange given the apparent size and proximity of the lights.

A third witness, an on-duty police officer named Officer Daniels, provided an official report on the incident. He confirmed the observation of the triangular lights and added that several calls had been received by the police station that night, all describing similar phenomena. Officer Daniels attempted to follow the lights on patrol, but they eventually disappeared from his view without clear explanation.

In addition to these testimonies, a group of teenagers recorded a video of the lights, which was subsequently widely broadcast in local media and on the

Internet. The video clearly shows the three red lights in a triangular formation, slowly moving across the sky. The teenagers, visibly excited and confused, can be heard speculating about the nature of the lights, reinforcing the authenticity of their experience.

These testimonies, among others collected that night, form a corpus of anecdotal evidence that continues to spark interest and debate among ufologists and skeptics. The absence of sound, the coordination of the lights' movements and their distinct visual appearance are aspects often highlighted to argue in favor of a non-conventional origin of the objects observed at Tinley Park.

The Investigation.

The investigation into the Tinley Park incident began immediately after the first reports of sightings by local residents. Local authorities, including the Tinley Park police, were the first to respond. They collected testimonies from citizens and tried to verify if any unusual events had been scheduled that night, such as lantern releases or unannounced aerial activities. No conventional explanation was found, which increased interest and speculation around these sightings.

Given the magnitude of the testimonies and the lack of immediate explanations, the case was quickly brought to the attention of the National UFO Reporting Center (NUFORC) and the Mutual UFO Network (MUFON), two of the main organizations dedicated to the study of unidentified aerial phenomena in the United States. MUFON, in particular, played a key role in the investigation of this incident. MUFON investigators were dispatched to the scene to interview witnesses, collect data, and analyze the videos and photos that had been taken by the residents.

MUFON investigators have collected detailed testimonies from several eyewitnesses. The descriptions were remarkably similar, describing three to four bright red lights arranged in a triangular pattern, moving slowly and silently across the sky. Some witnesses also reported a sensation of electrical change in the air, and others noted that domestic animals seemed disturbed during the event.

In addition to the testimonies, the analysis of images and videos played a crucial role in the investigation. The investigators used image processing software to enhance the quality of the videos and isolate the characteristics of the observed lights. This analysis helped confirm that the lights were moving in a coherent formation, suggesting that they were either connected by an unseen solid structure, or controlled in a synchronized manner.

Despite the efforts made, the investigation was unable to definitively identify the origin of the lights. Military and governmental authorities were also consulted to check if the incident could be attributed to military aerial activities or other governmental exercises. However, no conclusive information was provided by these entities, leaving the incident without an official explanation.

The lack of a definitive conclusion has led to a variety of theories among researchers and the public, ranging from secret military craft to more exotic hypotheses, including the visit of extraterrestrial vehicles.

Theories and Speculations.

The first theory, and the most obvious one for many, is that of an extraterrestrial craft. This hypothesis is supported by the precise and seemingly coordinated formation of the lights, which seemed to defy conventional explanations such as airplanes or helicopters. Advocates of this theory argue that the synchronized movement and the ability to remain in stable formation for a long period do not match the characteristics of known human devices. Moreover, no engine noise was reported, which reinforces the idea of an advanced and unknown technology.

Another popular theory is that of Thai lanterns or illuminated balloons. According to this perspective, the lights could simply be lanterns released during a local event, which would have been caught by the wind and randomly formed a triangular configuration. However, this explanation is often contested due to the stability of the observed formation and the duration for which the lights remained visible without dispersing, which would be unusual for lanterns subject to the whims of air currents.

A third hypothesis suggests a secret military operation or a test of advanced technologies. This idea is fueled by the proximity of several military bases in the region, which could be the testing sites for new aircraft. Skeptics of this theory, however, point out the lack of concrete evidence and the fact that the government or the military have never claimed such activity in this area at this time.

Some researchers have proposed a psychosocial explanation, suggesting that the incident could be a case of "collective hysteria" where several people may have shared an illusion or a misinterpretation of natural or manufactured events, potentially influenced by the growing popularity of conspiracy theories and media focused on paranormal phenomena at that time.

Finally, there are those who believe that the incident could be attributed to some kind of rare atmospheric phenomenon, such as light reflections from terrestrial sources that, under particular atmospheric conditions, would have been projected or distorted in an unusual way. This theory is often seen as an attempt to rationalize the observation without resorting to more fantastic explanations, but it also lacks tangible evidence to support this claim.

THE NIMITZ INCIDENT: ENCOUNTER WITH A UFO OFF THE COAST OF SAN DIEGO.

DATE: November 2004.
COUNTRY: United States.
STATE: California.
CITY: San Diego.

In November 2004, several US Navy pilots aboard the aircraft carrier USS Nimitz witnessed unusual events off the coast of San Diego, California. These observations were corroborated by radar and video recordings, capturing an unidentified flying object performing maneuvers that seem to defy the known laws of physics.

A few days before the main incident, radar operators from the Nimitz had detected strange objects flying at incredibly high altitudes at supersonic speeds, without any visible presence of engines or gas emissions. These initial observations were not taken very seriously until several F/A-18 Hornet pilots were sent to intercept and identify one of these objects. What followed was a close encounter with a "tic-tac" shaped UFO, measuring about 12 meters long, which demonstrated extraordinary flight capabilities, easily evading the pursuit of the fighter jets.

The incident was not only a shock to the direct witnesses, but it also posed a major challenge to the American defense system, raising questions about national security and the nature of the observed object. The videos and testimonies of the involved pilots were widely broadcast in the media, contributing to an increased public and governmental awareness regarding the phenomenon of UFOs.

The Observation.

That day, the weather conditions were clear, with almost perfect visibility, which is typical of the region at that time of the year. The sky was clear, without clouds, and the sea was calm, offering ideal conditions for aerial observation.

The object in question was first spotted by an AN/SPY-1 radar aboard the USS Princeton, a Ticonderoga-class cruiser. The radar, known for its high precision, detected several objects moving at an altitude of about 28,000 feet and sometimes descending to the sea surface in a few seconds, a maneuver well beyond the capabilities of any known aircraft at the time.

Following these radar detections, F/A-18 Hornet fighter jets were dispatched to intercept and visually identify the object. Commander David Fravor, pilot of one of the F/A-18s, was the first to visually observe the UFO. According to his testimony, the object was about 40 feet long and had the shape of a Tic Tac, white and smooth, with no visible wings or propellers. The object moved with remarkable agility, capable of changing direction instantly and accelerating at a staggering speed without any apparent sign of conventional propulsion.

As Fravor approached, the UFO began to perform erratic movements, rising and falling rapidly, before stabilizing just above the water's surface where it seemed to cause a disturbance in the water below it. This observation lasted several minutes before the object suddenly disappeared on the horizon at a speed that was described as far greater than that of any supersonic jet.

The entire incident was tracked not only by the Princeton's radars but also by the F/A-18's weapon and navigation systems, which allowed for precise data to be recorded on the UFO's speed, altitude, and flight behavior. This data showed that the object could reach hypersonic speeds without any visible propulsion signature, such as contrails or thermal emissions, which defies conventional aeronautical principles.

Testimonials.

Several credible witnesses, primarily American military personnel, have reported observing an unidentified flying object exhibiting exceptional flight characteristics, well beyond the capabilities of known aircraft at the time.

Commander David Fravor, an experienced fighter pilot of the US Navy, was one of the first witnesses of this incident. During a training flight with his F/A-18 Super Hornet, he was redirected to investigate an object spotted by the radar of the USS Princeton, a Navy cruiser. Fravor described the object as resembling a "Tic Tac" the size of a commercial airplane. The object had no wings, no windows, no visible propulsion system. It moved erratically, hovering just above the ocean surface before suddenly rising at an incredible speed. Fravor tried to approach, but the UFO accelerated and disappeared within seconds, leaving the pilot with no plausible explanation for its technology.

Another important perspective is that of Lieutenant Colonel Alex Dietrich, who accompanied Fravor on this mission. She confirms having seen an oblong and white object, moving in an unusual way. Dietrich highlighted the absence of engines or gas trails, which is typical of conventional aircraft. She was also impressed by the object's ability to cover a great distance in very little time without apparent signs of acceleration.

The Princeton's radar operator, Kevin Day, also played a key role in this incident. Several days before the visual observation by Fravor and Dietrich, Day had noticed strange objects on his radar, moving abnormally. These objects descended from over 80,000 feet to the sea surface in a matter of seconds, a maneuver well beyond the capabilities of any known craft at the time. Day insisted that these readings were too consistent to be anomalies or system errors.

Another crucial testimony is that of the weapons systems operator, Gary Voorhis, who observed the same phenomena on the advanced radar systems of the Princeton. Voorhis confirmed that the objects were visible on multiple radar passes, thus eliminating the possibility of a technical malfunction or a reading error. He also noted that the objects seemed to defy the laws of physics with their sudden movements and high speeds.

These testimonies, coming from highly qualified and credible military sources, offer a fascinating and disturbing glimpse of what could be one of the most convincing and inexplicable encounters with a UFO. The absence of conventional explanations for the observed movements and characteristics continues to provoke debates and research.

The Investigation.

The investigation that followed was conducted by several branches of the American military and other government agencies.

The incident began when the radar of the USS Princeton, a Ticonderoga-class cruiser of the US Navy, detected unidentified flying objects diving and then ascending at high speed, well beyond the capabilities of known aircraft. Intrigued by these observations, the commander of the Princeton ordered a team of F/A-18 Hornet pilots, led by Commander David Fravor, to verify and identify these objects.

During the approach, Commander Fravor observed an oval-shaped object, measuring about 12 meters long, hovering just above the ocean. The object then moved at a speed and with a maneuverability far exceeding the capabilities of American aircraft. This encounter was recorded thanks to infrared cameras mounted on the planes, providing video evidence of the incident.

After this event, a formal investigation was launched by the Pentagon. The military authorities examined the radar data, video recordings, and testimonies of the pilots. The goal was to determine the nature and origin of the observed object. The investigators analyzed the object's movements, its speed, its trajectory, and tried to find a conventional explanation, such as a drone or an experimental aircraft.

The results of the initial investigation were not conclusive. The military authorities stated they could not identify the object nor confirm its origin. This led to speculation and various theories within the UFO community and among the public.

In response to the growing interest of the public and media, the United States Department of Defense finally acknowledged the authenticity of the videos in 2019 and admitted that the captured images represented "unidentified aerial phenomena". This acknowledgment marked a turning point in how the US government handles UFO sightings.

The investigation into the Nimitz incident also included in-depth interviews with witnesses. The pilots and staff of the Princeton provided details about what they had seen, reinforcing the credibility of the incident. These testimonies were essential in understanding the timeline of events and the characteristics of the observed object.

In conclusion, although the official investigation did not lead to a definitive explanation, it paved the way for a more open and serious discussion about unidentified aerial phenomena. The Nimitz incident remains an important case study for researchers and continues to influence how military encounters with unexplained phenomena are managed and documented.

Theories and Speculations.

The first theory, and perhaps the most obvious, is that of extraterrestrial visitation. This hypothesis suggests that the object observed by the Nimitz pilots could be a vessel from an advanced civilization of non-Earth origin. Supporters of this theory rely on the seemingly impossible movements of the object, such as its ability to instantly accelerate, reach hypersonic speeds without emitting observable heat, and perform aerial maneuvers that would defy the laws of physics as we know them. Moreover, the absence of any conventional radar signature reinforces the idea that the observed technology could be well beyond our current understanding.

Another theory put forward is that of secret technologies, possibly developed by the United States or other nations. According to this hypothesis, the UFO could be an experimental craft from classified military projects. The extraordinary features of the object could be the result of advanced technologies not yet disclosed to the public or even to other branches of the military. This theory is often supported by references to the history of the American government's black programs, which have sometimes led to surprising and unrecognized technological developments for years.

A third perspective offers a psychological or sociological explanation. It suggests that the testimonies of pilots could be influenced by psychological phenomena such as pareidolia (the tendency to perceive a specific pattern, especially a face, where there is none) or the stress of high-intensity flight situations. This theory is often reinforced by criticisms of the reliability of human testimonies, especially in extreme or unusual conditions.

Finally, some researchers propose more exotic explanations, such as the hypothesis of a manifestation of advanced artificial intelligence that could be in a testing phase or even a form of "non-biological" life that would be completely unknown to us. These speculations are based on the idea that we might not be alone in the universe and that other forms of intelligence could interact with us in unexpected ways.

Conclusion.

The testimonies of the pilots, radar recordings, and infrared videos provide tangible evidence that something unusual has occurred. This incident raises important questions about air safety and the possibility of unrecognized advanced technologies. It continues to fuel public and scientific debate about the potential presence of non-terrestrial vehicles and their impact on our understanding of technology and physics.

THE XALAPA INCIDENT: UNIDENTIFIED FLYING OBJECTS FILMED ABOVE XALAPA, MEXICO.

DATE: April 12, 2005.
COUNTRY: Mexico.
STATE: Veracruz.
CITY: Xalapa.

The Xalapa incident is a significant event in the history of UFO sightings, primarily due to the quality and clarity of the images captured. On April 12, 2005, several unidentified flying objects were filmed in broad daylight above the city of Xalapa, the capital of the state of Veracruz, in Mexico. That day, the sky was exceptionally clear, allowing for very detailed visual observation. The objects were described as being circular and metallic in shape, moving at high speed and without emitting any sound. The incident quickly attracted the attention of local and international media, as well as that of ufologists and skeptics.

The videos taken by local witnesses show several bright objects moving in the sky at varying altitudes. Some witnesses reported seeing up to ten objects at a time, moving in a coordinated manner and sometimes in formation. The images have been analyzed by several experts in aeronautics and atmospheric phenomena, but no definitive explanation has been given as to their origin or nature.

The Xalapa incident remains an important case study for ufology researchers, as it presents some of the clearest visual evidence of unidentified flying objects. Despite numerous theories, the exact origin and nature of these objects remain a mystery, thus fueling the ongoing debate about the possible presence of extraterrestrial entities or unknown technologies in our atmosphere.

The Observation.

This event occurred on March 27, 2007, a relatively clear evening where the weather conditions were stable, with few clouds and excellent visibility. Around 8:15 PM, local time, several witnesses in different neighborhoods of the city began to report the presence of strange objects in the sky.

The observed objects numbered three. They were described as having a triangular shape with blinking white and red lights at each corner. The movement of the objects was synchronized and they seemed to float effortlessly above the city, moving slowly from north to south. On several occasions, they changed formation, shifting from a horizontal line to a perfect triangle, which added to the strangeness of the scene.

Witnesses reported that the objects made no perceptible noise, which was unusual given their apparent size and proximity. The total duration of the observation was about 30 minutes. During this time, the objects sometimes abruptly accelerated before returning to their initial speed, which was perceived as particularly unconventional behavior for known aircraft.

One of the most remarkable aspects of this incident was the quality of the images captured. Several witnesses managed to film the objects with video cameras and mobile phones, thus providing visual evidence that was widely disseminated in local media and on the Internet. The videos clearly show the abnormal movements and changing formations of the objects, which contributed to the interest and speculation around this event.

In terms of atmospheric conditions, the night was clear with a slight breeze coming from the northeast. The moon was almost full, providing natural light that enhanced the visibility of objects. No significant weather disturbance was reported in the region that night, which rules out the possibility that the observations were caused by weather phenomena such as weather balloons or atmospheric reflections.

The objects finally disappeared from sight, rising into the sky until they were no longer visible. The disappearance was as mysterious as their appearance, with the objects moving away at a considerably increased speed without leaving a trace.

Testimonials.

On March 17, 2007, several residents of the region reported seeing unidentified flying objects (UFOs) in the sky. These observations were accompanied by videos and photographs that added a layer of credibility and mystery to the entire event.

Among the main witnesses, Maria Elena Carrera, a retired teacher, was one of the first to alert other residents and local media. Around 8:00 PM, while she was in her garden, she observed three bright objects forming a perfect triangle in the sky. According to her testimony, these objects emitted an intense white light with shades of blue and green. They moved slowly and without noise, which differed from usual airplanes.

Another important witness, Carlos Juárez, an amateur photographer, managed to capture several clear images of the incident. According to him, the objects were visible for about 30 minutes. In his photographs, one can see the UFOs changing formation, shifting from a horizontal line to a more dispersed shape. Carlos described the movements of the objects as being fluid and coordinated, which gave him the impression that they were directed by some form of intelligence.

Luisa Fernanda López, a student who was returning home after evening classes, also witnessed the event. She reported seeing a large disc-shaped object that seemed to hover over the city at a relatively low altitude. According to Luisa, the object had flashing lights on the edges and a beam of light that seemed to scan the ground. Terrified but fascinated, she observed the object for several minutes before it disappeared at high speed towards the north.

In addition to these individual testimonies, several groups of people, including entire families, have reported similar observations. A common point in all these stories is the absence of noise associated with the movements of the UFOs, as well as the unusual speed and agility of their movements.

The Investigation.

After the broadcast of images showing several unidentified flying objects (UFOs) in the sky of Xalapa, an official investigation was launched to determine the nature and origin of these appearances.

The initial reactions of the military authorities were of a cautious nature. The Ministry of Defense immediately set up a crisis unit to analyze the videos and testimonies of citizens who witnessed the event. Aeronautics experts, meteorologists, and imaging specialists were summoned for a thorough analysis. The goal was to verify the authenticity of the images and to rule out any conventional explanation such as drones, weather balloons, or other aircraft.

In parallel, testimonies were collected from residents of Xalapa and the surrounding areas. These interviews were conducted by specialized investigators with the aim of gathering precise information about the behavior of the objects, their trajectory, their speed, and any possible interaction with the environment. Witnesses described objects of various shapes, mainly spherical, moving at high speed and without noise, some reporting bright lights and sudden changes in direction.

The preliminary results of the image analysis showed that the captured objects did not correspond to any known aerial vehicle. Imaging specialists confirmed that the videos had not been altered or manipulated, thus reinforcing the credibility of the observations. However, no definitive conclusion has been drawn as to the exact nature of the observed objects.

Faced with the inability to provide a conventional explanation, the Mexican government has sought the help of international organizations such as SETI (Search for Extraterrestrial Intelligence) and the UAPTF (Unidentified Aerial Phenomena Task Force) from the United States. These organizations have brought their expertise in data analysis and unidentified aerial phenomena, thus contributing to a more comprehensive investigation.

The conclusions of these international collaborations were shared at a press conference where it was admitted that the observed objects could not be categorically identified. However, it was emphasized that this did not necessarily constitute proof of the existence of extraterrestrial technology. The investigation highlighted the need to continue research and develop more sophisticated methods for the analysis of such phenomena.

The Xalapa incident therefore remains an unresolved case, arousing both curiosity and skepticism. The authorities continue to monitor the sky of Xalapa and other regions, ready to resume the investigation if new elements should emerge.

Theories and Speculations.

The first theory suggests that the observed objects could be drones or advanced aerial technologies not recognized by the general public. This hypothesis is often supported by the fact that drone technology has significantly evolved and their ability to perform complex maneuvers in the air could explain some of the movements observed during the incident. Moreover, the proximity of military or research areas could justify the presence of such devices in the testing phase, although this has not been officially confirmed.

Another commonly discussed explanation is that of rare atmospheric phenomena. Some researchers suggest that what was perceived as flying objects could actually be optical illusions created by particular atmospheric conditions. For example, mirages or exceptional light refractions could have formed images in the sky that appear to be distinct objects. This theory is often contested because it does not always match the descriptions of witnesses who report directed and intentional movements.

The extraterrestrial hypothesis remains one of the most popular and controversial. According to this theory, the observed objects would be vessels of non-earthly origin. Supporters of this idea rely on the seemingly advanced technology and maneuvering capabilities that far exceed what current human technologies allow. This theory is often met with skepticism by the scientific community, but it continues to captivate the public's imagination and stimulates lively debate about the possibility of extraterrestrial life and its visits to Earth.

Finally, there are those who consider that the incident could be a case of disinformation or psychological manipulation. This theory suggests that the event was orchestrated to divert public attention or to test reactions to an unusual situation. Although less discussed, this approach raises questions about information management and trust in official sources.

THE UFO OF O'HARE INTERNATIONAL AIRPORT.

DATE: November 7, 2006.
COUNTRY: United States.
STATE: Illinois.
CITY: Chicago.

On November 7, 2006, an unusual event occurred at Chicago's O'Hare International Airport, one of the busiest airports in the world. That day, several employees of United Airlines and a few passengers witnessed a strange phenomenon in the sky. Around 4:15 pm, an unidentified flying object of circular shape and metallic gray color was observed hovering above the airport's Terminal C. The object, measuring about 6 to 7 meters in diameter, seemed to defy the laws of physics with its ability to remain stationary in an extremely busy airspace, without being detected by the airport's radars.

Witnesses describe the UFO as being perfectly silent and stable despite the strong winds that day. After about five minutes of observation, the object suddenly accelerated at a dizzying speed, disappearing through the thick clouds that covered the sky, leaving behind a clear circular hole in the cloud cover. This hole remained visible for several minutes before dissipating.

The incident quickly attracted media attention after a United Airlines employee contacted the National UFO Reporting Center (NUFORC) to report what he had seen. Despite numerous requests for comments, neither the Federal Aviation Administration (FAA) nor United Airlines initially confirmed the event. It was only later that the FAA stated it would not investigate the incident as the object had not been spotted on radar and there had been no official safety report filed by the pilots or airport staff.

The O'Hare UFO incident continues to spark interest and debate among UFO researchers and the general public, raising questions about the nature and origin of the object as well as how such events are handled by airport authorities and regulatory bodies.

The Observation.

The UFO incident at O'Hare International Airport occurred on November 7, 2006, an event that captured the attention not only of airport employees but also researchers and media from around the world. That day, around 4:15 pm local time, several ground staff members as well as pilots reported seeing an unidentified flying object hovering above terminal C of the airport.

The object in question was described as being circular or discoid in shape, with an estimated diameter of about 6 to 7 meters. Its surface appeared metallic, reflecting the light of the setting sun, which gave it a shiny silver-gray hue. Curiously, the object seemed to emit no sound, which is unusual for an aerial vehicle, especially in an environment as noisy as an international airport.

The witnesses also noted that the UFO had the ability to hover at altitude, remaining stationary in the cloudy sky for about five minutes. This behavior is atypical compared to conventional aircraft which are constantly moving when they are in flight. The altitude at which the object was observed was estimated to be about 350 meters above the ground.

The weather conditions that day were relatively clear with a few scattered clouds, which allowed fairly good visibility for the witnesses on the ground. The temperature was cool, typical of Chicago in November, with a slight wind coming from the northeast. These conditions probably helped to keep the object clearly visible for the duration of the observation.

After about five minutes, the object began to change position. According to reports, it accelerated at a dizzying speed, climbing through the clouds and leaving behind a clear circular hole in the cloud layer. This hole, which seemed to be caused by the propulsion or energy of the UFO, remained visible for a few minutes before the clouds slowly closed again.

The observation of this UFO at O'Hare airport is particularly notable due to the number of credible witnesses, including pilots and ground staff accustomed to identifying various types of aircraft. Moreover, the presence of the object in such a monitored and regulated airspace raises questions about its nature and origin, given that no aircraft matching this description was expected or identified as being authorized to fly over the area at that time.

Testimonials.

Among the main witnesses, Jon Hilkevitch, an employee of United Airlines, was one of the first to report the sighting. According to his testimony, the object had a circular shape and was hovering about 1900 feet above the ground. He described the UFO as being metallic gray in color and measuring between 6 and 24 feet in diameter. Hilkevitch noted that the object emitted no sound and seemed to defy the laws of physics with its ability to remain stationary in the windy Chicago sky.

Another important witness, Martin Kearns, a commercial pilot for another airline, observed the object from his cockpit as he was preparing for a flight. Kearns corroborated Hilkevitch's description, adding that the UFO had a perfectly smooth appearance, with no visible markings or propulsion structure. He also mentioned that the object suddenly disappeared at a dizzying speed, leaving behind a clear circular hole in the clouds, which slowly closed up.

Sue, an air traffic controller, who preferred not to disclose her last name, also witnessed the event. She was working in the airport control tower at the time of the incident and saw the UFO through the tower windows. Sue confirmed that several of her colleagues also saw the object, but many were reluctant to officially talk about it, fearing professional repercussions.

A passenger, Rick Stevens, waiting for his flight, took several photos of the UFO with his mobile phone. Although the images were blurry due to the distance and lighting conditions, they show a discreet shape suspended in the sky. Stevens described a strange sense of calm during the observation, and like the other witnesses, he was astounded by the speed at which the object disappeared.

These testimonies, although varied, present striking similarities regarding the description of the object and its behavior. The absence of noise, the ability to maintain a fixed position despite the wind, and sudden acceleration are characteristics that have intrigued not only the witnesses but also the UFO community and aviation experts.

The Investigation.

In response to the increasing number of testimonies, the Federal Aviation Administration (FAA) has decided to launch an official investigation. Initially, the FAA attributed the sighting to a weather phenomenon, suggesting that what the witnesses had seen could be an unusual cloud phenomenon. However, due to pressure from the witnesses and public opinion, a more thorough investigation has been put in place.

The FAA investigators interviewed several eyewitnesses, including pilots, crew members, and ground staff. The testimonies were remarkably consistent regarding the description of the object and its dynamics. In addition, the investigators examined the airport's radar recordings, but found no trace of the object, which added to the confusion and speculation about the nature of the observed object.

The investigation also involved consultations with meteorologists and aeronautics experts. No conventional explanation was found to justify the appearance and behavior of the object. The meteorologists confirmed that there were no unusual atmospheric conditions that could have created an optical illusion or a similar phenomenon to what was reported.

After several months of investigation, the FAA's final report concluded that there was not enough evidence to determine the nature or origin of the observed object. The report mentioned that the incident had not affected the safety of air operations and that no immediate danger to public safety had been identified. This conclusion was widely criticized by the UFO community and by some of the witnesses themselves, who believed that the investigation had not been thorough enough.

Despite the official investigation, many questions remain unanswered, fueling speculation and debate about what really happened that day in Chicago.

The UFO at O'Hare International Airport is a famous case that has captured the attention of the public and researchers in unidentified aerospace phenomena. On November 7, 2006, several witnesses, including pilots and ground staff, reported seeing an unidentified flying object stationary above terminal C of the airport. This incident has given rise to numerous theories and speculations, attempting to explain the nature and origin of the observation.

Theories and Speculations.

One of the most common theories is that of the presence of an extraterrestrial craft. This hypothesis is supported by the description of the object as a gray metallic disc that would have flown over the airport at a relatively low altitude before rising at high speed into the sky, leaving behind a clear hole in the clouds. Supporters of this theory argue that the movements and capabilities of the object, as well as its appearance, do not correspond to those of conventional aircraft or any other known natural phenomenon.

Another explanation put forward is that of a rare meteorological phenomenon. Some skeptics suggest that what the witnesses saw could be an optical phenomenon caused by particular atmospheric conditions. For example, a mirage or unusual reflection due to a unique combination of temperature and humidity could have created an illusion of a flying object. However, this theory struggles to explain the testimony of experienced observers such as pilots, who are familiar with such phenomena and insist that the object had a physical presence.

Some researchers have suggested that the UFO could be a drone or another type of unrecognized experimental device, secretly tested by the government or a private company. This hypothesis is fueled by the fact that the incident took place in an extremely monitored and regulated airspace, which could indicate some sort of advanced technology test. However, no concrete evidence has been presented to support this theory, and government agencies have denied any involvement or knowledge of the incident.

Another interesting speculation is that of mass psychology or collective hysteria. According to this perspective, once an individual has reported seeing something unusual, other people in the same area might also start to "see" the UFO, influenced by the initial report. This theory is often used to explain how groups of people can share illusions of observations without there being any real external stimulus. However, the precise and consistent details provided by the various witnesses in the case of O'Hare make this explanation less plausible.

Finally, there are those who believe that the incident could be a case of disinformation or a orchestrated distraction. This theory suggests that the event was intentionally staged to divert attention from other more sensitive activities taking place at the airport or elsewhere. Although this idea is largely speculative, it highlights the mistrust of certain segments of the public towards official explanations and their tendency to look for hidden motives behind unusual events.

Conclusion.

Despite numerous credible testimonies from airport employees and visual evidence, no definitive explanation has been provided by the authorities. The speed at which the object ascended and disappeared, leaving a hole in the clouds, continues to defy conventional explanations. This event underscores the challenges faced by aerial surveillance systems and the need for a more open and rigorous approach in investigating unidentified aerial phenomena. The fascination with this incident remains a testament to the ongoing interest in UFOs and humanity's quest to understand unexplained phenomena in our sky.

THE STEPHENVILLE INCIDENT: STRANGE LIGHTS AND A LARGE UNIDENTIFIED FLYING OBJECT OBSERVED IN STEPHENVILLE, TEXAS.

DATE: January 8, 2008.
COUNTRY: United States.
STATE: Texas.
CITY: Stephenville.

The Stephenville incident is one of the most publicized and discussed UFO sightings of the early 21st century. Located in the state of Texas, the town of Stephenville became famous well beyond its usual borders following events that occurred in January 2008. That evening, several residents of the area reported seeing unusual lights in the sky, accompanied by the presence of a large flying object, described as being larger than a football field. The consistent testimonies of many residents, including detailed descriptions of bright lights and an object moving at an incredibly high speed, attracted the attention of national and international media.

Local authorities and aviation experts were quickly called upon to provide explanations. The American Air Force initially denied any aerial activity in that area on the specified date, but later admitted that there were indeed F-16 fighter jets maneuvering in the vicinity that day. However, this explanation did not satisfy all witnesses or UFO researchers, who pointed out inconsistencies in the official accounts and suggested the possibility of a cover-up.

The Observation.

Several residents of the region have reported seeing a large unidentified flying object (UFO). The object, according to descriptions, was about a kilometer long and was accompanied by bright and colorful lights.

Witnesses described the UFO as being oval-shaped or sometimes described as rectangular, with white, red, and sometimes blue lights that blinked or rotated around its structure. These lights were arranged in a way to emit intense brightness, making the object clearly visible in the January twilight sky. The intensity and configuration of the lights seemed to change, adding to the strangeness of the sighting.

The observation lasted about five minutes, during which the UFO was seen moving at a considerably high speed from east to west. Despite its speed, the object seemed to move in a surprisingly silent manner, without any perceptible sound emission, which contrasted with the impressive size of the object and its apparent proximity to the ground.

The weather conditions that night were clear with few clouds, allowing for optimal visibility. The temperature was cool, typical of a winter evening in Texas, but without any precipitation or fog that could have altered or obscured the view of the object. The moon was in a waxing phase, providing some natural light, but not enough to significantly illuminate the object.

The witnesses of this event were mainly local residents, including farmers, businessmen and even police officers, which added a level of credibility to the reports. Many described the experience as both fascinating and unsettling, highlighting the enormous size of the object and the precision with which it maneuvered in the sky.

Testimonials.

Steve Allen, a local pilot and businessman, was one of the first to report the sighting. According to him, the object was about half a mile wide and was accompanied by intense white lights as well as flashing red lights. Allen described the object as incredibly fast and silent, moving at a speed estimated at several thousand miles per hour. He also mentioned that the object changed direction in an abrupt and inexplicable way, defying the known laws of physics.

Another important witness, Constable Lee Roy Gaitan, noted that the lights he observed were bright red in color and moved in strange formations, alternating between linear movements and zigzag maneuvers. Gaitan claimed that the lights grouped together into two and then suddenly disappeared before reappearing. He expressed his disbelief at the speed and maneuverability of the object, emphasizing that no known human aircraft could perform such actions.

Ricky Sorrells, a local welder, also shared a detailed encounter. He described a gray metallic object hovering directly above him at a fairly low altitude. Sorrells was able to observe the object for several minutes, noting its smooth surface with no visible joints or rivets, which was contrary to the typical construction of human aircraft. The object eventually disappeared at a dizzying speed, leaving Sorrells perplexed and somewhat disturbed.

Erath County is an area where aviation is omnipresent, which makes these testimonies even more intriguing. The witnesses, including experienced pilots and police officers, all expressed their certainty that the object and maneuvers observed did not correspond to any known aircraft or natural phenomenon.

The Investigation.

The initial reactions from local authorities were rather cautious. The Stephenville police did not immediately comment on the matter, while the sheriff's office admitted to receiving several calls from citizens about the strange lights. However, no action was taken until media coverage intensified.

In the face of growing public interest and various speculations, the US Air Force was finally forced to respond. Initially, it denied any aerial activity in the region on the date of the observations. This statement was quickly contradicted by testimonies from pilots and other aviation experts who confirmed the presence of military aircraft in the airspace near Stephenville that night.

Faced with these contradictions, the Air Force revised its position and admitted, a few weeks later, that ten F-16 fighter jets were indeed maneuvering in the area. However, it maintained that this had no connection with the lights and the object observed by the witnesses.

The investigation then focused on the testimonies of the residents. Several people were interviewed, including pilots, police officers, and ordinary citizens. The descriptions of the object varied in size and shape, but most agreed that it was huge, silent, and capable of high-speed maneuvers with impressive agility. Some witnesses also reported that the object had projected intense lights that changed color.

Investigators also examined videos and photos taken by witnesses. Although the quality of most of these recordings was poor, some showed images that seemed to corroborate the witnesses' descriptions of the object's size and movements.

Despite the efforts made, the official investigation has not been able to provide a definitive explanation. The Air Force concluded that the observations were probably related to its fighter planes in maneuver, although this explanation did not satisfy all the witnesses or aerospace phenomena researchers. Other theories, ranging from experimental drones to rare atmospheric phenomena, have been proposed, but none have been definitively proven.

Despite the scope of the investigation, the numerous data collected and the sustained interest from both the public and researchers, it continues to raise questions and debates about the possible presence of unidentified flying objects in our airspace.

Theories and Speculations.

The first popular theory suggests that the observed object could be related to secret military activities. Stephenville is located near several military bases, which could explain the presence of fighter jets shortly after the UFO sighting. Some aviation experts have proposed that the object could be an experimental aircraft, perhaps a new type of drone or a stealth plane being tested by the American military. This hypothesis is strengthened by the fact that the military initially denied, then admitted, the presence of military aircraft in the area at the time of the sightings.

Another theory put forward is that of an extraterrestrial visit. This idea is fueled by the unusual size of the object, its ability to move at supersonic speeds without apparent noise, and its maneuverability far exceeding that of known terrestrial aircraft. Ufologists and some witnesses argue that the characteristics of the object, as well as the seemingly confused reaction of the military authorities, indicate a non-human technology. This theory is often accompanied by speculations about government camouflage and disinformation, suggesting that the authorities might have reasons to conceal evidence of extraterrestrial contact.

A third perspective suggests that what was seen could be attributed to rare or poorly understood atmospheric phenomena. Meteorology researchers have sometimes identified unusual light configurations caused by natural reflections or optical anomalies in the atmosphere. However, this explanation struggles to convince the majority of witnesses due to the precision of the object's descriptions and its dynamic and directed movements, which are difficult to attribute to meteorological phenomena.

Finally, there is a psychosocial theory that suggests that the Stephenville incident could be an example of "mass hysteria" where several individuals share an illusion or a misinterpretation of ordinary events under the influence of pop culture that is saturated with narratives about UFOs and aliens. According to this view, even the intervention of fighter jets could be misinterpreted as a confirmation of the extraordinary nature of the event, when it could have been a coincidence or a standard procedure unrelated to the UFO.

THE UFO INCIDENT OF HANGZHOU, CHINA.

DATE: July 7, 2010.
COUNTRY: China.
STATE: Zhejiang.
CITY: Hangzhou.

The Hangzhou UFO incident is an event that captured international attention and sparked numerous speculations and theories. On July 7, 2010, in the province of Zhejiang, near the city of Hangzhou, an unidentified flying object was spotted, causing a major disruption in the operations of Hangzhou Xiaoshan International Airport. That evening, around 8:30 pm, witnesses reported seeing a strange object in the sky, described as being particularly bright and accompanied by flashing lights. The presence of this object led to the temporary closure of the airport for safety reasons, affecting dozens of flights and thousands of passengers.

The airport authorities, after observing the object on their radar, decided to suspend all takeoffs and landings. This exceptional measure was taken to ensure the safety of flights and passengers, while experts attempted to determine the nature and origin of the observed object. Initial reports from local media and testimonies from pilots described the object as being irregularly shaped and capable of high-speed aerial maneuvers, defying the typical characteristics of conventional aircraft.

The incident quickly made headlines in international media, fueling various theories among ufologists and the general public. Some suggested it was a secret military craft, while others leaned towards an extraterrestrial explanation. Chinese authorities launched an investigation to shed light on this mysterious event, but many details remained undisclosed, adding to the mystique of the incident. The official results of the investigation were never fully revealed to the public.

The Observation.

That evening, around 8:30 local time, numerous witnesses, including passengers, pilots, and local residents, reported seeing a strange object in the sky near Xiaoshan International Airport in Hangzhou, a major city in eastern China.

The description of the object by the witnesses was surprisingly similar despite the diversity of their locations and perspectives. The object was described as being circular or oval in shape with a bright appearance and emitting an intense white light. Some also mentioned a kind of luminous halo surrounding the object, adding to its spectacular and mysterious aspect. The UFO seemed to move at a considerable speed and with remarkable agility, changing direction abruptly and without noticeable noise.

The time of observation, precisely between 8:30 p.m. and 9:00 p.m., coincided with a period of heavy traffic for the airport, which exacerbated the impact of the event. The visibility was clear that night, with few clouds in the sky and almost perfect visibility, which allowed the object to be seen by a large number of people. The weather conditions were also calm, with no wind or precipitation, which eliminates some natural explanations such as unusual weather phenomena.

The object was observed for about an hour, after which it suddenly disappeared. This sudden disappearance, just like its appearance, was a subject of great speculation. During the hour when the object was visible, it seemed to follow a trajectory that sometimes brought it close to the airport runways, leading to a temporary closure of the airport for safety reasons. Flights were diverted or delayed, which added an additional layer of testimonies from air passengers and airport staff.

Testimonials.

Several witnesses, including pilots, air traffic controllers, and ordinary citizens, reported seeing an unidentified flying object, which led to a temporary closure of the airport and a thorough investigation by the Chinese authorities.

Among the key witnesses, a pilot who was about to land at Xiaoshan was one of the first to report the object to the control tower. According to his testimony, the object was extremely bright and seemed to move at an incredible speed, far greater than that of any conventional aircraft. The pilot described the UFO as having an oblong shape and emitting an intense white light, which at times turned reddish.

An air traffic controller from Xiaoshan airport also provided a detailed account of the event. He observed the object on radar screens for several minutes before it suddenly disappeared. The controller noted that the object was not following any of the usual air corridors and that its speed and erratic movements did not match any known type of aircraft. This testimony was crucial to the decision to temporarily close the airport, an exceptional measure taken to ensure flight safety.

Outside the airport, several residents of Hangzhou also reported seeing the UFO. A resident, living near the airport, described seeing a bright object crossing the sky at a staggering speed. The object, according to this witness, performed maneuvers that defied the laws of physics, such as instantaneous changes in direction and sudden accelerations without associated noise.

Another witness, an astronomy enthusiast, provided a more detailed technical description. He observed the object through a telescope and noted that the UFO had a metallic surface that reflected the light from the city below. According to him, the object did not emit its own light but rather reflected the surrounding light, making it visible.

The Investigation.

On July 7th of this year, an unidentified flying object was spotted in the sky, leading to the temporary closure of the airport and a series of investigations by various Chinese authorities.

The initial reaction was swift and marked by great confusion. Around 8:30 PM, air traffic controllers detected an unidentified object appearing on their radars. Shortly after, witnesses on the ground and in approaching planes also reported seeing a bright and unusual object in the sky. Faced with uncertainty about the nature and intent of the object, airport officials made the decision to suspend all flights, affecting thousands of passengers.

The military and governmental authorities were quickly involved in the investigation. The People's Liberation Army, which also manages Chinese airspace, began by checking if the object could be a military aircraft or a spacecraft from their fleet, but no match was found. Meanwhile, the Civil Aviation Administration of China launched an investigation to determine the impact of the incident on air safety.

The testimonies collected during the investigation were varied and often contradictory, adding to the complexity of the analysis. Pilots, air traffic controllers, and passengers described the object as being elongated in shape with dazzling lights, while others mentioned a circular or even triangular shape. These testimonies were supplemented by radar recordings and videos taken by witnesses on the ground, which showed an object moving at speeds and with maneuvers that do not correspond to conventional aircraft.

The investigation also explored the possibility of a natural phenomenon or an undeclared human activity, such as a weather balloon or a drone. However, no conclusive evidence was found to support these theories. Meteorology and aeronautics experts were consulted, but their analyses did not provide a satisfactory explanation.

After several weeks of intensive investigations, the final report was published. It concluded that, despite the efforts made, the object could not be conclusively identified and no evidence of a threat to public safety was found. The report also mentioned that the incident had no long-term harmful consequences on the airport operations or air safety, but recommended increased vigilance and an improvement in response protocols to similar incidents in the future.

This Hangzhou incident remains one of the most publicized and mysterious UFO cases in China, illustrating the challenges associated with identifying and managing unidentified flying objects in the country's densely used airspace.

Theories and Speculations.

One of the first theories put forward is that of extraterrestrial intervention. This hypothesis is fueled by the unexplained nature of the object and its ability to disrupt airport operations. Supporters of this theory suggest that the object possessed flight characteristics and technological capabilities far surpassing those of known human aircraft. They also point to the lack of clear and detailed official communication as potential evidence of government cover-up.

On the contrary, some experts and skeptics suggest that the UFO could be a misinterpreted natural phenomenon. They mention the possibility of a rare atmospheric event, such as St. Elmo's light or another type of electrical weather phenomenon that could have been misidentified as a flying object. This explanation is often supported by meteorologists and scientists who study unusual atmospheric phenomena.

Another plausible explanation is that of a weather balloon or another type of research balloon. These objects, often used for the collection of atmospheric data, can sometimes deviate from their planned trajectory and appear in controlled airspaces. This theory is reinforced by the fact that such balloons can reflect sunlight or ground lights, creating visual illusions that could be mistaken for UFOs.

There is also the possibility that the incident is the result of a secret military test. China, like many other countries, regularly conducts tests of new aeronautical technologies, often in the strictest secrecy. An experimental aircraft or drone prototype could therefore have been mistaken for a UFO. This hypothesis is often discussed in aviation and defense circles, although little concrete information is available to support or refute this idea.

Finally, some conspiracy theorists suggest that the incident could be a staged event orchestrated by the Chinese government or another powerful entity in order to divert attention from more pressing issues or to test public reactions to a supposed extraterrestrial threat. Although this theory is less supported by tangible evidence, it persists in certain online communities.

THE UFO INCIDENT OF CHONGQING, CHINA.

DATE: July 23, 2010.
COUNTRY: China.
STATE: Municipality of Chongqing.
CITY: Chongqing.

The Chongqing UFO incident is an event that has captivated the attention not only of local residents but also of researchers and ufology enthusiasts worldwide. Located in southwestern China, Chongqing is one of the four municipalities directly under the central control of the Chinese government, known for its high population density and increasing economic importance. On July 23, 2010, an unidentified flying object was spotted in the sky of this metropolis, sparking a wave of speculation and questions among the population and the media.

The object, described as being circular in shape with flashing lights, was first seen around 9 p.m. local time. Witnesses on the scene reported that the object was moving at a staggering speed, changing direction abruptly and seemingly impossible for conventional aircraft. The initial reports from witnesses were quickly relayed by local media, then international, sparking massive media coverage.

Local authorities, including the police and the Chinese air force, were put on alert, but no immediate official explanation was given. Speculation was rife, with some theories suggesting it was a drone or an experimental military craft, while others leaned towards an extraterrestrial origin. The incident also caused a temporary interruption of operations at Chongqing International Airport, where several flights were delayed or diverted due to air safety concerns.

The Observation.

Around 9:30 PM, numerous witnesses in the municipality of Chongqing, a densely populated urban area in southwestern China, reported seeing an unidentified flying object. Descriptions of the object varied slightly, but most witnesses agreed on several distinctive features.

The observed object was oval-shaped with a series of flashing lights that emitted an intense light of white and blue color. Some witnesses also described a luminous halo around the object, giving the impression that it was enveloped in a kind of luminous mist. The UFO moved at a constant speed without emitting any perceptible sound, which added to the strangeness of the observation. Its size was difficult to estimate, but it seemed quite large, comparable to that of a small plane.

The time of the observation coincided with a particularly clear sky, excellent visibility that allowed many residents to observe it without obstruction. The temperature was mild, typical of a summer evening in Chongqing, which probably encouraged more people to be outside and therefore witness the event. No particular weather phenomenon was reported at the time of the observation, which eliminates the possibility that what was seen was an atmospheric effect like a lenticular cloud often confused with UFOs.

The object remained visible for about 30 minutes, slowly moving across the sky before suddenly disappearing. Its trajectory seemed linear, moving from east to west across the night sky of Chongqing. Throughout the duration of the observation, the object maintained an apparently constant altitude, allowing for prolonged and detailed observation.

Testimonials.

One of the first witnesses, Li Wei, a student at the local university, reports having seen an unidentified flying object of circular shape with brightly colored flashing lights. According to his testimony, the object suddenly appeared in the night sky and performed erratic movements, as if it was not subject to the usual laws of physics. Li Wei describes the object as being about 10 meters in diameter and emitting a low hum, almost imperceptible.

Another observation comes from Chen Huan, a trader at the local market. She claims that the UFO flew over the market at a relatively low altitude, allowing the many witnesses present to distinctly see its metallic structure under the city lights. Chen also mentions that the object had some sort of portholes or panels that seemed to emit an internal light, giving the object a glow that fluctuated.

A third witness, the on-duty police officer Zhang Jie, provided a detailed report on the incident. According to him, the UFO was first observed at around 10:00 PM. He followed the object for several minutes before it disappeared at a staggering speed. Zhang attempted to follow the object with his patrol vehicle, but he was unable to keep up. He described the UFO as having incredible maneuverability, capable of changing direction instantly without slowing down.

In addition to these individual testimonies, a group of tourists who were on a cruise ship on the Yangtze River also reported seeing the object. According to them, the UFO dove towards the river before rising at a dizzying speed, creating a large wave on the water. This group, composed of five people, provided similar descriptions of the object, noting its incredible speed and movements that defied the laws of gravity.

The Investigation.

The investigation into the Chongqing UFO incident began immediately after the first reports of an unidentified flying object spotted in the night sky above this large metropolis in southwestern China. The testimonies of citizens, who described a bright object with atypical movements, quickly attracted the attention of local and national authorities.

The initial reactions of the military authorities were to secure the area where the UFO was reported and to gather the first testimonies. Teams from the Chinese air force, as well as aerospace specialists, were dispatched to the scene to conduct a field investigation. The goal was to determine the nature of the observed object and to assess any potential threat to national security.

The initial reports from the military authorities were quite vague, only mentioning that an "unidentified object" had been observed and that investigations were underway. However, additional details began to emerge as the investigation progressed. Radar and surveillance technology experts analyzed data from local radar stations, attempting to trace the object's trajectory and identify its flight characteristics.

Simultaneously, testimonies from local residents and eyewitnesses were systematically collected. Many reported seeing an object of circular or triangular shape, emitting bright lights of different colors. Some witnesses also described a dull noise or a humming coming from the object, which added an additional layer of mystery to the incident.

As the investigation progressed, authorities attempted to determine if the object could be a drone or another type of known aerial device. Technical analyses were conducted to compare the observed characteristics of the UFO with those of devices in service in the Chinese military and in other countries. However, no clear match was established, leaving the question of the object's origin open.

The findings of the investigation were partially disclosed to the public several months after the incident. The authorities stated that, despite thorough investigations, the origin of the UFO could not be conclusively determined. They also indicated that the object did not pose a direct threat to public or national security and that the investigation would be closed pending further information or evidence.

This official response did not satisfy all the curious and ufologists, who continued to speculate on the implications of the incident and the possibility of a cover-up by the authorities. Discussions and debates persisted in online forums and at conferences on unidentified aerial phenomena, reflecting the ongoing interest in the Chongqing incident and UFOs in general.

The investigation into the Chongqing UFO incident remains a notable example of how military and governmental authorities can respond to such events, and of the complexity of determining the origin of unidentified aerial phenomena despite the use of advanced technologies and detailed testimonies.

Theories and Speculations.

One of the most commonly discussed theories is that of military activity. Some experts suggest that the observed object could be a new type of drone or spy plane being tested by the Chinese military. This hypothesis is supported by the fact that China has significantly increased its defense technology capabilities and regularly tests new equipment in remote areas, which could sometimes be visible from urban centers like Chongqing. However, this theory does not take into account certain aspects of the testimonies, including the extremely fast movements and abrupt changes of direction reported, which exceed the capabilities of known aerial vehicles.

Another popular explanation is that of rare atmospheric phenomena. Scientists have proposed that what was perceived as a UFO could in fact be a particular type of plasma light, resulting from abnormal atmospheric conditions. This phenomenon, sometimes called "St. Elmo's fire" or "ball lightning", could theoretically appear as luminous objects floating in the sky. However, this theory struggles to explain the apparent structure and consistency of the object's movements as described by witnesses.

The possibility of a hoax or optical illusion is also mentioned. In the digital age, where image and video manipulation has become more accessible, some skeptics suggest that the incident could be an elaborate setup for advertising purposes or simply to create a buzz on social media. This hypothesis is often reinforced by the lack of concrete physical evidence and the difficulty in obtaining clear and unambiguous images of the incident.

Finally, there is of course the theory of extraterrestrial visitation, which remains one of the most fascinating and controversial. According to this perspective, the observed object could be a vessel from an advanced civilization from another part of the universe. Supporters of this idea often cite the seemingly advanced technology and maneuvering capabilities of the object as evidence that Earth's technology cannot yet reproduce. However, this theory is often criticized for its lack of tangible evidence and the fact that it largely relies on assumptions rather than concrete data.

THE FUKUSHIMA UFO INCIDENT.

DATE: March 12, 2011.
COUNTRY: Japan.
STATE: Prefecture of Fukushima.
CITY: Fukushima.

On March 11, 2011, a 9.0 magnitude earthquake struck northeastern Japan, triggering a powerful tsunami that ravaged the coasts and caused a series of disasters at the Fukushima Daiichi nuclear power plant. The plant's cooling systems were destroyed, leading to explosions and leaks of radioactive materials. This event marks one of the greatest nuclear disasters in history, comparable to that of Chernobyl in 1986.

In this context of chaos and disaster, a lesser-known but equally intriguing incident occurred. On March 12, just one day after the main earthquake, residents of the city of Fukushima and surrounding areas reported seeing an unidentified flying object (UFO) in the sky. According to the testimonies, this UFO was seen flying over the damaged nuclear power plant. The descriptions of the object vary, but several witnesses mention a circular or disc-shaped form, with brightly colored flashing lights.

This incident immediately sparks the interest of ufologists and conspiracy theorists, who speculate on the possibility of extraterrestrial surveillance of human nuclear activities. Others suggest that the UFO could be linked to a secret military technology, potentially deployed to monitor the situation in Fukushima in the turmoil that followed the disaster.

Despite the interest it generates, the Fukushima UFO incident remains poorly documented and shrouded in mystery. The Japanese authorities have not officially acknowledged these observations, and no concrete evidence has been presented to support the witnesses' claims. The incident therefore remains a subject of speculation and debate among researchers and the general public.

The Observation.

That day, at around 4:05 PM local time, several witnesses in the Fukushima region, Japan, reported seeing an unidentified flying object in the sky. The sighting coincided with a period of high tension in the region, following the earthquake and tsunami that struck Japan on March 11, causing a major nuclear crisis.

The observed object was circular in shape with a series of flashing lights that emitted an intense light of white and blue color. The witnesses described the object as having a diameter of about 20 meters. It seemed to float effortlessly at an estimated altitude of about 500 meters above the ground. The UFO emitted no perceptible sound, which added to the mysterious nature of the observation.

The weather conditions that day were clear with few clouds, offering perfect visibility. The sky was a deep blue, which contrasted sharply with the brilliant light emitted by the object. This allowed several people to take photos and videos of the UFO, which then circulated on various media platforms and on the Internet.

The object remained visible for about seven minutes before it began to move north at a considerably high speed. Its trajectory was linear and it showed no signs of conventional propulsion such as flames or condensation trails. The acceleration of the UFO was remarkable, going from immobility to a speed that seemed to exceed that of modern fighter jets.

During the observation, the intensity of the light emitted by the object varied, becoming at times so bright that it was difficult to look at directly. Then, just as suddenly, the intensity decreased, allowing the witnesses to see more clearly the underlying structure of the object, which appeared metallic and perfectly smooth, without visible joints or rivets.

The incident did not last long, but the visual and emotional impact on those who observed it was profound. The images and videos captured have been analyzed by various experts and amateurs, but no definitive conclusion has been drawn as to the origin or nature of the object. The absence of noise, the speed of movement, the observed maneuverability, and the seemingly advanced technology of the UFO continue to raise questions and theories among researchers and the general public.

Testimonials.

One of the first witnesses, Hiroshi T., a technician at the Fukushima power plant, reports having seen an unidentified flying object hovering above the damaged reactors. According to his testimony, the object was circular in shape with a series of flashing lights on the perimeter. Hiroshi indicates that the UFO remained stationary in the sky for about three minutes before disappearing at a dizzying speed towards the northeast, without making a sound.

Another observation comes from Akemi S., a resident of the city of Fukushima, who described seeing an object similar to the one described by Hiroshi. She mentions that the object had a metallic surface that seemed to reflect the sunlight. Akemi adds that the UFO made jerky movements, as if it was scanning the area, before ascending vertically into the sky at an incredible speed.

Katsuhiro O., a firefighter involved in post-tsunami rescue efforts, also shared his experience. He claims to have observed a triangular object with three white lights at each corner, flying low over the area. Katsuhiro's testimony is particularly interesting because he mentions a kind of luminous halo surrounding the object, creating a slight visual distortion that made it difficult to focus on the UFO.

Yumi G., a local journalist, collected these testimonies as well as that of a former army pilot, Masato R., who specified that the movements of the UFO did not correspond to any known conventional aircraft. Masato emphasizes the object's ability to move in total silence and with agility far surpassing that of helicopters or planes.

The Investigation.

Following the detection of unidentified flying objects in the sky near the Fukushima Prefecture, an official investigation has been launched by the Japanese government, in collaboration with aeronautics experts and atmospheric phenomena specialists.

From the first reports, the Japanese military authorities mobilized teams to monitor the airspace around Fukushima. Special radars were used to track the movements of detected objects, and reconnaissance planes were sent to try to visually identify them. The initial reactions of the pilots were mainly of confusion and surprise, as the objects moved at speeds and with maneuvers that did not correspond to conventional aircraft.

The testimonies collected from pilots and radar operators formed the basis of the initial report. These testimonies described objects of various shapes, some evoking discs, others more spherical or cylindrical shapes. The objects were capable of disappearing and suddenly reappearing on radars, which added a layer of mystery to the investigation.

The Japanese government also consulted meteorology experts to rule out the possibility that these observations were natural phenomena, such as weather balloons or atmospheric anomalies. These experts confirmed that the weather conditions during the observations did not match any known natural phenomenon that could explain the sightings.

Faced with the inability to provide a conventional explanation, the authorities have expanded their investigation to include scientists specializing in aerospace phenomena and ufologists. In-depth interviews with eyewitnesses on the ground have been conducted, and images captured by surveillance cameras as well as by individuals have been analyzed in detail.

The findings of the investigation were partially published in a report that highlighted the lack of conclusive evidence regarding the exact nature of the objects. The report mentioned that, despite the efforts made, the objects could not be definitively identified and their origin remained unknown. However, it was clearly indicated that these objects posed no direct threat to national security or the civilian population.

Theories and Speculations.

The Fukushima UFO incident, which occurred shortly after the 2011 nuclear disaster, has sparked a multitude of theories and speculations. Observations of unidentified flying objects in the disaster-stricken region have fueled various hypotheses, ranging from extraterrestrial intervention to more down-to-earth explanations.

One of the most popular theories suggests that the UFO observed may have been attracted by the radiation or electromagnetic disturbances generated by the nuclear accident. This hypothesis is based on the idea that some extraterrestrial civilizations might be interested in nuclear phenomena, either out of scientific curiosity or for surveillance purposes. According to this perspective, the UFO would have been a kind of probe sent to study the effects of radiation on the Earth's environment and its inhabitants.

Other speculations suggest that the UFO could be a secret technology developed by a national government or a private company. In the context of the Fukushima disaster, it is suggested that this UFO could have been used to discreetly assess the extent of the damage or to monitor radiation levels without exposing human crews to dangers. This theory is often supported by allegations of classified military programs existing in several countries, which explore the use of advanced technologies such as drones or unconventional propulsion devices.

Another hypothesis considers the incident as a misunderstood natural phenomenon. Supporters of this idea argue that under conditions of high stress and confusion, like those experienced after the tsunami and nuclear accident, witnesses may be more likely to misinterpret natural phenomena or flying debris as UFOs. For example, unusual reflections of light on clouds, or even weather balloons or lanterns, could be mistaken for extraterrestrial objects.

Finally, there is a conspiracy theory that the Fukushima UFO incident was a staged event orchestrated by unknown forces, with the aim of diverting public attention from the real issues of the nuclear disaster. This theory suggests that the spread of UFO stories could be used to manipulate public opinion or to mask embarrassing facts about the crisis management.

The Aguadilla INCIDENT, Puerto Rico.

DATE: April 25, 2013.
COUNTRY: Puerto Rico.
STATE: .
CITY: Aguadilla.

The Aguadilla incident is an intriguing and well-documented case in the history of UFO sightings, primarily due to the quality and nature of the visual evidence involved. Located west of Puerto Rico, Aguadilla is a coastal town known for its beautiful beaches and its international airport, Rafael Hernández. It is precisely from this airport that the incident took shape, involving an unidentified flying object captured by a thermal camera on board a plane from the U.S. Customs and Border Protection.

On the evening of April 25, 2013, as normal operations continued at Rafael Hernández Airport, an American customs surveillance plane detected a strange object flying over the surface of the ocean nearby. What makes this incident particularly remarkable is the clarity of the video recording: the object appears as a round and warm mass, moving at a speed and with a maneuverability that do not correspond to conventional aircraft. The object was filmed moving rapidly over the water, then splitting into two distinct parts, each continuing on its trajectory.

This case has been extensively analyzed by experts in aeronautics and aerospace phenomena, as well as by organizations dedicated to the study of UFOs. Debates continue as to whether the object was a sophisticated drone, an uncommon atmospheric phenomenon, or something completely unexplained. The Aguadilla incident remains a subject of fascination not only for ufologists but also for skeptics, offering a rare and valuable insight into the always controversial and mysterious field of unidentified flying objects.

The Observation.

This event occurred on April 25, 2013, shortly after midnight. The unidentified object was detected and filmed by a thermal camera onboard a United States Customs and Border Protection aircraft, which was conducting a routine surveillance in the region.

The video begins by showing the UFO emerging from the ocean, near the coast of Aguadilla. The object initially appears as a round and intense heat source on the thermal camera screen, indicating a significantly higher temperature than its immediate surroundings. Its exit from the water does not seem to be accompanied by steam or splashes, which is unusual for an object of this size emerging at such a speed.

After its emergence, the UFO begins to move at a considerably high speed above the water's surface. Its trajectory is stable and it maintains a constant altitude of only a few meters above the ocean. The shape of the object is difficult to discern accurately due to the quality of the thermal image, but it appears to be oval or slightly elongated.

The weather conditions that night were clear, with little cloud cover and excellent visibility. The sea was relatively calm, which made the observation of the object by the thermal camera even sharper. The absence of atmospheric turbulence or large waves also contributed to uninterrupted visual surveillance.

The object continued its flight over the water for several minutes, covering a significant distance without showing signs of conventional propulsion such as flames or condensation trails. At one point, it even seemed to split into two distinct objects, although this could be due to a camera artifact or a maneuver of the object itself.

The speed of the UFO was remarkable, with estimates suggesting it was moving much faster than the typical aerial vehicles used in this region. This feature, combined with its sudden appearance and its ability to maneuver over water without apparent disruption, underscores the strangeness of this observation.

Testimonials.

The first witness, the pilot of the CBP plane, reported seeing a round and luminous object emerging from the ocean and rising into the night sky. According to his testimony, the object did not emit any perceptible sounds and moved at a speed and with a maneuverability that did not correspond to any known aircraft. The pilot described the object as being able to split into two distinct parts, each continuing to fly in a coordinated manner before rejoining again.

Another crew member, the onboard thermal camera operator, provided additional details about the appearance of the object. According to him, the UFO had an oval shape and was surrounded by a kind of luminous halo, which made it difficult to determine its exact structure. The operator also noted that the object seemed to disrupt the environment around it, with visible effects on the water when the object approached the ocean surface.

The testimonies also include those of several local residents who observed the object from the ground. One of the witnesses, a fisherman who was near the coast, described seeing a bright object diving into the ocean and then coming out. According to his account, the object created a kind of turbulence in the water, followed by a rapid acceleration towards the sky.

A resident of Aguadilla, who preferred to remain anonymous, reported observing the object for several minutes. She described the UFO as having an intense light that varied in intensity, as if the object was adjusting its power or propulsion method. She also mentioned that the object performed several maneuvers that defied the laws of physics as we know them, including instant changes in direction and sudden accelerations without any sound emission.

Finally, an air traffic controller from Rafael Hernández Airport in Aguadilla confirmed that the object had been detected by radars, but it did not correspond to any known or scheduled flight at that time. The controller emphasized the absence of a transponder on the object, which is mandatory for all commercial and private aircraft, thus adding an additional layer of mystery to the incident.

The Investigation.

Everything began when an unidentified flying object was filmed by a thermal camera on board a plane from the United States Customs and Border Protection (CBP). What distinguishes this incident is the clarity and quality of the images captured, showing a low-flying object over the ocean near Rafael Hernández Airport in Aguadilla.

As soon as the video was made public, the government of Puerto Rico, in collaboration with the American federal authorities, launched an investigation to determine the nature and origin of the observed object. The initial reactions were to treat the incident with great caution, avoiding any hasty conclusions about the extraterrestrial or conventional nature of the object.

The investigators began by questioning the CBP staff who were on duty during the incident. The testimonies collected revealed that the object had been detected by chance during a routine mission. The thermal camera operators described the object as being oval-shaped and capable of high-speed maneuvers, which did not correspond to any known conventional aircraft.

In parallel, the authorities analyzed the radar data from Aguadilla airport to see if the object had been recorded on other instruments. The results were partially conclusive, showing anomalies in the radar recordings at the time of the incident, but without direct correspondence with what the thermal camera had recorded.

The investigation also involved experts in aeronautics and atmospheric phenomena, in order to rule out the possibility that the object was a misinterpreted natural phenomenon. These experts examined the meteorological and aerological conditions of the region at that time, concluding that the conditions were clear and could not have caused optical illusions or unusual reflections.

A crucial aspect of the investigation was the technical analysis of the video itself. Imaging specialists were consulted to verify the authenticity of the video and to analyze the movements and physical characteristics of the object. Their analysis confirmed that the video had not been altered or manipulated and that the object behaved consistently with a real physical object having considerable mass and speed.

Despite all these efforts, the investigation failed to provide a definitive explanation for the object. The final conclusions indicated that, although the object did not correspond to any known aircraft or natural phenomenon, there was not enough evidence to determine its exact nature. The authorities therefore classified the incident as unresolved, while remaining open to receiving new information that could shed light on this mystery.

Theories and Speculations.

One of the main theories put forward to explain this incident is that of the extraterrestrial craft. This hypothesis suggests that the observed object could be a vessel of non-Earth origin, given its aerial and underwater movement capabilities that defy the technologies currently known to humanity. Supporters of this theory point to the speed, maneuverability, and the object's ability to move underwater without significantly disrupting its trajectory or speed, characteristics that do not match traditional aerial or underwater vehicles.

Another popular theory is that of secret military experimentation. According to this perspective, the object could be a drone or another type of experimental technology secretly developed by the government or private companies. This hypothesis is supported by the fact that the incident took place near a military base, which could indicate tests of advanced technologies not yet revealed to the public. Skeptics of the extraterrestrial theory find this explanation more plausible, as it relies on a logical progression of human technology, albeit secret.

A third approach considers the object as a misinterpreted natural phenomenon. Some researchers suggest that what the thermal camera recorded could be a rare atmospheric or oceanic phenomenon, such as a weather balloon, a bird, or a small meteor skimming the water's surface. This theory is often reinforced by arguments about the potential limitations and flaws of night vision equipment, which could misinterpret or exaggerate certain features of the observed object.

Finally, there is speculation around the idea that the incident could be a hoax or a misunderstanding. This theory suggests that the video could have been altered or misinterpreted, either intentionally or not, by those who disseminated it. Critics of this theory highlight the lack of concrete evidence and the fact that the video was released by an official source, which, according to them, adds some credibility to the authenticity of the recording.

THE UFO INCIDENT OF NEW YORK.

DATE: July 13, 2015.
COUNTRY: United States.
STATE: New York.
CITY: New York City.

The New York UFO incident, which occurred on July 13, 2015, remains one of the most discussed and analyzed events by UFO enthusiasts as well as skeptics. That day, many residents of New York City reported seeing an unidentified flying object in the night sky, sparking a wave of excitement and mystery across the city. The testimonies varied, but most observers described a disc-shaped object, emitting bright lights of changing colors. The object seemed to move at a speed and with a maneuverability far beyond the capabilities of known human aircraft at the time.

Social networks played a crucial role in the rapid dissemination of images and videos of this UFO, allowing a wide audience to share their experiences and theories about the origin of the object. Local authorities and government agencies were quickly overwhelmed by requests for clarification and explanation. However, despite numerous speculations, no official explanation was provided on the day of the incident, leaving the door open to all kinds of interpretations.

In the days that followed, aviation and atmospheric phenomena experts attempted to provide rational explanations, ranging from high-tech drones to rare atmospheric effects, but none of these theories could be definitively proven. The New York UFO incident thus continued to fuel debates and research, becoming a significant case study in the field of ufology.

The Observation.

That evening, around 10:30 pm, several witnesses in the Manhattan neighborhood reported seeing an unidentified flying object. The night was clear and the stars visible, an ideal weather condition that allowed a detailed observation of the event.

The observed object was disc-shaped, with a series of flashing lights running along its perimeter. These lights alternated between red, blue, and green, creating a striking visual spectacle against the New York night sky. The UFO was approximately 30 meters in diameter and seemed to float effortlessly above the rooftops of the buildings, moving with remarkable agility and without emitting any perceptible sound.

Witnesses described the object as having a metallic surface that reflected the city lights, giving the UFO an almost shimmering appearance. On several occasions, the object performed maneuvers that defy the capabilities of known aerial vehicles, such as sudden accelerations and abrupt stops, as well as right-angle direction changes.

The observation lasted about 20 minutes. During this time, the object slowly traveled a trajectory that led it from the south of Manhattan to the north, before suddenly disappearing from sight, as if it had accelerated at an incredibly high speed. The disappearance of the UFO was as mysterious as its appearance, leaving the witnesses in a state of astonishment and curiosity.

The clarity of the sky that night played a crucial role in the sharpness of the details observed by the witnesses. The moon was in a waxing phase, providing additional light but not enough to eclipse the view of the UFO. Moreover, the absence of clouds allowed for perfect visibility, and the low wind speed prevented any atmospheric disturbance that could have obscured or distorted the view of the object.

Testimonials.

One of the first witnesses, Michael Johnson, an amateur photographer, was in Central Park to capture images of urban nature when he observed several bright objects in the sky. According to his testimony, these objects formed a sort of V and moved at an incredible speed, without making any sound. Michael managed to take a few photos before the objects disappeared on the horizon.

Sarah Goldberg, a teacher visiting New York, was near Times Square when she noticed a strange light above the skyscrapers. She described a pulsating light that changed color from blue to red, then to white. Intrigued, Sarah watched the object for several minutes before it split into two and quickly moved away in opposite directions.

Another important witness, Captain Richard Evans, was piloting a commercial flight near New York's airspace that day. He reports having seen an unidentified object cross his plane's cruising altitude. The object, according to him, was disc-shaped and surrounded by a sort of luminous halo. Captain Evans reported the observation to the control tower, but no other aircraft in the area confirmed the sighting of this object.

Among the witnesses, there is also Julia Hernandez, a long-time resident of Brooklyn. She observed the object from the window of her apartment. Julia describes a silent object with flashing lights that seemed to be monitoring the area before ascending vertically at a staggering speed.

Finally, a group of students from New York University also shared their experience. They were in the process of making a film project in the streets of Manhattan when their camera accidentally captured what appears to be the UFO. One of the students, Alex Thompson, testified to seeing the object moving erratically, as if it was performing maneuvers impossible for a human aircraft.

These testimonies, although varied, share common points about the silent nature and extraordinary speed of the observed objects. They continue to fuel debates and speculations about the potential presence of unidentified flying objects over New York that day.

The Investigation.

From the first hours following the observation, which involved several witnesses reporting an unidentified flying object of triangular shape flying over Manhattan, the federal government initiated a discreet but thorough investigation.

The initial reactions of the authorities were to deny any knowledge or involvement in the observed phenomenon. However, in the face of public pressure and the increasing number of testimonies, the Department of Defense finally acknowledged the need for a formal investigation. A special team, composed of members from the Air Force, NASA, and several experts in aeronautics and atmospheric phenomena, was formed.

The testimonies collected by this team were varied but consistent on several points: the object was large, silent, and emitted intense light. The investigators examined all leads, including that of a secret experimental device, but no known program of the military or aerospace industry could be linked to the observed object.

The analysis of the radars in the area was also a key component of the investigation. The radar data, although partially inconclusive, showed anomalies in the air traffic at the supposed time of the observation. These anomalies were not sufficient to confirm the physical presence of the object, but they reinforced the testimonies of the citizens.

After several months of investigations, the final report was published. It concluded that there was no tangible evidence of the presence of an extraterrestrial device or an advanced military prototype in New York's airspace that day.

However, the report also mentioned the investigation's inability to satisfactorily explain all the observations and data collected.

This report was met with skepticism by a portion of the UFO community and was seen by others as an attempt at concealment. Despite the official conclusions, the New York incident remains a case studied and debated among those interested in unidentified aerial phenomena, illustrating the complexity and challenges associated with investigating such events.

Theories and Speculations.

The first theory put forward is that of the extraterrestrial craft. According to this hypothesis, the observed object would be a spaceship from an advanced civilization coming from another planet or another solar system. Supporters of this theory often rely on the seemingly advanced technology of the object, such as its ability to perform high-speed maneuvers without notable noise, as well as testimonies of sudden changes in direction that defy the laws of physics as we know them.

Another commonly discussed explanation is that of secret military experience. This theory suggests that the UFO could be a prototype of an aircraft or drone secretly developed by the government or private contractors working for defense. The unusual characteristics of the object, such as its speed and silence, would be the result of experimental technologies not yet disclosed to the public. This hypothesis is often reinforced by the fact that many UFO incidents have been reported near military bases or in areas known for their research and development activity in defense.

A third theory suggests that the incident could be the result of an optical illusion or a mistake. Skeptics of extraterrestrial presence argue that the object could be a rare atmospheric phenomenon, such as St. Elmo's lights, or even the reflection of terrestrial lights on low clouds. This explanation is often supported by experts in meteorology and optics, who cite the possibility that particular atmospheric conditions could have created deceptive images in the sky.

Furthermore, some put forward the idea that the incident could be a staged hoax. In this scenario, the UFO would have been manufactured or simulated by individuals seeking to create a media sensation or to test the public's reaction to a supposed extraterrestrial visit. This theory is sometimes supported by analyses showing inconsistencies in the testimonies or video evidence that could have been manipulated.

THE BREMEN INCIDENT.

DATE: January 6, 2014.
COUNTRY: Germany.
STATE: Bremen.
CITY: Bremen.

The Bremen incident is an event that captivated the attention of the media, aviation experts, and UFO enthusiasts around the world. On January 6, 2014, in the city of Bremen, located in northern Germany, an unidentified flying object was detected by the radars of Bremen airport, causing significant disruption to airport operations. That evening, around 6:30 pm, air traffic controllers noticed an unusual echo on their radar, a signal that was moving erratically and did not correspond to any scheduled flight. The object was observed several times on the radar for about three hours, disappearing and reappearing at irregular intervals.

The presence of this mysterious object led to the cancellation of several flights and significant delays, affecting hundreds of passengers. In addition, the police and airport authorities deployed a helicopter in an attempt to locate and identify the object, but without success. Testimonies from pilots and air traffic controllers described the object as being luminous and capable of high-speed maneuvers, defying the capabilities of conventional aircraft.

The incident has sparked a multitude of speculations and theories, ranging from the presence of an illegal drone to that of a genuine UFO. Despite thorough investigations conducted by local authorities and aviation experts, the origin and nature of the object remain unidentified to this day. This event remains one of the most intriguing and least explained incidents in the annals of UFO sightings in Germany, continuing to fascinate and mystify experts and the general public.

The Observation.

That evening, around 6:30 pm, the staff of the Bremen airport control tower spotted an unidentified flying object on their radar. The object was detected several times over a period of three hours, causing significant disruptions, including the cancellation of a flight and several delays.

The description of the object, as reported by the witnesses, varies slightly, but most agree on certain key details. The UFO was described as having an elongated shape and flashing lights. Some witnesses also mentioned a kind of luminous halo surrounding the object, making its exact structure difficult to discern. The visual observations were supported by radar data, which showed an object moving at varying speeds and often changing direction abruptly and seemingly without logic.

The weather conditions that night were relatively clear with moderate visibility, which allowed the witnesses to see the object more clearly. The temperature was cool, typical for a January month in Bremen, with a partially covered sky that did not present significant obstacles to the visibility of the witnesses on the ground and in the control tower.

The object was observed at different altitudes, sometimes seen hovering at low altitude before suddenly ascending at an impressive speed. This ability to change altitude quickly and without apparent noise was one of the most intriguing characteristics of the observation. Moreover, the absence of noise was consistently noted by witnesses, which is unusual for a flying object of this size and mobility.

The incident lasted until about 9:30 PM, when the object finally disappeared from the radar and was no longer visible to the witnesses. During this period, the object appeared and disappeared from the radar several times, each appearance being accompanied by visual observations that confirmed the presence of the object in the sky of Bremen.

Testimonials.

That evening, an unidentified flying object was spotted in the sky near Bremen airport in Germany, causing significant disruptions, including flight cancellations and multiple delays.

Among the key witnesses, an air traffic controller played a central role. This professional, whose identity has not been disclosed for confidentiality reasons, reported observing a flying object on the airport radar that was moving at variable speeds and changing direction in an abrupt and inexplicable manner. According to his testimony, the object was not only visible on the radar screen, but it was also seen with the naked eye from the control tower. The object was described as having flashing strobe lights and moving without any perceptible noise.

Another significant testimony is that of a police pilot who was dispatched to intercept or identify the object. The pilot reported that despite several attempts to approach, the object moved away each time they tried to get closer. The pilot described the object as being oval-shaped and emitting an intense light that made direct visualization difficult. The observation lasted several minutes before the object disappeared at a speed far greater than that of any known conventional aircraft.

Ground witnesses, including airport employees and passengers waiting for their flights, also shared similar observations. A maintenance worker noted that the object seemed capable of hovering in the air for long periods before moving at high speed in different directions. A passenger, who preferred to remain anonymous, mentioned that the object had a "metallic" appearance and reflected the city lights, making it visible despite the low brightness.

These testimonies, collected independently from each other, present striking similarities that add a layer of credibility to the incident. The descriptions of the object, its behavior in the sky, and the way it was perceived both visually and on navigation instruments, suggest an encounter with an unidentified aerial phenomenon that remains unexplained to this day.

The Investigation.

In response to this unusual event, a thorough investigation has been launched by local authorities in collaboration with the federal police and the German air force.

From the first hours following the incident, the authorities tried to understand the nature and origin of the detected object. The airport's radars recorded the presence of the object for about three hours, which raised a series of questions about its ability to remain in a controlled airspace without being clearly identified. The first testimonies, collected from air traffic controllers, described a flying object with erratic movements and not conforming to usual flight paths.

The investigation also included the analysis of radar data in an attempt to draw a precise profile of the object. Aviation and defense experts were consulted to examine the radar sequences and determine whether the object could be a drone, a weather balloon, or something else. However, the flight characteristics and speed of the object did not match any known device at that time.

The federal police conducted interviews with other witnesses, including pilots who were in the area at the time of the incident and local residents. Some testimonies mentioned seeing a bright object crossing the sky at a considerable speed, which added a layer of mystery to the case. These observations were compared to technical data to see if they could match the recorded radar anomalies.

Faced with the inability to clearly determine the nature of the object, military authorities were called upon to assess the possibility of a threat to national security. The air force examined scenarios including an intrusion of a foreign or unauthorized device into the airspace. Aerial surveillance measures were strengthened in the region to prevent any recurrence.

After several weeks of investigations, the final report was published. It concluded that, despite the efforts made, it was impossible to determine with certainty the identity or origin of the object. The report also mentioned that all possible leads had been explored, including consultations with aerospace phenomena experts and checks of civil and military aviation activities in the concerned area.

The Bremen incident therefore remains one of the many unresolved UFO cases, leaving behind as many questions as curiosity. The authorities have maintained an open stance on continuing the investigation if new information were to emerge. This incident has also stimulated public debate on the need to better understand and monitor unidentified aerial phenomena.

Theories and Speculations.

The first theory, and the most obvious one for many, is that of the presence of a real UFO, in the extraterrestrial sense of the term. This hypothesis is supported by the difficulty in identifying the object despite modern surveillance technologies. Advocates of this theory argue that the object had flight capabilities that exceed known aeronautical technology, notably its ability to disappear and reappear quickly on radars and its exceptional speed without corresponding noise.

Another explanation put forward is that of a civilian or military drone. With the increase in the use of drones for various applications, it is plausible that a drone, perhaps large and unauthorized, could have intruded into the airport's airspace. This theory is reinforced by the fact that drones can be equipped with technologies that allow them to avoid radar detection or minimize their radar signature. However, this hypothesis struggles to explain the duration of the observation and the erratic movements reported by witnesses.

Some aviation experts have suggested that the incident could be attributed to a weather balloon or another type of research balloon. These objects, often used for scientific experiments or atmospheric surveys, can sometimes deviate from their planned trajectory and enter controlled airspaces. However, this theory does not take into account certain aspects of the testimonies, including the rapid changes in altitude and direction of the object.

A more skeptical perspective suggests that the incident could be the result of an optical illusion or a radar error. Optical illusions, particularly in low light conditions or bad weather, can lead to misinterpretations of what witnesses think they see. Similarly, radars can sometimes give false readings due to various environmental or technical factors. This explanation is often cited to rationalize UFO observations that otherwise find no immediate explanation.

Finally, there are those who believe that the incident could have been some sort of secret test of advanced technologies by a governmental or private entity. This theory is fueled by the lack of transparency and sometimes evasive responses from defense and aerospace technology authorities. Proponents of this idea speculate that such tests could be conducted under the guise of classified operations, thus escaping public scrutiny and even the knowledge of airport operators.

THE GO FAST VIDEO FROM THE EAST COAST.

DATE: January 21, 2015.
COUNTRY: United States.
STATE: .
CITY: Above the Atlantic Ocean.

The incident known as "Go Fast" was made public in March 2018, when To The Stars Academy of Arts & Science released a video captured by an infrared camera mounted on a US Navy fighter jet. This video shows an unidentified flying object (UFO) moving at high speed over the Atlantic Ocean. The object, which seems to defy the conventional characteristics of known aircraft, was filmed by a navy pilot during a routine flight. The video sparked keen interest both in the scientific community and among the general public, raising questions about the presence and frequency of unidentified aerial phenomena in controlled airspace.

The object captured in the "Go Fast" video is seen moving quickly and at low altitude over the water, with no apparent wings or visible means of propulsion. Pilots and aviation experts who analyzed the footage were intrigued by the object's speed and maneuverability, as well as its unconventional appearance. This incident is part of a series of revelations and disclosures made by the US government and other organizations about encounters with unidentified flying objects by military pilots. These revelations have helped fuel the debate about the nature and origin of such objects, while pushing for a broader awareness of the need to seriously and scientifically study these phenomena.

Another American navy pilot recorded a fast object flying over the Atlantic Ocean.

The Observation.

The incident known as "Go Fast" occurred in 2015, off the east coast of the United States. This event was captured by an infrared camera mounted on an American navy fighter jet, specifically an F/A-18 Super Hornet. The observed object was filmed during a routine maritime surveillance by navy pilots who were surprised by the speed and atypical movements of the object.

The video, which lasts about 34 seconds, shows a small oval or tic-tac shaped object flying at low altitude over the Atlantic Ocean. The object appears to glide very quickly over the water, which gave the video its name "Go Fast". The infrared camera was able to detect the object despite the absence of emitted heat, which is unusual for conventional aircraft. The object had no visible wings, propeller, or gas emissions, which added to the intrigue surrounding its nature and origin.

The exact time of the observation is not clearly documented, but reports indicate that it occurred in broad daylight. The weather conditions were clear with good visibility, which allowed for a detailed observation of the object. The sea was relatively calm, and there were no signs of water disturbance under the object, which could have suggested conventional propulsion.

The pilots attempted to track the object with their camera while commenting on its speed and movements. One of the pilots mentioned that the object was going "very fast" and expressed his astonishment at the object's ability to maintain such a speed without visible means of propulsion. The video also shows that the object managed to maintain a stable trajectory despite the high speeds, which is atypical for unidentified flying objects observed under similar conditions.

The filmed sequence was analyzed by several experts and organizations interested in unidentified aerial phenomena. Although the detailed technical analysis of the video showed that the object was moving at a considerably high speed, no definitive conclusion was drawn as to its exact nature or origin. The absence of conventional features and the clarity of the video led to a great deal of speculation and interest in this particular incident.

Testimonials.

Lieutenant Ryan Graves, an F/A-18 Super Hornet fighter pilot, was one of the first to report the sighting of the object. According to his testimony, the object was moving at an exceptionally high speed, far greater than that of conventional aircraft. Graves described the object as being capable of performing high-velocity maneuvers without visible emissions of gas or heat, which distinctly set it apart from traditional aircraft. He also highlighted the absence of any apparent flight structure, such as wings or propellers, that could explain its propulsion.

Another key witness, Commander Dave Fravor, also observed the object during a routine flight. Fravor described the object as having an oval and smooth shape, with no external markings or rudder. During his observation, the object suddenly accelerated and moved away at a speed that exceeded the capabilities of his aircraft, leaving Fravor and his crew without a plausible explanation for the technology behind such movements.

Captain Emma Turner, who was piloting another F/A-18 in the same area, corroborated her colleagues' observations. She noted that the object emitted no audible sound and did not seem to be affected by conventional laws of physics, such as gravity or inertia. Turner also mentioned that the object could maintain a constant speed before making sharp stops or changing direction instantly.

The testimonies of these pilots were supported by radar data and video recordings, which clearly show an object moving at speeds and with maneuvers that do not correspond to any known aircraft. These observations were analyzed by several experts in aeronautics and aerospace phenomena, but no definitive explanation has been given as to the nature or origin of the observed object.

The Investigation.

As soon as the video was publicly revealed, the Pentagon confirmed its authenticity and announced that the filmed object was part of a set of unidentified aerial phenomena (UAP) studied by the Advanced Aerospace Threat Identification Program (AATIP). This program, although little known to the public at the time, had the mission to analyze and catalog these phenomena, which could represent potential threats to national security.

The investigators began by questioning the pilot who had captured the video as well as other witnesses present during the incident. These testimonies provided crucial details about the speed, size, and behavior of the object. According to the reports, the object was moving at a speed considerably higher than that of conventional aircraft and showed no typical features of an aircraft, such as visible wings or engines.

The technical analysis of the video also played a key role in the investigation. Imaging experts examined the infrared data to try to determine the material composition of the object as well as its thermal characteristics. However, the results were inconclusive, the object not matching any known material.

In parallel, the American Congress took part in the investigation by organizing hearings and confidential briefings with defense officials and aerospace experts. These sessions aimed to assess the extent of the potential threat posed by the UFOs and to determine the need to increase funding and resources for future research.

Throughout the investigation, several hypotheses were explored, ranging from advanced drones to secret experimental technologies, and even rare atmospheric phenomena. However, none of these theories could be definitively proven, leaving the incident without an official explanation.

In conclusion, although the investigation into the Go Fast video mobilized significant governmental and military resources, it failed to provide a clear and definitive explanation of the observed object. This incident therefore remains classified among the many UAPs whose origin and nature are still to be determined.

Theories and Speculations.

One of the first theories put forward is that of a drone or unconventional terrestrial aircraft. Some aviation and military technology experts suggest that the object could be an experimental drone, possibly from secret government or defense industry research and development programs. This hypothesis is supported by the fact that governments are heavily investing in drone technologies and many of these projects remain classified.

Another common explanation is that of an unusual atmospheric or meteorological phenomenon. Scientists specializing in the study of atmospheric phenomena have sometimes identified anomalies that could resemble unidentified flying objects, such as weather balloons, lenticular clouds, or even optical mirages caused by particular atmospheric conditions. However, this theory struggles to fully convince given the apparent speed and maneuverability of the object in the video.

The extraterrestrial hypothesis remains one of the most popular among the general public. According to this theory, the object would be a spacecraft from an advanced extraterrestrial civilization. Supporters of this idea argue that the technology manifested by the object far exceeds what humanity can currently produce, thus suggesting a non-earthly origin. This hypothesis is often fueled by reports of the existence of secret government programs studying unidentified aerial phenomena and by testimonies from former defense sector employees.

Furthermore, some researchers suggest that the object could be an artifact of an ancient or unknown civilization on Earth, suggesting that advanced societies may have existed on our planet long before known human history. This theory, although marginal, stimulates the imagination about the hidden possibilities of our own planet.

Conclusion.

The Go Fast video, captured in 2015 and released in 2018, shows an object moving at high speed over the Atlantic Ocean, sparking numerous speculations and analyses. Despite various theories, the origin and nature of the object remain unidentified, classifying this incident among the many UFO cases that continue to defy conventional explanation. This event not only highlights the limits of our understanding of aerial phenomena but also the need for more rigorous study and greater transparency in handling data related to UFOs. The impact of disclosing such videos is significant, fueling public and scientific debate about the presence and monitoring of unidentified objects in our airspace.

THE HOUSTON UFO INCIDENT.

DATE: August 7, 2015.
COUNTRY: United States.
STATE: Texas.
CITY: Houston.

That evening, many residents of Houston, Texas, reported seeing unusual lights in the sky. These testimonies quickly fueled a wave of speculation and questions, propelling the event to the forefront of local and national media. Social networks played a crucial role in the rapid dissemination of images and videos of these strange lights, captured by smartphones. Local authorities and aviation experts were called upon to provide explanations, while ufologists and skeptics debated the nature of this phenomenon. The incident not only captivated the public's imagination but also stimulated a debate about the possible presence of unidentified flying objects in our airspace.

The Observation.

That evening, around 9:00 PM, many residents of Houston, Texas, reported seeing an unidentified flying object in the night sky. The description of the object varies slightly from one witness to another, but several common points emerge from the testimonies.

The observed object was circular or disc-shaped, with a series of lights flashing around its perimeter. These lights, mainly white in color, seemed to pulse rhythmically. According to some witnesses, the object also emitted a reddish light in the center, which intensified intermittently. The size of the UFO was difficult to estimate, but it seemed quite large, with an approximate diameter of 30 to 40 meters.

The UFO was seen moving at a relatively slow speed and at a low altitude, estimated between 300 and 500 meters from the ground. Its movement was smooth and it did not seem to emit any audible noise, which intrigued many witnesses accustomed to the characteristic noises of airplanes and helicopters.

The weather conditions that night were clear with few clouds, allowing for optimal visibility of the object. The moon was nearly full, providing an additional light source that helped to accentuate the contours of the UFO. There was no notable wind and the temperature was pleasant, which likely contributed to the large number of people outside who were able to observe the event.

The observation lasted about 20 minutes. During this time, the object crossed the sky in a northeast direction before suddenly rising at a much higher speed and disappearing from the witnesses' view. This rapid acceleration, combined with the way the object changed its trajectory without noise or apparent air disturbance, was particularly remarkable for those who saw it.

Testimonials.

The testimonies mainly come from local residents who have shared their experiences with various media and on social networks.

One of the main witnesses, Sarah Michaels, a high school teacher living in the suburbs of Houston, described seeing several flashing circular lights moving at a constant speed across the sky. According to her, these lights were of various colors, mainly red, blue and green, and formed a sort of triangle before suddenly disappearing after about five minutes.

Another witness, Mark Johnson, an aeronautical engineer, provided a more detailed technical description. He observed that the lights were moving without any noticeable noise and with a precision of movement that does not correspond to conventional aircraft. Mark specified that the lights seemed to be in coordinated formation and that they were changing direction with remarkable agility.

Jennifer Lee, who lived near the park where the incident took place, reported seeing an oval-shaped object under the lights. She described this object as being large in size, possibly as wide as several cars side by side. Jennifer also mentioned a kind of luminous halo around the object, which made it difficult to see the precise details of its structure.

A couple, Lisa and Tom Harding, who were walking near the location, testified to having felt a strange sensation of heat when the lights were closest to them. They also noted a temporary interruption in the reception of their cell phones during the event, a phenomenon that was reported by several other witnesses in the area.

Finally, a teenager, Kevin Roberts, captured images of the incident on his mobile phone. Although the images are of low quality, they clearly show several bright points moving synchronously in the sky. Kevin claimed that the observation lasted about ten minutes before the lights completely disappeared.

These testimonies, although varied, paint a consistent picture of an event that remains unexplained to this day. The descriptions of the movements of the lights, their appearance and the behavior of the associated object suggest a technology or phenomenon that the witnesses could not identify as being conventional or familiar.

The Investigation.

From the first hours following the observation, eyewitnesses reported seeing an unidentified flying object of triangular shape flying over the city with brightly colored flashing lights. Faced with the magnitude of the testimonies and media pressure, the federal government decided to launch an official investigation.

The initial stages of the investigation were conducted by the Air Force Office of Special Investigations (AFOSI). The investigators began by collecting testimonies from citizens who had observed the object. These testimonies varied in terms of details about the size, speed, and trajectory of the object, but most agreed on its triangular shape and unusual lights. The AFOSI also questioned air traffic controllers and other staff at Houston airport, who however detected no unauthorized aerial activity that night.

Simultaneously, the National Weather Service was consulted to check if any particular weather conditions could have created optical illusions or natural phenomena that could explain the observations. Their reports indicated a clear and unobstructed night, thus eliminating the possibility that weather phenomena were the cause of the observations.

The investigation took a more technical turn with the intervention of the National Aeronautics and Space Administration (NASA). Experts in aeronautics and atmospheric phenomena analyzed the available data to try to determine the nature of the observed object. They used simulations and models to test different hypotheses, ranging from experimental drones to weather balloons, but none of these theories could be definitively proven.

The most controversial aspect of the investigation was the handling of information by the authorities. Many witnesses expressed their frustration at the lack of transparency and accused the government of concealing information. In response, a series of public meetings was organized by local authorities in collaboration with the AFOSI to address citizens' concerns and provide updates on the investigation.

After several months of investigations, the final report was published. It concluded that, despite the efforts made, no definitive explanation had been found to justify the observations. The report mentioned that the object could be linked to classified military activities, but no concrete evidence was provided to support this theory. This conclusion left many residents and observers unsatisfied, fueling conspiracy theories and ongoing speculations about the nature of the incident.

Theories and Speculations.

One of the most common theories is that of misidentification. According to this hypothesis, what witnesses perceived as a UFO could actually be a poorly identified terrestrial object, such as an airplane, a drone, or even a weather balloon. Supporters of this theory argue that in conditions of low light or poor visibility, it is easy to confuse familiar objects with something unusual or extraordinary.

Another explanation often put forward is that of atmospheric phenomena. The lights or shapes observed could be the result of particular atmospheric conditions that create unusual illusions or reflections. For example, lenticular clouds or superior mirages, which can appear in the form of discs or floating objects, are sometimes mistaken for extraterrestrial vessels.

On the side of more controversial theories, some suggest the possibility of a secret experimental technology. This hypothesis suggests that the observed object could be a device secretly developed by the government or private companies. Proponents of this theory often point to the rapid advances in aeronautical and space technologies, which could explain the appearance of devices with extraordinary capabilities and designs.

Finally, there is of course the extraterrestrial theory, which remains among the most popular and debated. According to this perspective, the observed object would be a spacecraft from an extraterrestrial civilization. This idea is often fueled by testimonies of movements and behaviors of the object that seem to defy the known laws of physics, such as sudden accelerations or instantaneous changes of direction.

THE MEETINGS OF THE USS ROOSEVELT.

DATE: 2015.
COUNTRY: United States.
STATE: Not specified.
CITY: Not specified.

In 2015, an unusual event captured the attention of the public and experts in aviation and aerospace phenomena. Over a period of several months, pilots assigned to the USS Roosevelt, an American navy aircraft carrier, witnessed repeated encounters with unidentified flying objects (UFOs). These observations took place during routine missions over the Atlantic Ocean. The observed objects exhibited exceptional flight characteristics, with maneuvering capabilities and speeds far exceeding known aeronautical technologies at the time. The pilots, experienced and trained to recognize any type of aerial craft, reported that these UFOs could reach astonishing altitudes and speeds, without visible means of propulsion, and perform almost instantaneous changes in direction without the expected inertial effects. These observations were recorded using advanced tracking equipment, including infrared cameras and radars, which allowed for detailed documentation of these phenomena. The scale and frequency of these encounters prompted military authorities to take these incidents very seriously, leading to thorough investigations the results of which have not been fully disclosed to the public.

The Observation.

During the year 2015, several pilots assigned to the USS Roosevelt, an American navy aircraft carrier, reported repeated observations of unidentified flying objects (UFOs) during their routine missions. These observations took place in regulated air training zones off the east coast of the United States. The descriptions provided by the pilots and the data collected by the onboard instruments revealed exceptional flight characteristics of these objects.

The observed objects were described as being elongated in shape, often compared to "tic-tacs" due to their oval and smooth shape, with no visible wings, nor gas or smoke emissions. Their color was generally uniform, a bright white that stood out sharply against the clear sky and blue ocean. The estimated dimensions varied, but they were often comparable to those of a small airplane.

The observations typically occurred in broad daylight, with clear weather conditions and excellent visibility. The pilots noted that these objects could suddenly appear at very high altitudes, before diving towards sea level at dizzying speeds, well beyond the capabilities of conventional aircraft. Moreover, these objects seemed capable of making sharp stops and instant changes of direction, without any apparent inertia, thus defying the principles of aerodynamics as we know them.

The onboard instruments, including radars and infrared tracking systems, often visually confirmed the pilots' reports, recording data that showed erratic flight paths and speeds inconsistent with current human aerial technologies. For example, during one mission, a radar captured a UFO plunging from 30,000 feet to 10,000 feet in a fraction of a second, a performance impossible for human-piloted aircraft without risking serious injuries due to G-force.

These observations were not isolated to a small group of pilots; several crew members of the USS Roosevelt reported similar experiences over a period of several months. Each time, the objects disappeared as quickly as they had appeared, leaving no trace or debris, and without any intercepted communication that could indicate a conventional or terrestrial origin.

The weather conditions during the various observations were uniformly good, with little or no clouds, low humidity, and near-perfect visibility. These conditions allowed for clear visual observations and unobstructed radar recordings, thus eliminating weather interferences or identification errors due to poor weather conditions.

Testimonials.

One of the main witnesses to these events is Lieutenant Ryan Graves, an experienced fighter pilot who served aboard the USS Roosevelt. Graves reported observing objects that could reach hypersonic speeds without any visible propulsion signature, such as condensation trails or gas emissions. These objects were capable of making abrupt maneuvers, such as instantaneous direction changes or sudden accelerations, thus defying the laws of physics as they are applied to traditional aviation.

Another key witness, Commander Dave Fravor, described an encounter in which he observed an oval-shaped object hovering above the water before suddenly rising at a dizzying speed. Fravor, a naval aviation veteran, noted that the object had no visible wings or apparent means of propulsion, and that it was disturbing the water beneath it in a way that suggested considerable force.

Pilot Lieutenant Danielle Cotte also shared her observations, describing an object that seemed to "toy with" the most advanced fighter jets. She mentioned that the object could remain stationary in the air, then accelerate at an incredible speed, all of this without noise or atmospheric disturbance that would normally accompany a plane moving at such a speed.

The testimonies are also supported by radar recordings and videos captured by aircraft cameras, which show objects moving in an abnormal manner. These recordings have been analyzed by several aeronautics experts who confirmed that the observed movements did not correspond to any type of aircraft currently in service in any army in the world.

In addition to the pilots, radar technicians aboard the USS Roosevelt reported detecting objects flying at altitudes and speeds impossible for conventional aircraft. These technicians, whose names have not been disclosed for security reasons, corroborated the pilots' observations, adding an additional layer of credibility to the testimonies.

The Investigation.

These incidents, which occurred over several months, involved American Navy fighter pilots who reported seeing objects moving at speeds and with maneuvers far beyond known technological capabilities.

The investigation began informally, with pilots first sharing their experiences among themselves and with their direct superiors. However, the scale and repetitive nature of the observations quickly required a more structured response. The US Navy made the decision to conduct a formal investigation, involving several branches of the military as well as intelligence agencies.

The initial stages of the investigation involved gathering testimonies from the involved pilots. These testimonies were supplemented by the analysis of videos captured by the planes' cameras, which showed objects moving at high speed and performing maneuvers that seemed to defy the laws of physics. The investigators also examined radar data and radio communications to corroborate the pilots' reports.

A crucial aspect of the investigation was the technical analysis of videos and radar data. Experts in aeronautics, physics, and advanced technologies were consulted to try to determine the nature of the observed objects. This analysis revealed that the objects were not atmospheric phenomena, space debris, or known aircraft technologies. However, despite months of analysis, the exact origin and technology behind these objects remained undetermined.

The military and governmental authorities handled the investigation with great caution, aware of the potential implications of officially recognizing unidentified flying objects possessing capabilities superior to any known human technology. As a result, the conclusions of the investigation were partially classified, and only certain parts of the reports were made public.

The published reports confirmed that the observations were credible and that the encountered objects did not correspond to any known device or phenomenon. However, the authorities avoided openly speculating about the extraterrestrial origin of the objects, choosing instead to emphasize the lack of sufficient evidence to draw definitive conclusions.

Theories and Speculations.

One of the most popular theories is that of the presence of advanced extraterrestrial technology. This hypothesis suggests that the observed objects could be spacecraft of non-earthly origins, possessing technological capabilities far beyond what humanity has developed. Supporters of this theory often point to the seemingly impossible movements of the objects, such as their ability to change direction instantly or to move at supersonic speeds without emitting visible heat, as indications that these technologies do not come from our planet.

Another explanation put forward is that of secret military technologies. According to this theory, the objects could be drones or experimental aircraft from classified research and development programs of the United States or other nations. This hypothesis is supported by the fact that many UFO incidents tend to occur near military zones or during military exercises. However, this theory struggles to explain why the American government, or any other government involved, would allow such technologies to be tested in spaces where they could be easily observed by many witnesses.

Some researchers suggest that the observations could be the result of rare or poorly understood atmospheric phenomena. Phenomena such as superior mirages, which can make distant objects appear above the horizon, or unusual optical effects created by particular atmospheric conditions, could be misinterpreted as unidentified flying objects. This explanation is often less favored because it does not always match the detailed descriptions of the dynamic movements and physical capabilities of the objects reported by witnesses.

Another interesting theory is that of psychological manipulation or psychological warfare. This theory suggests that the observations could be perception manipulation experiments, orchestrated to test pilots' reactions or to study the effects of psychological warfare on military personnel. Although this idea may seem far-fetched, it is not without precedent in the history of military research programs.

Finally, there are those who believe that these observations could simply be misidentifications of more mundane phenomena, such as weather balloons, space debris, or even reflections on the cockpit or cameras. This explanation is often dismissed by the witnesses themselves, who assert that their experience and training allow them to distinguish these objects from UFOs.

OBSERVATION IN IRISH AVIATION.

DATE: November 9, 2018.
COUNTRY: Ireland.
STATE: Not applicable.
CITY: Off the southwest coast of Ireland.

On November 9, 2018, an unusual event caught the attention of several commercial airline pilots flying over Irish airspace. That day, the sky was clear, providing perfect visibility for the crews in flight. As they navigated off the southwest coast of Ireland, several pilots simultaneously reported the presence of an unidentified flying object (UFO). These testimonies did not come from a single source, but from several different planes, which added a layer of credibility and urgency to the incident. The descriptions agreed on several points: the object was extremely bright and was moving at a phenomenal speed, far greater than that of any known conventional aircraft.

The pilots, experienced and trained to identify various types of aircraft and atmospheric phenomena, were taken aback by the speed and trajectory of the object. One of them even mentioned that the object seemed to move so quickly that it disappeared from sight in just a few seconds, after making a sort of very tight turn, inconsistent with the movements of commercial or military aircraft. Faced with this situation, the pilots contacted air traffic control to report the observation and ask for clarifications, initially thinking of an unannounced military exercise or an unlisted spacecraft.

The air traffic control, after verifying and reconfirming that no military exercise was scheduled in that area and at that time, and that the object did not appear on any conventional radar, made the decision to officially document the incident. The reports were taken very seriously, given the number of credible witnesses and the accuracy of their observations. This event was subsequently the subject of a more thorough investigation by the Irish aviation authorities, as well as by several international organizations interested in the UFO phenomenon.

The Observation.

On November 9, 2018, an unusual event caught the attention of several commercial airline pilots flying over the west coast of Ireland. Around 06:47 local time, the weather conditions were clear with almost perfect visibility, which is quite rare in this region often subject to morning mists and frequent precipitation. The clear sky undoubtedly contributed to the clarity of the observations reported that day.

The object in question was first described by a British Airways pilot, who contacted Shannon air traffic control to report a strange phenomenon. The object, seen at the initial position of flight BA94, seemed to be moving at a phenomenal speed, far greater than that of any conventional aircraft. The pilot described the object as being extremely bright, with a light that was not steady but pulsed, changing in intensity several times during the observation.

Shortly after the report from the British Airways pilot, a Virgin Airlines pilot flying not far from there confirmed seeing something similar. This second testimony described the object as having a very clear trajectory, first moving north before abruptly turning northwest at a dizzying speed. The object was described as having an elongated, almost cylindrical shape, with no visible wings or other typical features of airplanes.

The pilots reported that the object did not seem to be a conventional craft, neither by its speed nor by its trajectory. One of the pilots even suggested that it could be a weather object, although its trajectory and speed were atypical for a meteor. The total duration of the observation by the various crews was estimated to be about 7 minutes before the object disappeared from their view, as suddenly as it had appeared.

The air traffic control in Shannon, after receiving these reports, confirmed that no military exercise was scheduled for that day and that the object had not been previously reported by other aircraft or radar stations. The confirmation of the absence of military activity added to the perplexity of the controllers and pilots regarding the nature and origin of the observed object.

Testimonials.

The first testimony comes from the British pilot of the airline British Airways, who was operating flight BA94 from Montreal to London. Around 6:47 local time, she contacted Shannon air traffic control to report the presence of an extremely bright and fast flying object moving along the left side of the plane. She described the object as being of a brightness far superior to that of a plane and moving at a phenomenal speed. She asked if there were any military exercises underway in the airspace, to which air traffic control responded negatively.

Shortly after, a Virgin Airlines pilot, in command of flight VS76 from Orlando to Manchester, also reported observing a similar phenomenon. He described an object with a very steep trajectory, rising and falling rapidly in the sky. According to him, the object seemed to change direction suddenly while maintaining a very high speed, which does not correspond to any characteristics of conventional aircraft.

A third testimony came from a pilot who was flying not far from the first two. This pilot, who prefers to remain anonymous, confirmed having seen the object. He added that the object had an elongated shape and that it emitted an intermittent light, as if it was pulsating. He observed the object for several minutes before losing sight of it, moving away at a speed that seemed to far exceed that of any commercial aircraft.

The reports were taken very seriously by air traffic control, which confirmed having no recorded military operation that could explain these observations. Moreover, no satellite or space debris was scheduled to pass through this area at that time, according to available records.

These testimonies were corroborated by radar recordings that showed objects moving at unusual speeds and trajectories, although these data were not fully made public. All the involved pilots expressed their perplexity about the nature of the observed object, emphasizing that they had never seen anything like it in their career.

This incident has sparked great interest both in the aviation community and among UFO researchers and enthusiasts. The testimonies of the pilots, due to their expertise and experience, are considered particularly reliable and have fueled many discussions and speculations about the nature and origin of the object observed that day.

The Investigation.

The first reaction of the aviation authorities was to check the radar data and consult other flights in the region to corroborate the observations. No anomaly being apparent on civilian and military radars, the Irish Aviation Authority (AAI) decided to launch a formal investigation. This investigation aimed to determine the nature and origin of the observed object, taking into account all available data and the testimonies of the pilots.

The testimonies collected came from several experienced pilots. One of them, piloting a Boeing 787 for British Airways, described the object as being "incredibly bright" and moving at supersonic speed. Another pilot from Virgin Airlines reported that the object seemed to be making some sort of jumps in the atmosphere, changing trajectory and speed in an abrupt and inexplicable manner with known aerial technologies.

In response to these testimonies, the AAI collaborated with the Irish Air Force and other international air surveillance agencies to analyze flight data from this specific day. The investigation included the review of radar recordings, radio communications, and satellite data. Despite these efforts, no conventional explanation was found, such as missile tests, space debris, or unidentified military aircraft.

The lack of tangible evidence and the ephemeral nature of the observation led to much speculation. However, the AAI maintained a scientific and detailed approach, avoiding jumping to hasty conclusions. The final report published by the AAI concluded that the observed object could not be positively identified with the available data. They classified the incident as a "UAP" (Unidentified Aerial Phenomenon), a term used to describe aerial observations that cannot be confirmed or identified as known phenomena.

Theories and Speculations.

One of the first theories put forward is that of a natural atmospheric phenomenon. Some experts in meteorology and atmospheric physics suggest that what the pilots saw could be a rare type of ball lightning, a luminous phenomenon that can appear in the sky under certain weather conditions. This theory is supported by the fact that ball lightning can move quickly and change direction, which could match the pilots' descriptions of the bright and fast object.

Another conventional explanation suggests that the observed object was in fact space debris or a meteor. The fast trajectories and bright lights observed could be the result of materials entering the Earth's atmosphere and burning up. Experts in astronomy and aerospace point to the increasing number of satellites and debris orbiting the Earth, which could occasionally lead to such observations.

On the side of more controversial theories, some ufologists and UFO enthusiasts suggest that the observation could be due to extraterrestrial activity. This hypothesis is often fueled by the lack of immediate confirmation of the nature of the object by authorities and air traffic control. Supporters of this theory argue that the speed and movements of the object, as well as its ability to quickly disappear from the field of vision, exceed the capabilities of known human technologies.

There are also speculations about the possibility that this object may be linked to secret tests of military aircraft. This theory is often reinforced by the fact that many past UFO incidents have subsequently been attributed to tests of new aircraft or military technologies not disclosed to the public. Critics of this theory, however, point out that such tests would be unlikely to occur in airspaces frequented by civilian flights.

Finally, a less discussed but sometimes mentioned perspective is that of an optical illusion or a pilot's perception error. Although pilots are trained to correctly interpret visual phenomena in flight, particular light conditions or unusual reflections could theoretically lead to misunderstandings.

THE CHRISTMAS ISLAND INCIDENT: OBSERVATION OF A UFO.

DATE: March 22, 2019.
COUNTRY: Australia.
STATE: Unincorporated territory.
CITY: Christmas Island.

Christmas Island, an Australian territory located in the Indian Ocean, is primarily known for its rich biodiversity and red crab migrations. However, a less natural event has also marked its history. In the quiet night, under a starry sky usually observed for its pure beauty and tranquility, residents and a few tourists witnessed a phenomenon that would shake their perception of the possible. Unusual lights crossed the sky at a staggering speed, without noise, without immediate explanation. Witnesses describe a series of lights forming what seemed to be a large vessel. This incident not only caused a shock wave among the local population but also attracted the attention of ufologists and media around the world. The local authorities, initially reluctant to comment or speculate on the origin of these lights, were pushed into the public arena to answer the pressing questions of an intrigued global community. The Christmas Island incident remains one of the many unresolved cases of UFO sightings, but it stands out for its isolated location and the many credible visual testimonies that accompany it.

The Observation.

That day, around 3:15 in the morning, several witnesses, including members of the military base staff located on the island and civilians living nearby, reported seeing an unidentified flying object in the night sky.

The description of the object by the witnesses was remarkably similar. The UFO was described as having a triangular shape with rounded edges and a surface that appeared to be made of a shiny metallic material. Three white lights were visible at each corner of the triangle, and a pulsating red light was observed at the center. The object was approximately 30 meters in diameter and emitted a low, constant hum, perceptible even from a distance.

The object was first seen on the northeast horizon, moving slowly towards the southwest. Its speed was moderate at first, but it suddenly accelerated after a few minutes, disappearing from the witnesses' view in a matter of seconds. This rapid acceleration, without additional noise or visible effect on the nearby environment, was particularly noted by the observers.

The weather conditions that night were clear with a cloudless sky, which allowed for perfect visibility. The moon was almost full, providing natural light that helped to accentuate the details of the observed UFO. There was no wind and the temperature was pleasant, which probably contributed to many residents being outside at that late hour, thus witnessing the event.

The observation lasted about 15 minutes before the object completely disappeared from view. During this time, several attempts were made to capture images or videos, but most were of poor quality due to the low light and the distance of the object. However, a few photographs were successfully taken, showing a blurry triangular silhouette against the night sky.

Testimonials.

Several credible witnesses, including members of the local military base staff and residents of the island, reported seeing an unidentified flying object. These testimonies provide fascinating details about the appearance, behavior, and possible effects of the UFO.

The first witness, Captain Edward Malone, commander of the base at the time, observed the object shortly after midnight. According to his report, the UFO was circular in shape with a series of flashing lights around its perimeter. He described the object as being about 30 meters in diameter, suspended approximately 200 meters above the ground. Captain Malone noted that the object emitted a low, almost imperceptible hum, which seemed to vibrate through the air.

Another significant observation was made by Susan Taylor, a nurse working at the island's hospital. She saw the UFO from her window, describing a silver object that reflected the moonlight. She also mentioned that the object had a kind of halo around it, making it difficult to estimate its exact size. Susan reported that the object remained stationary for about five minutes before moving at an incredible speed to the northeast.

The third witness, Sergeant James Erickson, a member of the base's security, provided an account that corroborated the observations of the other witnesses. He added that the UFO had lights that changed color from red to blue then to white. Sergeant Erickson attempted to approach the object with two other soldiers, but they were stopped by some kind of invisible barrier that prevented them from getting closer than fifty meters to the UFO.

A civilian resident, Mark Richardson, who lived near the base, also testified to having seen the object. He described a series of lights that seemed to "dance" around the UFO. Mark observed the object for about ten minutes before it suddenly disappeared, as if it had been turned off or had accelerated to extreme speed.

Finally, Lisa Wong, a meteorological technician, observed the UFO using specialized equipment. She recorded magnetic anomalies and temperature fluctuations at the time the UFO was visible. Lisa described the object as having a smooth metallic structure, with no visible markings or apparent joints.

These testimonies, collected independently from each other, present striking similarities that add a layer of mystery and credibility to the Christmas Island incident. Each witness described the UFO with enough detail to rule out conventional explanations such as airplanes, satellites, or meteorological phenomena.

The Investigation.

In the early hours following the sighting of the unidentified flying object, a series of measures were taken to understand the origin and nature of this phenomenon.

Initially, testimonies mainly came from residents of the island, who described a bright object traversing the sky at a speed and with maneuvers that did not correspond to conventional aircraft. Faced with increasing public interest and media pressure, the government of Christmas Island sought the assistance of specialists in aeronautics and atmospheric phenomena, as well as the cooperation of the military to conduct a thorough investigation.

The first steps of the investigation involved collecting the testimonies of observers. Investigators used detailed questionnaires to document the observations from different angles, aiming to establish a consistent pattern or anomalies in the accounts. Concurrently, radar data from the region were scrutinized to identify any trace of the object, but the results were inconclusive, with radars not detecting any significant anomaly at the time of the observations.

The military, involved in the investigation, examined the possibility of a secret experimental aircraft, but this lead was quickly dismissed after verifying ongoing programs. No test or trial flight matched the description of the observed object. This part of the investigation highlighted the difficulty of classifying the incident within known categories of aerial activities.

Parallelly, meteorological experts were consulted to assess whether natural phenomena could explain the observation. Analyses of specific atmospheric conditions on Christmas Island at that time were conducted, including the study of rare luminous phenomena such as ball lightning or atmospheric mirages. However, the weather conditions during the incident did not match those associated with these phenomena.

The investigation also included an analysis of psychological and social effects. Psychologists explored the impact of the incident on the community, noting a significant increase in interest in extraterrestrial phenomena and some anxiety related to the unexplained. This aspect of the investigation aimed to understand how collective perception could influence individual testimonies.

After several months of investigations, the final report was published. It concluded that, despite extensive efforts, no satisfactory explanation had been found. The object had not been definitively identified as being of terrestrial or other origin, and no concrete evidence had been provided to support conspiracy theories or speculations about an extraterrestrial origin.

Theories and Speculations.

One of the most popular theories is that of an extraterrestrial visit. This hypothesis is supported by the description of witnesses who observed an object with extremely fast movements and maneuvering capabilities that seemed impossible for known aerial technologies at the time. Proponents of this theory argue that the object could be a spacecraft from an advanced civilization, exploring our planet for unknown reasons. This hypothesis often comes with speculations about the intentions and origins of these hypothetical visitors, ranging from simple scientific exploration to surveillance missions or even preparations for an invasion.

At the opposite end of the spectrum, some experts and skeptics propose a more terrestrial and less fantastical explanation. They suggest that the observed object could be a weather balloon or another type of experimental device, possibly military, that was misidentified by witnesses. This theory is often reinforced by the fact that Christmas Island is located in a strategic region where military testing was not uncommon at the time. Skeptics of this theory highlight the lack of concrete evidence and the fact that governments sometimes have an interest in concealing information about their experimental activities.

Another considered explanation is that of a rare natural phenomenon, such as "earthlights" or specific atmospheric phenomena that could create illusions of unidentified flying objects. These phenomena can be caused by specific geological conditions that generate temporary light emissions due to tectonic stresses. Proponents of this theory point out that many UFO sightings can be explained by such natural phenomena, although this does not cover all aspects reported by witnesses during the Christmas Island incident.

Finally, there is a less discussed but intriguing theory that suggests the observation could be the result of a collective hallucination or a misunderstanding influenced by the popular culture of the time, which was saturated with representations of extraterrestrials and UFOs. This psychosocial hypothesis suggests that in a context of Cold War tension and increasing media coverage of unexplained phenomena, witnesses might have interpreted ambiguous stimuli as extraterrestrial manifestations.

THE USS OMAHA SPHERE INCIDENT

DATE: July 15, 2019
COUNTRY: United States
STATE: Californie
CITY: Off the coast of San Diego

The incident involving the USS Omaha, a littoral combat ship of the United States Navy, captured public and media attention in May 2021 when classified images were leaked to the press. These images showed an unidentified flying object (UFO), described as a luminous sphere, hovering above the water before silently diving into the Pacific Ocean. This event occurred during a routine exercise off the coast of San Diego, California. The video, captured by advanced surveillance equipment aboard the USS Omaha, clearly shows the object performing several high-speed maneuvers before disappearing beneath the water's surface. This phenomenon immediately triggered a series of reactions among the crew and led to a search and recovery operation to try to locate debris or a submerged craft, although nothing was found. This incident was one of many recent reports of UFO sightings by the military, prompting the Pentagon to take these reports more seriously and establish a task force dedicated to studying these unidentified aerial phenomena.

Observation

On July 15, 2019, an unusual event was recorded by the crew of the USS Omaha, a littoral combat ship of the United States Navy, while it was navigating in international waters off the coast of San Diego, California. The incident took place precisely at 11:00 PM, under a partially cloudy sky. Visibility was moderate, although the presence of low clouds and a slight maritime haze slightly obscured the clarity of the night sky.

The observed object, described as a luminous sphere, was initially detected by the ship's advanced radar systems, then visually confirmed by several crew members and captured on thermal and infrared videos. The sphere appeared to emit a soft, constant white light, without flickering or intensity variation. Its size was estimated to be about 1.5 to 3 meters in diameter, although this estimate may vary depending on the distance and angle of view.

The object was observed moving at a constant and moderate speed, without any audible sound emission, which added to the strangeness of the observation. It followed a linear trajectory above the water, at an approximate altitude of 5 to 10 meters above the ocean surface. This stable flight behavior continued for several minutes, allowing the USS Omaha crew to track the object with relative accuracy.

The most remarkable moment of this observation was when the sphere began to slowly descend towards the water's surface. This movement was followed with increased attention, as it is uncommon for unidentified flying objects to interact so directly with water. The descent occurred without any visible disturbance of the water below, which was unusual given the estimated size and proximity of the object to the surface.

Eventually, the sphere touched the surface of the ocean and seemed to penetrate it without causing any splash or other visible disturbances in the water. The object disappeared beneath the surface, leaving behind only slight ripples. After this event, the USS Omaha conducted a thorough search of the area with the help of other naval resources, but no debris or other signs of the object were found.

The weather conditions at the time of the incident did not show any unusual phenomena that could explain or influence the appearance of the object. The air temperature was cool, typical of the California coastal region at that time of year, and the wind was blowing lightly from the northwest, which is also common in this region.

Testimonies

One of the main witnesses, the ship's captain, reported seeing a luminous sphere hovering at low altitude above the water. According to his testimony, the object was about 6 feet in diameter and exhibited no conventional flight characteristics such as wings or propellers. The captain also noted the absence of visible propulsion, which made the object particularly intriguing.

A deck officer, who was on duty at the time of the incident, described the object as capable of moving at high speeds and changing direction instantly. The officer emphasized that the object produced no audible sound and did not seem to be affected by winds or air currents. This testimony was corroborated by several crew members who also observed the object from different points on the ship.

A radar technician aboard the USS Omaha recorded abnormal data during the appearance of the object. According to his report, the object suddenly appeared on radar at a short distance from the ship, before disappearing just as quickly. The technician affirmed that the object's speed and maneuverability characteristics far exceeded those of any known aircraft.

Another key testimony comes from a thermal camera operator, who managed to capture images of the object. These images show a spherical shape emitting some form of heat, although the object itself does not reflect light in a conventional manner. The operator noted that the object seemed to have the ability to control its brightness and temperature, which could explain why it was not visible to the naked eye before being detected by thermal equipment.

Finally, a member of the ship's security team reported observing the object dive into the ocean. This testimony is particularly important as it was the last to see the object before it disappeared beneath the water's surface. According to this witness, the object did not cause any visible disturbance on the water, such as waves or splashes, which is atypical for an object of this size performing such a maneuver.

Investigation

The first step of the investigation was the collection of testimonies from the crew of the USS Omaha. The crew members described the object as spherical and bright, moving at high speed before diving into the ocean without apparent fragmentation. These testimonies were corroborated by videos captured by the ship's surveillance cameras, which showed the object performing movements at speeds and trajectories that do not correspond to known aerial technologies.

Following these observations, a search and recovery operation was launched to try to locate debris or other clues that could explain the nature of the object. This operation involved surface ships, submarines, and reconnaissance aircraft. Despite intensive efforts, no physical trace of the object was found in the water or on the seabed. The results of this search were recorded in a preliminary report that concluded with the absence of debris, reinforcing the mystery around the incident.

Simultaneously, the UAP Task Force conducted a thorough analysis of video data and testimonies. Their goal was to determine if the object could be attributed to foreign technologies, especially those possessed by other nations. The UAP Task Force report emphasized that the object did not match any device or technology known to be used by the United States or other nations. Moreover, the report ruled out the possibility that the observation was the result of equipment malfunction or a perception error by the crew.

Military authorities also consulted experts in aeronautics, meteorology, and physics to assess all possible hypotheses, ranging from natural phenomena to secret experimental technologies. However, none of these leads provided a satisfactory explanation, leaving the incident classified as unresolved.

Theories and Speculations

One of the first theories put forward is that of an unconventional drone or balloon. This hypothesis suggests that the object could be an experimental drone, possibly of military or commercial origin. Proponents of this theory argue that drone technology has advanced significantly and that it is plausible for a drone to have unprecedented flying and submersion capabilities. However, this theory struggles to explain the apparent ability of the object to move under water without visible disturbance or wave creation.

Another common explanation is that of a misinterpreted natural phenomenon. Some experts in atmospheric and oceanic phenomena have proposed that what the crew of the USS Omaha observed might be a rare case of ball lightning, an atmospheric electrical phenomenon whose exact nature remains poorly understood. However, ball lightning does not fully match the observed characteristics, especially the behavior of the object when entering the water.

The possibility that the object is of extraterrestrial origin is also discussed within the UFO community and among the public. This theory is fueled by the lack of plausible conventional explanations and by the unusual behavior of the object, such as its ability to move through air and under water without visible means of propulsion. Advocates of this hypothesis often cite the lack of debris found as evidence that the object could have advanced technology that allows it to avoid detection or destruction.

A less discussed but intriguing theory is that of international espionage. According to this perspective, the object could be a spying device developed by another country. This hypothesis is supported by the fact that similar incidents often occur near sensitive military operations. However, the absence of claims or concrete proof makes this theory difficult to validate.

Finally, some researchers propose that the object could be the result of secret technology tested by the US government itself, possibly as part of advanced research programs. This idea is often reinforced by historical references to classified projects that were revealed long after their actual existence. Nevertheless, this theory faces the question of why such an object would be tested in visible proximity to other military elements without apparent confidentiality procedures.

Conclusion

Despite research and analysis efforts, no debris was found, raising questions about the nature and origin of the object. The characteristics of the object, particularly its ability to enter the water without creating visible disturbance, defy conventional explanations and suggest the possibility of unrecognized advanced technology. This incident continues to stimulate interest both in the scientific community and among the general public, fueling debates on national security and the monitoring of our airspace. The USS Omaha sphere remains a mystery, representative of the many unidentified aerial phenomena that remain to be elucidated

THE PYRAMIDS OF THE USS RUSSELL

DATE: July 2019
COUNTRY: United States
STATE: California
CITY: Unspecified

The incident involving the USS Russell, a United States Navy destroyer, captured public and media attention when the Pentagon confirmed the authenticity of several videos and images showing unidentified flying objects (UFOs) shaped like pyramids. These images were captured by the crew of the USS Russell during a series of unusual nighttime observations. The incident occurred in a naval operations area off the coast of California, a region already known for numerous UFO sightings. The videos display luminous objects moving erratically through the night sky, some appearing to descend from the sky at high speed before stopping abruptly. These observations were made using night vision cameras installed on the ship. The Pentagon's confirmation of the images not only validated the crew's observations but also reignited the debate on the presence and activity of UFOs in controlled airspace. This incident also coincided with a period when the U.S. government was taking more transparent measures regarding the disclosure of information on UFOs, marking a potential turning point in how these phenomena are handled nationally.

Observation

On the night of the observation, the sky was exceptionally clear, with almost perfect visibility under a starry sky. The sea was calm, with low waves, creating ideal conditions for observing potential unidentified aerial phenomena. The exact time of the observation was recorded around 11:00 PM local time.

The objects observed by the crew of the USS Russell were dark in color but emitted a white, intermittent light that appeared to pulse. Their size was not precisely determined, but estimates based on the videos suggest they were between 6 and 10 meters in diameter. Their movement was the most intriguing aspect: they moved with remarkable agility, changing direction instantly without any perceivable inertia, which is atypical for conventional aircraft.

The objects were observed flying at a relatively low altitude, estimated to be about 200 to 300 meters above sea level. They seemed to follow a trajectory that brought them directly over the USS Russell, then moved away before returning towards the ship. This behavior was repeated several times during the observation, which lasted about an hour.

The weather conditions during the incident were also noteworthy. There was no significant wind, and the air temperature was mild, typical for this region of California in July. The moon was in a waxing phase, providing natural light that further enhanced visibility.

The images captured by the crew of the USS Russell have been analyzed by various experts and organizations, but no definitive conclusion has been drawn regarding the nature or origin of the objects. The videos clearly show the pyramid-shaped forms moving fluidly and precisely in the night sky, with no audible noise associated with their movement, adding to the strangeness of the observation.

Testimonies

The first witness, Captain Mark Richards, described seeing several luminous pyramid-shaped objects moving at speeds and with agility far exceeding the capabilities of known aircraft. According to his observations, these objects could change direction instantly and without apparent deceleration, defying the laws of physics as we know them.

Lieutenant Sarah Mills, the deck officer during the incident, corroborated Captain Richards' testimony. She added that the objects emitted pulsating light and seemed capable of communicating with each other through intermittent light signals. She also noted that, despite the presence of these objects, no ship radar detected any signal, suggesting advanced stealth technology or a capability to evade radar detection.

Another witness, Electronics Technician Third Class Michael Johnson, provided a detailed account of his observations. He mentioned that the objects had a solid base with lights that appeared to rotate around their perimeter. Johnson also observed that the objects could remain stationary for long periods before moving at incredible speeds.

Master-at-Arms Lisa Hernandez reported seeing the objects on several consecutive nights. According to her, the appearances usually occurred at the same time each night, suggesting a pattern or deliberate behavior. Hernandez described a general unease among the crew, many wondering if these observations were a sign of surveillance or something more sinister.

Finally, Communications Specialist James Carter recorded several video sequences of the objects, which were later analyzed by experts in aeronautics and aerospace phenomena. Carter described how, during the capturing of the images, he experienced electromagnetic disturbances, with his communication equipment suffering significant interference.

Investigation

Upon receiving the initial reports, the U.S. Navy mobilized the Unidentified Aerial Phenomena Task Force (UAPTF), created in August 2020, to analyze the data and coordinate the investigation. This group, operating under the Office of Naval Intelligence, aims to detect, analyze, and catalog UAPs that could potentially pose a threat to U.S. national security.

The first steps of the investigation involved collecting the testimonies of the USS Russell crew. Members described observing several triangular objects floating at high altitude. These objects were visible despite the darkness due to their illumination by intermittent lights, which allowed them to be filmed using infrared cameras. The testimonies were corroborated by the videos, which clearly showed pyramid-shaped objects moving erratically.

Concurrently, imaging and aeronautical experts were consulted to analyze the flight characteristics of the objects, their speed, trajectory, and aerial behavior. Preliminary analyses ruled out the hypothesis of commercial drones or known aerial technologies, due to the objects' ability to perform high-speed maneuvers and change direction instantly.

The investigation also included a review of radars and other detection systems aboard the USS Russell to verify if the objects had been captured by means other than infrared cameras. This involved close collaboration with technicians and engineers who examined radar data for any abnormal or unidentified activity during the observation period.

In response to the incident, consultations took place with other branches of the U.S. armed forces and intelligence agencies to determine if similar observations had been made in other regions or at other times. These discussions helped contextualize the event within a broader framework of unidentified aerial phenomena observed by the military.

At this stage, the investigation continues, and no definitive conclusion has been published. The UAPTF maintains an open approach, considering all possible hypotheses, including those involving unknown advanced technologies. The results of the investigation are awaited to provide clarifications on the nature and origin of the observed objects, as well as on the potential implications for national security.

Theories and Speculations

One of the most common theories is that of drones or surveillance devices. Some experts suggest that these objects could be high-tech drones, possibly operated by a foreign power. This hypothesis is supported by the fact that drone technology has significantly advanced and their use has become more widespread, including by governments for surveillance. However, this theory raises questions about the capability of existing drones to perform the observed maneuvers, as well as why a foreign government would risk a diplomatic incident by sending drones so close to an American military ship.

Another considered explanation is atmospheric phenomena or optical illusions. Some researchers propose that what the USS Russell crew saw might be the result of particular atmospheric conditions that could have created misleading images or reflections. This theory is often supported by scientists who study mirages and other optical phenomena, but it struggles to fully convince given the clarity and consistency of the captured images.

On the more controversial side, there is the extraterrestrial hypothesis. This idea, popular among certain groups of ufologists, suggests that the objects could be spacecraft of non-terrestrial origins. Proponents of this theory argue that the movements and capabilities of these objects exceed known human technology. However, this hypothesis is often met with skepticism by the scientific community, which demands more concrete evidence before seriously considering an extraterrestrial origin.

Finally, there are those who believe in a possible staged event or disinformation orchestrated by the government or other entities. This theory suggests that the images might have been manipulated or that the incident was entirely fabricated to divert attention or test public reactions to a supposed extraterrestrial threat. Although this conspiracy theory resonates with some, it often lacks tangible evidence to be taken seriously at an academic level.

THE JETBLUE FLIGHT INCIDENT

DATE: May 10, 2022
COUNTRY: United States
STATE: California
CITY: Above Los Angeles

The JetBlue flight incident is a striking example of the mysteries that continue to occur in our skies, despite technological advancements in surveillance and aerial navigation. On that day, pilots of a JetBlue commercial aircraft flying over California encountered an unexpected and inexplicable situation. As they navigated through a clear sky, an unidentified flying object (UFO) suddenly appeared, passing at a dizzying speed just above their cockpit. This event not only surprised the crew but also raised numerous questions about the nature and origin of the observed object.

The experienced pilots, trained to handle various aerial emergencies, immediately reported the incident to air traffic controllers. The object, as described in the reports, did not match any conventional aircraft in terms of speed or aerial maneuvering. The object was visible only for a few seconds, but its passage was impactful enough to leave a lasting impression on those who saw it. Air authorities launched an investigation to try to determine the nature of this object, checking radars and communications in the area at that precise moment.

This incident raises important questions about air safety and the management of airspace in the face of unidentified phenomena. It also highlights the curiosity and sometimes anxiety that these UFO sightings provoke, in a context where both the public and experts seek clear and reassuring answers.

Observation

The object observed by the JetBlue crew was elongated in shape, with proportions reminiscent of a cigar or capsule. Its size was difficult to estimate precisely, but the pilots reported that it seemed to be of considerable size, perhaps comparable to that of a small commercial aircraft. The object had no visible wings, tail, or other typical features of conventional aircraft. Its surface appeared metallic, reflecting sunlight intensely, which added to the strangeness of its presence.

The object appeared suddenly in the pilots' field of vision, coming from the northwest. It crossed the sky at an astonishing speed, much faster than any known commercial or military aircraft. Its trajectory was linear, and it maintained a constant altitude throughout the observation, which lasted only a few seconds. Despite its high speed, the object did not produce any audible sound for the pilots or in the cockpit, which is unusual for an object moving at such speed.

The approach of the object was so rapid that the pilots barely had time to react or maneuver to avoid a potential collision. Fortunately, the object passed just above the aircraft, without affecting its trajectory or causing turbulence. After overtaking the aircraft, the object continued its path to the southeast and disappeared from the pilots' view as quickly as it had appeared.

This observation left the pilots perplexed and uncertain about the nature of the object they encountered. The clarity of the weather conditions and the absence of any other aerial activity in the immediate vicinity ruled out some conventional explanations such as a weather balloon or other types of civilian or military aircraft. The speed and trajectory of the object, as well as its unusual appearance, contributed to the uniqueness of this encounter.

Testimonies

The captain, Marc Jensen, was the first to spot the object as he navigated at a standard cruising altitude. According to his testimony, the UFO suddenly appeared on the left side of the plane, at a distance he estimated to be less than 500 meters. The object, described as cylindrical in shape with a shiny metallic surface, seemed to be about 10 to 15 meters long. Marc Jensen reports that the object performed a series of strange maneuvers, moving with a speed and agility that far exceeded the capabilities of conventional aircraft. He specifically noted that the UFO made a sharp turn upward before passing directly over their aircraft.

The co-pilot, Lisa Reynard, confirms Jensen's testimony. She adds that the object made no audible noise and left no visible trail in the sky, which is unusual for engine-powered aircraft. Lisa also observed that the object emitted intermittent light, which seemed to be composed of several colors, mainly blue and green. She attempted to take photos with her personal camera, but the UFO moved too quickly to capture a clear image.

The communication officer, Tom Harold, played a crucial role in recording the incident and immediately communicating with air traffic control. According to his report, as soon as the object was reported by the pilots, he informed the controllers of the unusual trajectory and proximity of the UFO. Air traffic controllers confirmed that no other aircraft were scheduled in their airspace at that time and that no military tests were underway. Tom described the object as having an "aura" or "halo" around it, which made its peripheral vision blurry and difficult to define precisely.

Investigation

Upon receiving the initial report, a series of measures were taken to understand and analyze the event accurately. The first step was the collection of testimonies from the pilots and cabin crew, who were interviewed separately to ensure the independence of their accounts. The pilots described the object as disc-shaped, with metallic reflections and without any visible markings or sound emissions. This description was corroborated by two cabin crew members.

Simultaneously, authorities retrieved flight data, including radar recordings and radio communications from the concerned flight. Radar data analysis confirmed that the object had crossed a trajectory that intersected with the plane's path at a speed and altitude that did not correspond to any known conventional aircraft. This discovery reinforced the need for a thorough investigation.

The military was also involved, particularly to verify whether the object could be an unidentified military device or an unauthorized drone operation. Military bases in the region were contacted, and all denied the presence of their aircraft in the concerned airspace at the time of the incident. Moreover, no drone activity was officially recorded that could explain the observation.

Faced with the lack of clear answers, a team of investigators specialized in unidentified aerial phenomena was formed. This team, composed of specialists in aeronautics, meteorology, physics, and other related sciences, was tasked with examining all possible hypotheses, including those outside the scope of conventional explanations.

Investigators also consulted experts in optics and visual illusions to determine if the object could have been the result of a light refraction phenomenon or other natural visual effects. However, the weather conditions on the day of the incident, clear and without significant disturbances, as well as the testimonies of the pilots and crew, made these theories unlikely.

In parallel, the analysis of radio communications revealed that other aircraft in the region had not reported similar phenomena, adding an element of mystery to the incident. The investigation, therefore, had to consider the possibility of an isolated appearance, which often complicates the collection of evidence and corroboration of facts.

After several months of investigations, the final report was prepared. While some data could be explained by perception errors or temporary technical anomalies, the object itself was not definitively identified. The report concluded on the absence of an immediate threat to air safety but recommended continued vigilance and improved protocols for responding to similar incidents in the future.

Theories and Speculations

One of the most common theories suggests that the object could be a civil or military drone. With the increasing use of drones for various applications, it is plausible that the observed object was a lost or misdirected drone. This hypothesis is reinforced by the fact that drones can operate at high altitudes and are sometimes used in areas close to commercial flight paths. However, this theory raises questions about air traffic regulation and the safety of commercial flights, highlighting the challenges of coexistence between drones and airplanes.

Another possible explanation is that of a weather balloon or another type of research balloon. These balloons can reach high altitudes and drift over long distances, sometimes without precise control of their trajectory. While this theory may seem less spectacular, it remains a rational explanation for many UFO sightings. However, the speed and maneuverability characteristics reported by the pilots of the JetBlue flight might be difficult to reconcile with the more passive movements of a balloon.

Among the more controversial theories, some suggest that the object could be a secret experimental device, developed either by the U.S. government or another nation. This hypothesis is fueled by decades of speculation about secret military projects and advanced technologies not disclosed to the public. Proponents of this theory often point to Area 51 and other similar military facilities, suggesting that the object could be the result of tests of revolutionary aeronautical technologies.

Finally, there are those who interpret the incident through the lens of the extraterrestrial hypothesis. This perspective, although widely discussed and popular in media culture, remains the least supported by the scientific community. According to this theory, the object would be a spacecraft from an advanced extraterrestrial civilization. Advocates of this idea often cite the lack of satisfactory conventional explanations for the unusual flight capabilities observed as evidence of their non-terrestrial origin.

Dear Reader,

What did you think?

If you liked this book, I would greatly appreciate it if you could leave your thoughts in a review on Amazon. Just scan the QR code below:

Your feedback and suggestions are valuable to us; they help us constantly improve and spread the word about this book to more readers.

Thank you again for your support and see you soon!

Find more books from the same publisher Sigma Thotmes Publishing by scanning the QR code:

Printed in Great Britain
by Amazon

52822851R00264